The Cambridge Companion to Film Music

This wide-ranging and thought-provoking collection of specially commissioned essays provides a uniquely comprehensive overview of the many and various ways in which music functions in film soundtracks. Citing examples from a variety of historical periods, genres and film industries – including those of the USA, UK, France, Italy, India and Japan – the book's contributors are all leading scholars and practitioners in the field. They engage, sometimes provocatively, with numerous stimulating aspects of the history, theory and practice of film music in a series of lively discussions which will appeal as much to newcomers to this fascinating subject as to seasoned film-music aficionados. Innovative research and fresh interpretative perspectives are offered alongside practice-based accounts of the film composer's distinctive art, with examples cited from genres as contrasting as animation, the screen musical, film noir, Hollywood melodrama, the pop-music and jazz film, documentary, period drama, horror, science fiction and the western.

PROFESSOR MERVYN COOKE teaches film music, jazz, twentieth-century music and composition at the University of Nottingham. He has edited *The Cambridge Companion to Benjamin Britten* (1999), *The Cambridge Companion to Jazz* (2002, co-edited with David Horn) and *The Cambridge Companion to Twentieth-Century Opera* (2005). He has also published *A History of Film Music* (Cambridge University Press, 2008) and *The Hollywood Film Music Reader* (2010), and co-edited volumes 3–6 of *Letters from a Life: The Selected Letters of Benjamin Britten* (2004–2012).

DR FIONA FORD completed her doctoral thesis on *The Film Music of Edmund Meisel (1894–1930)* at the University of Nottingham and has wide experience of researching contemporaneous original scores for silent film and early scores for sound films. She has written a book chapter on Edmund Meisel for *The Sounds of the Silents in Britain: Voice, Music and Sound in Early Cinema Exhibition* (2012, ed. Julie Brown and Annette Davison) and a chapter on *The Wizard of Oz* for *Melodramatic Voices: Understanding Music Drama* (2011, ed. Sarah Hibberd).

The Cambridge Companion to

FILM MUSIC

....

EDITED BY

Mervyn Cooke
and
Fiona Ford

CAMBRIDGE
UNIVERSITY PRESS

CAMBRIDGE
UNIVERSITY PRESS

University Printing House, Cambridge CB2 8BS, United Kingdom

One Liberty Plaza, 20th Floor, New York, NY 10006, USA

477 Williamstown Road, Port Melbourne, VIC 3207, Australia

4843/24, 2nd Floor, Ansari Road, Daryaganj, Delhi - 110002, India

79 Anson Road, #06-04/06, Singapore 079906

Cambridge University Press is part of the University of Cambridge.

It furthers the University's mission by disseminating knowledge in the pursuit of education, learning and research at the highest international levels of excellence.

www.cambridge.org
Information on this title: www.cambridge.org/9781107476493

© Cambridge University Press 2016

First published 2016

A catalogue record for this publication is available from the British Library

Library of Congress Cataloging in Publication data
Cooke, Mervyn. | Ford, Fiona.
The Cambridge companion to film music / edited by Mervyn Cooke and Fiona Ford.
Cambridge, United Kingdom : Cambridge University Press, [2016] |
Includes bibliographical references and index.
LCCN 2016026629 | ISBN 9781107094512
LCSH: Motion picture music – History and criticism.
LCC ML2075 .C3545 2016 | DDC 781.5/42–dc23
LC record available at https://lccn.loc.gov/2016026629

ISBN 978-1-107-09451-2 Hardback
ISBN 978-1-107-47649-3 Paperback

In memory of
Sergio Miceli
1944–2016

Contents

Figures

Music Examples

Tables

Notes on Contributors

James Buhler teaches music and film sound in the Sarah and Ernest Butler School of Music at the University of Texas at Austin. He is co-editor (with Caryl Flinn and David Neumeyer) of *Music and Cinema* (2000) and co-author (with David Neumeyer and Rob Deemer) of *Hearing the Movies* (2010), now in its second edition. He is currently completing a manuscript entitled *Theories of the Soundtrack*.

David Butler is Senior Lecturer in Screen Studies at the University of Manchester. He is the author of *Jazz Noir: Listening to Music from* Phantom Lady *to* The Last Seduction (2002) and *Fantasy Cinema: Impossible Worlds on Screen* (2009). He has written widely on the ideological function of music in film and television, especially in film noir and science fiction, and his current research is focused on the life and work of Delia Derbyshire, one of the pioneering figures in British electronic music, whose tape and paper archive was donated to the University of Manchester on behalf of her estate.

Mervyn Cooke is Professor of Music at the University of Nottingham. The author of *A History of Film Music* (2008) and editor of *The Hollywood Film Music Reader* (2010), he has also published widely in the fields of Britten studies and jazz: his other books include *Britten and the Far East* (1998), several co-edited volumes of Britten's correspondence and studies of the same composer's *Billy Budd* (1993) and *War Requiem* (1996). He has edited previous Cambridge Companions devoted to Britten, twentieth-century opera and (with co-editor David Horn) jazz, and has published two illustrated histories of jazz for Thames & Hudson. He has recently completed an analytical study of the ECM recordings of jazz guitarist Pat Metheny.

David Cooper is Professor of Music and Technology and Dean of the Faculty of Performance, Visual Arts and Communications at the University of Leeds. He is the author of monographs on Bernard Herrmann's scores for *Vertigo* (2001) and *The Ghost and Mrs. Muir* (2005), a large-scale study of Béla Bartók (2015) and co-editor (with Ian Sapiro and Christopher Fox) of *Cinemusic? Constructing the Film Score* (2008). He is currently Principal Investigator of a major research project on the Trevor Jones Archive, funded by the UK Arts and Humanities Research Council.

Kate Daubney is the Series Editor of the Film Score Guides published by Scarecrow Press. She established the series in 1999 (with Greenwood Press) as a way for film musicologists to analyse the composition and context of individual scores by drawing more widely on the often hard-to-access archival and manuscript resources of composers both living and dead. She is also a scholar of the film scores of Max Steiner and the author of the first Film Score Guide (2000), devoted to Steiner's music for *Now, Voyager*.

Annette Davison is Senior Lecturer at the Reid School of Music, University of Edinburgh. Her research focuses primarily on music for screen and has been published in a range of journals and essay collections, including two for which she was co-editor (with Erica Sheen and Julie Brown). She is the author of the monographs *Hollywood Theory, Non-Hollywood Practice: Cinema Soundtracks in the 1980s and 1990s* (2004) and *Alex North's* A Streetcar Named Desire: *A Film Score Guide* (2009). She has begun to explore music for short-form promotional media. Her essays on the main-title and end-credit sequences for multi-season North American television drama serials can be found in *The Oxford Handbook of New Audiovisual Aesthetics* (2013), the journal *Music, Sound, and the Moving Image* (2014) and in the Danish journal *SoundEffects* (2013), where she analyzes viewer behaviour in relation to these sequences. Current research includes the role of music in sponsored film and advertising.

George Fenton is one of the world's leading composers of music for film, television and theatre, with a distinguished career spanning half a century. He began composing professionally in the mid-1970s for theatre productions by the Royal Shakespeare Company and the National Theatre, then worked extensively for BBC TV where he wrote many well-known signature tunes and scores for popular drama series. His later music for the BBC Natural History Unit achieved a new high standard for the genre and won several awards for *The Blue Planet* (2001) and *Planet Earth* (2006). The success of his first feature-film score, for *Gandhi* (1982), launched a career in the movies which was to include Academy Award nominations for *Gandhi*, *Cry Freedom* (1987), *Dangerous Liaisons* (1988) and *The Fisher King* (1991). He has maintained a prolific and highly varied output of music for both mainstream and independent productions in the United States and United Kingdom, and recently composed (with Simon Chamberlain) a stage musical based on the film *Mrs Henderson Presents* (2005).

Caryl Flinn is Professor and Chair of the Department of Screen Arts and Cultures at the University of Michigan. She is the author of *Strains of Utopia: Nostalgia, Gender, and Hollywood Film Music* (1992), *The New German Cinema* (2003), *Brass Diva: The Life and Legends of Ethel Merman* (2007) and *The Sound of Music* (BFI Film Classics, 2015), and co-editor (with David Neumeyer and James Buhler) of *Music and Cinema* (2000). Her work also appears in the anthologies *Melodrama: Stage, Picture, Screen* (1994), *Camp: Queer Aesthetics and the Performing Subject* (1999), *Film Music: Critical Approaches* (2001), *Teaching Film* (2012), *A Companion to Rainer Werner Fassbinder* (2012) and *The Oxford Handbook of New Audiovisual Aesthetics* (2013).

Fiona Ford is an independent researcher currently working on Max Steiner's pre-Hollywood career and his early years at RKO (with particular emphasis on his score for *King Kong*). She completed her undergraduate Music degree at the University of Oxford in the mid-1980s, returning to academia at the University of Nottingham in the new millennium. Her postgraduate research interests focused on the film music of Dmitri Shostakovich (MA, 2003) and Edmund Meisel (PhD, 2011). She has published on the use of pre-existing music in Shostakovich's score to *Hamlet* and Herbert Stothart's *The Wizard of Oz*, as well as Meisel's lost soundtrack for *The Crimson Circle* and his famous accompaniment to Sergei Eisenstein's *Battleship Potemkin*.

Peter Franklin retired in 2014 as Professor of Music at Oxford, where he is an Emeritus Fellow of St Catherine's College. He writes on late-romantic symphonies and post-Wagnerian opera and film, and is the author of *A Life of Mahler* (1997) and *Seeing Through Music: Gender and Modernism in Classic Hollywood Film Scores* (2011). His book *Reclaiming Late-Romantic Music: Singing Devils and Distant Sounds* (2014) is based on the lectures he gave as Visiting Bloch Professor of Music at the University of California at Berkeley in 2010.

Krin Gabbard taught at Stony Brook University from 1981 until 2014. He is currently an Adjunct Professor of English and Comparative Literature at Columbia University. Otherwise he is busy playing his trumpet and writing a memoir about his parents. His books include *Jammin' at the Margins: Jazz and the American Cinema* (1996), *Black Magic: White Hollywood and African American Culture* (2004) and *Hotter Than That: The Trumpet, Jazz, and American Culture* (2008). His current project is an interpretative biography of Charles Mingus. He lives in New York City with his wife Paula.

Stephen Glynn, a film writer and teacher, is currently an Associate Research Fellow at De Montfort University, UK. His books on film music include studies of *A Hard Day's Night* (2005) and *Quadrophenia* (2014) and *The British Pop Music Film* (2013).

Guido Heldt studied in Münster, Germany, at King's College, London, and at Oxford. After completing a PhD on early twentieth-century English tone poems (Münster 1997), he worked at the Musicology Department of the Free University Berlin (1997–2003) and as a visiting lecturer in the History Department of Wilfrid Laurier University, Waterloo, Ontario (2003), before joining the Department of Music at the University of Bristol in 2004. His work has focused on film music and narrative theory (he is the author of *Music and Levels of Narration in Film*, 2013), composer biopics, music in German film and on a range of other film-music topics. He is currently working on a monograph about music and comedy in film and TV.

Timothy Koozin is Professor and Division Chair of Music Theory at the Moores School of Music, University of Houston, Texas. His research interests include music and meaning, popular music, film music and music instructional technology. His writings appear in *Perspectives of New Music*, *Contemporary Music Review*, *Music Theory Online* and *College Music Symposium*. His edited collection of essays on the film music of Fumio Hayasaka and Tōru Takemitsu was published as a special issue of the *Journal of Film Music* in 2010. Koozin is co-author of two music-theory textbooks with companion websites: *Techniques and Materials of Music* (2014, enhanced seventh edition) and *Music for Ear Training* (2001, now in its fourth edition). He is a former editor of *Music Theory Online*, the electronic journal of the Society for Music Theory.

Hannah Lewis is Assistant Professor of Musicology at the University of Texas at Austin. Her research interests include film music, music and visual media, twentieth-century avant-garde and experimental music and musical theatre.

She has presented at national and regional meetings of the American Musicological Society and the Society for American Music, and her work has appeared in the *Journal of the American Musicological Society, Journal of the Society for American Music* and *American National Biography*. She is currently writing a book about music in French cinema during the transition to synchronized sound.

Stan Link is Associate Professor of the Composition, Philosophy and Analysis of Music at Vanderbilt University's Blair School of Music, where he teaches composition, theory and interdisciplinary courses on film, art, literature and music. The author of numerous essays and papers on subjects ranging from musical horror to dancing nerds, he is also an active composer of acoustic and electroacoustic music performed in the United States, Europe and Australia. Stan lives in Nashville, Tennessee, with his wife, the musicologist Melanie Lowe, and their daughter, Wednesday.

Miguel Mera is Reader in Music at City University, London, and a member of BAFTA. His film scores have been screened at festivals and cinemas around the world, including the feature film *Little Ashes* (2008), which won the Schermi d'Amore Rose Prize for Best Film at the Verona Film Festival. He is the co-editor (with David Burnand) of *European Film Music* (2006), *The Routledge Companion to Screen Music and Sound* (with Ron Sadoff and Ben Winters, forthcoming) and a special edition of *Ethnomusicology Forum* (2009), exploring global perspectives in screen-music studies. He is also the editor of a special edition of *Music and the Moving Image* (2009), developing concepts relating to audiovisual 'reinvention', and is the author of *Mychael Danna's* The Ice Storm: *A Film Score Guide* (2007). Miguel has also undertaken empirical research applying eye-tracking methodologies to the study of film-music perception.

Sergio Miceli, who died in 2016, was at the time he wrote his contribution to this volume a retired Full Professor of History and Aesthetics of Music at the Conservatory 'Luigi Cherubini', Florence, Italy. He was formerly Adjunct Professor of History of Film Music at Florence University and the University of Rome, 'La Sapienza'. He also taught film music with Ennio Morricone at the Accademia Musicale Chigiana in Siena, with Franco Piersanti at the Scuola Civica di Musica in Milan, and at the Centro Sperimentale Cinematografia (CSC) in Rome. He was a member of the editorial boards of *Music and the Moving Image* and the Russian journal *MediaMusic*. His publications include *Morricone, la musica, il cinema* (1994), *Musica e cinema nella cultura del Novecento* (2010) and *Film Music: History, Aesthetic-Analysis, Typologies* (2013); and, with Morricone, *Composing for the Cinema: The Theory and Praxis of Music in Film* (2001; English translation 2013).

Mekala Padmanabhan studied at the Universities of Victoria and North Dakota, and received her doctorate from the University of Nottingham. She is an independent scholar and Diploma Examiner (Music) for the International Baccalaureate Organization, with research expertise in Tamil film music and popular culture, as well as late eighteenth-century Viennese lied, Haydn and German poetry and aesthetics. In 2013 she was a Visiting Research Fellow at the

AHRC Centre for Music Performance as Creative Practice, University of Cambridge. Her publications include an essay exploring musical creativity in Tamil film-music orchestras, to appear in Tina K. Ramnarine's *Global Perspectives on the Orchestra: Essays on Collective Creativity and Social Agency* (forthcoming), and 'Dedications to Haydn by London Keyboard Composers around 1790' in *Widmungen bei Haydn und Beethoven: Personen – Strategien – Praktiken* (2015).

Danae Stefanou is Assistant Professor of Historical Musicology at the School of Music Studies, Aristotle University of Thessaloniki, Greece, where she also directs the Critical Music Histories research group, and is a member of the Cognitive and Computational Musicology team. She previously studied at the Universities of Nottingham (MA) and London (PhD), and was a Research Fellow and Visiting Lecturer at Royal Holloway, University of London. Her research explores a broad range of twentieth- and twenty-first-century sonic practices, with a particular focus on experimentalism, noise and free improvisation, and has been published in various journals, Grove Music Online and several edited volumes, including *Made in Greece: Studies in Popular Music*, ed. Dafni Tragaki (forthcoming).

Robynn J. Stilwell is Associate Professor in Music at Georgetown University. Her research interests centre on the meaning of music as cultural work. Publications include essays on Beethoven and cinematic violence, musical form in Jane Austen, rockabilly and 'white trash', figure skating, French film musicals, psychoanalytic film theory and its implications for music and for female subjects, and the boundaries between sound and music in the cinematic soundscape. Her current project is a study of audiovisual modality in television and how the latter draws from and transforms its precedents in film, theatre, radio and concert performance, with an eye towards the aesthetic implications for technological convergence.

Claudio Vellutini is a postdoctoral resident scholar and Visiting Assistant Professor at the Jacobs School of Music, Indiana University (Bloomington). He received his PhD in Music History and Theory from the University of Chicago, where he also collaborated with the Center for Italian Opera Studies. He is the recipient of an Ernst-Mach Fellowship from the Österreichisches Austauschdienst, the exchange agency funded by the Austrian Federal Ministry of Science and Research (2012–13), and of an Alvin H. Johnson AMS 50 Dissertation Fellowship from the American Musicological Society. His research focuses on the cultural and reception history of Italian opera, particularly in nineteenth-century Vienna, and on contemporary opera staging. He has published in the *Cambridge Opera Journal* (2013) and *19th-Century Music* (2014).

Paul Wells is Director of the Animation Academy at Loughborough University, where he is a Professor, and Chair of the Association of British Animation Collections. He has published widely in animation studies, including his book, *Animation, Sport and Culture* (2014). Paul is also an established writer and director of film, TV, radio and theatre, conducting workshops and consultancies worldwide based on his book *Scriptwriting* (2007). His credits include the documentary film *Whispers and Wererabbits: Claire Jennings* (2014) and a feature script currently in production.

Ben Winters is Lecturer in Music at The Open University. He is the author of *Music, Performance, and the Realities of Film: Shared Concert Experiences in Screen Fiction* (2014) and *Erich Wolfgang Korngold's* The Adventures of Robin Hood*: A Film Score Guide* (2007), and has published on film music in journals including *Music & Letters*, *Journal of the Royal Musical Association* and *Music, Sound, and the Moving Image*. His book chapters include contributions to James Wierzbicki (ed.), *Music, Sound and Filmmakers* (2012) and Erik Levi (ed.), *The Impact of Nazism on Twentieth-Century Music* (2014). Current projects include co-editing Ashgate's Screen Music series and co-editing (with Miguel Mera and Ron Sadoff) *The Routledge Companion to Screen Music and Sound* (forthcoming).

Acknowledgements

The editors are greatly indebted to Vicki Cooper, formerly Senior Commissioning Editor for Music and Theatre at Cambridge University Press, for her customary helpfulness and perseverance in seeing this volume cheerfully into press, and to her successor Kate Brett for overseeing the final stages of production. Along the way we have benefitted enormously from the skills of former assistant editor Fleur Jones, practical assistance from Emma Collison, Christofere Nzalankazi and Lorenza Toffolon, and the professional expertise of copy editor Matthew Bastock. We are also indebted to our project manager for the production process, Sri Hari Kumar at Integra Software Services.

This book owes its existence to the considerable efforts of Peter Franklin and Robynn Stilwell in getting the concept up and running some years ago, and we are grateful to them both for their constant support during the editorial process and for their staunch membership of our team of distinguished contributors. As the book took shape, we were also helped by valuable input from Alison Arnold, Emilio Audissino, Jan Butler, Richard Dyer, David Neumeyer and Renata Scognamiglio, and by timely technical assistance from David Ford for Table 17.1. Caryl Flinn expresses her appreciation to Mervyn Cooke, Fiona Ford, Joseph DeLeon, Herb Eagle, Adrian Martin, Katy Peplin and, especially, to Leah Weinberg, whose illuminating responses to earlier versions of Chapter 15 contributed to the final draft. In connection with Chapter 18, Danae Stefanou wishes to thank Yannis Kotsonis for invaluable feedback on her contribution and JLG for indirectly encouraging the improvisation of music, noise and silences. For essential assistance with Chapter 19, Annette Davison wishes to thank Johanna Blask (Paul Sacher Foundation), Hans Werner Henze, Elaine Kelly, John Marshall, Ulrich Mösch, Christa Pfeffer, Nicholas Reyland, Tina Kilvio Tüscher and Schott Music.

A version of Chapter 21 was presented at the Performance Seminar Network Third International Conference at the AHRC Centre for Music Performance as Creative Practice (CMPCP), University of Cambridge (July 2014), with financial support from the *Music & Letters* Trust and CMPCP; the English translations of Tamil quotations and poems in this chapter are by Mekala Padmanabhan, who is grateful to Ramesh Vinayakam for granting access to his score for *Ramanujan* and giving his permission to reproduce excerpts from it here. The musical examples in

Chapters 14, 17 and 20 are aural transcriptions prepared by the authors; those in Chapter 17 have been approved by Ennio Morricone, whose archival holdings only contain material from *C'era una volta il West* (1968) onwards. We are grateful to Faber Music Ltd (both in their own right and on behalf of Chappell and Co. Ltd), Alfred Music (on behalf of Warner Bros.) and Hans Werner Henze and the Paul Sacher Foundation for permission to reproduce copyrighted material, as detailed in the individual captions for figures and music examples. We particularly wish to thank Brett Service (Curator of the Warner Bros. Archives at the School of Cinematic Arts, University of Southern California) for his assistance with preparing the facsimiles in Chapter 3.

Sadly, our distinguished contributor Sergio Miceli died in July 2016, while this book was in press. He had shown a tremendous interest in the project throughout its development, and a formidable attention to detail in preparing his own contribution to it, and it is an honour for us to be able to dedicate our symposium to the memory of the leading Italian film musicologist of his generation.

Introduction

MERVYN COOKE AND FIONA FORD

One of the authors represented in this collection of essays notes in passing that the concept of a 'companion' volume might these days be in danger of being considered a little old fashioned, as indeed the idea of 'film' is itself somewhat passé in the exciting and technologically unpredictable age of digital audio-visual media in which we live. Yet film music and the music of other related screen media, and the increasingly prolific field of film-music studies, are nowadays so diverse in their aims and achievements – and potentially bewildering in their rich variety – that even seasoned aficionados (including the present editors) sometimes feel the need for a little companiable guidance through the veritable labyrinth of possibilities offered by the intelligent and resourceful combinations of sound and image by which we are constantly surrounded. In assembling this book, it has been fascinating for us to see how all our contributors have helped continue to shape our necessarily flexible perceptions of how film music is made, how it might be considered to function and how it is appreciated.

In planning this book, one of our priorities was to concentrate on the practicalities of film-music production as much as on the theorizing and analysis which the composition of such music has long since generated in both academia and the media. Included here, therefore, are a leading contemporary film composer's reflections on his career and the state of the industry from a personal perspective (Chapter 5), some thumbnail discussions of how other living composers view both their cinematic art and scholars' varying attempts to come to terms with it (Chapter 7), as well as detailed accounts of the development of film-sound technology and the various ways in which soundtracks have been assembled across the decades (Chapters 1 and 2). The manner in which one celebrated film composer of Hollywood's Golden Age conducted his music in recording sessions is subjected to fascinatingly close scrutiny (Chapter 3), debunking in the process the tired myth that a creative genius in the film industry can simply stand up in front of a hard-pressed orchestra and risk blowing a huge budget by waving his arms around and hoping it will all come right in the end. Composers, orchestrators, arrangers, performers, conductors, music directors and music editors are a constant presence throughout these essays as a reminder that the often sophisticated film scoring which continues to generate reams of discussion is for the most part the intense product of exceptionally hard graft – a fundamentally collaborative process, often carried out to punishingly tight and in some cases even health-threatening deadlines – all accomplished at the very heart of a high-pressure commercial industry.

As well as examining how film music is actually made, our anthology considers the various ways in which it might be interpreted and analysed. Analytical processes not only cover its many and varied dramatic functions, which began life in the three broad categories of 'synchronization, subjugation and continuity', as our historical account of the transition from silent cinema to the sound film demonstrates (Chapter 1), but also embrace considerations of wildly differing musical styles, compositional techniques and cultural contexts. One of the delights of studying the extraordinary panoply of film-scoring possibilities is the way in which we need to switch from (for example) an appreciation of the genealogy of cowboy-associated folk tunes (Chapter 14) to the complexities of esoteric twelve-note serial manipulations (Chapter 19), or from well-worn classical styles to dynamic rock music – sometimes even within the same film (Chapter 17) – or from contrasting subgenres of jazz (Chapters 11 and 12), both symphonic and authentic, to the dauntingly large soundworld of pop. Once regarded as a rather dubious type of film scoring by die-hard traditionalists for whom the only viable music track was a finely crafted and leitmotif-based orchestral score, pop scoring and hit songs in all sorts of styles have been truly ubiquitous in movies across the decades, starting in the silent era, blossoming in early sound musicals and the swing era, coming prominently to the fore in the age of rock'n'roll and culminating in the many exciting developments in modern pop-scoring methods from the 1960s to the present day. The present essays vividly demonstrate the sheer variety of ways and genres in which such music has been handled: these include one of the best-loved instances of a hit song in a melodrama of the early 1940s (Chapter 8), the life and times of the British pop-music film (Chapter 4) and telling examples of the exploitation of pop music in CGI animation (Chapter 9), horror and science fiction (Chapter 13).

The theoretical side of film-music scholarship is a particularly daunting area of the subject, covering as it does general considerations of music's contribution to film narrative and of the often complex and sometimes intractable relationships between music, sound and dialogue. The summary of film-music theories provided here (Chapter 6) offers a comprehensive account of attitudes both classic and right up-to-date – as well as a vivid illustration of the formidable extent to which film musicology has burgeoned since the first wave of scholars disseminated their groundbreaking (and still widely cited) work in print in the 1980s and 1990s. While some theorizing about movie soundtracks, both old and new, might be felt to be somewhat divorced from reality, many modern scholars have also continued the more traditional, positivistic pursuits of delving meticulously into archives to study and analyse primary source materials, and the interviewing of composers in order to establish exactly how their film scores are created (Chapter 7). Contemporary film scholarship has also been distinguished – though it was certainly a long time coming – by the increasing attention paid in English-language publications to national film industries other than that of the United States, and to a wide range of non-Anglophone films. While Hollywood output is inevitably well represented in our collection, we also include studies of films from the United Kingdom (Chapters 4 and 16), Italy (Chapter 17), France (Chapter 18), Germany (Chapter 19), Japan (Chapter 20) and India (Chapter 21). Treatments of genres particularly associated with Hollywood, such as the musical (Chapter 15), the western (Chapter 14), film noir (Chapter 11), horror and science fiction (Chapter 13), as well as the silent film (Chapter 1) and Golden Era classics (Chapters 3 and 8), are offset by illuminating considerations of the Italian revisionist western (Chapter 17) and the ways in which other genres, notably the musical and animation, have developed in the UK (Chapters 4 and 16) and the Tamil film industry (Chapter 21), in many respects rather differently from their US counterparts. At many moments we are also reminded that some of the most significant innovations in film sound have occurred in the often experimental context of independent 'art' cinema (see, for example, Chapters 16 and 18), which studiously avoids the standardized practices attendant upon the fundamentally commercial considerations which have dominated mainstream film production for more than a century.

If we have in recent years come a little closer to understanding how film music is made, how it functions and how it is interpreted, there is one further area of fascination which has only recently begun to be properly considered: what can film music actually *feel* like? The sometimes peculiarly visceral effect of film scoring, especially that couched in disconcerting modernist idioms and forms of *musique concrète*, is tantalisingly explored in a number of contributions (Chapters 10, 13 and 18) and serves as a timely reminder that there are still crucial aspects of our subject which are as yet little understood and likely to be the focus of much future research.

PART ONE

Making Film Music

1 Evolving Practices for Film Music and Sound, 1925–1935

JAMES BUHLER AND HANNAH LEWIS

The transition from silent to synchronized sound film was one of the most dramatic transformations in cinema's history, radically changing the technology, practices and aesthetics of filmmaking in under a decade. This period has long been a subject of fascination for filmmakers, scholars and fans alike. From *Singin' in the Rain* (1952) to *The Artist* (2011), the film industry itself has shaped a narrative that remains dominant in the popular imagination. The simplistic teleological view of the transition – and the inevitability of the evolution of sound towards classical Hollywood sound practices that it implies – has been revised and corrected by numerous scholars (Bordwell *et al.* 1985; Gomery 2005). But a narrative of continuity that posits its own idealized teleology is just as much a distortion as one founded on total rupture, as Gomery, for instance, simply replaces the great men of filmmaking with the great men of finance, and Bordwell, akin to André Bazin's myth of total cinema (Bazin 2005 [1967], 17–22), draws the idea of a sound film from a transhistorical idea of cinema itself, though what Bazin links to deep focus and long takes, Bordwell links to editing.

While the film industry's transition was swift, it was neither crisis-free nor particularly systematic, especially with respect to technology and aesthetics. Donald Crafton notes that the transition to sound was 'partly rational and partly confused' (1997, 4), and Michael Slowik adds that 'sound strategies differed from film to film', which resulted in 'a startling array of diverse and often conflicting practices' (2014, 13). The relationships between film and sound (particularly music) had to be negotiated, and the introduction of synchronized sound prompted a range of audiovisual approaches and opinions about the new technology and its aesthetic implications. The 'transition' period was therefore a time of pronounced experimentation but also of surprisingly rapid aesthetic and economic codification within the film industry. On the one hand, the range of reactions and approaches to sound in different national contexts points to the contested nature of synchronized sound during the transition era and its implications for cinema as art, industry and entertainment. On the other, an international consensus, led by the American industry, had formed around proper sound practices, the so-called classical style, by the late 1930s. Roger Manvell and John Huntley, for instance, argue that filmmakers had by 1935 mastered the soundtrack sufficiently to the point that they 'had become fully aware of the dramatic powers of sound' (1957, 59). This emerging consensus allowed for considerable variation in national practices but set limits and high technical standards for films that aimed for international distribution.

Early History of Sound Film: Experimentation and Development (1900–1925)

A diversity of sound and music practices characterized the era of early cinema (Altman 2004, 119–288). As film found a more secure footing as a medium of entertainment and narrative film increasingly dominated the market, musical accompaniment became more closely connected to the film. The importance of musical accompaniment – 'playing the pictures' – consequently increased with this codification of narrative filmmaking technique, as a means of representing and reflecting the narrative. Although the practice of 'playing the pictures' was quite varied, it was structured around three general principles: synchronization, subjugation and continuity.

Synchronization involved fitting the music to the story, through mood, recurring motifs and catching details pertinent to the narrative. Mood related music to dramatic setting, usually at the level of the scene. Motif entailed a non-contiguous musical recurrence linked to a narratively important character, object or idea and topically inflected to reflect the action. Catching the details, which would evolve into 'mickey-mousing' in the sound era, involved exaggerated sound or music and an exceptionally close timing with the image, as in the vaudeville practice of accompanying slapstick comedy with intentionally incongruous sound. Subjugation required that music be selected to support the story and that music should never draw attention to itself at the expense of the story. This principle ensured that the accompaniment was played to the film rather than to the audience. Through subjugation, music could also serve to mould the audience's own absorption in the narrative. The musical continuity of the accompaniment likewise encouraged spectators to accept and invest in the film's narrative continuity (Buhler 2010).

These three principles structured the three dominant modalities of 'playing the picture' during the silent era: compilation, improvisation and special scores. Compiled scores, whether based on circulated cue sheets or assembled by a theatre's musical staff, were especially common, and a whole division of the music-publishing industry was organized to support this concept. The publishing firms not only supplied original music composed to accompany conventional moods, but they also offered catalogues and anthologies of music indexed by mood and topic to facilitate compilation scoring. The most famous American anthology was Ernö Rapée's *Motion Picture Moods for Pianists and Organists* (1924). Compilation was the preferred practice of accompaniment in the early years and, even in the 1920s, it remained the basic method for orchestral performance.

Improvisation was the accompaniment practice over which the film industry had the least control. Typically performed on a piano or organ, an improvised score was left to musicians to invent on the fly. As with compiled scores, the improvisation would introduce shifts in musical style to fit the need of any given scene, and improvisers would commonly work well-known tunes into their accompaniments. But the results varied greatly depending on the musicians in charge, resulting in the stereotype of the inept small-town pianist. Variable accompaniment practices left to the devices of local musicians were seen, according to Tim Anderson, as '"problems" that needed to be solved', as the film industry moved towards greater standardization of exhibition in the 1910s (1997, 5).

Some 'special' scores – scores created and distributed to go with specific films – began to appear in America in the 1910s, and increased in frequency and prominence in the 1920s. Notable special scores for American films include Joseph Carl Breil's for *Birth of a Nation* (1915), Mortimer Wilson's for *The Thief of Bagdad* (1924), William Axt's and David Mendoza's for *The Big Parade* (1925), and J. S. Zamecnik's for *Wings* (1927). The increased prevalence of special scores was part of the film industry's attempts to standardize and systematize musical practices. Over the course of the 1910s and 1920s, movie exhibition became increasingly stratified, and film music reflected this disparity: many urban deluxe theatres devoted considerable resources to maintaining large music libraries and musical personnel, including substantial orchestras and Wurlitzer organs, but small town theatres could hardly afford to do the same, as Vachel Lindsay, among others, ruefully noted (1916, 189–97).

In Europe, cinema occupied a somewhat different cultural position, alongside its commercial and popular associations. In France, Camille Saint-Saëns composed a score in 1908 for *L'Assassinat du Duc de Guise*, the first production of the 'Film d'Art' company, which was formed with the idea of making prestige pictures that might attract a higher class of patron (Marks 1997, 50–61). Other French composers soon demonstrated an interest in composing for cinema, most notably Erik Satie and members of Les Six. In the 1920s, surrealist artists and writers not only took inspiration from the cinema but also worked with it seriously as a medium. Additionally, ciné-clubs and journals devoted to filmmaking indicate film's potential as high art in the eyes of French filmmakers and musicians. In Germany, too, silent film had a close relationship to modernist movements in the plastic arts, and original film scores to accompany these artistic films were quite common. Mostly original film scores were composed for such well-known expressionist films as Robert Wiene's *Das Cabinet des Dr. Caligari* (1920; score by Giuseppe Becce) and Fritz Lang's *Metropolis* (1927; score by Gottfried Huppertz). The Viennese-born composer Edmund Meisel composed scores for German and Soviet films, including Sergei Eisenstein's *Battleship Potemkin* (1925), one of the most influential Soviet films of the silent era (Ford 2011). Additionally, German artists like Oskar Fischinger experimented in 'visual music', further linking music and the moving image through abstract visual art (Moritz 2004; Cooke 2008, 58).

European film-music practices were as diverse as they were in America, and accompaniment followed the same three principles of synchronization, subjugation and continuity, and was also organized by the same three modalities of compilation, improvisation and original score. In Germany, compilation was particularly formalized, with original compositions, anthologies and catalogues indexed by topics and moods along American lines. (Becce's volumes of Kinothek music were especially popular.) In 1927, Hans Erdmann, Becce and Ludwig Brav published the *Allgemeines Handbuch der Film-Musik*, a two-volume compendium of silent-film dramaturgy, hermeneutic theory of music and systematic sorting of musical works according to the needs of a music director of a cinema. Although it appeared late in the silent era and so never had a chance to establish its principles in theatres, the *Handbuch* does represent a particularly well-formulated theory of mature silent-film practice (Fuchs 2014). Its basic idea of a musical dramaturgy, related to traditional forms of theatre but with specific problems unique to film, also seems to have been absorbed by the composers of sound film as they worked to establish a place for music on the soundtrack.

Ultimately, the American studio system, with its drive towards standardization in order to control both labour costs and quality, found it increasingly advantageous to pursue experiments in synchronizing film with recorded sound. Filmmakers and inventors had been interested in mechanically linking sound and music with image since the earliest days of cinema. Thomas Edison, for instance, always claimed his inspiration for the motion picture had been the phonograph, 'to do for the eye what the phonograph does for the ear' (Edison 1888). In 1895, he developed the Kinetophone, joining his Kinetoscope with a phonograph, and in 1913 his firm released a second version of the Kinetophone that allowed for better synchronization. In France, Léon Gaumont developed the Chronophone, a sound-on-disc technology that he patented and exhibited publicly in

1902 (Gaumont 1959, 65). Significant early research into sound synchronization occurred in Germany as well: in 1900, Ernst Ruhmer of Berlin announced his Photographophone, evidently the first device successfully to reproduce sound photographed on film (Crawford 1931, 634), and Oskar Messter's Biophon apparatus was exhibited at the 1904 World Exposition in St. Louis (Narath 1960, 115). In the end, these systems had little more than novelty appeal, owing to major difficulties with synchronization and amplification.

A feverish pace of electrical research in the 1920s led to renewed effort in the development of synchronized sound, alongside a number of mass media and sound technologies. Donald Crafton refers to sound film's various 'electric affinities' – including electricity and thermionics, the telephone, radio, television and phonography – that developed prior to or alongside sound-synchronization technology as part of the research boom following the First World War (1997, 23–61). Perhaps most importantly, the invention of radio tubes led to a much more effective means of amplification. Companies and laboratories experimented with both sound-on-disc and sound-on-film playback technologies. Sound-on-disc sometimes (but not invariably) involved simultaneously recording a phonograph disc and a nitrate image, which were mechanically played back in sync, and sound-on-film consisted of an optical recording of the soundtrack – a physical writing of the sound onto a photographic strip that ran alongside the images. Sound-on-disc initially had somewhat better sound fidelity, and it drew on the long-established recording techniques of phonography, along with its industry and equipment. Sound-on-film, on the other hand, was better for on-location shooting, as the apparatus was more portable and the sound easier to edit. Although sound-on-film ultimately won out, for years both systems remained equally viable.

In 1919, three German inventors – Joseph Engl, Hans Vogt and Joseph Massolle – patented Tri-Ergon, an optical recording system first screened publicly in 1922 (Kreimeier 1996, 178). Meanwhile, in America in 1923, Lee de Forest, working with Theodore Case, patented and demonstrated a system with optical recording technology called Phonofilm. Early Phonofilms included a short speech by President Calvin Coolidge and performances by the vaudeville star Eddie Cantor and African-American songwriting duo Sissle and Blake. Several scores were also recorded and distributed for the Phonofilm system, including Hugo Riesenfeld's for James Cruze's *The Covered Wagon* (1923) and for Lang's *Siegfried* (1924). Although de Forest's system provided some publicity for the technology of synchronized sound film, the system remained mostly a novelty. While the recording process was already quite advanced, as can be heard on extant Phonofilm films, issues remained with Phonofilm's exhibition and economics. Most importantly, not enough theatres were equipped with the Phonofilm playback equipment. De Forest claimed that as many as fifty theatres had been wired for his system in 1924 (Crafton 1997, 66), but major film companies, which also controlled much of the theatre market, were unwilling to risk production with Phonofilm, and this reluctance made the system commercially unsustainable.

Innovation, Introduction and Dispersion of Synchronized Sound Technology (1926–1932)

Vitaphone

Substantial change arrived with the public success of Vitaphone. Western Electric, a subsidiary of AT&T (American Telephone and Telegraph Company), developed this sound-on-disc system. Western Electric formed a partnership with Warner Bros., a modest but growing studio at the time. According to Crafton, 'The Vitaphone deal was one of several tactics designed to elevate the small outfit to the status of a film major' (1997, 71). Their target market was midsize movie theatres with a capacity of 500–1000 – those theatres too small to afford big names in live entertainment, but large enough to afford the cost of installing sound equipment. (Warner Bros. did not end up following this strategy, since their first sound films were screened at larger, more prominent theatres, and the popularity of the talking picture radically altered the longer-term economic planning.)

Warner Bros. planned to use Vitaphone to replace live orchestral musicians with standardized recordings of musical accompaniment and to offer 'presentation acts' in the form of recorded shorts to provide all theatres with access to the biggest stars. In a lecture given at Harvard Business School in early 1927, Harry Warner recounted:

> [M]y brother [Sam] ... wired me one day: 'Go to the Western Electric Company and see what I consider the greatest thing in the world' ... Had he wired me to go up and hear a talking picture I would never have gone near it, because I had heard and seen talking pictures so much that I would not have walked across the street to look at one. But when I heard a twelve-piece orchestra on that screen at the Bell Telephone Laboratories, I could not believe my own ears. I walked in back of the screen to see if they did not have an orchestra there synchronizing with the picture. They all laughed at me. (Warner 1927, 319–20)

Using Vitaphone to record synchronized musical scores for their feature films, Warner Bros. aimed to codify film-music practices, replacing the diversity of live silent-film accompaniment with more standardized, high-quality musical performances.

For the Vitaphone debut, Warner Bros. recorded a synchronized musical accompaniment and some sound effects for *Don Juan* (1926), a silent costume drama starring John Barrymore that the company already had in production. The accompaniment was compiled by well-known silent-film composers Axt and Mendoza, both of whom worked at the Capitol Theatre, and was performed by the New York Philharmonic. On 6 August 1926, the film premiered at the Warner Theatre in New York along with a programme of shorts, including the New York Philharmonic playing Wagner's *Tannhäuser* Overture (1845) and performances by violinists Mischa Elman and Efrem Zimbalist and by Metropolitan opera singers Marion Talley, Giovanni Martinelli and Anna Case. All shorts that evening were classical performances, with the exception of Roy Smeck, 'The Wizard of the String'.

As can be seen from this first programme, Warner Bros. emphasized Vitaphone's connections to high culture at the time of its introduction, explicitly linking sound-film technology and classical music as a means of establishing Vitaphone's cultural prestige and gaining public acceptance of the somewhat unfamiliar medium. In his recorded public address that opened the programme, Will Hays, president of the Motion Picture Producers & Distributors of America, reinforced this point: 'The motion picture too is a most potent factor in the development of a national appreciation of good music. That service will now be extended, as the Vitaphone shall carry symphony orchestrations to the town halls of the hamlets' (quoted in Barrios 1995, 22). Film critic Mordaunt Hall's review in the *New York Times* implied that this tactic for gaining public acceptance of the new technology was at least somewhat successful. He stated that the 'Warner Brothers are to be commended for the high-class entertainment', and claimed that the programme 'immediately put the Vitaphone on a dignified but popular plane' (Hall 1926a).

The second Vitaphone premiere, which occurred exactly two months later on 6 October 1926, contrasted with the first in tone and cultural register (Barrios 1995, 26–7). This time the programme of shorts consisted primarily of vaudeville and popular performances (including a performance by Al Jolson in *A Plantation Act*). As was typical of deluxe theatre practice, the programme was designed to prime the audience for the night's feature film, a slapstick comedy called *The Better 'Ole* (1926) starring Syd Chaplin. In his review of *The Better 'Ole*, Hall was not troubled by the popular tone of the programme, noting that the 'series of "living sound" subjects are, in this present instance, in a far lighter vein, but none the less remarkable' (Hall 1926b). The third Vitaphone feature, *When a Man Loves* (1927), which included an original score by famed American composer Henry Hadley (Lewis 2014), did not debut until

3 February 1927, and the programme that premiered with this film split the difference of the first two, mixing shorts of high- and low-brow genres (Barrios 1995, 29–30). A potpourri of genres continued into the 1930s, although the number of classical-music shorts steadily declined. Jennifer Fleeger has argued that the variety of musical shorts in particular – some featuring opera, others jazz – was crucial since 'opera and jazz provided Hollywood sound cinema with both "high" and "low" parentage, and in the case of Warner Bros., multiple tales of inception that gave the studio room to remake itself' (2009, 20; 2014a).

Movietone, RKO and RCA Photophone

Following the success of Vitaphone, other companies quickly followed suit. Fox's Movietone, an optical recording system developed by Theodore Case and Earl Sponable, was the next technology introduced to the American public, in the spring of 1927. As a sound-on-film process, Movietone was capable of portable synchronized recording, and Fox quickly exploited this potential, beginning with the release of sound-enhanced newsreels. In September 1927, Fox began releasing feature films that, like the Vitaphone features, used Movietone to provide synchronized continuous scores and some sound effects. The first three were 7th *Heaven*, *What Price Glory* and *Sunrise: A Song of Two Humans* (Melnick 2012, 288–96; Bergstrom 2005, 192). All three carried scores compiled by Rothafel, Rapée and the musical staff at the already famed Roxy Theatre. Each of these films also modelled a slightly different conception of how Movietone might be exploited for feature films. 7th *Heaven* and *What Price Glory* were both re-releases designed to market and distribute the 'Roxy touch'. Both films also featured theme songs penned by Rapée and aimed at the sheet-music market. 'Charmaine', the theme of *What Price Glory* based on a song Rapée had written in the teens (Melnick 2012, 263), proved an exceptional hit. The Movietone score for *Sunrise* (1927), by contrast, was designed for longer-run exploitation (*ibid.*, 295). It was the only film of the original trio that premiered with its Movietone score and a full programme of Movietone shorts, similar to the strategy Warner Bros. had developed for its Vitaphone features. This score, which was received enthusiastically by critics, featured no theme song and was usually attributed to Riesenfeld until Bergstrom (2005) decisively challenged this view, and additional research by Melnick (2012) conclusively showed that Rothafel, Rapée and the musical staff at the Roxy were responsible for both this score and those for the other early Movietone features.

Photophone, another optical system, this one developed by RCA (a subsidiary of General Electric and owner of NBC, the nation's largest radio network), was introduced soon after Movietone. The first film with a Photophone soundtrack was *Wings*, a Paramount production that evidently combined live accompaniment with recorded sound effects featuring propellers and aircraft engines (Marvin 1928). Distributed initially as a road show with up to six soundtracks for effects, *Wings* was the most popular film of 1927, and it won the Academy Award for Best Engineering Effects (for Roy Pomeroy, who was responsible for the sound).

The Jazz Singer

By the end of 1927, both Warner Bros. and Fox were regularly producing sound films, but the economic certainty of sound film was not yet assured. Insufficient theatres had been wired for sound, and public interest was showing signs of waning in the first half of 1927. In order to drum up enthusiasm, Warner Bros. announced they were producing a film with Al Jolson. This became *The Jazz Singer* (1927), the first feature with directly recorded synchronized dialogue.

While *The Jazz Singer* was a turning point for sound film, proving its long-term economic viability and prompting a number of studios to turn their attention to synchronized sound, its importance has been somewhat overstated in popular narratives of the transition to sound. Consensus now seems to be that it was not *The Jazz Singer* but *The Singing Fool* (1928) – Jolson's second feature film and a much greater commercial success – that was decisive in convincing studios to convert to talking pictures. Furthermore, *The Jazz Singer* was not itself a major aesthetic departure: it merely brought the aesthetics of the Vitaphone shorts into the narrative world of a feature film, presenting what commentators at the time called a 'vitaphonized' silent film (Wolfe 1990, 66–75; Gomery 1992, 219). Yet the story of *The Jazz Singer* as the first talking film remains seductive. Its narrative – about a Jewish singer (Jack Robin) and his cantor father who opposes his son's desire to sing jazz songs – seems to equate the technology of synchronized sound with modernity and youth, and silent film with the older, traditional generation (Rogin 1992). It seems an almost too perfect allegory of the transition to sound.

Beyond that, however, little scholarly attention has been given to the reasons why this film with so little talking in it has come to serve as the point of origin for the talking film. And it seemingly occupied this position already in 1928. Crafton notes that 'newspaper and magazine reports of the time consistently regarded *The Jazz Singer* as a breakthrough, turn-around motion picture for Warner Bros. and the genesis of the talkies', and that the film was 'an immediate hit' (Crafton 1996, 463, 468). Indeed, in a paper delivered to the Society of Motion Picture Engineers, *New York Times* reviewer Hall sketched this history of the transition: 'it is now the familiar

Movietone news reel and the financially successful Vitaphone version of Al
Jolson's "Jazz Singer" that caused Hollywood to rush so wildly to sound,
when many had given it the cold shoulder when the Warner Brothers
launched their first Vitaphone program' (1928, 608). At that same conference, William A. Johnston stated forthrightly that 'nothing revolutionary happened until "The Jazz Singer" came along. That is the picture that
turned the industry talkie. Al Jolson and a song did the trick' (1928, 617).

Ultimately, the commercial success of *The Jazz Singer* gave Warner
Bros. the prerogative to continue experimenting with and releasing sound
films. In 1928 they released the first 100 per cent talkie, *Lights of New York*,
and then had a juggernaut hit with *The Singing Fool*. Other studios
followed, rapidly moving towards producing sound films of their own.

Hollywood Adjusts to Sound

The period from 1927 to 1930 was one of much uncertainty and experimentation as the industry adjusted to the technology, economics and
emerging aesthetics of sound film. In 1927, AT&T and their subsidiary
Western Electric founded ERPI (Electrical Research Products Inc.) to
handle rights and standardize costs. ERPI installed sound technology in
theatres and studios, and all major companies signed on. Soon after, RCA
formed its own studio, RKO Pictures, to exploit its Photophone sound
film, and the company also competed with ERPI in wiring theatres. After
some initial patent disputes – due to its work in radio, RCA held strong
patent positions – the two sides agreed to cross-license the basic technologies, allowing all films to be played on either system. This consolidation
further quickened the pace of Hollywood's transition.

Initially, there were three kinds of sound films: films with synchronized
scores and sound effects, part-talkies and 100 per cent talkies. The first
category featured music and sound effects that were post-synchronized.
Essentially, these films followed silent-film strategies, recording music and
sound effects that could have been performed live, using sound as spectacle
or special effect. Examples of synchronized sound films include Warner
Bros.' *The First Auto* (1927) and MGM's *White Shadows in the South Seas*
(1928). While spoken dialogue was not a part of this kind of film, sometimes the voice was added to the soundtrack off-camera or in post-
synchronization, in the manner of a sound effect, such as in *The First
Auto*, parts of *The Jazz Singer, White Shadows in the South Seas* and *Wild
Orchids* (1929). At the other end of the spectrum was the 100 per cent
talkie, emerging out of the aesthetics established in the Vitaphone shorts.
The emphasis on spoken dialogue in the early talkies resulted in a general

aesthetic shift towards the comprehensibility of dialogue, sometimes at the expense of music or other sound effects. Regular production of 100 per cent talkies did not begin until 1929, perhaps in part because recording equipment and trained personnel to operate it remained in somewhat short supply (K. F. Morgan 1929, 268).

In between was the part-talkie, which was widespread in 1928 and 1929. Part-talkies were a varied lot, and as early as 1929 they were already being discounted as an expedient 'due to recording and production problems' (*ibid.*, 271). Many, the so-called goat glands, had begun production as silent films but had dialogue scenes added (Crafton 1997, 168–9, 177). Talking (or singing) scenes in such films could heighten the spectacle and play to the novelty of synchronized sound, much like Technicolor sequences that were also occasionally added to films during this period, although the part-talkie's shifts from intertitles to spoken dialogue and back with little warning often strike audiences today as jarring. The disparaging contemporaneous term 'goat gland' suggests that the lack of integration of the talking sequences also disturbed critics (and perhaps audiences) of the time, though the way the term was deployed indicates that the critics understood 'talking' as an interpolation – a gimmick that had been added to a silent film akin to the description of *The Jazz Singer* as 'vitaphonized' – rather than as a conflict between opposing film aesthetics (as such films are usually evaluated today).

Some part-talkies such as *The Singing Fool, Noah's Ark* (1928) or *Weary River* (1929) thoroughly integrated talking and silent sequences, and such films could not be as easily converted into silent films without substantial re-editing (though each did appear in a silent version, and in each case the silent version is, like the goat glands, shorter than the sound version). These part-talkies are films apparently conceived as full hybrids with some thematic thought given to which scenes would better appear silent and which would be suited for spoken dialogue or musical performances. In *Lonesome* (1928), masterful parallel editing, which follows Jim and Mary in turn, accelerates towards the couple's eventual union at Coney Island, and this point of conjunction is emphasized by a shift from the silent-film technique of the parallel editing to the talking-film technique of their initial encounter. Although the spectacle of the talking film obviously means to affirm the romance as something transformational for the new couple, the actual technique of talking film here makes the dialogue scene appear (to a modern audience) laboured instead, with much of the viva-cious energy, dynamism and music of the silent sequences suddenly drained away during the talking.

As the novelty of spoken dialogue began to wear off, a craze for musical films began. Musicals offered a new kind of film spectacle, featuring elaborate song and dance numbers, frequently advertised as 'all singing, all dancing and all talking'. Stage talent was brought to the screen in droves, as actors with singing experience, Broadway songwriters and stage directors all found in Hollywood a lucrative source of income and a chance to reach much larger audiences. Many of these early musicals were revues such as *The Hollywood Revue of 1929* (1929), *The Show of Shows* (1929), *Paramount on Parade* (1930) and *King of Jazz* (1930), all of which essentially strung together a series of shorts. Such films offered studios opportunities to stage elaborate musical spectacles without having to worry about a connecting narrative and the different approach to capturing dialogue that narrative film required. Like the Vitaphone shorts on which Warner Bros. had honed its techniques, the individual numbers of a revue could be conceived as stage acts, and so dialogue captured with stage diction could simply mark the recording of an act. In this respect, one important innovation of *The Broadway Melody* (1929), one of MGM's first talking features and winner of the second Academy Award for Best Picture, was the way it distinguished stage and backstage in terms of sound design realized as the approach to recording. It proved an important model for the backstage musical, although Warners' musical part-talkies starring Jolson (*The Jazz Singer* and *The Singing Fool*) also largely follow this model. In the backstage musical, the dramatic action happened behind the scenes, and the musical numbers, often in colour and thematically unrelated to the principal action, would thus be given diegetic justification as performance. Operettas such as *The Desert Song* (1929), *The Love Parade* (1929) and *The Lottery Bride* (1930) were another important type of musical film during the transition era. Additionally, film musicals often exploited the synergy between the film and popular-music industries. As Katherine Spring has shown (2013), popular songs were ubiquitous during the transition period, even in non-musical films; and sometimes, as in *Weary River*, it is hard to tell the difference between a dramatic film and a musical.

Shifts in recording practices and sound editing affected the emerging aesthetics of sound film. Originally all sounds were recorded live on set; many accounts (and production photographs) reference musicians situated just off-screen. This posed many challenges regarding microphone placement and mixing. It also usually resulted in longer takes, since there was less fluidity with editing than had been possible in silent film. Various improvements ultimately led to sound editing and mixing taking place in post-production. Filming to playback – the recording of a song in the studio in advance, to be played back and lip-synced by the actors while the image was shot silent – was the method used by Gaumont to produce Chronophone films, and it was purportedly used in *The Jazz Singer* to cover Jolson's canting (Crafton 1997, 240), but it was sometimes difficult to achieve a convincing illusion of precise synchronization, and the technique also posed logistical problems for complicated scenes such as production numbers. The first commonly cited example of pre-recording was *Broadway Melody*, and after 1929 the practice became common (Barrios 1995, 60; Crafton 1997, 236).

Dubbing and re-recording had been possible if not always completely feasible since 1927, but there was a loss of recording fidelity, especially with sound-on-film (Jacobs 2012). Warners, the only studio using sound-on-disc, had a working re-recording process by 1928 that allowed music underscoring (Slowik 2014, 64–73). As J. P. Maxfield explained,

> The whole process [of Vitaphone rerecording] has been improved by the use of semi-permanent records of special material with a needle carefully fitted to the groove. This improvement has gone so far that no measureable surface noise is added in the process of dubbing.
>
> ('Discussion', in H. A. Frederick 1928, 728)

Maxfield's description makes clear, however, that Vitaphone dubbing was a convoluted process that had to be done in real time. As such, the practice did not become widespread until the early 1930s, when techniques for reducing the ground noise of film had developed sufficiently to allow reliable re-recording with sound-on-film. Early on, voice dubbing would often be done directly on the set, rather than through pre-recording or re-recording (Larkin 1929). In *The Jazz Singer*, for instance, the father's one word of dialogue and Jolson's piano playing were evidently both dubbed in live off-camera ('Open Forum' 1928, 1134).

Of course, film-music composition also underwent substantial change. Initially, the organization of music departments in Hollywood was somewhat ad hoc. In the late 1920s, the Hollywood studios either called upon composers with experience in silent-film scoring from deluxe theatres or they recruited composers, orchestrators and arrangers with experience on Broadway, including songwriters for film musicals. The composers from the deluxe cinemas, such as Riesenfeld and Mendoza, were assigned to score the synchronized silent films, whereas those who had specialized in arranging and composing Broadway production music, such as Max Steiner, Louis Silvers, Herbert Stothart and Alfred Newman, were assigned to the musicals and talking pictures. These initial assignments would have important consequences as studios quickly eliminated silent-film production, leaving a set of composers trained more on Broadway than in the silent cinema to establish the musical conventions of the Hollywood sound film. As talking pictures rapidly took over, musical accompaniment shifted from the wall-to-wall scoring characteristic of silent cinema to becoming increasingly intermittent. Nevertheless, this shift seems not to have been wholly a product of inadequate technologies of re-recording, as scholars have long presumed, since many talking films from before 1930, including the first all-talking *Lights of New York*, have extensive music underscoring dialogue (Slowik 2014, 89–93; Buhler and Neumeyer 2014, 25–6). Instead, the shift seems better explained by the kinds of films being made between 1930 and 1932 – more contemporary drama – and filmmakers' uncertainty over how closely the musical practice of the sound film should follow that of the silent film. In essence, wall-to-wall music threatened to make sound film appear a little too much like silent film.

Although the technology improved quickly during the transitional period, its advance was also highly disruptive to established working conditions, and those most threatened with displacement by the new technology hardly welcomed its arrival. Labour disputes, especially with musicians, were widespread. Many theatre musicians were laid off as orchestras and organists were replaced with synchronized soundtracks. The musicians' union fought for the continuation of live music, but without much success (Kraft 1996, 47–58; Cooke 2008, 46–7). At the same time, the new technology prompted a need for studio musicians; and, as a result, many of the best musicians moved to Hollywood.

Additionally, standardization came somewhat more slowly than was optimal because many theatres had initially invested in sound-on-disc and did not want to pay to convert to sound-on-film. Furthermore, although sound-on-film did not suffer from potential synchronization issues as did sound-on-disc, the former initially had more problems with sound quality in exhibition. At first, many major studios released films on both formats, a procedure that continued through the mid-1930s. Nevertheless, the Wall Street Crash of 1929 and subsequent deep and prolonged economic downturn profoundly affected the industry (as it affected nearly all aspects of American life), forcing studios to streamline their productions, to limit experiments and to focus on codification of best practices. By the start of 1931, Warner Bros. had joined the other Hollywood studios and begun converting to production using sound-on-film, and the production of silent films in Hollywood was also mostly over, with the exception of a few holdouts like Charlie Chaplin.

As sound-film technology became increasingly standardized, so did production practices. David Bordwell has emphasized the way the film industry worked to re-establish many of the regular production techniques from the silent film that had been disrupted with the coming of sound. These included, in particular, scene construction based on editing and single-camera shooting. The early sound film had used the soundtrack as the master shot to establish continuity in a scene. The image could be edited to the master continuity of the soundtrack, either by filming the scene with multiple cameras from various positions and with lenses of different focal lengths or through the use of cut-ins, especially reaction shots of characters listening. Through improved blimping, microphones, film stock, techniques of re-recording and other technology, the need for the audio master shot became less pressing (Bordwell *et al.* 1985, 301–6).

Innovation and Resistance in Europe (1929–1931)

While the transition to sound in the United States was rapid, the dissemination of the technology around the world was wildly uneven due to the large capital investments required and the financial uncertainty caused by the Great Depression. Because most theatres in Europe were wired for sound after 1929, the Depression created an economically chaotic situation as exhibition practices lagged behind production practices, and many sound films were initially shown silent at many theatres (Kreimeier 1996, 182). Furthermore, the change was, in many ways, controlled and dictated by American production and distribution companies. The United States had dominated world markets since the First World War, and American companies' patents on sound synchronization technologies gave them a distinct advantage over the film industries of other countries, except perhaps in Germany, where the film industry took advantage of its control over key sound-film patents (Gomery 1976; Gomery 2005, 109–13). The reaction to synchronized sound in Europe provides a particularly rich story of competition, resistance and innovation in the aftermath of widespread technological change (Gomery 2005, 105–14).

Even as Hollywood adjusted to the changes brought on by synchronized sound, American companies sought to expand their reach (and their profits) through international distribution of sound films. They saw Europe in particular as an available market. The installation of sound equipment and distribution of sound films in countries that had not yet developed the technology to do this themselves promised to be lucrative. Engineers in Europe, however, had also made progress on sound-synchronization technology: more than fifteen sound systems were competing in Europe during the transitional period and, by 1928, the primarily Dutch-owned Tobis was formed, controlling most of the important patents in Europe, including the Tri-Ergon system (Kreimeier 1996, 178–9). Ufa, AEG and Siemens and Halske then launched the company Klangfilm to organize the German industry's response. In 1929, Tobis and Klangfilm came to an agreement, and they began jointly marketing their technology as Tobis-Klangfilm, aiming to corner the European market and shut out American companies. Tobis-Klangfilm sought to stall the American film industry's impending control of the international market, disputing patents in the hope of obstructing what they saw as an inevitable 'talkie invasion' by the American companies (Gomery 1980, 85) – not just studios, but also the activity of firms like ERPI that posed a major threat to more basic industrial concerns. In the summer of 1930, representatives from Tobis-Klangfilm and members of the American film industry conferred on neutral ground in Paris. An international cartel resulted from this 'Paris Agreement', and the German and American companies agreed to split up much of the world for patent rights and charge films royalties for distribution within each territory. As German and American companies held the decisive patents, other national film industries were at the mercy of foreign firms for the technology to produce and exhibit sound films. Resistance to the change was particularly widespread in countries like France due to fear that national cinematic practices would diminish.

Because the European transition to commercial sound-film production came somewhat later than in the United States (initially running two to three years behind), and perhaps because they had the American model to react to or because they needed to play catch-up, Europeans developed a number of innovative sound films as they made the transition. In England, *Blackmail* (1929) was originally planned as a silent film, but the quick inroads sound film was making in British theatres required that director Alfred Hitchcock re-conceive the film with dialogue sequences. As was commonly the case during the transition era, a silent version was also released for theatres not yet equipped with sound. The lead actress (Anny Ondra) had a heavy Czech accent, so Joan Barry was hired to speak the dialogue off-camera, essentially dubbing the film live because techniques of post-synchronization were not yet well developed (Belton 1999).

Walter Ruttmann devised an innovative audiovisual aesthetic in his first sound film, *Melodie der Welt*. Adapting the approach he took in his silent *Berlin: Die Sinfonie der Großstadt* (*Berlin: Symphony of a Great City*; 1927), Ruttmann created an audiovisual 'symphony', a collage of recorded diegetic sounds corresponding to the montage of images from around the world. The soundtrack sounds almost like a prototype for *musique concrète*. Ruttmann also experimented with sound-only films. In 1931, Lang directed his first sound film, *M*, a wonderfully strange hybrid that combines silent-film technique (including fully silent sequences), a kind of voice-over narration to connect different locations, and off-screen sound to heighten suspense. Though Lang's approach to sound in *M* might, like Hitchcock's work on *Blackmail*, seem related to the technical challenges of synchronized sound film, it should be noted that by 1931 films coming out of the German film industry had achieved a high technical standard with respect to dialogue. Although shooting more dialogue without showing moving lips than American films from the time, deft handling of synchronized dialogue is nevertheless demonstrated in *Die Drei von der Tankstelle* (*Three Good Friends* or *Three Men and Lilian*; 1930), Erik Charell's *Der Kongreß tanzt* (*The Congress Dances*; 1931) and Pabst's *Westfront 1918: Vier von der Infanterie* (*Comrades of 1918*; 1930), *Die 3 Groschen-Oper* (*The Threepenny Opera*; 1931) and *Kameradschaft* ('Comradeship'; 1931). If *M* was not an improvised solution to challenges posed by inadequate technology, it seems instead an experiment to avoid the obviousness of sync sound without reverting wholly to silent-film technique.

While establishing close and convincing synchronization remained a continual concern, and American films generally began a shot with a sync point of flapping lips and dialogue before passing to reaction shots, European films were on the whole less obsessed with such close dialogue synchronization and frequently shot dialogue from behind, where synchronization could be much looser. In early cases, like *Blackmail* and Augusto Genina's *Prix de beauté* (*Miss Europe* or *Beauty Prize*; 1930), this seems to have been an expedient to allow dialogue to be added during post-production to footage shot silent. But the practice continued in later films, most notably in René Clair's three Parisian operettas. In general, Clair explored an approach to sound film that also downplayed dialogue in favour of other sound elements. Apparent especially in his 1931 film *Le Million*, his first sound films use minimal dialogue, instead utilizing audiovisual counterpoint and songs to propel the action forwards. Clair does not completely avoid dialogue, but he associates it with the negative forces of economic necessity and the law. He also frequently shoots dialogue with the principal characters facing away from the camera. This strategy of loose synchronization endows the voice with a certain lightness – as though it is only barely contained by the speaking body and might break free at any moment (Fischer 1977; Gorbman 1987, 140–50; Cooke 2008, 62–4). Clair's world, inspired by vaudeville stage comedies, is comic and giddy, ruled by happenstance.

The experimental tradition of filmmaking in the Soviet Union continued for a time with sound. Dziga Vertov was the first Soviet director to make a sound film in the USSR: *Enthusiasm*, released in 1931. In the film, on-location sound and mechanical sound effects are woven together to create a collage, as was the case with Ruttmann. Vertov's experimental approach to the soundtrack combined with the subject of Soviet miners, thereby reflecting the broader values of Soviet filmmakers that had begun with silent films like his earlier *Man With a Movie Camera* (1929) and Eisenstein's *Battleship Potemkin*.

Vococentrism and the Codification of Practices (1931–1935)

After 1930, due in part to adverse economic pressures from the Great Depression, codification of effective practices for producing sound film became an ever more important goal of the industry, especially in the United States. This had the effect of curtailing the spirit of experimentation, and the wide-ranging practices of the early years gave way to an increasingly ordered set of practices defined by the principles of 'vococentrism' (Chion 1999, 5; Neumeyer 2015, 3–49). Despite calls for continued development of the possibilities of asynchronous sound by theorists, experiments in sound design that pushed against the default vococentrism of synchronized dialogue such as films by Chaplin, Clair, Lang, Pudovkin and Eisenstein frequently yielded excellent and provocative films but little real influence on the direction of mainstream filmmaking. Whether in the United States or internationally, in the years after 1930 commercial sound film increasingly simply meant talking film, and the vococentrism of talking film meant a high preponderance of synchronized dialogue.

In practice, however, vococentrism dominated because it was a robust yet flexible principle. If vococentrism insisted on the centrality of dialogue on the soundtrack, this did not mean that dialogue was uniformly ubiquitous or that sync dialogue featured prominently at every moment in the talking film. Certainly, some films were edited primarily on the basis of dialogue, so that each new line motivated a cut and almost all of the soundtrack was taken up by dialogue. But the power of the reaction shot was understood almost immediately, as was the potential for sound effects, and to some extent music, to complement and contextualize the voice, to make a setting for it. As Clair noted in his appreciative remarks about *The Broadway Melody*, 'We hear the noise of a door being slammed and a car driving off while we are shown Bessie Love's anguished face watching from a window the departure we do not see' (Clair 1953, 94). Since Michel Chion draws vococentrism from an analogy with the face, it is worth lingering on this comparison. If the face dominated the cinematography and editing of narrative film, this did not mean that every shot was a close-up, or that every shot revealed a face (except perhaps in a metaphorical way: the face of things, the face of the world), or even that every shot containing a face centred it. The centricity of the face in classic style was instead interpretive: it presumed that the reading of the image would be guided by the placement and displacement of the face within and from the frame. A similar situation pertained to the voice and the soundtrack. Vococentrism meant understanding the soundtrack in terms of the setting of the voice, and the expressive potential of the reaction shot lay at least in part in the way that it shifted the audiovisual interpretive significance of the voice from cause (the source of the dialogue in the speaking body) to its effect (on a particular listener).

Even as the industry rapidly standardized practices that favoured voco-centrism, sound film continued to be widely distrusted by many who worked in the industry, both in Europe and America. If American companies moved quickly to convert to sound, the rapidity of the transition by no means indicated any kind of consensus surrounding its desirability over silent film. Many still understood sound film, especially dialogue, as contrary to the spirit of cinema. Europeans, notably Soviet and French directors, were particularly resistant. In the USSR, Eisenstein, Pudovkin and Alexandrov, three prominent directors, wrote an influential statement in 1928 attacking Hollywood's approach to sound film before they had even seen one of its films. Rather than having image and sound slavishly bound in synchronized dialogue, the Soviet directors advocated a counterpoint between image and sound, a relationship that they believed was the audiovisual equivalent of the dialectical montage for which Soviet films had become justly famous (K. Thompson 1980; Eisenstein, Pudovkin and Alexandrov 1928). Initially, Clair – well known for the visual style of his silent films – was also strongly opposed to the talking film, fearing synchronized dialogue in particular would destroy the expressive power of the image. He likewise advocated setting sound contrapuntally against the image in order to resist a naturalistically constructed synchronization grounded in realism, writing that 'if *imitation* of real noises seems limited and disappointing, it is possible that an *interpretation* of noises may have more of a future in it . . . We do not need to *hear* the sound of clapping if we can *see* the clapping hands' (Clair 1953, 91–4, emphases in original).

The opposition between talking film as slavish synchronization and sound film as a site for inspired counterpoint, or asynchronous sound, as its best antidote was picked up by most film theorists of the time, including Béla Balázs and Rudolf Arnheim. According to Balázs, sound film should 'approach the reality of life from a totally different angle and open up a new treasure-house of human experience' (1970 [1952], 197). Arnheim, by contrast, questioned the efficacy of asynchronous sound in many instances and focused as much on the power of synchronization as its redundancy: synchronized sound transformed film, the act of synchronization opening a divide between foreground elements in the image and the background. Sound film, he noted, 'endows the actor with speech, and since only he can have it, all other things are pushed into the background' (1957, 227). As Arnheim was quite aware – and none too pleased – the synchronization of the sound film had the effect of imposing an ordering hierarchy on the image: synchronized objects were important objects, and dialogue added another level that made vococentrism the technical principle that implemented sound film's irreducible anthropocentrism. In the silent film, by contrast, the world was not divided by a capacity to articulate meaning through talk; an essential continuity between people and things was assured in their common muteness, the universal condition of the silent image. With such a hierarchy of sounds established, the focus on the voice ensured the centrality of the human figure and its subjectivity in the sound film's new economy of meaning and intention. Music and sound effects, then, set the voice within the economy of human meaning.

Vococentrism can therefore be understood as an effective reworking of the three principles of silent-film music, recast as powers within the hierarchal order of foreground and background. Centricity rewrites the principle of synchronization as a marker of import, the site of meaning that assures the appearance of subjectivity and its hegemonic status. Continuity becomes the power of background, the guarantor that the image presents only a view, a fragment of a world that extends indefinitely beyond the frame. Continuity also establishes the more or less neutral ground of asynchronous sound against which the synchronization of the foreground figure stands out in contrast. Finally, vococentrism redeploys subjugation to unlock its full syntactical power, that of the hierarchy itself; but subjugation pertains not simply to music and effects *vis-à-vis* the voice or the soundtrack *vis-à-vis* the image, but ultimately to the subjugation of everything to narrative, the cinematic form of meaningful action. Vococentrism, then, is the principle of the voice of narrative, which organized the codification of classical style.

Conclusion: The Emergence of the New Art

The traditional historical narrative of film music places the end of the transition to sound in 1933 with Steiner's score for *King Kong*, which is typically considered to be the first classical Hollywood film score and responsible for beginning an era of relatively standardized approach to composing for films. This narrative is, of course, an oversimplification. Slowik argues that Steiner's practice in the early 1930s was less an innovation than an extension and codification of methods that had developed in the silent film and had continued as a minority practice through the transitional period. Writing on Steiner's scores for *Symphony of Six Million* and *The Most Dangerous Game* (both 1932), Slowik states 'Steiner's primary contribution was to reintroduce the theme-driven score in a dramatic context, an approach that had fallen out of favor with the advent of the 100 percent talkie' (2014, 204). Nathan Platte's work on

[handwritten margin note: anthropocentrism = considering human beings as the most significant entity of the universe; interpreting or regarding the world in terms of human values and experiences]

Steiner's early scores during this period likewise makes it clear that many innovations that have been assigned to *Kong* in standard film-music histories had predecessors in earlier scores by Steiner and others (Platte 2014). Nevertheless, the music for *Kong* seems much more consistent with the practices that would dominate Hollywood film music during the classic era than do the sound-film scores that came before it – with the possible exception of *Symphony of Six Million* (*ibid.*, 321, 328; Long 2008, 88) – and indeed many that come after it. Steiner's innovations would seem to belong to the manner in which he evoked but also broke with silent-film practice in a way that enabled him to forge an underscore predicated on sound film. But this practice did not emerge immediately in Steiner's music, and, as Slowik and Platte both note, *Kong* still retained strong affinities to transitional accompaniment practices quite continuous with those of the silent film.

Like *The Jazz Singer, Kong* was perhaps primed to become a signal event, and to serve as the moment of origin for the classic Hollywood film score, because its soundtrack thematized its problem and so could be allegorized into a general solution. Slowik notes structural affinities between *Kong* and the earlier *Symphony of Six Million* with respect to music: both films initially develop an opposition of space articulated with music (island, ghetto) and without music (city, uptown). *Six Million* begins in the ghetto and returns to it, and throughout music remains bound to the ghetto, which is rendered exotic and pathetic in virtue of its musicality. *Kong* inverts this arrangement, beginning with the city devoid of music, devoid of life; the exotic island is then suffused with music, and Kong's forced appearance in the city has the effect of releasing music into it (Buhler *et al.* 2010, 331). According to Slowik, 'What marked *King Kong* as unusual was not a *musical* decision to tie music to fantasy but rather a *narrative* decision to depict urban reality and exotic fantasy in the same film and to blend them together in the final act' (2014, 234). And Slowik rightly notes that Steiner's score for the film is fully consistent with film-music practice that had developed at the end of the transitional period. Yet this revisionist claim, although broadly correct, is akin to the one that would minimize the influence of *The Jazz Singer* in the transition to sound; neither claim accounts for the fact that these stories began circulating almost immediately. They may well form crucial pieces in the mythology of sound film, but the myth was already forming at the moment of origin. If Steiner could quickly represent *Kong* as having opened a new path for music in film (1937, 220), it is likely that he seized on this film and not his previous or later work for a reason, even if he had a strong self-interest in promoting his own work.

While films like *The Jazz Singer* and *Kong* have become iconic in the history of film sound and film music for their innovations framing the transition period, the myths surrounding these films obscure a much richer history: one of codification and experimentation, of unexpected continuity and major disruption and of negotiation and confrontation. The shift occurred in markedly different ways in Hollywood and in Europe, and the technology's dissemination to the rest of the world reveals further dimensions and complexities to the story of the transition. Emily Thompson, for instance, in her study of the installation of sound technology around the world, writes that sound film 'provided a powerful new means by which to articulate national agenda, and the end result was not a single, standardized and unified modern voice but a cacophony of competing signals and messages' (2004, 192). Within this period, the role of music and sound in cinema shifted in many dramatic ways, but emerging out of the transition period the major principles motivating their use remained. The maintaining of these principles was by no means inevitable, as producers, directors and composers around the world negotiated the role of music and sound in the soundtrack; moreover, experiments with the soundtrack did not cease after the transition period. Many of the most innovative uses of sound in later films came from directors and composers who bucked the trends of established practices. Yet the manner in which film music and sound practices were standardized by the mid-1930s reveals certain constants from the silent to the 'classical' era of filmmaking: sound film, organized under the principle of vococentrism, ultimately had the effect of tightening the already powerful grip of narrative on cinema.

2 'Pictures That Talk and Sing'
Sound History and Technology

DAVID COOPER

Synchronization sometimes went disastrously wrong in early experiments to join sound and film, particularly if these two components were reproduced separately and got out of step, say due to the film having been damaged, a section removed and the ends joined together. Austin Lescarboura, managing editor of *Scientific American* from 1919 to 1924, devoted a chapter of his book *Behind the Motion-Picture Screen* (first published in 1919) to the topic of 'Pictures That Talk and Sing' and described a scene from the film *Julius Caesar* (1913) – an early Shakespeare adaptation presented in the Kinetophone sound system with sound provided by synchronized Edison sound cylinders – in which an actor 'suddenly sheathed his sword, and a few seconds later came the commanding voice from the phonograph, somewhere behind the screen saying: "Sheathe thy sword, Brutus!"' (Lescarboura 1921, 292). The audience's response was, understandably, one of hilarity.

Lescarboura, with considerable prescience, foresaw that the principles involved in new photographic methods of recording sound – then still at an experimental stage – would 'some day form the basis of a commercial system' (*ibid.*, 300). Early attempts at 'sound on picture' (such as Lee de Forest's Phonofilm) suffered from problems of noise, but by 1928 many of these had been resolved and a soundtrack that had reasonable fidelity became available through Movietone, which, like Phonofilm, had the advantage of the soundtrack actually lying on the print beside the pictures, thus removing the problem of 'drift' between two separate, albeit connected, mechanisms. The fascinating period during which filmmakers came to terms, in various ways, with the implications of the new technology is charted in detail in Chapter 1 of the present volume.

According to John Michael Weaver, James G. Stewart (a soundman hired by RKO in 1931 and chief re-recording mixer for the company from 1933 to 1945) recalled that the first sound engineers in film wielded considerable power:

> during the early days of Hollywood's conversion to sound, the production mixer's power on the set sometimes rivalled the director's. Recordists were able to insist that cameras be isolated in soundproof booths, and they even had the authority to

cut a scene-in-progress when they didn't like what they were hearing.

(Weaver 1993, 12)

Stewart noted that the impositions made by the sound crew in pursuit of audio quality in the first year of talkies had a detrimental effect on the movies, bringing about 'a static quality that's terrible'. Indeed, one might argue that film sound technology, from its very inception, has been driven forward by the attempt to accommodate the competing demands of sonic fidelity and naturalness.

Peter Copeland has remarked how rapidly many of the most important characteristics of sound editing were developed and adopted. By 1931, the following impressive list of techniques was available:

> cut-and-splice sound editing; dubbing mute shots (i.e. providing library sounds for completely silent bits of film); quiet cameras; 'talkback' and other intercom systems; 'boom' microphones (so the mike could be placed over the actor's head and moved as necessary); equalization; track-bouncing; replacement of dialogue (including alternative languages); filtering (for removing traffic noise, wind noise, or simulating telephone conversations); busbars for routing controlled amounts of foldback or reverberation; three-track recording (music, effects, and dialogue, any of which could be changed as necessary); automatic volume limiters; and synchronous playback (for dance or mimed shots).

(Copeland 1991, 21)

Re-recording, which was used less frequently before 1931, would become increasingly prevalent through the 1930s due to the development of noise-reduction techniques, significantly impacting on scoring and music-editing activities (Jacobs 2012).

The Principles of Optical Recording and Projection

A fundamental principle of sound recording is that of transduction, the conversion of energy from one form to another. Using a microphone, sound can be transformed from changes in air pressure to equivalent electrical variations that may then be recorded onto magnetic tape. Optical recording provides a further means of storing audio, either through the changes in density, or more commonly the changes in width of the developed section of a strip of photographic emulsion lying between the sprocket holes and the picture frames. Figure 2.1(a) displays one of a number of different formats for the variable-width track with a solid black edge on the left-hand side, which is termed the unilateral variable area, shown in Figure 2.1(b). Other alternatives (bilateral, duplex and push-pull variable areas) have solid edges on the right side or on both sides. In variable-density recording, the photographic emulsion can take on any state between undeveloped (black – no light passes

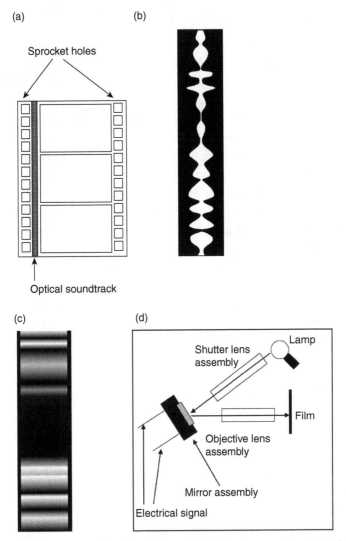

Figure 2.1 35 mm film with optical soundtrack (a), a close-up of a portion of the variable-area soundtrack (b), a close-up of a portion of the variable-density soundtrack (c) and a simplified schematic view of a variable-area recorder from the late 1930s (d), based on Figure 11 from L. E. Clark and John K. Hilliard, 'Types of Film Recording' (1938, 28). Note that there are four sprocket holes on each frame.

through) to fully developed (clear – all light passes through). Between these two states, different 'grey tones' transmit more or less light: see Figure 2.1(c). In digital optical recording tiny dots are recorded, like the pits on a CD.

The technology for variable-area recording, as refined in the 1930s, involves a complex assembly in which the motion of a mirror reflecting light onto the optical track by way of a series of lenses is controlled by the electrical signal generated by the microphone: see Figure 2.1(d). If no signal is present, the opaque and clear sections of film will have equal areas, and as the sound level changes, so does the clear area. When the film is subsequently projected, light is shone through the optical track and is received by a photoelectric cell, a device which converts the illumination it receives back to an electrical signal which varies in proportion to the light impinging on it, and this signal is amplified and passed to the auditorium loudspeakers. The clear area of the soundtrack, between the two opaque sections shown in Figure 2.1(b), is prone to contamination by particles of dirt, grains of silver, abrasions and so on. These contaminants, which are randomly distributed on the film, result in noise which effectively reduces the available dynamic range: the quieter the recording (and thus the larger the clear area on the film soundtrack), the more foreign particles will be present and the greater will be the relative level of noise compared to recorded sound. Much effort was expended by the studios to counter-act this deficiency in optical recording by means of noise reduction in the 1930s, the so-called push-pull system for variable-area recording being developed by RCA and that for variable-width recording by Western Electric's ERPI (see Frayne 1976 and Jacobs 2012, 14–18).

Cinematography involves a kind of sampling, each 'sample' being a single picture or frame of film – three such frames are shown in Figure 2.1(a) – with twenty-four images typically being taken or projected every second. Time-lapse and high-speed photography will also use differ-ent frame rates. Early film often had much lower frame rates, for instance 16 frames per second (fps). The illusion of continuity generated when the frames are replayed at an appropriate rate is usually ascribed to persistence of vision (the tendency for an image to remain on the retina for a short time after its stimulus has disappeared), though this is disputed by some psychologists as an explanation of the phenomenon of apparent or strobo-scopic movement found in film: as Julian Hochberg notes, 'persistence would result in the superposition of the successive views' (1987, 604). A major technical issue which the first film engineers had to confront was how to create a mechanism which could produce the stop-go motion needed to shoot or project film, for the negative or print must be held still for the brief time needed to expose or display it, and then moved to the next frame in about 1/80th of a second. Attempts to solve this intermittent-motion problem resulted in such curious devices as the 'drunken screw' and the 'beater movement', but generally a ratchet and claw mechanism is found in the film camera.

Some film projectors still use one of the most ingenious of the early inventions, modelled on the 'Geneva' movement of some Swiss watches and called the 'Maltese Cross movement' because of the shape of its star wheel: see Figure 2.2. The wheel on the right has a pin (a) and a raised cam with a cut-out (b). As this cam-wheel rotates on its central pivot, the

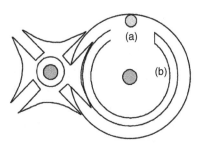

Figure 2.2 The Maltese Cross or Geneva mechanism.

star wheel on the left (which controls the motion of the film) remains stationary until its wings reach the cut-out and the gap between the wings locks onto the pin. The star wheel is now forced to turn by a quarter of a rotation, advancing the film by one frame. Unlike the intermittent motion required for filming and projection, sound recording and replay needs constant, regular movement. A pair of damping rollers (rather like a miniature old-fashioned washing mangle) therefore smoothes the film's progress before it reaches the exciter lamp and the photoelectric cell, which generate the electrical signal from the optical track and hence to the audio amplifier and the auditorium loudspeakers. As the soundtrack reaches the sound head some twenty frames after the picture reaches the projector, sound must be offset ahead of its associated picture by twenty frames to compensate.

Soundtracks on Release Prints

Early sound films only provided a monophonic soundtrack for reproduction, and this necessarily limited the extent to which a 'three-dimensional' sound-space could be simulated. This was an issue of considerable importance to sound engineers. Kenneth Lambert, in his chapter 'Re-recording and Preparation for Release' in the 1938 professional instructional manual *Motion Picture Sound Engineering*, remarks:

> Most of us hear with two ears. Present recording systems hear as if only with one, and adjustments of quality must be made electrically or acoustically to simulate the effect of two ears. Cover one ear and note how voices become more masked by surrounding noises. This effect is overcome in recording, partially by the use of a somewhat directional microphone which discriminates against sound coming from the back and the sides of the microphone, and partially by placing the microphone a little closer to the actor than we normally should have our ears.
>
> (K. Lambert 1938, 76)

Whilst it was possible to suggest the position of a sound-source in terms of its apparent distance from the viewer by adjustment of the relative levels of the various sonic components, microphone position and equalization, film-makers could not provide explicit lateral directional information. If, for instance, a car was seen to drive across the visual foreground from left to right, the level of the sound effect of the car's engine might be increased as it approached the centre of the frame and decreased as it moved to the right, but this hardly provided a fully convincing accompaniment to the motion. In order to create directional cues for sound effects, further soundtracks were required. Lest there be any confusion, the term 'stereo' has not usually implied two-channel stereophony in film sound reproduction, as it does in the world of audio hi-fi (the Greek root *stereos* (στερεός) actually means 'solid' or 'firm'); rather, it normally indicates a minimum of three channels. As early as the mid-1930s, Bell Laboratories were working on stereophonic reproduction (though, interestingly, no mention is made of these developments in *Motion Picture Sound Engineering* in 1938), and between 1939 and 1940 Warner Bros. released *Four Wives* and *Santa Fe Trail*, both of which used the three-channel Vitasound system, had scores by Max Steiner and were directed by Michael Curtiz (Bordwell *et al.* 1985, 359).

Disney's animation *Fantasia* (1940), one of the most technically innovative films of its time, made use of a high-quality multi-channel system called Fantasound. This system represented Disney's response to a number of perceived shortcomings of contemporaneous film sound, as was explained in a 1941 trade journal:

(a) Limited Volume Range. – The limited volume range of conventional recordings is reasonably satisfactory for the reproduction of ordinary dialog and incidental music, under average theater conditions. However, symphonic music and dramatic effects are noticeably impaired by excessive ground-noise and amplitude distortion.

(b) Point-Source of Sound. – A point-source of sound has certain advantages for monaural dialog reproduction with action confined to the center of the screen, but music and effects suffer from a form of acoustic phase distortion that is absent when the sound comes from a broad source.

(c) Fixed Localization of the Sound-Source at Screen Center. – The limitations of single-channel dialog have forced the development of a camera and cutting technic built around action at the center of the screen, or more strictly, the center of the conventional high-frequency horn. A three-channel system, allowing localization away from screen center, removes this single-channel limitation, and this increases the flexibility of the sound medium.

(d) Fixed Source of Sound. – In live entertainment practically all sound-sources are fixed in space. Any movements that do occur, occur slowly. It has been found that by artificially causing the source of sound to move rapidly in space the result can be highly dramatic and desirable.

(Garity and Hawkins 1941, 128)

In its final incarnation, the Fantasound system had two separate 35 mm prints, one of which carried four optical soundtracks (left, right, centre and a control track). Nine optical tracks were utilized for the original multitrack orchestral recordings (six for different sections of the orchestra, one for ambience, one containing a monophonic mix and one which was to be used as a guide track by the animators). These were mixed down to three surround soundtracks, the playback system requiring two projectors, one for the picture (which had a normal mono optical soundtrack as a backup) and a second to play the three optical stereo tracks. The fourth track provided what would now be regarded as a type of automated fader control. Tones of three different frequencies (250 Hz, 630 Hz and 1600 Hz) were recorded, their levels varying in proportion to the required levels of each of the three soundtracks (which were originally recorded at close to maximum level), and these signals were subsequently band-pass filtered to recover the original tones and passed to variable-gain amplifiers which controlled the output level: see Figure 2.3 for a simplified diagram. The cinema set-up involved three horns at the front (left, centre and right) and two at the rear, the latter being automated to either supplement or replace the signals being fed to the front left and right speakers.

As part of the research and development of the sound system, Disney engineers also invented the 'Panpot', or panoramic potentiometer, a device to balance the relative level of sounds in the left, centre and right channels that has become a fundamental control found in every modern mixing console. Using the Panpot, engineers could 'steer' sound across the sound-space, allowing them to produce the kind of lateral directional information discussed above. Given a cost of around $85,000 to equip the auditorium, it

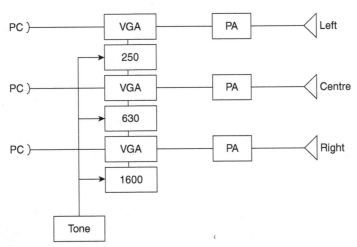

Figure 2.3 A simplified block diagram of the Fantasound system (after Figure 2 in Garity and Hawkins 1941). PC indicates photocell, PA power amplifier and VGA variable-gain amplifier.

is perhaps unsurprising that only two American movie houses were willing to invest in the technology required to show *Fantasia* in the Fantasound version, although eight reduced systems, each costing $45,000, were constructed for the touring road shows which used a modified mix of orchestra, chorus and soloists respectively on the three stereo tracks (see Blake 1984a and 1984b; Klapholz 1991).

Stereo sound in film was intimately tied to image size, and in CinemaScope – Twentieth Century-Fox's 2.35:1 widescreen format which dominated 35 mm film projection from the early 1950s – the soundtrack complemented the greater dramatic potential of the picture. The numbers 2.35:1 indicate the aspect ratio of the width and height of the projected picture, that is, the image width is 2.35 times the image height. (The Academy ratio which prevailed before widescreen films became popular is 1.33:1.) CinemaScope was not the first widescreen format: Cinerama, which was used for the best part of a decade from 1952, had a seven-track analogue magnetic soundtrack with left, mid-left, centre, mid-right and right front channels, and left and right surround channels.

CinemaScope films have four audio tracks, one each for right, centre and left speakers at the front of the auditorium, and one for effects. These are recorded magnetically rather than optically, with magnetic stripes between the sprocket holes and the picture, and between the sprocket holes and film edge. (A 70 mm format called Todd-AO, which had six magnetic soundtracks, was also available.) *The Robe*, Henry Koster's Biblical spectacle of 1953 with a score by Alfred Newman, was the first film to be released by Fox in the CinemaScope format. Although around 80 per cent of American cinemas were able to show films in CinemaScope by 1956, only 20 per cent had purchased the audio equipment required to reproduce the magnetic tracks, and viewers had the mixed blessing of a superior widescreen image and an inferior monophonic optical soundtrack. Theatre managers were reluctant to adopt magnetic reproduction, not merely because of the up-front cost of installing the equipment, but also because of the much greater hire charge for magnetic prints, which were at least twice as expensive as their optical equivalents.

A revolution in film-sound reproduction occurred in the 1970s with the development by Dolby Laboratories of a four-channel optical format with vastly improved sound quality. Dolby had found an ingenious method of fitting the three main channels and the effects channel into two optical tracks, using 'phase steering' techniques developed for quadraphonic hi-fi. Ken Russell's critically pilloried *Lisztomania* of 1975 was the first film to be released using the new format called Dolby Stereo, and it was followed in 1977 by George Lucas's *Star Wars* (later renamed *Star Wars* Episode IV: *A New Hope*) and Steven Spielberg's *Close Encounters of the Third Kind*,

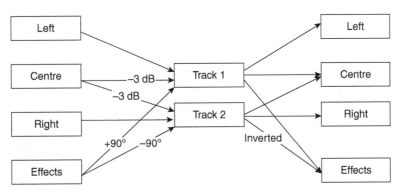

Figure 2.4 A simplified diagram of the Dolby Stereo system. On the left side are the four source channels, in the centre are the two film soundtracks derived from them and on the right are the four output channels played in the cinema.

both of which made great use of the potential offered by the system. Dolby Stereo involves adding the centre channel (dialogue, generally) equally to both left and right tracks, but at a lower level (-3 dB), the surround channel also being sent to both tracks, but 180° degrees out of phase relative to each other (on one the surround signal is +90°, on the other it is -90°). A matrixing unit reconstructs the four channels for replay through the cinema's sound-reproduction system: see Figure 2.4.

Dolby Laboratories improved the frequency response and dynamic range of the analogue optical audio tracks in 1987 by introducing their 'SR' noise-reduction process, and in 1992 a digital optical system with six channels was made available, which had the standard three front channels, one for low-frequency effects and two separate left and right rear channels for surround sound. Dolby's consumer formats, which have similar specifications to their cinema-sound products, have seen wide-scale adoption, though competing multichannel digital formats include DTS (Digital Theater Sound) which, in an approach that looks back to Vitaphone, uses six-channel sound stored on external media and synchronized to the film by timecode, and Sony's SDDS (Sony Dynamic Digital Sound), which employs the ATRAC (Adaptive Transform Acoustic Coding) compression technology designed for MiniDisc.

The technical improvements in sound quality have required cinema owners to invest in their projection and reproduction equipment if they wish to replay multichannel film sound adequately. A standard for such equipment, and the acoustics of the theatres which use it, was established by Lucas's company Lucasfilm, certified cinemas being permitted to display the THX logo, and required to apply annually for re-certification. The standard covers such diverse issues as background noise, isolation and reverberation, customer viewing angle, equipment and equipment installation. THX can be seen, perhaps, as an attempt to complete the democratization of the cinema, for unlike the picture palaces of days gone by, every seat in the house should provide a similar (though not identical) hi-fidelity aural experience, which ideally relates to that of a soundtrack reproduced on a digital format with high-quality headphones.

In late 1998, agreement was reached between Dolby Laboratories and Lucasfilm THX for the introduction of a 6.1 surround-sound format called Dolby Digital-Surround EX, which includes a centre-rear speaker for more accurate placement of sound at the rear of the auditorium. The format, initially employed in 1999 on the first film in Lucas's second *Star Wars* trilogy, Episode I: *The Phantom Menace*, brought together two of the major players in film sound in an attempt to improve the sonic quality of the cinematic experience even further.

Cinema sound has continued to be a major focus for technical development, including the introduction of further digital formats such as Dolby Surround 7.1 (which employs a pair of surround channels on each side) in the release of *Toy Story 3* (2010); Barco Auro 11.1 (which places the 5.1 system on two vertical levels with an additional overhead channel) in *Red Tails* (2012); and Dolby Atmos full-range surround with up to sixty-four channels on separate levels in *Brave* (2012).

Soundtracks at the Post-Production Stage

The soundtrack of the final release of a film is mixed from three basic types of audio material: dialogue, music and effects. These three elements (known as 'stems') are usually archived on separate tracks by the production company for commercial as much as artistic reasons: many films are also released in foreign-language versions and it would be expensive to re-record music and effects as well as dialogue, which is added by actors in an ADR (automatic dialogue replacement) suite as they watch a looped section of the film. The quantity of sound actually recorded on set or on location and used on the final soundtrack varies between productions, partly for pragmatic and partly for aesthetic reasons. At one extreme, all dialogue and effects may be added during post-production (after the main filming has been completed), and at the other, only location sound may be used. Although one of the first films to have a soundtrack created entirely in post-production was Disney's Mickey Mouse short *Steamboat Willie* (1928), the transition to this being the norm for most live-action sound films took another decade (K. Lambert 1938, 69). If the film is recorded on a sound stage in a studio, much of the dialogue will probably be of acceptable quality, whereas audio collected on location may suffer from background noise, rendering it unusable. For example, in Ron Howard's *Willow* (1988), 85 per cent of the dialogue was added in post-production, whereas in Spielberg's *Indiana Jones and the Last Crusade* (1989), only 25 per cent was (Pasquariello 1993, 59). James Monaco notes that in some instances Federico Fellini had not even written the dialogue for his films until shooting had finished (1981, 106).

Sound-effects tracks can be subdivided into three main categories: spot effects, atmospheres and Foley. Spot (or hard) effects may be specially recorded or taken from effects libraries on CD or other digital media, and include most discrete sounds of relatively short duration: dogs barking, engines starting, telephones ringing and so on. Atmospheres (or wild tracks, so called because they are non-synchronous with the action) are of longer duration than spots (though a hard-and-fast line between the two types can be hard to draw), may be recorded on set or specially designed and are intended to enhance the aural impression of a particular space or location. Foley effects are named after Jack Foley, who pioneered the recreation of realistic ambient sounds in post-production at Universal in the late 1920s. Foley artists work on a specially designed sound-proofed and acoustically dead recording stage where they watch the film on a monitor and perform the sound effects in sync with the action to complement or replace the background sounds recorded on set. Creature sounds, many of which must be invented to supply the language of extinct or fantastic animals (for example, the dinosaurs of Spielberg's 1993 film *Jurassic Park*, or the aliens in *Star Wars*), form a further sub-category of effects. These may derive from real animal sounds which are recorded and processed or superimposed – for example, Chewbacca in *Star Wars* is in part a recording of walruses.

An alternative strategy for dealing with effects tracks is to consider them in terms of the apparent location of their constituent elements in a flexible three-dimensional sound-space. Thus it is possible to discriminate between a sonic foreground, middleground and background that can dynamically mirror the equivalent visual planes (irrespective of whether the sources are in view). The accurate construction of these sound-spaces became more significant with the development of sound systems like Dolby Stereo and Dolby Digital in which finer detail could be distinguished, and the re-equipping of cinemas with high-quality reproduction equipment according to the THX standard. Sound designers such as Alan R. Splet, who worked closely with director David Lynch on his films from *Eraserhead* (1976) to *Blue Velvet* (1986), showed just how creative an area this can be, for their work often went beyond the naturalistic reproduction of sound-spaces, at times adopting a role analogous to that of nondiegetic music. Lynch's own telling remark that 'people call me a director, but

I really think of myself as a sound-man' underlines this trend to place the sonic elements on an equal footing to that of the visuals (Chion 1995b, 169).

During the dub, a final stereo mix is produced from the dialogue, effects (including atmospheres and Foley) and music tracks, and this is used to generate the soundtracks on the release print. The dub is normally a two-stage process, the first of which involves a pre-mix in which the number of tracks is reduced by combining the many individual effects and dialogue tracks into composite ones. In *Indiana Jones and the Last Crusade*, for instance, twenty-two tracks were sometimes used for Foley alone; for the television show *Northern Exposure* (CBS, 1990–95), up to sixty-nine analogue tracks held music, dialogue and effects; and twenty-eight eight-track recorders were used for effects on Roland Emmerich's 1998 blockbuster *Godzilla* (James 1998, 86). The pre-post-prodmix results in individual mono or stereo tracks (four or six, depending on the system) for dialogue and effects (Foley, spots and atmospheres), and these are mixed with the music tracks by three re-recording mixers at the final dub to generate the release soundtrack. A track or group of tracks called 'music and effects' (M&E) is also mixed from the individual music and effects tracks to retain decisions made by the director and editors about the relative levels of the individual components, for the reason explained above.

Synchronization

In every case, the soundtrack must be locked or synchronized to picture, and this has provided problems since the earliest sound films with a score. For dialogue and effects tracks it is largely a matter of matching a visual image with its sonic correlate (for example, the sound of gunfire as the trigger of a gun is pressed, or engine noise as a car's ignition switch is turned). Often there will be an unambiguous one-to-one mapping between image and sound, and difficult as the operation may be for the editor, there is a 'correct' solution. This is not necessarily the case with music, for although the technique of tight synchronization between image and music (mickey-mousing, otherwise known as 'catching the action') is frequently found, there will generally be a much subtler relationship between the two.

Steiner has often been credited with the invention of the click track, as an aid to his work on the score to John Ford's *The Informer* (1935), though in his unreliable and unpublished memoirs he makes various unsubstantiated claims about his invention or use of the click track for earlier RKO films produced in 1931 and 1932 (Steiner 1963–4). It seems that Disney's crew had used a similar device some time earlier, to assist the synchronization of animated film and music, filing patents in 1928, 1930 and 1931. In *Underscore*, a 'combination method-text-treatise on scoring music for motion picture films or T.V.' written by the prolific composer Frank Skinner in 1950, the main uses of the click track in the classic Hollywood film were enumerated:

1 To catch intricate cues on the screen by writing accents to fall on the corresponding clicks, which will hit the cues automatically.
2 To speed up, or make recording easier, if the music is to be in a steady tempo. This eliminates any variation of tempo by the conductor.
3 To record the correct tempo to dancing, such as a café scene which has been shot to a temporary tempo track to be replaced later. The cutter makes the click track from the original tempo track.
4 To lead into a rhythmic piece of music already recorded. The click track is made in the correct tempo and the number of bars can be adjusted to fit.
5 To insert an interlude between two pieces of music, if rhythmic, to fit perfectly in the correct tempo.
6 To record any scene that has many cues and is difficult for the conductor. The music does not have to be all rhythmic to require the use of a click track. The composer can write in a rubato manner to the steady tempo of clicks.

(Skinner 1950, iv)

Although the technology used to generate the click track may have changed over the years, its function is still much the same for scores using live musicians.

The click track produces an audible metronomic tick calibrated to the prevailing tempo at any point in the score, and this is fed to the conductor (and normally the other musicians) by means of a distribution amplifier and headphones. In its earliest form, it required holes to be punched in the undeveloped (opaque) optical track on a film print. As film normally travels at 24 fps, if a hole is punched in the optical track next to the first sprocket hole of every twelfth frame, an audible click is produced each time a hole passes the sound head (every half a second), producing a metronome rate of 120 beats per minute. In order to provide a greater range of possible tempi, holes can be punched in any of eight different positions on a frame – next to a sprocket hole, or between sprocket holes (see Figure 2.5). Thus, for example, to set a tempo to 128 beats per minute, a hole is punched every 11 frames.

Given that each 1/8th of a frame of film represents approximately 0.0052 seconds, it is possible to calculate the length of time, and thus film, that a crotchet will take at any metronome mark. For example, if the metronome mark is 85, each crotchet will last for 60/85 seconds (around 0.706 seconds). Dividing this latter figure by 0.0052 gives just

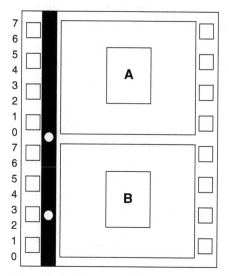

Figure 2.5 Punched holes in the optical soundtrack. The punch in frame A is at the top of the frame, the punch in frame B is at the 3/8 frame position. Numbers at the left-hand side of the frame indicate the frame position for punches. (Note that the film is travelling downwards, so the numbering is from the bottom of the frame upwards.)

over 135, and dividing again by 8 (to find the number of frames) produces the figure 16⅞th frames. *Accelerandi* and *rallentandi* may also be produced by incrementally decreasing or increasing the number of 1/8th frames between punches, although this can require some fairly complicated mathematics. For many years, film composers have used 'click books' such as the Knudson book (named after the music editor Carroll Knudson, who compiled the first such volume in 1965), which relate click rates and click positions to timings, allowing the estimation of where any beat will lie in minutes, seconds and hundredths of a second.

As well as the audio cues provided by a click track, several forms of visual signal, known as streamers, punches and flutters, can be provided. Until the 1980s, streamers were physically scraped onto the film emulsion as diagonal lines running from left to right, over forty-eight to ninety-six frames (two to four seconds of film). Figure 2.6 illustrates a streamer running over nine frames – normally these would extend over three, four or five feet of film, and the line would look less oblique than it does here. When projected, during which process the film runs downwards and the image is inverted, a streamer appears as a vertical line progressing from the left to the right of the screen, terminated by a punched hole in the film (roughly the diameter of a pencil) which displays as a bright flash. Flutters offer a subtler and looser means of synchronization than the click track. Here clusters of punches in groups of three, five or seven are placed on a downbeat or at the

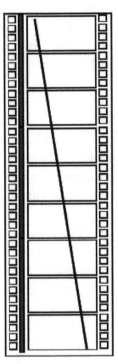

Figure 2.6 Schematic illustration of the visual cue known as a streamer, shown running over nine frames.

beginning of a musical cue, each punched frame having an unpunched frame as a neighbour (the pattern of punched [o] and unpunched [-] frames can be imagined as forming one of the following sequences: o-o-o, o-o-o-o-o or o-o-o-o-o-o-o). This method of 'fluttering' punches was devised by prolific film composer and studio music director Alfred Newman, and has been called the Newman system in his honour.

Almost invariably in contemporary film work, some form of computer-based system will generate the click track and visual cues in conjunction with a digital stopwatch on the conductor's desk. Auricle: The Film Composer's Time Processor, released in 1985 by the brothers Richard and Ron Grant, combined most of the time-based facilities required by the composer, including streamers in up to eight colours, allowing differentiation between varying types of cue. More recently, software applications such as Figure 53's Streamers have been widely adopted by composers and studios.

For many film composers, the real significance of such software is its ability to calculate appropriate tempi to match hit points. These are visual elements to be emphasized, often by falling on a strong beat or through some other form of musical accentuation. It is not difficult to calculate a fitting tempo and metre when there are only two such hit points, but the maths can become considerably more complicated when there are three or more irregular ones. Appropriate software permits the composer to construct the rhythmic and metrical skeleton of a cue rapidly.

Time Code

Much of the functionality of such software is premised on SMPTE/EBU (Society of Motion Picture and Television Engineers/European Broadcasting Union) time code. This offers a convenient way of labelling every frame of video by reference to its position in terms of hours, minutes, seconds and frames (hh:mm:ss:ff) relative to a start-point, and is available in two basic forms: vertical interval time code (VITC) and linear or longitudinal time code (LTC). There are a number of different and incompatible standards for time-code frame-rate: 24 fps for film, 25 fps for British and European video (PAL/SECAM) and 29.97 and 30 fps for American and Japanese video (NTSC).

Frame rates for video are related to the mains frequency. In the United Kingdom this is 50 Hz, and the frame rate is set to half this value (25 fps) whereas in the United States, which has a 60 Hz mains frequency, 30 fps was originally established as the default rate. With the development of colour television, more bandwidth was required for the colour information, and so the frame rate was reduced very slightly to 29.97 fps. Given that there are only 0.03 frames fewer per second for 29.97 fps than for 30 fps, this appears a tiny discrepancy, but over an hour it adds up to a very noticeable 108 frames or 3½ seconds. Thus 'drop frame' code was developed: the counter displays 30 fps, but on every minute except 0, 10, 20, 30, 40 and 50, two frames are dropped from the count (which starts from frame 2 rather than 0).

To accommodate these different rates, time code must be capable of being written and read in any version by a generator. In each case, a twenty-four hour clock applies, the time returning to 00:00:00:00 after the final frame of twenty-three hours, fifty-nine minutes and fifty-nine seconds. By convention, time code is not recorded to start from 00:00:00:00, but shortly before the one-hour position (often 00:59:30:00 to allow a little 'pre-roll' before the start of the material) to avoid the media being rolled back before the zero position, and confusing the time-code reader.

SMPTE/EBU time code is found in every stage of production and post-production, except in initial photography on analogue film, for it is not possible to record it on this medium; instead, 'edge numbers' sometimes called Keykode (a trademark of Kodak) are used, marked at regular intervals during the manufacturing process in the form of a barcode. Most film editing is now digital and takes place on computer-based systems, which have almost entirely replaced the old flatbed 16 mm and 35 mm editing tables such as the Steenbeck (which in turn ousted the horizontal Moviola). Computer-based editing is described as a non-linear process, because there is no necessary relationship between the relative positions of the digital encoding of the discrete images and their storage location, which is dependent upon the operating system's method of file management. An important aspect of editing performed on a non-linear system, whether the medium is video or audio, is that it is potentially non-destructive: instead of physically cutting and splicing the film print or magnetic tape, the operator generates edits without affecting the source data held in the filestore. This will normally involve the generation of some kind of play list or index of start and stop times for individual takes which can be used by the computer program to determine how data is to be accessed.

Sound, picture and code are transferred to the computer where editing takes place and an edit decision list (EDL) is created, which indicates the start and end time-code positions of every source section of the picture or sound and their position in the composite master. Where analogue film is still used, this list (see Table 2.1 for an example) is employed to cut the original negative from which the projection print will finally be made once its time-code values have been converted back to Keykode frame positions.

Composers now generally work away from film studios, often preparing the complete music track in their own studios using a version of the film in a digitized format to which a MIDI-based sequencer is synchronized. Functionality provided by sequencers has become increasingly sophisticated and most not only record and play MIDI data, but also digital-audio data files recorded from a live source such as an acoustic instrument or generated electronically. The integration of MIDI and digital recording and editing has greatly simplified the problems of synchronization for the composer and

Table 2.1 *A section of an edit decision list (EDL).*
V and A indicate video and audio, respectively. V1, V2, A1 and A2 are four different source tapes of video and audio.

Cue	Type	Source	Source in	Source out	Master in	Master out
1	V	V1	06:03:05:00	06:04:09:21	00:01:00:00	00:02:04:21
2	A	A1	01:10:01:05	01:11:03:20	00:01:00:00	00:02:02:15
3	V	V2	13:20:05:00	13:20:55:00	00:02:04:21	00:02:54:21
4	A	A2	01:22:00:12	01:22:05:22	00:02:29:00	00:02:34:10
5	A	A1	06:05:10:03	06:05:29:05	00:02:35:01	00:02:54:03

sound editor, for interactions between the two sources of musical material can be seamlessly controlled. This is particularly relevant to the fine-tuning of cues, especially when the composed music is slightly longer or shorter than required. In the analogue period there were two main methods of altering the length of a cue: by physically removing or inserting sections of tape (possibly causing audible glitches) or by slightly speeding it up or slowing it down. In the latter case, this produces a change of pitch as well as altering the duration: faster tape speed will cause a rise of pitch, slower speed a fall. This may be reasonable for very small changes, perhaps a sixty-second cue being shortened or extended by one second, but larger modifications will become audibly unacceptable; for instance, shortening a one-minute cue by three seconds will cause the pitch to rise by almost a semitone, and produce a marked change in timbre.

MIDI sequences preclude this problem, for the program can simply recalculate note lengths according to the prevailing tempo, and this will cause the cue to be appropriately shortened or lengthened. Digital signal-processing techniques offer an equivalent method of altering digital-audio cues called time stretching, which does not result in a change of pitch. At one time such procedures were only available on expensive equipment in research institutes and large studios, but the enormous increase in the power of computer processors and reduction in the cost of computer memory and hard-disk space has made them readily accessible to the composer working on a personal computer or hardware sampler.

Music and the Processes of Production

It is customary to consider the making of a film as being divided into three phases called pre-production, production and post-production. Depending on the nature of the film, the composition and recording of musical components may take place in any or all the phases, though the majority of the musical activities will usually take place in post-production. If music is scored or recorded during pre-production (generally called pre-scoring or pre-recording), it will almost certainly be because the film requires some of the cast to mime to an audio replay during shooting, or for some other compelling diegetic reason. Oliver Stone's *The Doors* (1991), a movie about Jim Morrison, is a good example of a film with a pre-recorded soundtrack, some of it being original Doors material and the rest being performed by Val Kilmer, who plays the lead role (Kenny 1993). Production recording of music has become generally less common than it was in the early sound films, largely because of the problems associated with the recording of hi-fi sound on location or on sets not optimized for the purpose. Bertrand Tavernier's jazz movie 'Round Midnight (1986), with a score by Herbie Hancock, is a somewhat unusual example, being shot on a set specially built on the scoring stage where orchestral recordings normally take place (Karlin and Wright 1990, 343).

For the majority of films, most of the nondiegetic music is composed, orchestrated, recorded and edited during post-production. By the time the composer becomes involved in the process, the film is usually already in, or approaching its final visual form, and thus a relatively brief period is set aside for these activities. Occasionally composers may be involved much earlier in the process, for example David Arnold was given the film for the 1997 Bond movie *Tomorrow Never Dies* reel by reel during production (May to mid-November), very little time having been allocated to post-production. Karlin and Wright indicate that, in 1990, the average time allowed from spotting (where the composer is shown the rough cut and decides, with the director, where the musical cues will happen) to recording was between three and six weeks. James Horner's 1986 score for James Cameron's *Aliens*, which has 80 minutes of music in a film just short of 140 minutes in duration, was completed in only three and a half weeks, and such short time scales remain common. Ian Sapiro has modelled the overall processes associated with the construction of the score at the level of the cue in his study of Ilan Eshkeri's music for *Stardust* (2007) and this is illustrated in Figure 2.7 (Sapiro 2013, 70).

Directors often have strong feelings about the kind of music they want in their films, and their predilections will govern the choice of composer and musical style. As an aid during the film-editing process, and as a guide for the composer during spotting, temp tracks (i.e. temporary music tracks), which may be taken from another film or a commercial recording, and will have some of the characteristics they require, are often provided. In some cases, these temp tracks will form the final soundtrack, most famously in Stanley Kubrick's *2001: A Space Odyssey* (1968), for which Alex North had composed a score, only to have it rejected in favour of music by Richard Strauss, Johann Strauss and Ligeti (see Hubai 2012 for a detailed study of rejected scores). If a film is rough-cut to a temp track, it may take on aspects of the rhythmic structure of the music, limiting the composer's freedom of action.

Spotting results in a list of timings and a synopsis of the accompanying action called timing notes or breakdown notes (see Table 2.2) that are given to the composer. Like the edit decision list discussed above, these notes provide a level of detail which not only suggests the kind of musical codes to be employed (given that the majority of films and television programmes rely upon the existence of commonly accepted musical forms of signification), but also gives information about its temporal character (metre and rhythm). Cues are listed according to the reel of film in which they appear (each reel of film being 1000 feet or just over

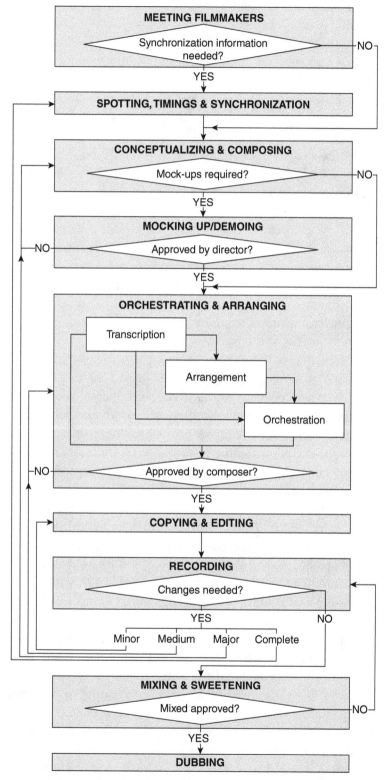

Figure 2.7 Ian Sapiro's model of the overall processes associated with film scoring as a decision matrix.

Table 2.2 *Timing sheet for cues in an imaginary film.*
2M2 refers to the cue number (second musical cue on the second reel of film). Time is total elapsed time from the beginning of the cue in minutes, seconds and hundredths of seconds.

Title:	'Leeds Noir'	
Cue:	2m2	
Time code	Time	Action
		Night-time outside a large urban building. Eerie moonlight shines on wet road.
01:45:30:00	0:0.0	Music starts as boy and girl stare morosely into each other's eyes.
01:45:44:05	0:14.21	Ambulance passes with siren sounding.
01:46:01:00	0:31.00	Man emerges from office doorway.
01:46:02:20	0:32.83	Pulls out his large leather wallet.
01:46:08:23	0:38.96	Gives boy £20.00 note and takes package.
01:46:44:00	1:14.00	End of cue.

eleven minutes), are identified as being a musical cue by the letter M and are numbered according to their order in the reel.

As already implied, the 'factory' conditions of music production prevailing in the classic Hollywood system have partly given way to a home-working freelance ethos, with composers operating from their own studios. Certainly, high-budget films often still employ a large retinue of music staff including a music supervisor taking overall control, a composer, orchestrators, copyists and a music recordist, with orchestral musicians hired in for the recording sessions; but many lower-budget movies and television programmes have scores entirely produced by the composer using synthesized or sampled sounds ('gigastrated'), and returned to the production company on digital files ready for final mixdown. While this reduces the cost of the score dramatically, and lessens the assembly-line character of the operation, some of the artistic synergy of the great Hollywood partnerships of composers and orchestrators may have been lost. Although it may be theoretically possible, using a sequencer connected to sound libraries, to produce scores of the density and finesse of those written by Hollywood partnerships such as Max Steiner and Hugo Friedhofer, or John Williams and Herb Spencer, the short time frame for a single musician to produce a complex score can restrict creativity.

New Technology, Old Processes

Since the 1980s, digital technology has infiltrated almost every aspect of the production and reproduction of film, and in the second decade of the twenty-first century the major US studios such as 20th Century Fox, Disney and Paramount moved entirely to digital distribution. Despite this, the processes that underpin filmmaking have remained remarkably stable, and although pictures and TV shows may no longer be released on physical reels of celluloid, many of the concepts and much of the terminology from the analogue period retain currency. Equally, while the function of film music has been more elaborately theorized concurrently with the period of transition from analogue to digital, the role of the composer in US and European mainstream film and cinema, and of his or her music, has changed less than might have been expected in this technologically fecund new environment. While there certainly have been some radical developments, particularly at the interface between music and effects, the influence of 'classical Hollywood' can still be strongly detected in US and European mainstream cinema, an indication, perhaps, of both the strength of those communicative models and the innate conservatism of the industry.

3 The Composer and the Studio
Korngold and Warner Bros.

BEN WINTERS

Discussing issues of authorship in the context of film scores is inherently complex. Even leaving aside the question of music's dependence on other audio-visual information for its narrative meanings, the very creation of a film score is often itself a collaborative process. Composers may work with other musicians to produce a score, and they might also frequently be required to co-operate with producers, directors, editors, recording engineers or other members of a film's creative team. In Hollywood, at least, this collaboration seems to have been most institutionalized during the studio system of the 1930s and 1940s, a time when each of the major studios had its own music department. Scores might have been credited to an individual but they were often the product of a staff of composers, orchestrators and arrangers, all under the guiding hand of a department chief in constant contact with a producer or studio head. This presents us with a very different picture of music composition from that commonly encountered in much Western musicology. It is only relatively recently that musicologists have explored opera and ballet as essentially collaborative in nature; still many more creative personalities have arguably been involved in film-score production and presentation. In this chapter, then, I aim to explore the interaction between film composer and movie studio during the studio era of Hollywood, concentrating on Erich Korngold's working relationship with Warner Bros. After exploring the implications of a wider contextualized account of film-score composition, I will sketch a picture of the workings of a typical studio music department – including the activities of studio-employed orchestrators. The second half of the chapter deconstructs a particularly entrenched myth about the way in which Korngold worked with the technology of the scoring stage – a vital part of the production process. The resulting revised picture suggests a composer who, despite his background in the world of Viennese opera and concert music, was fully embedded in the collaborative world of film-score production and, moreover, engaged fully with its medium-specific technology.

For my friend, Dr Celia Blacklock (1981–2014).

Collaborative Approaches to Art

Contextualizing composers within a community of creative personae certainly downplays the authorial power traditionally accorded them; and although Western musicology is now far more willing to recognize the complexities of authorship discourse, the figure of the 'genius' composer continues to cast a long shadow. Film studies, too, laboured for many years under the burden of a mode of thinking that privileged the creative efforts of individuals, most commonly a film's director. Gradually discredited by the theoretical impact of structuralism in the 1960s and, later, post-structuralism, this *auteur* theory gave way among scholars to a greater emphasis upon collaboration in their discussion of studio-era filmmaking – though *auteur* theory continues to be of importance to non-dominant groups (Staiger 2003). Its attractiveness in the first place, though, rested on its ability to resolve, albeit simplistically, a fundamental question of film theory: how can an industrialized, collaborative product be interpreted as art?

With a few exceptions, early film scholars had regarded collaboration with suspicion, as somehow threatening to the interpretation of cinema as art. Inheritors of a Romantic aesthetic of authorship, they found alien the notion of a collective creative process. Instead, the studio system was seen as a factory-like destroyer of artistic integrity, the commercial 'whore' of Wall Street, restricting the creative talents of the true defender of cinematic art, the director. Indeed, the factory analogy was often overplayed to reinforce the achievements of the director in overcoming these obstacles. There were a few, however, who proposed an alternative view. The anthropological studies of Leo Rosten (1941) and Hortense Powdermaker (1951), for example, stressed the complexity of human relationships within the studio system, resisting the rigid application of industrial models and assigning creativity to a collective body of people. In the 1980s, film studies embraced this view of authorship, acknowledging (in André Bazin's immortal phrase) 'the genius of the system' (Bazin 1985 [1957]), as an extract from Thomas Schatz's study of the same name demonstrates. Auterism, argues Schatz, effectively stalled

> film history and criticism in a prolonged state of adolescent romanticism …
> But the closer we look at Hollywood's relations of power and hierarchy of
> authority during the studio era, at its division of labor and assembly-line
> production process, the less sense it makes to assess filmmaking or film style
> in terms of the individual director – or *any* individual, for that matter.
>
> (Schatz 1989, 5; emphasis in original)

In contrast, the image of the studio system as the factory-like destroyer of creativity in the musicians associated with film was, until relatively recently, firmly entrenched – despite balanced contributions to the debate by figures such as Lawrence Morton (1951). This is attested by disapproving references in the literature to the changes made to the work of composers Bernard Herrmann or Aaron Copland by their respective studios (see, for example, Kalinak 1992, 151–8). Gradually, though, such a position has been challenged. In addition to my own work (2007) on Korngold's score for *The Adventures of Robin Hood* (1938), other recent contributions by Nathan Platte (for example, 2011, 2012, 2014), David Neumeyer and Platte (2012) and Hannah Lewis (2014) have helped enrich our understanding of film composition in studio-era Hollywood film. Through close critical engagement with archival sources, such studies often reveal Hollywood scores to be provocative sites for creative collaboration rather than battlegrounds for the competing authorial claims of individuals. In their guarded rejection of an uncomplicated individual authorship in favour of a sociological examination of a complex of relationships, the approaches pioneered by film studies have provided musicology with a useful model to apply to the study of a film's score. For studio-era film music, this requires investigating direct creative contributions to the score by non-musician elements at the studio (such as a producer or studio executive), in addition to tracing the more prosaic interactions between composer and music department.

Everyday Working

Although the working practices of a Hollywood music department varied from studio to studio, the basic structure remained consistent. Under the control of a musical director, employees might carry out a number of tasks, such as securing the legal rights to use copyrighted music, liaising with recording engineers or preparing cue sheets for composers. Composers and orchestrators themselves were often under studio contract like any other member of staff, and therefore required to turn their hands to whatever assignment came their way and to relinquish all control or ownership of the material produced. Indeed, a typical contract might include the following clause:

> All material composed, submitted, added or interpolated by the Writer pursuant to this agreement shall automatically become the property of the Corporation, which, for this purpose, shall be deemed the author thereof, the Writer acting entirely as the Corporation's employee . . . [The writer grants to the corporation] the right to use, adapt and change the same or any part thereof and to combine the same with other works of the Writer or of any other person to the extent that the Corporation may see fit, including the right to add to, subtract from, arrange, rearrange, revise and adapt such material in any Picture in any manner. (Adorno and Eisler 2007 [1947], 124)

Max Steiner, one of Warner Bros.'s most prolific composers between 1936 and 1965, certainly recognized the authorial power of the studio:

> A thousand and one things can happen to a music sound track from the time it leaves the composer's brain until it is heard by the audience. I have had pictures which did not require any music whatsoever, according to the producers. Some of these turned out to be 100 per cent underscoring jobs. On other pictures I was told that a certain film could not be released without an entire underscoring job, and I would work for weeks, day and night. When the finished product left the studio to go to the exchanges, only 60 per cent of all the music written remained. (Steiner 1937, 231)

This studio ownership was something initially enshrined in award ceremonies. When *Anthony Adverse* (1936) won the Academy Award for Best Musical Score on 4 March 1937, the award was presented to music-department chief Leo Forbstein. Korngold, as the score's composer, did not even rate a mention (B. Carroll 1997, 266, 285). Though this practice was to change later, it gives an insight into the industry's efforts to maintain corporate control over its output at this time.

The work of composers was also monitored closely by their music-department head and, in some cases, the producer. Unsurprisingly, this was not always to the composer's liking. Kate Daubney has pointed out that Steiner fell out with David O. Selznick over the constant re-editing of *Gone With the Wind* (1939), and she draws our attention to a remark halfway through a cue in Steiner's short score for *They Died With their Boots On* (1941): 'Music stops – if it were *my* picture' (2000, 17). Indeed, Platte has recently explored Selznick's role in shaping the scores of Steiner, Dimitri Tiomkin and others, noting 'his persistent involvement throughout the scoring process' (2012, 123). Similarly, Hal B. Wallis, the executive in charge of production at Warners, is known to have provided copious notes to his music department, and his undoubted ability for understanding music's role in film is evidenced by his remarkably specific cutting notes for *Casablanca* (1942):

> From Hal B Wallis [presumably to music director Leo F. Forbstein]
> Cutting Notes
> Reel #2
>
> **Casablanca Sep 2 1942**
> Start the piano as Ilsa and Laszlo come in the door. You can stop the piano playing at the table with Ilsa when Renault brings Strasser over to the table. Then don't start the music again until Sam introduces the guitar player. When Ilsa calls Sam over to play, let that go just as it is until the scene is interrupted by Renault coming back, saying: 'Oh, you have already met Rick'. Now, at that point, when Rick and Ilsa exchange glances, on the first of their close-ups, start an orchestration using 'As Time Goes By'. And *score* the scene. Let Steiner do this. And carry this right through the Exterior until the lights go out.

Music Notes Sep 2 1942

On the *Marseillaise*, when it is played in the cafe, don't do it as though it was played by a small orchestra. Do it with a full scoring orchestra and get some body to do it. You should score the piece where the Gendarmes break the door in and carry right through to the dissolve to the Police Station.

In the last reel, the last time Bogart looks off and we cut to the plane I would like to see a dramatic pause in the music, just before the cut to the plane. Then as we cut to the plane, emphasize the motor noises and then, when you cut back to the scene, resume the music. (Behlmer 1986, 216)

This close collaboration between employer and employee was, in any case, nothing new in music, and the Hollywood studio system merely highlighted and exaggerated relationships of power to which composers had always been subject. One only has to think of the long history of composer patronage or, for example, the detailed instructions to which Tchaikovsky worked in his ballet collaborations to find parallels that could be almost as prescriptive. The dominance of the ballet master in Tchaikovsky's time, and his contractual authority over a composer (Wily 1985, 1–10), perhaps suggests a direct forerunner of the relationship between composer and movie producer. Nor was it, necessarily, a negative intrusion into the creative process. No matter what Steiner may have thought, Wallis's contribution to the music of *Casablanca* was both important and effective.

In a rather more obvious example of the fragmentation of authorial control, the smaller major studios (Universal, Columbia and United Artists) and low-budget studios (such as Republic) would often choose a more economical approach to scoring that made use of multiple composers, classical music libraries and a stock of pre-written original musical material (sometimes called 'library music'). Randall Larson (1985, 17) has indicated how Universal's music department, for example, re-used original feature-film music from *Bride of Frankenstein* (1935) in the serials *Flash Gordon* (1936), *Buck Rogers* (1939) and *Radio Patrol* (1937). When James Dietrich supplied music for Universal's 1932 horror film *The Mummy*, director Karl Freund replaced half of the score with stock melodies from the studio's library, including extracts from Tchaikovsky's *Swan Lake* (*ibid.*, 27). Indeed, such was the level of co-operation between members of Universal's music department, 'quite often a single score would be created by an entire cadre of composers, each one taking a hand in the composition, orchestration and what-not in order to get it done in time' (*ibid.*, 37). Such collaborative practices were not restricted to the smaller studios: Steiner is known to have contributed to some scores at RKO at the beginning of his career without receiving a screen credit (Daubney 2000, 9), and David Raksin (1989) described in detail the 'team composition' undertaken at Twentieth Century-Fox. This must have been commonplace in the culture of creative collaboration engendered by the studio system.

Among the unsung heroes of a studio's music department were the orchestrators, some of whom were not given screen credit for their contributions. Korngold's score for *The Adventures of Robin Hood* (1938), for example, was orchestrated by Hugo W. Friedhofer and Milan Roder, yet only principal orchestrator Friedhofer is mentioned in the title credits. Obviously, composers may have preferred to orchestrate their own music, but the time constraints involved in producing a film score in, perhaps, a matter of weeks made the orchestrator a necessary and significant member of the creative team. Friedhofer describes the process of working with Korngold thus:

> Well it was a very, very close association. He always liked to look at the scores. We'd discuss the sketches very thoroughly. He had a fantastic way of playing the piano with an orchestral style, so you could almost sense what he was hearing in the orchestra ... [In] the first few [films we worked on], he gave me half a dozen of his sketches, we discussed them, and then I took them home and orchestrated them.   (Danly 1999, 40)

> As time went on, he came to rely more and more on my discretion in the matter of color and voicing, and in many instances would discuss with me the orchestrations of sections which were to be farmed out to other orchestrators.
>   (B. Carroll 1997, 251–2)

Friedhofer also worked with Steiner in an equally close relationship, though he reports once disagreeing with the composer over the orchestration of a particular passage. Rather tellingly, it was Steiner who relented in the end:

> I remember once, only, that we had problems. It was on a picture called *Green Light* [1937] ... There was a character ... who had a slight limp in one leg ... [and] Max wrote this kind of limping theme ... [He] read [my orchestration] through and was very unhappy, for some reason or other ... And he started tinkering with the orchestration, and apparently spent two hours, trying this way, trying it that way ... Finally ... he said, 'All right, fellows. Let's forget all about that. Let's try the original version again.' So they did, and then he liked it.
>   (Danly 1999, 45)

Orchestrators were genuinely creative collaborators who interacted with their composers, offering suggestions and improvements; on occasion, they were even called upon to compose (*ibid.*, 63). Their contributions to the overall sound of the studio-era film score should not be underestimated.

Korngold and Warner Bros.

Even with an awareness of the working realities of the studio system, however, there is still perhaps a temptation to buy into an image of at least some film composers rooted firmly in romanticized notions of creativity. Korngold, as one of the canonic names of early classical Hollywood film music, is particularly susceptible to a sort of mythmaking that seeks to ascribe to him the characteristics many associate with the act of composition in a less obviously commercial sphere. In particular, Korngold's relationship with the technology of film has often been portrayed as that of a genuine artist coming face-to-face with the realities of an industrial product, and as a result certain dubious ideas have been propagated as fact. Michael Haas's recent study of Jewish composers banned by the Nazis thus claims that, whereas Alfred Newman and Steiner 'supplied music by the minute and used stopwatches to measure to the second what was required … Korngold's practical mastery was unheard of … Most astonishingly, he knew instinctively how much music was needed for, say, twelve inches of film, and never used a stopwatch' (2014, 198). Similarly, in Mervyn Cooke's history of film music, we read: 'While recording, Korngold scrupulously avoided click-tracks and stopwatches, preferring to rely on his innate musicality to aid the process of synchronization' (2008, 95).

These statements draw on a long tradition. Jessica Duchen, for example, talks in her Korngold biography of 'an unerring instinctual understanding of the relationship between music and time'; claims that Korngold never used cue sheets, on which a technician would have written the exact timing for a scene; and finally concludes that 'Korngold refused mechanical aids of all types' (1996, 152). According to Kathryn Kalinak, Korngold 'shunned the standard devices for synchronization' (1992, 96), while Russell Lack talks about the composer 'effortlessly' matching music to picture cues (1997, 128). One of the earliest and ostensibly most authoritative sources for this view, given his personal correspondence with the composer, is that written by Tony Thomas. In his book *Music for the Movies*, originally published in 1973, Thomas states that Korngold 'never used timing sheets, cue marks, or earphones. If a sequence called for forty-two and two-thirds seconds, he would write a piece of music and conduct it so that it would fill forty-two and two-thirds seconds' (1997, 172; cf. 1973, 130–1, where the text reads 'cue marking on the screen' rather than 'cue marks').

All these accounts seem to stress an innate, effortless ability to manipulate music to very precise degrees without the assistance of technology. This is the mark of Korngold's greatness as an artist, it seems, transcending naturally the world of the so-called hack composer – who in contrast worked with stopwatches, cue sheets and click tracks, which represent both the technology-mediated everyday world and the Hollywood industrial product. It is a view so ingrained in large parts of the Korngold and film-music literature that it is almost the first thing anyone thinks to mention about him; and yet, as a portrait of the composer, it is simply not supported by the evidence. Examining the materials held in the archives of Warner Bros. reveals that not only did Korngold use cue sheets, but he also appears to have worked routinely with timing aids on the scoring stage after 1938, both to provide tempo indications and to aid music's synchronization with image.

As I have revealed elsewhere, Korngold certainly used both typed and handwritten cue sheets (some in his own hand) when working on *The Adventures of Robin Hood*. The seven extant cue sheets range from simple breakdowns of scenes, in which the duration of shots is specified, to more lengthy and complex cues – including an especially elaborate one for the climactic duel between Robin and Sir Guy written in Korngold's own hand (Winters 2007, 83–5). Moreover, in addition to timing information, on some sheets a music editor has also noted down lengths of film in feet and frames – which certainly suggests an engagement with the Moviola, a device on which composers or editors could measure footage. Nor was this compositional aid restricted to *Robin Hood*. Cue sheets held in the Erich Wolfgang Korngold Collection at the Library of Congress from other Warner Bros. films – for example, *The Sea Hawk* (1940) and *Devotion* (1946) – reveal similar or greater levels of detail, and include holograph pages or annotations in Korngold's hand in addition to prepared typed sheets. Thomas's statement that Korngold never worked with cue sheets might therefore have been a misreading of the sort of evidence provided by the composer's widow, Luzi Korngold. Luzi states that Korngold's technique of composition differed from other film composers in that they worked with cue sheets, whereas he was assigned a projection room so he could consult the film itself (1967, 67). At no point, however, does she suggest that these two methods of composition – the use of cue sheets and consulting the film – were mutually exclusive. That Korngold did not rely on cue sheets supplied by technicians and a stopwatch to compose his scores seems certain, but that he did use them at some point in the process seems equally incontrovertible. Indeed, an interview article with Korngold that appeared in a 1937 issue of *Etude* magazine reported: 'even Korngold, while he worked on the film "Anthony Adverse" ... had to work with stop watch in hand; for in such cases accurate and precise timing is of paramount importance' (Arvey 1937).

Perhaps the most beguiling aspect of the myth surrounding Korngold's working practices at Warner Bros. is the notion that he required no mechanical aids to assist him when conducting during recording sessions. In preferring to rely on his innate abilities, the myth seems to say, he asserted his creative independence from the Hollywood industrial product. Certainly, Luzi Korngold stated that her husband never worked with a click track (a sequence of audible beats much like a metronome: see Chapter 2) but rather accompanied the image as if working with opera singers – where, of course, such timing aids were neither available nor necessary (1967, 68). This assertion is not obviously contradicted by any of the manuscript materials. Yet the click track was not the only synchronization device available to a conductor, and evidence from the manuscript full scores of a number of post-1938 films held in the archives of Warner Bros. – including *The Sea Hawk, Kings Row* (1942), *The Sea Wolf* (1941) and *The Constant Nymph* (1943) – suggests that this part of the myth can also be questioned. The scores reveal a number of pencil marks in Korngold's hand, which are often placed before the beginning of a cue or, significantly, at a change of tempo. They are combined with the vertical strokes with which Korngold routinely notated his beat patterns, suggesting they were connected with his conducting activities, and consist of a series of circles with an associated number that likely indicate regularly spaced punches made in the visual part of the celluloid. When the film passed over the projector lamp, each punch would create a brief flash of light on screen, thus providing a kind of intermittent visual equivalent of the more constant audio click track. The number above or below the circle gave a frame rate for the spacing of the punches, and thus can easily be interpreted as a metronome mark. Since the punch spacing could be altered as necessary, it was a far more flexible system than that offered by the click track, which at the time offered only fixed-frame spacing rather than the variable click track of later years.

It seems fairly clear that these punches may have had two functions. First, they established tempo at either the beginning of a cue or at the time of a tempo change (indeed, they often seem to occur during a fermata, preparing Korngold for his next tempo). Figure 3.1 shows an example of this from *The Sea Wolf*, cue 4A. The warning punches at the beginning occur every 10 frames. For film running at 24 fps (and thus 1440 frames per minute), this would give Korngold four flashes of light at a tempo of 144 beats per minute and thus the *Allegro* crotchet beat of the cue's common time. The punches' other function is more intriguing: they assist precise synchronization of image and music. In an early scene from *Kings Row* in which Parris Mitchell appears at the window of his childhood home to greet his grandmother, the music is closely aligned both with the scene's jump cuts and the panning movement of the camera. Figure 3.2 shows some detail from Korngold's full score for part of that section. On beat

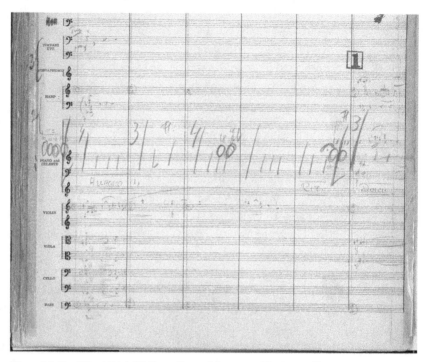

Figure 3.1 Detail from Erich Wolfgang Korngold's score to *The Sea Wolf*, cue 4A. © WB MUSIC
CORP. (ASCAP). All Rights Reserved. Reproduced by kind permission of Alfred Music (on
behalf of Warner Bros.).

three of bar 2 we are shown Parris's grandmother, and on the downbeat of
bar 3 we switch back to Parris. The duration of the shot of the grandmother, however, requires a lengthening of the second half of bar 2, and it
is in this bar that Korngold indicates punch markings on the second and
fourth beat (at a distance of 20 frames, which equates to 72 beats
per minute). The music is audibly slower in this bar. The next bar, however, is marked *Più mosso* in the composer's hand, and the punch in bar 4
(presumably occurring 18 frames after the calculated downbeat) acts to
ensure Korngold has reached the required tempo; indeed, the music rather
rushes through the first two beats of this bar, as if he had not been quite fast
enough in the previous three beats of *Più mosso*. Korngold must ensure
that the beginnings of subsequent bars are precisely aligned with the point
at which the camera finishes its panning shot as it tracks Parris moving
from window to window. Both the synchronization of chord change with
the view of Parris's seated grandmother and the alignment of downbeats
with the end of the camera's panning shot are aided by the visual punches
that have been marked in Korngold's hand in the full score.

A second example from *Kings Row* also involves the close synchronization of each bar of music with changes in the image. The scene involves

Figure 3.2 Detail from Korngold's score to *Kings Row*, cue 1D. © WB MUSIC CORP. (ASCAP). All Rights Reserved. Reproduced by kind permission of Alfred Music (on behalf of Warner Bros.).

alternating shots of Parris and the reclusive Mrs Tower, as he takes his leave after Cassie's birthday party. Figure 3.3 shows some detail from the full score for the passage, which reveals that Korngold's markings allow for changes between punch rates of 16 frames, 14 frames and 20 frames. In other words the first bar is at 90 beats per minute, the second at almost 103, with the third slower at 72 beats per minute. Evidently Korngold had written this particular passage with the camera work very much in mind, but the length of the shots required some subtle alterations to his tempo on the scoring stage to make the fit precise. Rather than simply rely on his skill as a conductor, he has used the technology available to assist him.

Clearly, then, the idea that Korngold shunned mechanical timing aids is simply incorrect – though he may admittedly have used them less consistently than his colleagues. It is worth considering, though, from where these misleading ideas concerning the composer's relationship with the technology used at Warner Bros. spring, for they clearly have their origins somewhere, no matter how distorted they have become. The picture is a complex one. Luzi Korngold, for instance, reports a story in which the composer asks Henry Blanke upon first visiting the studio how long a foot of film takes to be projected (1967, 67), supposedly revealing (as Brendan

Figure 3.3 Detail from Korngold's score to *Kings Row*, cue 1E. © WB MUSIC CORP. (ASCAP). All Rights Reserved. Reproduced by kind permission of Alfred Music (on behalf of Warner Bros.).

Carroll has claimed) that Korngold had 'instinctively worked out his own mathematical method of scoring a scene' (1997, 279). Another important piece of the puzzle is provided by the critic Josef Reitler's oft-cited story, in which Korngold – suffering a particularly pedestrian performance of his opera *Die tote Stadt* (1920) under the baton of Franz Schalk – turns to his companion ten minutes before the end of the first act, and announces 'I've finished.' Again, Duchen takes this as further proof of Korngold's 'unerring instinctual understanding of the relationship between music and time' (1996, 152), though it is perhaps just as likely an example of the composer's quick wit. Finally, we have the oral history of Friedhofer, the composer's trusted orchestrator at Warner Bros. Friedhofer certainly states that Korngold 'had [the tempos] in his head, and was infallible about it. He had a built-in sense of the speed at which something should move' (Danly 1999, 42–3). Moreover, he contrasts this with Steiner, who after running the picture once or twice would henceforth depend entirely on cue sheets and who also used click tracks a great deal when recording. Nevertheless, Friedhofer certainly makes no blanket statements along the lines that Korngold shunned mechanical timing aids or never worked with cue sheets.

In retrospect, even without the evidence provided by the full scores, we should always have been suspicious of these technology-shunning claims of Thomas and others. Indeed, the myth flies in the face of common sense. Korngold's abilities would have to be practically infallible to ensure he did not require numerous takes to match picture to music exactly – and these are scores that are often closely aligned with visual action. For a studio that thrived on its efficient working methods (stories abound of Jack Warner walking round the back lot turning off light switches to save electricity), the thought that a composer-conductor would be allowed to waste potentially thousands of feet of film attempting to get a perfect match between music and image without using any mechanical means whatsoever seems a little far-fetched – even for an artist of Korngold's stature. Specific evidence was always there, however. Ernst Korngold told Kalinak that although his father did not use a click track he did remember punches and streamers (see Chapter 2) in recording sessions for 'insurance'. The comment is somewhat buried in an endnote in Kalinak's book *Settling the Score* (1992, 222 n. 39). Likewise, Friedhofer's oral history, which describes Korngold's composition process in great detail, provides a good deal of corroborating evidence. He recounts the composer watching the film before going home and inventing themes, returning to watch and improvise on a piano, before making some very rough sketches, which he'd take home and refine. Korngold would then

> come back the next day and check and double-check for timing and what-not. Never any marks on the film until he was about ready to record. Then he would go in and sit with the film editor, and have the punches and what-not put on the film, the warning signals and so on, and also certain interior cues, to indicate changes of tempo. And his scores were always marked sort of in synchronization with the marks on the film, itself. (Danly 1999, 42)

In other words, the manuscript evidence merely confirms a picture that, although relatively clear in the primary evidence, has been somewhat glossed over in existing secondary accounts. Although Korngold may not have liked timing aids, Thomas's portrayal of a man with 'very little mechanical aptitude' (1997, 171), who possessed an almost superhuman ability to do away with them when composing and recording his scores, seems somewhat wide of the mark. But why has this myth persisted? What function does it serve?

In the mid-1980s, Andreas Huyssen – postmodern theorist of the 'great divide' – argued for a connection between the aims and techniques of the historical avant-garde and those of Western mass culture (Huyssen 1986). In its attempt to close the gap between art and life, the historical avant-garde had attempted to destroy a bourgeois vision of art that rested on the autonomy of artistic creation, one that emphasized its natural or organic qualities. Huyssen's point was that, like the mass culture that followed and partially fulfilled this utopian project, the avant-garde relied on technology to achieve its aims; and in that sense, it found its zenith in photography and film. The prevailing image of Korngold as film composer, though, appears to be reliant on those very aspects of bourgeois art that both the avant-garde and mass-culture movements sought to critique. Moreover, as the great émigré artist, Korngold is often presented in contrast to his fellow Viennese composer, the Warner Bros. workhorse Steiner (see, for example, Haas 2014, 266). Friedhofer, as I indicated above, explicitly contrasts their working methods, noting Steiner's reliance on cue sheets and his use of the click track – although he also suggests that Steiner used the click track in ingenious ways (Danly 1999, 43). This depiction of a contrasting pair of composers, one of whom writes and records his music effortlessly without the need of technology, while the other sweats over cue sheets and click tracks, is a powerful one that has notable precedents. As Bruno Nettl has revealed, similar imagery surrounds popular conceptions of a more illustrious Viennese pair, Mozart and Beethoven. Mozart is the composer associated with some supernatural power, who could compose without trying, and was a superb improviser (the instinctual composer); the Beethoven myth, on the other hand, suggests that music did not come easily, that it had to be worked at (Nettl 1989, 7–8).

Nettl outlines the myth partly in order to debunk it, and it seems clear that a similar Mozart myth has surrounded Korngold in Hollywood – though Steiner is perhaps too genial a character to occupy the Beethoven position fully, a role that in some respects appears to fit the irascible Herrmann better. Korngold, of course, had been named Erich Wolfgang in honour of Mozart, and Ernest Newman had compared Korngold with his namesake as far back as 1912 (Duchen 1996, 53–6) – and clearly it was his status as a *Wunderkind* that had prompted the comparison. This association appears to have continued to shape his image in later years. Thus, as with the popular reception of Mozart, Korngold in Hollywood has been ascribed an almost supernatural power to transcend the everyday world of his contemporaries; to improvise rather than work mechanically; and to fulfil that very role of the bourgeois artist that the mass-culture movement was supposed to critique. To investigate the reasons why this myth of Korngold as artist has taken hold over the image of Korngold the technologically savvy studio employee, despite the evidence to the contrary, would reveal much about the discourse surrounding film-music history and its relationship with musicology. In any case, what the archival materials provide is a more nuanced picture of Korngold as studio musician, one which suggests that for all his misgivings about the medium, he embraced the technological aspect of film in order better to achieve his artistic aims.

Conclusion

This chapter has sought to highlight the complexity of relationships involved in authoring a film score during the period of the Hollywood studio system, and in the case of Korngold to challenge the prevailing picture of the composer's relationship with the technology of film-score production. As such, it has asked questions about the medium's relationship with other forms of compositional activity. The haze of misinformation surrounding Korngold's relationship with the technology of music recording and synchronization is a reminder that further archival work in this area is needed. The constantly shifting relationships between composer and other creative elements at a movie studio – or between composer and the technology of score production – are both complex and, in every case, unique; and while a study of these structures is clearly important to an understanding of the role of the composer within the movie-making process, we would do well to remember that Hollywood has never quite worked with the smooth precision of the assembly line to which it aspired. Powdermaker described it as operating in a constant atmosphere of crisis, reliant on accidental finds from radio and theatre and adapting to situations as they arose rather than planning ahead (1951, 33). We also ought to remember, then, the warnings from film studies in over-stressing ideas of industrial practices in an attempt to redress a perceived imbalance:

> The time has come to dispense with the assembly-line analogy for studio
> production. Although the moguls no doubt wished their operations could
> be as efficient and predictable as those of a Ford plant, their product mitigated
> against standardization.   (Jewell 1995 [1984], 46)

All the same, musicology needs to acknowledge that the composer can be regarded as just one of many possible creative contributors to a film's score, albeit a very important one; and that the score can be seen as the product of collaboration between film makers, musicians, technicians and the technical characteristics of the medium itself. Undoubtedly, the developing recording technologies of the early 1930s and the need to avoid competing with dialogue comprehension placed certain restrictions on composers; but only if one regards the film score as an idealized conception in the composer's head that is realized imperfectly by its presentation in the cinema might we see the technologies and processes of production in terms of interference or artistic butchery, as used to be the case. Instead, if we see the film score as a multi-layered artefact that can manifest itself in a number of different ways – including the recorded version heard in the cinema – and in a manner that negotiates subtly between ideas of art and industry, then the authorial contributions of other musicians (including orchestrators), the restrictions or synchronization opportunities offered by the technology itself and even the comments of non-musicians (such as Wallis in the case of *Casablanca*) must be acknowledged. Human interaction between creative individuals may characterize the process as much as a conflict between the authorial artist and a faceless corporation. In the case of Korngold, the tendency of scholars to repeat myths about the composer's engagement with the mechanisms of film-score production that emphasize the composer's 'high-art' credentials is both a gentle warning to us about the constant need to question the assumptions we may make about the processes of composition and, simultaneously, a fascinating insight into the perceived status of film music as art.

4 Can't Buy Me Love?

Economic Imperatives and Artistic Achievements in the British Pop-Music Film

STEPHEN GLYNN

Genre theory has long adopted the biological model of a generic life-cycle, a paradigm especially pertinent to films centred on popular music which, operating in a narrow social and cultural time frame, adhere closely and concisely to such cyclical trends. The heyday of the British pop-music film, here categorized as fiction films in which British pop musicians both star and in which their music features diegetically, is broadly concurrent with what Arthur Marwick termed the 'Long Sixties' (1998, 7) and exemplifies the full life-cycle of a distinct sub-genre: it begins with the uncertain steps to copy or co-opt existing musical codes and conventions (1956–64); it flourishes into a more expressive, culturally diverse format accommodating a critical self-questioning (1964–7); finally it deconstructs, here shifting from toe-tapping narcissism to politicized allegory (1967–70). Employing Richard Dyer's terminology (1981, 1484), this chapter will illustrate the economic and artistic progression of the British pop-music film in its 'primitive', 'mature' and 'decadent' phases, and briefly attend to its intermittent afterlife, demonstrating that any analysis of the visual grammar of popular music must be sensitive to the financial, institutional and social factors that shape its development as a cultural form.

With a perceived diet of Norman Wisdom comedies and nostalgic war films, mainstream British cinema in the 1950s was, as Jeffrey Richards notes, 'in ethos and outlook, in technique and approach ... essentially conservative, middle class and backward-looking' (1992, 218). In 1956, therefore, it had little inclination to embrace the arrival of rock'n'roll, a loud, vulgar and American phenomenon that was in every aspect anathema to the indigenous film industry. Even US studios, unsure of the new music's longevity and fearful of a moral backlash, had fought shy of rock movies, leaving smaller independents to fill the void. But the international box-office success of Stan Katzman's low-budget exploitation feature *Rock Around the Clock* (1956), though infamously occasioning dancing in the aisles and the slashing of cinema seats, quickly prompted British studios to broach the subject.

Tommy Steele and Cliff Richard

For George Melly, 'The rise of Tommy Steele in the middle 50s [was] the first British pop event' (1972, 4). Equally, the first British pop-music film arrived on 30 May 1957 with the release of *The Tommy Steele Story*, produced by middle-ranking Anglo-Amalgamated and directed by middle-aged Gerard Bryant. Speed was clearly the essence since, with song-writing partners Lionel Bart and Mike Pratt, Steele penned fourteen new songs in seven days, while filming was completed in just three weeks – the swift editing and distribution ensuring that, at a total cost of just £15,000, the film opened two weeks ahead of the concurrent production by E. J. Fancey, *Rock You Sinners*. Such alacrity was not employed, however, to trump the jazz-inflected Tony Crombie and his Rockers, who starred in Fancey's film, but rather to promote Steele's imminent second major British tour. *The Tommy Steele Story* thus constituted just one further element in a lucrative cross-media marketing campaign that included UK Top Ten tie-in single hits with 'Butterfingers' and 'Water Water' and, as noted by Trevor Philpott, 'Tommy Steele shoes, shirts, blouses, panties, skirts, ear-rings, bracelets, pullovers and sweaters' (*Picture Post*, 25 February 1957). Extracted from this fashion and finance matrix, though, *The Tommy Steele Story* is generically interesting for its hesitant attempts to forge a cinematic correlation for its 'new' musical numbers. To a large extent the film grammar is conservative, relying on song-performance syntax derived from the classical Hollywood musical. As in the burgeoning Elvis Presley cycle, the new sub-genre's musical sequences were predominantly based on lip-synced performances by the singer which, supported by minimal onscreen instrumentation (usually an unplugged guitar), sought to articulate the illusion of 'real' diegetic performance. Just occasionally the film attempts a more creative visualization, as in the presentation of 'I Like' which modifies the Hollywood *bricolage* number of dancing with adjacent props, as in the 'Moses Supposes' number from *Singin' in the Rain* (1952). At other moments Steele's debut offers a more original – and ambivalent – investigation of the new cultural form. The images accompanying 'Elevator Rock' are essentially a variant on the established rise-to-fame montage, but whereas the traditional version invariably celebrates mass distribution, Britain's first pop-music film is (perhaps) less adamant that (inter)national dissemination beats a homely Bermondsey production. It is a scene of skilful compression that visualizes the commodification of Steele, taking us from the song's studio recording to its successive pressing on 78 rpm discs and thence to a shop's shelves replete with song sheets, each showing a guitar-wielding Tommy, before, over the closing bars, a self-referential *Melody Maker* headline proclaims the 'Film Offer to Tommy Steele'. With its graphic and rhythmic editing, the scene economically conveys the speed of the pop star-making process, and while the admiration of volume (a pleasure-surge from the sheer weight of product) is probably the ostensible motivation for the display of Steele's records and sheet music, an opposing response (the emotional disassociation resulting from this process of commodification) can also be identified.

The Tommy Steele Story proved itself the 'sure-fire blockbusting bonanza' its attendant posters had promised. Playing safe with its casting and conveying a positive image of fun-loving youth, within four months the film had made a clear £100,000 profit – a cultural phenomenon meriting not only a review in the august UK film journal *Sight & Sound*, but instigating a set of cinematic responses. First came the pastiche film *The Golden Disc* (1958), featuring the anaemic coffee-bar copy-cat Terry Dene, derided by Donald Zec as 'dreary and fumbling' (*Daily Mirror*, 14 March 1958), and decidedly not doing what it said on the label. It was followed by the parodic *Expresso Bongo* (1959), adapted from Wolf Mankowitz's West End play and a coruscating debunking of the new pop-star phenomenon, featuring Cliff Richard as the eponymous teenage sensation. His Bongo Herbert is no Steele-like repository of new-generation optimism: boorish and opportunistic, he forms instead a bridge to concurrent troublesome youth paradigms, social-problem films given extra resonance – and adolescent audience appeal – with the addition of seditious rock'n'roll numbers, as in *Beat Girl* (1960), where Adam Faith evaded the censors by singing in adolescent argot of having 'Made You'.

Expresso Bongo was another box-office and critical success, hailed effusively by William Whitebait as 'easily, so far, our best musical' (*New Statesman*, 5 December 1959). It also showcased the cinematic/commercial potential in promoting Cliff as the 'British Elvis'. And swiftly, like Elvis, Cliff was – largely through his film depictions – 'tamed' for mainstream audience appeal. For the national media in the late 1950s, an interest in rock'n'roll primarily signified a proclivity for juvenile delinquency, as when Cliff's leather-clad coffee-bar rocker snarled his up-tempo 'Living Doll' in *Serious Charge* (1959). Yet his trilogy of pop-music films in the early 1960s illustrates the acceptance of cardigan-wearing teenagers as 'just good kids', a social rapprochement that reinforces the absorption of rock'n'roll into more acceptable – and therefore profitable – strands of popular music. *The Young Ones* (1961), *Summer Holiday* (1963) and *Wonderful Life* (1964) are key to this merger of rock'n'roll with established modes of entertainment, both in sound (through the musical styles deployed) and in vision (through the images presented of the young). With six-figure budgets from the major studio ABPC (Associated British Picture Corporation), all three films are, for the first time in the sub-genre, prestigious productions employing colour and a widescreen format. They also announce that, while the 1950s had been a time of postwar negativity, the 1960s were going to be different.

And so it proved as, in many ways, this new-decade Technicolor trilogy, rather than its 'exploitative' coffee-bar predecessors, revealed itself unflinchingly formulaic: each film's narrative structure centres on a parent–child conflict; each film contains a set-piece confrontation where Cliff – spokesman for the younger generation – highlights their efficiency and responsibility; in each film's harmonious conclusion, the adults concede that the kids are alright. Freed from the nefarious influences of Marlon Brando, James Dean and Elvis, these films found inspiration from the earlier wholesome trinity of Mickey Rooney, Judy Garland and Gene Kelly. This strategy is clear from the first film, *The Young Ones*, which from the outset signals its provenance and purpose with the set-piece passed-along song-and-dance number, 'Friday Night'. The generic role model is evident in the hiring of American choreographer Herbert Ross to work on the first two productions, while all three films are built around the songs written by Peter Myers and Ronald Cass in an idiom highlighting their mainstream musical intentionality. Each film apes the Hollywood tradition with energetic dances, choreographed songs and duet numbers between the male and female leads. Each film offers the *de rigueur* medley section and, eager to pull in all market sectors, finds room to include at least one rock'n'roll number. And hence a surprise: 'We Say Yeah', part of the climactic youth club-saving concert in *The Young Ones*, is arguably the most raunchy, transgressive song treatment in a British pop-music film thus far. Especially given its tame surrounding narrative and musical discourse, it is an audacious scene, providing an affective cinematic correlation as Cliff's call to teenage rebellion – 'momma says no, daddy says no / they all gotta go / coz we say yeah' – is intercut with ecstatic female fans screaming back their affirmation, while a mid-song cut-back to their idol with a new low-level camera position provocatively provides what Rick Altman terms a 'crotch shot' (1987, 223). The pace of editing and juxtaposition of images accentuate the sexuality of the performance and the 'danger' of the rock performer, in a manner far more priapic than the chaste Steele and Dene. It is a brief moment when Cliff really rocked, a belated sign of the path not chosen.

That single number was sufficiently 'contained', however, for the film to be beaten only by *The Guns of Navarone* (1961) in the UK's top grossing films for 1962, thereby establishing Cliff as the nation's top box-office draw, surpassing even Elvis. The soundtrack album matched the film's commercial success, selling over 100,000 copies as it topped the UK charts for six weeks in early 1962, and remaining in the Top Ten for ten months (Coryton and Murrells 1990, 47). The critical response was, in large part, euphoric, Paul Dehn opining that 'I pick my words as cautiously as I burn my boats: this is the best screen-musical ever to have been made in

England' (*Daily Herald*, 16 December 1961). *Summer Holiday* performed even better, breaking all box-office records for a British-financed film for 1963. *Wonderful Life*, though, coming in at a relatively disappointing number five in 1964's top-grossing films, was to prove a bathetic and definitive conclusion of the first, 'primitive' phase of the British pop-music film. Others were ready to take up the mantle of positive rebellion, extending Cliff's 'We Say Yeah' threefold.

The Beatles

Susan Hayward writes that 'until the 1960s and 1970s the musical did not question itself – it indulged in narcissistic auto-satisfaction. Arguably, the rock musical of the 1960s started the questioning of the codes and conventions of the genre' (1996, 246). The Beatles' *A Hard Day's Night* (1964), directed by Richard Lester, is the key film in this generic interrogation. Its genesis, though, was again baldly economic: on discovering that EMI had failed to cover film soundtracks in their contract with the Beatles, United Artists quickly offered the group a three-picture deal – solely in order to obtain three potentially lucrative soundtrack albums. Thus, in its conception, the acknowledged apogee of the British pop-music film was akin – *pace* Technicolor Cliff – to all its generic predecessors: a low-budget exploitation movie to milk to the maximum the latest ephemeral musical craze. But what a craze it became. The Beatles' British success had been swift but incremental: in America, 'Beatlemania' was instant and enveloping, as evidenced by the response to the group's debut film and its motivational music. The momentum created by radio previews led to advance orders of over two million soundtrack albums, making *A Hard Day's Night*, while still at the presses, America's biggest-selling album to date, guaranteeing its number one position in the charts and ensuring the film's £200,000 budget had already been doubled in profits. This LP hysteria fed back into film demand, with America alone demanding 700 prints, and Britain 110, while globally a record 1500-plus prints were made, leading United Artists to announce proudly that *A Hard Day's Night* would have a saturation exhibition, with 'more prints in circulation than for any other pic in history' (Carr 1996, 47). The demand for product associated with the Beatles meant that *A Hard Day's Night* became the first film in history to ensure a profit while shooting was still in progress.

The opening chord of 'A Hard Day's Night' – a G7 with added ninth and suspended fourth – has, for Ian MacDonald, 'a significance in Beatles lore matched only by the concluding E major of "A Day In The Life", the two opening and closing the group's middle period of peak creativity' (1994, 102). It also heralds the opening of a middle phase in the British pop-music film, a phase that consistently problematizes the status of pop fame and the media machinery that promotes it. As part of such media, these 'mature' films are aware that they contribute to the mythologizing of its stars but simultaneously subject the process to a critical analysis. This doubleness, this refusal of decisiveness, is omnipresent in *A Hard Day's Night*, beginning with its paradoxical title and embedded in its generic characteristics, both established musical comedy and cutting-edge (quasi-) documentary realism. Lyrically, songs like 'Can't Buy Me Love' explore ambivalent forms of emotional/economic exchange, echoing those between artist, audience and their exploitation film, while Lester's knowing use of verbal and photographic clichés increasingly undermines any potential for cinematic realism. From the outset, the ostensible *cinéma-vérité* style is questioned, exposing the duality resultant from shooting in public spaces: are the Beatles just acting or actually fleeing their ubiquitous fans, or are such distinctions redundant given their effect on young extras? Granted coveted behind-the-scenes access, the film explores responses to this unprecedented pop cultural happening by the (for once) surprised media machine and charts the reactions of the fan-base furthering this mass hysteria. More particularly, this 'process' movie allows us to observe the effect of Beatlemania on the boys themselves – and reveals it to be far from an unalloyed pleasure. The film's opening frames thus signal a generic distinction from standard rags-to-riches biopics like *The Tommy Steele Story*: here running towards the audience are identifiable celebrities, already bearing the burdens of stardom; here are Lester's 'revolutionaries in a goldfish bowl' (Gelmis 1971, 316).

Although for the most part conventionally motivated, *A Hard Day's Night*'s cinematic correlation of the Beatles' songs also advances the pop-music film genre to new levels of sophistication. The opening title track immediately signals how the film will repeatedly avoid imitative diegetic performance, while a break with conventional presentation models is underlined in the train-carriage rendition of 'I Should Have Known Better': as musical instruments suddenly, surreally replace the Beatles' deck of cards, the song's articulation both employs and evades the diegetic mode, removing any generic consistency and installing an alternative, duplicitous viewing strategy. Primarily, however, the filming to accompany 'Can't Buy Me Love' constitutes the breakthrough moment for the pop-music film (see Table 4.1 at the end of this chapter) and encapsulates its mid-cycle paradigm shift. Coming after half an hour of intensifying claustrophobia, structurally the song signifies an enormous release of energy; when Ringo Starr sees a door marked 'Fire Escape', the sign works like a signal, sending the group hurriedly down the external staircase to the field below (see Figure 4.1).

Figure 4.1 *A Hard Day's Night*: 'We're out!' The British pop-music film's liberation from imitative diegetic performance.

What follows was directly inspired by Lester's earlier short *The Running, Jumping and Standing Still Film* (1959), starring Peter Sellers and Spike Milligan. As the Beatles caper in Goon-like abandon, suddenly freed from the burdens of nationwide touring, Lester employs diverse film speeds and camera angles to convey the quartet's musical catharsis. When they jump over discarded props, the film momentarily accelerates to aid their rush-and-tumble into the open air. An aerial shot follows one of the boys up and down a long path but abjures a terminal 'sight gag' – the sense of achieved release signifies sufficiently. When filming joins the group dancing together, Paul McCartney dashes towards the camera, smiling at the audience as he breaks the ultimate actor's taboo. Not all their movements are captured on the hoof, however: the slow-motion shot of a jumping John Lennon, McCartney and George Harrison references the group's extant iconography, in particular Dezo Hoffmann's Sefton Park photo of the leaping quartet. Their fun is abruptly ended, however, as a large middle-aged man appears, adorned with raincoat and wellingtons. The groundsman here replays the role of the policeman at the conclusion to Gene Kelly's 'Singin' in the Rain' routine: he represents an Apollonian authority that will not brook such Dionysian self-expression. His reprimand – 'I suppose you know this is private property' – has an extra resonance since the Beatles' treatment as *public* property has occasioned their escape. The tension between public figures and private spaces artistically motivates the Beatles' variant on Lester's surreal short – and simultaneously confirms the group's economic potential. Within *A Hard Day's Night* the scene comprises the most complete example of Lester's empathy with the music, a full visual correlative to the ambivalent sentiments contained in McCartney's composition. More widely, just as the group escape their virtual imprisonment, so is the musical number liberated from its generic restrictions, with subsequent films legitimized to use pop songs in the manner that instrumental music had traditionally been employed, as mood enhancement.

The critics certainly caught the mood. At home, Michael Thornton expressed his relief that this was not 'the usual kind of British pop musical in which a series of hit songs are linked loosely by an incredible plot and unspeakable dialogue', and instead judged it as possessing 'all the ingredients of good cinema – wonderful photography, imaginative direction, and excellent character performances' (*Sunday Express*, 13 July 1964), while in the ultimate – and enduring – critical soundbite, American Andrew Sarris described the film as 'the *Citizen Kane* [1941] of jukebox musicals' (*Village Voice*, 27 August 1964). The linking with an American masterpiece is doubly apposite since it offers not only a qualitative evaluation but also (if indirectly) a quantitative assessment, since *A Hard Day's Night* would become the first British pop-music film to succeed in the US market. There was a concomitant domination of the music charts as the 'Can't Buy Me Love' and 'A Hard Day's Night' singles topped both UK and American charts, while the soundtrack album – the film's sole reason for existing – achieved unparalleled results: it remained at number one in the British album charts for 21 weeks, selling 700,000 copies in the first year of its release, while European sales surpassed one million; in America advance orders of one million were soon doubled in sales as it headed the album chart for fourteen weeks. United Artists' initiative proved an overwhelming success with global sales of the soundtrack to *A Hard Day's Night* roughly totalling four million (Coryton and Murrells 1990, 97).

This important commercial momentum was maintained with the box-office returns for *Help!* (1965), the Beatles' spy-spoof sophomore feature with Lester, which totalled close to $6 million in the United States and $14 million worldwide. In the United Kingdom, the film was the second highest money-maker of 1965, bettered only by *Mary Poppins* (1964). Its economic performance was on a par with *A Hard Day's Night*, though expectations had, in truth, been higher with a now-established global phenomenon to market. Contemporaneous critical reception echoed the overall sense of anti-climax, Thornton's piece typical in noting how 'this isn't a nose-diving flop, that's for sure. But there is nowhere in evidence the special exciting quality of *A Hard Day's Night*' (*Sunday Express*, 1 August 1965). For all its 'Swinging London' colour surface difference, *Help!* nonetheless furthers a key trope of *A Hard Day's Night*: while earlier British pop-music films presented young men on the make – be they pop stars or juvenile delinquents – here they have made it, and again seem uncertain if the effort has been worthwhile. The effort certainly pays off in the musical numbers, notable for conveying much of the comedy's melancholy. One of many musically upbeat but lyrically sad numbers, 'Ticket To Ride' is generally considered the most inventively filmed sequence in *Help!* and the cinematic sibling of 'Can't Buy Me Love'. Lester again employs the Beatles' music as a nondiegetic accompaniment – here to Alpine action sequences – but now brings into play a radical rhythmic montage: completely fashioned post-production, its cutting for pace and rhythm obviates the need for pre-arranged choreography. Pauline Kael thought that *Help!* was Lester's 'best edited, though not necessarily best film' (1994, 221), and this editing is most effectively employed in the skilful cinematic correlation for Lennon's first ever heavy-metal track. Too skilful, perhaps? Extrapolating from Lester, John Boorman's inventive Dave Clark Five debut feature *Catch Us If You Can* (1965), with its opening pop-art montage ceding to a picaresque flight from the media spotlight, would signal the sub-genre's economic shift to a marginal status. Its rejection of narrative also signified the rejection of audiences – as even the Beatles discovered with the bewildered response to their television film *Magical Mystery Tour* (1967). And yet, aesthetically, after this radical mid-decade shift, pop-music films could not get back to the accessible narrative naiveties of *The Golden Disc* or *Summer Holiday* and retain any semblance of credibility. As Andy Medhurst noted, 'The British pop film, in all its endearing awkwardness, was pretty much dead' (1995, 68–9).

Psychedelia and *Performance*

Nonetheless, the sub-genre soldiered on, increasingly solipsistic – and chemically supported. If the 'primitive' pop-music film was fuelled by nothing more threatening than a frothy cappuccino and its 'mature' phase, most noticeably *Help!*, enjoyed the impetus of 'speed' ampheta-mines, the later 1960s saw a move to more serious experimentation with cannabis and LSD, drugs to elongate thought and amplify emotions. This was no era for the ingénu: instead, for the privileged few with their large and loyal following, record and film companies were happy to join the trip. They had no need to co-opt their contracted charges into exploitation quickies, and the creative longevity now accorded to the musical elite was meticulously/pedantically recorded in *One Plus One* (US title *Sympathy For the Devil*; 1968), Jean-Luc Godard's diptych on the garlanded Rolling Stones and grassroots political action. Equally pop-polemical, Peter Watkins's heavily mediated *Privilege* (1967), starring ex-Manfred Mann lead Paul Jones, critiqued the supposedly bottom-up rebellious nature of rock as it followed a state-manipulated pop star who, rather like Cliff, provides a hegemonic catharsis and channelling of teenage energies – and income – with his bad-boy persona yielding to religious evangelism. In Steve Shorter's Leni Riefenstahl-inflected stadium rock performances of 'Free Me', we encounter a further shift in the sub-genre's employment of musical performance. Removed from the flimsy storylines of Lester's movies and relegated to an ambient soundtrack in *Catch Us If You Can*, here, as in other third-phase pop films, the musical numbers serve primarily to advance the narrative and its attendant, alternative ideological programme. This musical narration would return in George Dunning's *Yellow Submarine* (1968), the ultimate in pop-art influence on the British pop-music film. The eclectic feature-length cartoon signifies sufficiently as a family fantasy on the forces of good overcoming evil, but can also be read as an allegorical play on late-1960s states of mind and statecraft: as Bob Neaverson describes it, 'an underground parable of how the psychedelic Beatles (symbols of the peaceful and apolitical forces of hippy counter-culture) overcome the forces of state power to establish a new regime of karmic awareness and universal goodwill' (1997, 88). Whether one saw the eponymous vessel as a pretext for the saturation marketing of ancillary product including alarm clocks, snow-domes, watches and 'the world's first ever full colour paperback' (Buskin 1994, 84), or a coded reference to the hippy-favoured narcotic pill Nembutal, *Yellow Submarine* was indubitably a critical success: for Ian Christie it was 'an absolute joy … the best film the Beatles never made' (*Daily Express*, 17 July 1968). Whilst the film was also a great commercial success in the United States, bettered that year only by *Funny Girl* (1968), UK's Rank got a whiff of drugs – understandably since the images accompanying 'Only A Northern Song', 'It's All Too Much' and the exuberantly rotoscoped 'Lucy in the Sky with Diamonds' are comprehensible only when experienced as audio-visual recreations of hallucinogenic states – and pulled the film from mainstream distribution. Equally unacceptably, *Yellow Submarine*'s soundtrack album, no longer the main motivation for a Beatles movie, only yielded (relatively) indifferent financial results worldwide.

Any optimistic 'flower power' overtones from the Fab Four's collective cartoon politics would be crushed in the solo film venture from the Rolling Stones' Mick Jagger, a work that completed the British pop-music film's synthesis of music and violence and was adjudged by Sarris 'the most deliberately decadent movie I have ever seen' (*Village Voice*, 30 July 1970). *Performance* (1970), directed by Donald Cammell and Nicolas Roeg, was bankrolled by Warner Bros. entirely on the promised participation of Jagger as star and soundtrack writer – the vague agreement that he would do eight numbers and act out a publicity-generating recreation of the Stones' Redlands drugs bust sufficed for the immediate granting of a $1.5 million budget. And so, in a sub-genre predominantly known for the studio exploitation of audience and artist, the economic momentum finally moved into reverse as Warners unwittingly underwrote what was, in essence, a home movie for co-director Cammell and his – admittedly well-heeled and well-connected – Chelsea-set friends. That funding was the project's high point: the troubled shooting, editing and shelving of the film for close on two years culminated in a mere fortnight's American release in August 1970 and a similarly brief UK sortie the following January before it was consigned to the vaults. Jagger had only come up with a single composition, so no face- and finance-saving Stones-related soundtrack album was forthcoming either. *Performance* subsequently found its way into the cult pantheon and academic exegesis has largely focused on its echoes of the Krays and Richardsons and its dismantling of the gangster genre, but a major thrust is its self-conscious replaying of motifs from the British pop-music film. *Performance* is narratively rooted in the musical domain, a setting authenticated not only by the casting of Jagger but also by its location in Notting Hill, the cradle of UK rock'n'roll lifestyle as recorded in Colin MacInnes's 1959 novel *Absolute Beginners*. Adjudged from a socio-musical perspective, *Performance*'s 'merging' of the pop-music film and gangster movie re-presents the late-1960s subsuming of a pastoral voice by an antiphonal violence; in so doing, it conclusively unites the opposing strands of the sub-genre's 'primitive' phase, the pop-star vehicle and the social-problem film. References to the exotic legend of the Old Man of the Mountain in his Persian fortress bring together the ageing rock star and now senior delinquent in the common etymological root of drop-out and hit-man, the *hashishin* and assassin. A dozen years on, *Performance* reworks the fun-loving and troublesome youth figures in 'real-time' adult disillusionment.

For want of Jagger-filled compositions, *Performance* forges an assembled soundtrack by mixing in musical textures from various cultures: Ry Cooder's slide guitar alternating with synthesizers and Indian *santoor* music adds an aural eclecticism that matches the Powis Square décor created by Christopher Gibbs. Nonetheless, Jagger's sole solo number, 'Memo from Turner', remains the film's centrepiece and a generic valediction as, initially dressed like a 1950s Ted with mutton-chop sideburns and slicked-back hair, he leads *Performance* less into a gangster's interrogation than a compendium of the British pop-music film in its 'primitive', 'mature' and 'decadent' phases. 'I remember you in Hemlock Road in 1956' dates the sub-genre's beginnings, while Turner's reminder that 'you were a faggy little leather boy / with a smaller piece of stick' succinctly depicts the cinema-seat slashing rock'n'roller of the era. The second verse offers a resumé of the corporate and mediated middle period: 'Weren't you at the Coke convention / Back in 1965 / And you're the misbred greying executive / I've seen so heavily advertised.' Finally, Turner's ironic plea for understanding – 'come now, gentlemen, your love is all I crave' – deflates the Summer of Love, the Beatles and the cartoon karma of *Yellow Submarine*. *Performance* so polarized critical opinion that the *New York Times* ran contrasting reviews on consecutive weeks, with Peter Schjeldahl's piece entitled 'The Most Beautiful Film of All?' (16 August 1970) countered by John Simon's less interrogative 'The Most Loathsome Film of All' (23 August 1970). Despite such diversity in reception, the film possessed a singular finality: for John Walker, '*Performance* put a hole through the head of the 1960s' (1985, 95). It did the same for the British pop-music film, its Borgesian maze of intertextuality incorporating a closing summation of the whole, now moribund, sub-genre.

Afterlife

Nonetheless, the British pop-music film has shown brief spasms of resuscitation, an intermittent afterlife that repeatedly investigates its previous generic incarnations. This can be categorized as a fourth 'historical' or 'revisionist' phase, largely equivalent to 'alternative' or 'youth heritage' cinema (Glynn 2013, 6). It is first evident in *That'll Be The Day* (1973), the debut feature of teen idol David Essex, which, as well as revisiting the early days of British rock'n'roll, returned fully to the sub-genre's blatantly commercial roots with co-producer David Puttnam striking a deal with America's Ronco record company whereby, in return for funding, the film would feature rock classics exploitable via an extensively advertised tie-in soundtrack album. The deal struck, Puttnam and writer Ray Connolly copiously revised the script, adding regular radios or record players to scenes, thereby creating Britain's first 'retro' rock movie, a music film not frantically chasing present trends but employing a pop-heritage soundtrack to fabricate a period setting and facilitate a commercially synergistic compilation LP, which reached number one in a two-month chart stay. It would prove, aesthetically and economically, a lasting template. The sequel, *Stardust* (1974), offered a raunchy riposte to the lifestyle portrayed by Lester in *A Hard Day's Night*, its cod-Beatles biography revealing a grubby rock decadence *in situ* from the beginning. Its backstage model of the unscrupulous management exploitation of Steve Shorter-style innocents would continue through the glam of Slade in *Flame* (1974) and the (post-)punk of Hazel O'Connor in *Breaking Glass* (1980). These

commercially limited exposés of corporate cynicism and the more remu-
nerative Who rock operas *Tommy* (1975) and *Quadrophenia* (1979) would
synthesize in *Pink Floyd: The Wall* (1982), lauded in the United States –
Roger Ebert adjudged it 'without question the best of all serious fiction
films devoted to rock' (*Chicago Sun-Times*, 24 Februry 2010) – but derided
in Britain. For example, Paul Taylor warned, with a wit sadly absent from
the film, of the problems with generic inbreeding: 'Crossing *Privilege* with
Tommy couldn't result in anything shallower. All in all, it's just another
flick to appal' (*Time Out*, 29 July 1982).

The afterlife of the pop-music film would next take a postmodern turn,
beginning with the absolute financial disaster of *Absolute Beginners* (1986),
a historicized 'primitive' coffee-bar musical that revisited the décor and
dirty tricks of *Expresso Bongo*, but effectively ruined Goldcrest Films, its
bloated £8.4 million budget clawing back just £1.8 million from UK
cinemas and less than $1 million in the United States. Far more successful
was the 'mature' postmodernism of the Spice Girls' movie *Spice World*
(1997), a backstage musical from a group matching the Beatles for popularity that replicated the getting-to-the-concert-on-time plot line of
A Hard Day's Night – with a *Summer Holiday* London double-decker
bus thrown in for good measure. The film's rampant self-reflexivity permitted the 'straight' showcasing of the Spice Girls and their songs in modes
ranging from nondiegetic to full performance while simultaneously parodying the make-up of the pop-music marketing and media discourses
that founded and followed their celebrity; it also saw PolyGram's modest
$25 million budget (mostly spent on 'star' appearances enjoying pop-
music film 'baggage') bring back over £11 million at the UK box-office,
$30 million in the United States and $75 million worldwide. To that must
be added *Spice World* the album, which broke existing records in shifting
over seven million copies in its first two weeks, with final sales topping
ten million. The first major studio pop-group exploitation music film since
the sub-genre's halcyon days in the 1960s, *Spice World*'s commercial
success – and critical plaudits, Matthew Sweet unironically commending
'an uproarious pantomime of ironies' that fused 'the recursively self-
referential qualities of Fellini's 8½ [1963] with the disposable peppiness
of *Help!*' (*Independent on Sunday*, 28 December 1997) – prompted the
inevitable epigonic *Seeing Double* (2003), 'starring' the similarly constructed S Club 7. There was no space, though, for an *Expresso Bongo*-
style parodic response, since *Spice World* itself so knowingly displayed its
ironic attitude towards its cinematic and musical heritage. A distaff variant
on Lester's pop-music films, it proved an increasingly rare generic convergence of economic imperatives and artistic achievement. Apart from
geriatric rockers Status Quo's disastrous *Bula Quo!* (2013), for Trevor

Johnston '[n]ot so much a movie, more a pub chat that got way out of hand' (*Time Out*, 3 July 2013), the new century, caring too much for money, has fought shy of trying to replicate the formula.

Table 4.1 *Chart run-down: the top ten musical sequences in the British pop-music film.*

10.	*Expresso Bongo*: 'The Shrine on the Second Floor'– Liberace-like campness
9.	*Catch Us If You Can*: 'Having a Wild Weekend' – an elegy to the ecstasy of dance
8.	*Tommy*: 'Acid Queen' – rock decadence (in a good way)
7.	*Privilege*: 'Free Me' – toe-tapping totalitarianism
6.	*Beat Girl*: 'Made You': cool? Straight from the fridge, daddy-o!
5.	*Help!*: 'Ticket to Ride' – Eastmancolor meets Eisenstein
4.	*The Young Ones*: 'We Say Yeah' – consummate rock'n'roll from Cliff Richard
3.	*The Tommy Steele Story*: 'Elevator Rock' – ambivalent beginnings
2.	*Performance*: 'Memo from Turner' – summative endings
1.	*A Hard Day's Night*: 'Can't Buy Me Love' – the 'eureka' moment, as big as the Beatles.

5 'A Film's First Audience'

The Composer's Role in Film and Television

GEORGE FENTON IN CONVERSATION
WITH MERVYN COOKE

George Fenton (b. 1949) began composing professionally in the mid-1970s for theatre productions by (amongst others) the Royal Shakespeare Company and the National Theatre. His early work with playwright Alan Bennett on *Forty Years On* (1968) and with Peter Gill at London's Riverside Studios led to numerous commissions for BBC TV where, in addition to other Bennett productions, he wrote signature tunes for all the regular BBC news bulletins (including the *One O'Clock News, Six O'Clock News, Nine O'Clock News, Newsnight* and *BBC Breakfast*) and several popular drama series (*Bergerac, Shoestring, The Monocled Mutineer*). Fenton's later scores for the BBC Natural History Unit achieved a new high standard for the genre, utilizing full orchestra and choir rather than the low-budget synthesized music which had been in vogue in the 1980s. His groundbreaking music for *The Blue Planet* (2001) won Ivor Novello, BAFTA and Emmy awards for Best Television Score, while *Planet Earth* (2006) was awarded an Emmy and a Classical Brit. The phenomenal popularity of these wildlife scores resulted in recordings and live touring performances with major orchestras, including the Berlin Philharmonic and Philharmonia, featuring large-screen HD projections of the BBC footage and presented at diverse venues ranging from regional concert halls to the Hollywood Bowl.

Fenton's early work with Gill at Riverside Studios came to the attention of Michael Attenborough, who introduced him to his father, the distinguished actor and film director Richard Attenborough. For the latter, Fenton composed his first feature-film score – for *Gandhi* (1982) – the success of which auspiciously launched a career in the movies characterized by an unusual stylistic versatility, and which was to include Academy Award nominations for *Gandhi, Cry Freedom* (1987), *Dangerous Liaisons* (1988) and *The Fisher King* (1991). Alongside his steady output of scores for mainstream productions in both the United States and United Kingdom, many of which are discussed below, Fenton has continued to work extensively with the independent British director Ken Loach, their collaborations including *Ladybird, Ladybird* (1994), *Land and Freedom* (1995), *My Name is Joe* (1998),

The Wind that Shakes the Barley (2006), *Route Irish* (2010) and *Jimmy's Hall* (2014).

* * *

MERVYN COOKE:

It's often struck me that film music might be more varied and dramatically interesting if more film composers came to the medium with prior experience of working in the theatre. How do you feel your own early experiences composing for the stage fed into your film scoring?

GEORGE FENTON:

I think it helped me a great deal. In both theatre and film, music is part of a collaboration. In the theatre one experiences the benefits and pitfalls of the collaborative process in a living way. You get live feedback from actors because they literally move, speak and dance to what you write. But what you write is also in service to the text, and I learnt a great deal about process and dramatic structure as a result. A sense of why plays work, some better than others, about pacing, etc. The difference is that theatre and sometimes European film are writers' media, whereas film – particularly American film – tends to be a director's medium; but there are similarities in the authorship and the need to 'read' the play or film so, yes, I consider it to have been a lucky start for me.

MC:

Your music first became very widely known in the shape of memorable signature tunes for TV drama series and the BBC's flagship current-affairs programmes, to the point where by the 1980s almost everybody in the UK must have heard several Fenton tunes without even realizing it. How did you approach writing signature tunes for these very different genres?

GF:

Because I began in the theatre, I approached all these projects in a visual way – either literally, or sometimes in my imagination. It's hard to explain how to visualize a news jingle, but I would literally spend hours trying to capture in my head the sound of the *Nine O'Clock News* headlines or *Newsnight*: what those headlines might be, what BBC News meant around the world. Similarly, with something like *Bergerac* [BBC, 1981–91] I would think endlessly about the place, the stories, the character of the detective. Who was he? Was he cool? If so, how cool? What was his tempo? Hopefully, as you dive deeper and deeper into the particular, you reach the point where what you're writing becomes a musical issue only: you are in a quite particular place and therefore there is a chance that what you write will have a sense of itself, and is perhaps less likely to date.

MC: What are the similarities and differences between composing music for television dramas and feature films?

GF: The answer used to be simple: one is for the theatre, one is for the living room. The difference between a captive audience in a controlled space, or not. Nowadays, thanks to the improvements in home reproduction and the streaming of both, it's much harder to distinguish between them – other than perhaps in the projects' ambitions – and I think that a feature film is self-defining in its arc whereas TV, no matter how good – and some of it is spectacularly good – is always shaped according to a slot. For the composer, I can see these shapes affect things like spotting [deciding where the music cues will be located]. Also, TV traditionally offers smaller budgets, but it's still a great platform for composers.

MC: Looking back on your early film work with the benefit of hindsight, are you aware of approaching scoring tasks differently these days, with the benefit of decades of experience? Did you ever make any rookie errors you'd care to recount?

GF: I don't think I've changed my *modus operandi* much, other than nowadays I can pre-lay tracks in my own home, so I am usually better prepared now. I miss the excitement of analogue technology, though. Of course, I made lots of wrong choices, but I still do. I never look back on a score, however recent, without reservations. Where I think I have improved is in helping people to play what I've written. To my shame I once brought a session to a stuttering halt by very nicely telling a senior musician that the instrument he was playing wasn't totally in tune. It wasn't, but my comment was a mistake because I wasn't specific enough and therefore it was no help. It rendered him almost incapable of playing, which otherwise he did brilliantly, so it got us nowhere.

MC: Alongside your scores for Hollywood and big-budget European productions, you've maintained a firm allegiance to the work of the independent British director Ken Loach. How did your longstanding collaboration with him come about, and how do you find the contrast between working for him and for more mainstream projects?

GF: Ken, or rather his producer, simply rang me and asked me to go and meet him. I was amazed because I thought of myself as far too 'commercial', but my heart leapt when they called. I rate Ken as one of the most interesting and gifted film makers ever. He has a clarity in his work that is unswerving, and it is that clarity that challenges one to do it justice with the score. He is not anti-music, not at all; in fact he loves music and is himself very musical, but he doesn't like the artifice of music in film. This is sometimes difficult to navigate because the mere use of music itself is an artifice; but then so are the camera and the cut. What is fascinating is trying to respond and speak truthfully to the film and not to inflate or sensationalize it. I suppose he makes one ask questions about 'why?', about assumptions, about truth, which affects how one thinks and creates.

MC: For Loach, you often feature intimate instruments such as solo guitar. Hollywood generally cries out for a big orchestral, or quasi-orchestral, sound, but some composers – for example, Thomas Newman – aren't comfortable with the idea that a conventional orchestra is ideal for modern film scoring. Have you ever resisted using a full orchestra when the expectation was that you would do so? Conversely, have you ever encouraged the use of an orchestra when a director didn't envisage it?

GF: Phil Joanou was very surprised when I played him the demo of the front title for his film *Heaven's Prisoners* [1996] that it wasn't orchestral – but he liked it anyway. I think in general you can rely on the movie to give you the line-up. The tendency now in contemporary films is to combine orchestral and non-orchestral elements – the best of both worlds? – but in some ways this has become as ubiquitous as the orchestra itself. I try not to have any preconceptions.

MC: Do you ever set out to achieve a specifically British sound in your film music? I'm thinking, for example, of Richard Attenborough's *Shadowlands* [1993], with its clear Anglican and Elgarian associations in the score. On the other hand, when writing for American films do particular transatlantic musical stereotypes sometimes suggest themselves?

GF: Yes, I certainly did in *Shadowlands*, but I think that probably the influence of English music is embedded in my writing unless I deliberately avoid it in favour of another idiom, and America offers lots that I have used. *Sweet Home Alabama* [2002], for example, and *The Long Walk Home* [1990]. In *84 Charing Cross Road* [1987], I tried to create the transatlantic distance between the main characters by idiom, which eventually theoretically became one voice.

MC: You're particularly renowned for your scoring of period dramas, such as *Dangerous Liaisons* [1988], *The Madness of King George* [1994], *The Crucible* [1996], *Dangerous Beauty* [1998] and *Stage Beauty* [2004]. Do you generally follow the Miklós Rózsa principle by researching musical styles appropriate to the relevant historical periods and, if so, how important do you feel this kind of 'authenticity' to be in modern film scoring?

GF: I do a certain amount of research. I think it's good to know the subject's musical territory, but I don't get particularly hung up on it. I think I tend to use it to find if there are elements or colours, certain instruments, which will work and make the score specific to that particular film. *Dangerous Liaisons* has a lot of period music, some dating from slightly earlier than the story's historical setting, but the score owes its tone to the framing: the composition of the shots is deliberately like Hitchcock's *Notorious* [1946]. After identifying how we could use period music, particularly comically, director Stephen Frears suggested that it was all going to be a bit dry, so why not score it like Hitchcock's *North by Northwest* [1959; music by Bernard Herrmann]! So I tried to combine a highly charged Herrmannesque approach with the forces of an earlier orchestra to give it some sense of uniformity, and that ended up being the score's central concept.

Sometimes, though, I do write completely within the idiom – for example, in *Stage Beauty* – perhaps in the moments when the music is more exposed in a montage where the picture might allow for a more formal structure, as it would for a song. Too many cadences can make a sequence less fluid, but sometimes the formality can be fun. The sequence in *Stage Beauty* where Charles changes the law begins in a mock serious way and then becomes serious. At the beginning I stayed in period (I even quoted sixteen bars of Purcell in the middle as a kind of test to my cue) and then developed the music into a different and darker tone. But honestly I think the transitions are decided by the film and aren't necessarily premeditated. Also, so many of these choices are subjective.

MC: Did you at any stage of your career feel you were being typecast, and is this tendency a common problem in the industry generally?

GF: Had I decided to settle in Hollywood I think I would have been, but thanks to living in London I am much freer. I can still work in theatre. And I would never have had the experience of composing for natural-history documentaries either. In general, I like the variety. It makes me feel I'm still learning things.

MC: In recent years your music has become widely appreciated in the shape of your resourceful orchestral scores for high-profile BBC Natural History Unit programmes, such as *The Blue Planet, Planet Earth* and *Frozen Planet* [2011], and their feature-film spin-offs. The groundbreaking project here was *The Blue Planet,* for which you departed from the then current fashion of using synthesizers for the scoring of wildlife documentaries. What motivated the use of a full orchestra and a choir, and was it something of a gamble in economic terms?

GF: At the time I was offered *The Blue Planet* I was very busy in LA. And my financial situation was secure enough not to have to worry that by employing an orchestra I was effectively working for slightly less than nothing. I often think about this and how different it would have been had I needed to pay myself! But I saw it as something that was good for the soul. Wonderful material, and inspiring both musically and personally. However the idea to score it with a big orchestra came from producer Alastair Fothergill. I had worked for him before and he had always loved the occasional 'bigger' moments when I evoked a large orchestral sound even in a modest way. So he wanted the scale and I was able to oblige, but throughout I always knew there was something very special about the project.

MC: How did the concept of touring your wildlife scores with live screenings and top-level professional orchestras come about? How much do you need to adapt your cues for the concert-hall experience? And how do you account for the great popularity of these concerts internationally?

GF: The BBC Concert Orchestra had asked if I would like to conduct a concert of the *Blue Planet* music. When I mentioned this to Jane Carter at the BBC she replied that I should play with the picture, having watched me record the score. It sounds simple enough but actually to adapt the music to play as concert pieces, to edit the pictures to make sense without a commentary and to give the evening an arc of its own is a complicated process. That said, I always believed that the results could be popular in their own right. A composer is a film's first audience. Much of what he or she writes is a vocalized response to the material: 'this bit's amazing', 'this bit's hilarious', etc. Watching *The Blue Planet*, I thought that if I put it on a big screen and the orchestra played, people would just dig it in an immersive way. What's interesting is that so much of the musical thought was informed by David Attenborough's voiceover; and yet, when it's not there, the response of the audience (because it isn't controlled by the narrator) is quite different, and their experience is very different to seeing the original films themselves. The concerts have proved incredibly popular, and with each new show I've done more and more picture editing as well as music editing and rewriting. They've become a journey of their own.

MC: As most of today's BBC documentaries on the natural and scientific world have scores that are clearly Fentonesque, are you proud of this legacy or do you sometimes feel (as my co-editor Fiona memorably puts it) like a Dr Frankenstein figure who inadvertently unleashed an uncontrollable monster?

GF: If a composer wants to borrow or be influenced or imitate something I've written, I feel flattered because I am flattered to be part of their journey just as others have been part of mine. However, if producers or directors are asking people to write like me I find it depressing that they think things have to be a certain way in order to tick a box. So then I feel like the 'experiment' went wrong.

MC: What do you think about the regular complaints that background music has overwhelmed the dialogue in recent BBC documentaries and dramas? Is the solution essentially just a question of improving the sound mixing and training for the presenters and actors [see, for example, D. Cohen 2011] or can some of the blame be put on how the music has been constructed? Why has audibility depreciated despite all the technological advances over the past twenty-five years?

GF: I think someone needs to take a long, hard look at sound mixing on TV. In some of the drama the dialogue is completely inaudible. My feeling is that the problem arises because the mixers have no 'average' setup to mix for. Is it a small TV with one speaker, a laptop or a 5.1 surround-sound home-cinema system? Since it's more satisfying, they tend to mix things so they sound good on the last of these. Not surprisingly, they want their work judged in the best possible conditions. But for a fuller answer you would need to ask a mixer.

MC: You've written scores for many American romantic comedies, including some directed by the late Nora Ephron [*You've Got Mail*, 1998; *Bewitched*, 2005]. Comedy scoring is traditionally cliché-ridden; for example, the widespread use of what Thomas Newman terms 'scurrying pizzicato strings', which he says are 'always good for a laugh' [Schelle 1999, 282]. Many of these clichés are now firmly enshrined in mind-numbingly formulaic reality-TV shows. Are such overworked musical gestures hard to avoid in the comedy genre in particular?

GF: There's nothing wrong with the use of pizzicatos, but I think their overuse is largely down to the fact that they sample very well, so they tend to be used a lot on keyboards. They perhaps are a romantic-comedy cliché now – and I may have been partly responsible for that, for which I apologize! – but hopefully my use of them never plumbed the depths that they have since reached. All films benefit from freshness in the score, a sense of enthusiasm, and those seem good starting points, particularly for comedy. But just as there are 'do's' in romantic comedy, more to do with harmony than instrumentation, there are also 'don'ts' because of peculiar prejudices amongst producers (oboe 'too sad'; clarinet 'too jazzy'). These feelings are difficult to understand for a musician but, hey, film is collaborative. Nora used to say 'jazz is the enemy of comedy!' It was funny, but not a joke.

MC: In spotting sessions, do you sometimes resist requests to furnish a particular scene with music when you don't feel it to be necessary? (The most extreme instance of this would perhaps be Malcolm Arnold's refusal to write anything except main-title music for *No Highway* (1951), on the grounds that adding music would otherwise 'ruin a good script and a good film' [see Burton-Page 1994, 53.])

GF: I tend more to move the starts and stops from their prescribed spotting, either from the notes or more usually the temp track. But, yes, in comedy particularly it is important to realize that audiences like a gap in which to laugh and too much music can be detrimental. I am a great believer in the actors being able to bat themselves in and the score should have the chance to do the same, so the early part of the film usually involves the most debate. I don't often refuse to write for a scene but I do encourage directors to let them play it without music if it seems better. Quite often they feel nervous of not having music just because they aren't confident in what they've got.

MC: How have technological developments affected film composing during your career? Have your working habits changed over the years in consequence?

GF: The technology has had a radical affect on every aspect of film. CGI digital cameras, colour timing, digital editing, and in music the advent of sequencers, samplers, Pro Tools [digital audio workstation software, similar to a multi-track tape recorder and mixer], etc. have changed the way one works; and yet for me they haven't changed things as much as for others. I think this is because I had a traditional method which was click-track tables, pencil and paper, so although I now have many different options as to how to (and how fully to) experiment, demo, etc., because I predate a lot of the technology – however interesting and inspiring some of it is – I normally end up in the same place as I always have, and I make my decisions finally that way. I still jot things down a lot – but equally nowadays I'd probably be lost without modern technology in trying to do my job.

MC: When working with electronics, have you ever had the chance to integrate sound effects and music in a meaningful whole? In general, are you provided with adequate information in advance about where dialogue and sound effects are likely to coincide with your music?

GF: I like the opportunity to use sound as part of the landscape of the score. I had the chance with *Company of Wolves* [1984] and certainly in some of the Natural History Unit films such as 'The Deep' [episode 2] in *The Blue Planet*. As regards sound effects generally, I think there is a better dialogue now between departments than there has been previously, although the lines still get blurred and this is a subject all of its own.

There are numerous complainants out there who dislike the use of music in natural-history documentaries, the normal complaint being that these films are 'natural', so why not have natural sound? This response plays very well into the increasingly thin line between effects and music. Most natural-history films do not use sync sound. It's impractical to record, and in many environments – such as the ocean – pointless because there is no noise. [For further on the 'silent' ocean and various musical responses to it, including Fenton's score for *Deep Blue* (2003) – the feature-length theatrical spin-off from *The Blue Planet* – see Cooke 2015.] So the sound of a marlin or killer whale swooshing past the camera with the thunderous low-end roar of an airliner is completely fictitious. Although these effects can be enormously useful in portraying scale, they are still effects; and where the problem sometimes arises is when those effects include ambience that has tones or pitches. Traditionally, the effects editors will work with the dubbing mixer for many days before they start to integrate the music and, whilst they may be making some brilliant and eerie sounds that are highly atmospheric, effects normally only speak to the moment. If the score, which not only speaks to the moment but is also trying to control the narrative arc, is one that integrates soundscapes or is trying to produce a similar effect with instruments then there can be a conflict. There have been occasions when I've felt that the effects editor has treated musical sample libraries as though they were a new toy box of effects, which inevitably compromises the score: firstly by the conflicting use of notes or clusters or percussion hits, but possibly more because the appetite for filling the moment means there is no space or silence (which frequently *is* real) available to the composer – and I would say that silence is one of the most important elements in music. However, if the two departments work together, as we do with the natural-history films I've done for the BBC, then it can be inspiring and collaborative and produce a soundscape where you sometimes can't tell where the score starts and the effects stop. Then it's very rewarding all round.

MC: What roles do synthesizers and computers play in the scores you've written since your more traditional orchestral scoring has been so much in demand? Are electronics more likely to feature in the eccentric worlds of films such as Terry Gilliam's *Zero Theorem* [2013], or do they still have a viable place in more conventional assignments?

GF: I tend to approach each film with an open mind. Certainly synthesizers are invaluable because they offer a massive range of textural and rhythmic possibilities, and beyond that they offer a very real solution for films where the budget won't stretch to an orchestra. It's hard sometimes to disentangle how one arrives at the palette for a score. I think it just slowly emerges and each composer will take a slightly different path. In general my interest is more in electronic sounds, analogue synths, etc., rather than imitative sounds.

MC: How often are you asked to work on the basis of temp tracks which don't use your music? Is this method useful to a composer, and are you able to give any specific examples from your experiences?

GF: I prefer that the temp track is not my music, and then sometimes it can be helpful in taking you out of yourself. A good recent example was *The Lady in the Van*, directed by Nicholas Hytner, which I have just finished. [The film was released in the UK in November 2015.] The temp track was deliberately all classical music, i.e. Beethoven, Schubert, Shostakovich, etc., because Nick felt that the film should not have 'film' music. In the end it did have film music, but the score inherited that sensibility, the formal and structural feeling of the temp, and I hope feels different to most scores as a result.

MC: With Neil Jordan's *Interview with the Vampire* [1994], you infamously fell victim to the all-too-common phenomenon of the summarily rejected score. (Somewhat perversely, the Internet Movie Database summarizes your career thus: 'He is known for his work on *Gandhi* (1982), *Groundhog Day* (1993) and *Interview with the Vampire: The Vampire Chronicles* (1994)'!) Have you ever been called in to write a score to replace someone else's rejected score? And has it ever happened to you since *Interview*?

GF: *Interview* was the only occasion that it's happened to me – so far – although it might be about to happen any minute now! There is always the potential for it happening again, for whatever reason. I think it made me more cautious for a while, more conventional, but also it coincided with my doing lighter films, so the demands changed. I've been asked many times to replace other scores. I accept it, as we all do, as being an unhappy fact of life, but I have never agreed to replace a score without first talking to the composer whose work I have been asked to replace. Just as a courtesy and because usually the decision to drop the score has nothing to do with the quality of what they wrote.

MC: There seem to be occasional acts of homage in your scores to illustrious predecessors in film scoring: I'm thinking of the Nino Rota-like music at the start of *Groundhog Day* [1993] and the Rózsa-like noir scoring of *Final Analysis* [1992], for example. Were these allusions conscious, and are there other examples in your work?

GF: My work is littered with attempts to emulate my heroes. The homage in *Groundhog Day* was totally deliberate, perhaps the Rózsa influence less conscious, but certainly down to my general love of the European Hollywood composers. In *Valiant* [2005], there is a homage to Korngold. I hope in all these cases it sounds like me paying homage rather than my writing a pastiche.

MC: Do you ever have the chance (or feel the need) to read scripts in advance, or visit sets or location shoots for inspiration? Not all film composers find these activities beneficial: Richard

Rodney Bennett said he went on location to Dorset with the cast and crew of *Far From the Madding Crowd* [1967] and just 'sat there and sneezed and had no musical ideas at all' [Daniel 2000, 153].

GF: As the film's first audience, the composer's first response to a film is important and therefore too many preconceptions based on books or scripts can get in the way of that first moment when you see a cut of the film, and water down your instinctive response. Conversely, being exposed to a film at an early stage sometimes allows one to get into the general musical landscape. Richard Attenborough always included me early on, but more in the filming than in the background. It was immensely helpful to absorb the feeling of the subject. Sometimes, though, I prefer to see the picture for the first time when there is a cut and then immediately start work.

MC: How does the realization that most film-goers won't be paying close attention to the intricacies of the score affect your approach in composing the music? Do you feel it's important for a single score to have a long-term trajectory that can work its magic subliminally? Or do certain assignments require a more music-of-the-moment approach in the interests of variety and immediacy?

GF: I think there's a case for both. But ultimately I hang on to the thought that the music is there for a reason and whether its effect is noticeable or subliminal shouldn't make any difference to how hard one should work on it, or that it shouldn't be defensible within the context of the score's overall arc. 'Musical' scores have a way of resonating, even if the audience may not be constantly conscious of it.

MC: It's noticeable that in many of your film scores you write substantial end-credit cues that are not merely the potpourri recyclings of existing cues which are much more common at this point in a film. Why is this, and does it worry you that so many people in the cinema walk out during the first seconds of the credits music?

GF: One reason is that it's a chance just to play the music without any sync issues, so it's quite liberating. I don't mind if people walk out because I dislike the way that the end crawl has become such a pointless waste of time. The requirement to

credit every composer, animator, etc., is equivalent to listing every member of the orchestra and every employee of the
recording studio. It's out of hand and has made the whole
thing an indulgence. I suppose I really write end titles for the
families of the music department (who are always at the very
end) while they wait patiently for their loved ones' names to
appear.

MC: Do you feel it's important to keep up with contemporary
        trends in film scoring, or with so much experience now
        behind you is it possible simply to pursue your own instincts?
        And what are your thoughts on the general state of film music
        today?

GF: I try to keep up. Whether it changes me I don't know. Writing
        involves constant choices and one's choices are so subjective.
        There are many composers I admire, and their solutions
        certainly make me think again about how and what I write.
        But there are also many who I feel don't really have their own
        voice and I think suffer from trying to make their scores
        sound like 'that other score' before they've had the chance
        to bring their own musical influences to bear. Highly useful
        though the [softsynth] libraries of (for example) Omnisphere
        and Zebra are, they are the least interesting aspects of
        contemporary scores – particularly some which are little
        more than that. Given that film music is primarily music, I
        think it's important to be influenced by music away from
        film – orchestral works or tracks or folk music, rather than
        only other film scores. That's the history of film music and I
        think today's most exciting new scores are influenced in that
        way too.

PART TWO

Approaching Film Music

6 Film-Music Theory

GUIDO HELDT

Theory Tangles

'Film-Music Theory' is the obvious title for this chapter, but it may also mislead. Its simplicity suggests that there *is* something we can call 'film-music theory', an established body of thought a survey can chart. But arguably there is not, and the first thing to do is to identify some of the blank areas on the map of film-music theory, and some of the obstacles that stand in the way of colouring them in.

The least problematic word in the title is 'music', but it, too, hides questions, gaps and blind spots. Can film-music theory limit itself to music, or is music so closely interwoven with other film sound that they are one object for theory? Michel Chion criticized the idea with the formula 'there is no soundtrack': that just because music, speech and noises are all types of sound does not mean that they have to form a coherent whole (1994, 39–40; 2009 [2003], 226–30). On the other hand, Chion has done more than most to think about film sound and music within the same theoretical horizon – a characteristic approach from the perspective of film studies, which tends to see music as a subcategory of film sound. It is a valid hierarchy, but it can obscure the specifics of music in film. Musicologists, on the other hand, tend to treat music as a thing unto itself, though one at times linked to other film sound. A minor question about the relationship of music and sound in film is whether we always know which is which; an example such as Peter Strickland's *Katalin Varga* (2009), with its tightrope walk between *musique concrète* and sound design, shows how that ambiguity can become creatively fertile (see Kulezic-Wilson 2011 and J. Martin 2015). Uncertainty regarding the sound–music relationship affects this chapter too; depending on the context, it sometimes considers both and sometimes focuses on music.

Some kinds of music in film have been more thoroughly theorized than others: the scarcity of systematic discussion of pre-existing music in film is the most obvious example. The most comprehensive study is by Jonathan Godsall (2013); there is work on 'classical' music in film (for example, Keuchel 2000 and Duncan 2003), and on directors known for their use of pre-existing music, such as Stanley Kubrick, Jean-Luc Godard and Martin Scorsese (see Gorbman 2007; Gengaro 2012; McQuiston 2013; Stenzl 2010;

Heldt *et al.* 2015). Another gap opens up if we change perspective and look at music not as a functional element of film. While it undoubtedly is that, a focus on function overlooks the fact that film has also been a major stage for the composition, recycling, performance, contextualization and ideological construction of music. It would be a task not for film musicologists, but for music historians to give film music a place in the story of music in the twentieth and twenty-first centuries.

The word 'film' is more of a problem. In the rapid expansion of screen-media musicology over the last generation, from the fringes of musicology and film studies to a well-established field with its own journals, book series, conferences, programmes of study, etc., music in the cinema has become an almost old-fashioned topic, at least from the vantage point of those working on music in television, in video games, on the internet, in audiovisual art and so on. (See Richardson *et al.* 2013 for a survey.) Yet even if this were an old-fashioned *Companion to Film Music*, it would still need to consider the problem: what we mean by 'film' is becoming fuzzy, and what film musicology has considered in depth or detail is less than what one can now categorize as film. Most of us have an ostensive idea of a 'film' – a narrative feature film, around two hours long, shown in a cinema – and most film musicology deals with such films. Yet films have had a second home on television since the 1950s; most of us have seen more movies on the box via direct broadcasts or video than in the cinema. The involvement of television broadcasters in film production means that this is not just a secondary use, but is built into the economic foundations of filmmaking. And what about music in TV films – is it within the remit of film musicology or that of the emerging field of television-music studies? And where in the disciplinary matrix are we when we flip through the TV channels and stumble upon the movie *Star Trek* (2009) and then upon an episode of the television series *Star Trek: The Next Generation* (1987–94)? Multimedia franchises are yet another solvent eating away at 'film'; in such a world, the idea of film musicology as a separate field may have had its day. Moreover, with the digital shift in filmmaking and exhibition, the very term 'film' has become anachronistic. ('Movie' has always been more telling, and it may be only linguistic pusillanimity that has kept it from becoming academically common.) Digital technology drags film out of its former home in the cinema and transforms it into a dataset fit for an increasingly diverse multi-platform media world.

On the other side of the methodological problem, much of what we can see and hear in the cinema has been largely ignored by film musicology: short films, abstract and other experimental films, documentaries, adverts, trailers and so on. There is literature on cartoons (see, for example, Goldmark 2001 and 2005; Goldmark and Taylor 2002; Jaszoltowski

2013), but other forms have languished in the shadows. Music in advertising has been studied more from the perspective of television – understandable given its role in the economy of the medium (see Rodman 2010, 77–101 and 201–24; B. Klein 2010) – though most insights translate to cinema adverts; music in documentaries has only produced a smattering of studies (Rogers 2015 is the most substantial, though 'rockumentaries' and other music documentaries have found interest: see T. Cohen 2009; Baker 2011; Wulff *et al.* 2010–11); and music in film trailers and in other filmic paratexts, such as main-title and end-credit sequences, is only just emerging as a field of study (see Powrie and Heldt 2014 for a summary and bibliography). And then there is 'theory', where things get more tangled. In the sciences, 'theory' is a relatively straightforward concept: a model of part of the world that allows us to make predictions that can be empirically tested, and where experimental falsification allows theories to be improved to become better models. This summary glosses over complications in the reality of theory formation and testing, but may help to throw art theories into relief. Art theories, too, model aspects of the world in order to explain how they 'work'. But while the sciences have an established 'scientific process', a particular nexus of theory, empirical testing and reality (however idealized), that relationship is looser in the arts, where the career of theories rests on a less tidy set of circumstances: on their inherent plausibility; on their fit with other theories; on their analytical power; on their originality or their capacity to generate original interpretations; on trends and fashions in a discipline and in the wider academic landscape (especially for small disciplines such as film studies or musicology, which historically have depended heavily on ideas from elsewhere); and on political, ethical and aesthetic stances that introduce a prescriptive element to some theories that has no equivalent in the sciences.

Closest to the scientific model is the cognitive psychology of the effects of film music. (For summaries of research, see Bullerjahn 2014 and Annabel J. Cohen 2010 and 2014.) Music theory is another tributary, informing how musicologists analyse the structures of music in films: harmonic structures from local chord progressions to film-spanning frameworks; metric, rhythmic and phrase structures that may affect how music relates to on-screen movement or editing; or motivic and thematic relationships. All of this is the small change of music analysis and usually goes without saying; only recently has music theory approached film musicology with more complex instruments (see Lehman 2012, 2013a and 2013b; and Murphy 2006, 2012, 2014a and 2014b). A different appropriation of music theory – on the general level of music as an abstract system – is music as a metaphor for formal aspects of film, in a move away from understanding film as recording or representation of reality (see

Bordwell 1980), a variant of the more common metaphor of the 'language' or 'grammar' of film (for example, Spottiswoode 1935; Metz 1971 and 1974 [1968]; Arijon 1976).

But mostly, 'theory' means film theory, and the challenge it poses to film musicology is its diversity (see, for example, Stam and Miller 2000, Simpson *et al.* 2004 and Braudy and Cohen 2009 for anthologies; Elsaesser and Hagener 2010 for an unusual account; and Tredell 2002 for a historical overview). There is media theory, dealing with technological and communicative, but also institutional and economic aspects of cinema; there are theories of the ontology of film, of film language, of authorship, of aesthetics, of narratology, with regard to narrative systems and with regard to the story patterns they generate; there are semiotics and pragmatics; there is genre theory; there are psychological theories on a spectrum from psychoanalytical approaches, often close to cultural theory, to empirical psychology; there are sociological theories, including engaged 'critical' theories; theories of performance, within film and of film; theories of film and cultural identities, and of different national and regional cinemas; theories of audiences and spectatorship, of gender, of emotion, of time and so on. There is also 'Theory', that 'blend of Marxism, psychoanalysis and structuralism' (Macey 2001, 379) that became prominent in Anglophone film studies in the 1970s (see Buhler 2014b for an overview of sound and music in relation to parts of Theory, and Bordwell and Carroll 1996 for critiques). The situation is complicated by the fact that theoretical thinking does not need to generate theories in a strong sense; much film-studies scholarship that does not aim to theorize as such still contributes to the initiative: to the development of ideas that may eventually be adopted in theories.

How film-music theory might fit into this jagged panorama (or widen its frame) is not yet clear. Is it another glass pebble in the theoretical kaleidoscope, contributing its own bit to the picture? Or should music be absorbed into film theories and become as integral to them as music often is to film? In the audiovisual art of film, sound is part and parcel of all these theoretical perspectives, and music intersects with most of them. So far, sound has played only a peripheral role in film studies, and film musicology has mostly been a thing apart, a situation to which musicologists are accustomed, separated as they are from colleagues elsewhere in the academy by musical notation and theory and its arcane symbols, concepts and terminology. However cosy that may be at times, it is also dangerously isolating. If film musicology wants to be productive in film studies, it has to grow into it, and film-music theory into film theory. That puts an onus on film scholars to accept it as something with which they need to engage if they want to do their job properly, and an onus on film musicologists to make themselves understood. That does not preclude studies reliant on expert musical knowledge – they make the widening of the horizon possible. But the arcana need to serve a purpose, and the results need to be communicated so that others can use them.

Theories in History

The challenge for film-music theory has been exacerbated by the unstable currents of artistic and academic developments. Film is only 120 years old, and sound film (as a commercially viable mass medium) less than 90, and beyond the aesthetic change that is a constant in the history of any art, revolutions in technology and media mean that film has been a moving target for theory. Film studies as an academic concern is only two generations old and has imported many ideas (and scholars) from other disciplines. That influx may have been stimulating, but there has been scant time for a disciplinary identity to emerge, much less so for a peripheral topic such as music. And while there have been major studies of film music since Kurt London's in 1936, for decades these were few and far between; only since the 1980s has development picked up and formed a new sub-discipline (though whether one subordinate to film studies or to musicology is not clear). That the birth of modern film musicology is often identified with the special issue 'Film/Sound' of *Yale French Studies* (Altman 1980) proves the point of the heterogeneous disciplinary history that makes film-music theory precarious; that the title of the special issue omits music – though five of its articles are about it – shows its peripheral place in film studies at the time (and to this day).

This chapter can only offer a whistle-stop tour of some milestones in the uncertain unfolding of film-music theory and try to trace how questions and ideas are threaded through the history of such theory. This neither amounts to a history nor a metatheory of film-music theory; given the sketchy nature of the matter, the chapter cannot be but a sketch itself.

Chasing After Film: The Accidental Theory of Silent-Film Music

Until about two generations ago, the honour of theory was accorded to practices understood as (high) art. But film started life not as art; it began as technological sensation and spectacle, and continued as (sometimes quite cheap) entertainment. During the first quarter of the twentieth century, music in silent film was theorized only in passing, as a by-product of the practice of making music for film. A venue for such accidental theorizing was the development in the 1910s of organized collections of titles, incipits or stock music deemed suitable for film accompaniment, such as the *Kinotheken* series in Germany (see Altman 2004, 258–65, for their early development). The implicit assumptions that governed their categories for music could be analysed as a cryptotheory of the semiotics of film music in its own right and the introductions to such collections often also contain, intentionally or not, nuggets of nascent film-music theory. 'The pianist should create a tone poem that forms a frame, as it were, for the picture', advises one compiler (True 1914, 2), and what can be understood as a prod for cinema pianists to take pride in their work can also be read as an acknowledgement of a key function of music in film: to bind the fragmented structure of shots and cuts in the visual images into a whole.

The purpose of such collections made a critical view unlikely; introductions usually describe what their authors see as best practice without judgement. An example is Ernö Rapée's 1925 *Encyclopedia of Music for Pictures*. What Rapée describes would, two decades later and translated into the conditions of sound film, provide the aim for the sarcastic critique of the first chapter of Theodor Adorno's and Hanns Eisler's *Composing for the Film* (2007 [1947]): music provides setting, atmosphere or emotion; Chinese music is for Chinese characters and English music for English ones; characters have themes (Rapée does not yet call them leitmotifs) chosen according to a system of musical clichés: the music shadows the film and does what it does in the most obvious way. (See excerpts from Rapée in Cooke 2010, 21–7; Hubbert 2011, 84–96; and Wierzbicki *et al.* 2012, 39–52.)

A counter-example is Hans Erdmann, Giuseppe Becce and Ludwig Brav's *Allgemeines Handbuch der Film-Musik*, which frames its 'thematic scale register' – classifying pieces of music by a multi-level system of moods – with a critique of silent-film practice and its 'style-less potpourris' of worn-out clichés (1927, vol. 1, 5). At the end of silent cinema, Erdmann, Becce and Brav justify their advice for matching music to film with a rudimentary version of what James Buhler (taking his cue from Francesco Casetti) calls an 'ontological theory' of film music: one that 'attempted to determine [the] nature and aesthetic possibilities' of film music by trying to determine the nature of film itself, an attempt that would become important in the transition to sound film (2014a, 190–4). Erdmann, Becce and Brav 'explain' the integral role of music in film by locating film between drama and music: to the former it is linked by 'the representational objective, the material content', to the latter by its 'wordlessness' that makes it 'averse to pure thought' (1927, vol. 1, 39; my translation). While the reasons for music's integral role in film were historical rather than aesthetic – music was common in other forms of dramatic storytelling, and it was part of the performance contexts in which film first appeared – it was still tempting to justify it by looking for a common denominator of film and music. Carl Van Vechten, for example, in 1916 found it in comparing the wordless action of film to ballet: 'and whoever heard of a ballet performed without music?' (2012 [1916], 20); and the idea of movement linking images and music is still used by Zofia Lissa (1965, 72–7). The flipside of Erdmann, Becce and Brav's critique is their call for coherence: 'incidental music' (that is, music as diegetic prop) should be historically credible, and 'expressive music' should not 'chase after film scenes like a poodle', but shape the emotional trajectory of the film (1927, 46); music is understood to possess its own formal and stylistic integrity that combines with the images to form the film. (For background to the *Handbuch*, see Comisso 2012 and Fuchs 2014.) The 'style-less potpourris' were still an issue when Rudolf Arnheim, writing in 1932, bemoaned that music chasing after film scenes coarsened their effect because it had not been part of the balancing of continuity and contrast at their conception (2002 [1932], 253–4).

Counterpoints: The Challenge of Sound Film

Silent film is more musical than sound film, but the challenge for theorists of early sound film was that it is musical in a different way. The sound of a silent film is not part of the film text, but is added *in situ* as part of the performance of the film (even though the brain may combine the visual and auditive layers into the experience of a whole). Sound film offered the possibility for sound and music to disappear into the images: 'realistic' diegetic sounds could be understood as their counterpart, and music lost its visible presence in the cinema and could become 'unheard melodies' (Gorbman 1987). One may wonder what would have happened had Edison succeeded and film had been furnished with synchronous sound from the start: would film theory have taken its cues from theories of drama? Probably only up to a point, as its patchwork of shots and cuts gives film a fundamentally different structure. But film theory carried the origins of the medium with its silent images and musical layer across the transition to sound, most obviously in the idea of film as an essentially visual art. That in 2003 Chion still felt the need to blow the trumpet of sound with the book title *Art sonore, le cinéma* (published in English as *Film, a Sound Art*, 2009) shows the long shadow of the idea. (A music-specific variant of the problem is found in Noël Carroll's 'Notes on Movie Music', which set music apart from 'the film' and categorized both as complementary 'symbol systems' [1996, 141].)

For film theorists, the transition to sound sharpened the question of what film was good for – a question not so much about film's ontology as one about its aesthetic potential. The technical recording process involved in most cinematic images (and sounds) made it tempting to ascribe to film a unique capacity for capturing reality – the view of mid-century theorists such as André Bazin, for whom 'the guiding myth' of cinema is 'an integral realism, a recreation of the world in its own image, an image unburdened by the freedom of interpretation of the artist' (2005 [1967], 21), or Siegfried Kracauer, who distinguished between 'basic and technical properties of film' and saw as its basic property that film is 'uniquely equipped to record and reveal physical reality', while of the technical properties 'the most general and indispensable is editing' (1961, 28–9).

For Bazin, sound film 'made a reality out of the original "myth"', and it seemed 'absurd to take the silent film as a state of primal perfection which has gradually been forsaken by the realism of sound and color' (2005 [1967], 21). But for theorists who had grown up with silent film, its relative lack of realism focused attention on 'the freedom of interpretation of the artist' enabled by the 'technical properties' of film – an achievement threatened by the illusion of realism which synchronous sound made that bit more insidiously perfect. And so Sergei Eisenstein, Vsevolod Pudovkin and Grigori Alexandrov feared that the realism of sound film might lead to sterile '"highly cultured dramas" and other photographed performances of a theatrical sort' that would damage the aesthetic of montage which early Soviet films had developed, because 'every adhesion of sound to a visual montage piece increases its inertia as a montage piece, and increases the independence of its meaning'; they called instead for an 'orchestral counterpoint of visual and aural images' (Eisenstein *et al.* 1928, 84); Arnheim warned that sound film was inimical to the work of 'film artists . . . working out an explicit and pure style of silent film, using its restrictions to transform the peep show into art' (1957, 154); and Béla Balázs wrote that sound film was still a 'technique' that had not 'evolved into an art' (1970 [1952], 194–5). Such scepticism was justified by film's rapid move towards using speech and noises primarily in a 'realistic' manner (though exceptions such as René Clair's films in the early 1930s show that creative solutions were possible, as did cartoons, which were freed from some of the expectations of realism).

One consequence of the shock of synchronized sound was to make theorists map how such sound could relate to images. There were two crucial issues: the degree to which sounds could be understood as realistic with regard to images, and the degree to which images and sounds converged or diverged conceptually. True to the title of the book, the most elaborate system was developed in Raymond Spottiswoode's *Grammar of Film* (1935, 48–50 and 173–96). Spottiswoode places sound on different polar scales: it can be realistic or unrealistic in kind or intensity; realistic sound can have an on-screen or off-screen source (the latter he calls 'contrapuntal' sound; 174–8); sound can be objectively unrealistic (voice-over or nondiegetic music) or subjectively unrealistic (representative of a character's perception). The second distinction is that between 'parallel' and 'contrastive sound': sight and sound 'convey[ing] only a single idea' or 'different impressions' (180–1).

Spottiswoode's first set of distinctions is, in different versions and with a variety of terms, still part of the toolbox of film musicology: diegetic and nondiegetic music; on-screen and off-screen music; music representing objective reality or subjective perception (from Chion's 'point of audition' [1994, 89–94] to 'internal' or 'imagined' diegetic music, 'metadiegetic music' and, conceptually wider, 'internal focalization'; for a summary see Heldt 2013, 119–33). Distinctions added later are, for example, that between on- and off-track music (between music heard and music implied by other means; Gorbman 1987, 144–50), and that between on- and off-scene diegetic music (between music that is diegetic with regard to the storyworld overall and music that is diegetic in a specific scene; Godsall 2013, 79–82), and temporality is introduced with the concept of displaced sound and music (see Bordwell and Thompson 2010, 280–98; Buhler *et al.* 2010, 92–113; Heldt 2013, 97–106).

Spottiswoode's distinction between parallel and contrastive sound also had its career in film-sound theory (with 'contrast' often replaced by 'counterpoint', building on Eisenstein, Pudovkin and Alexandrov's audio-visual 'counterpoint'; Nicholas Cook returns to 'contrast' [1998, 98–106]; see also Chion 1994, 35–9). Whatever the terms, the distinction underlies Eisenstein's statement that 'synchronization does not presume consonance' and takes account of 'corresponding and non-corresponding "movements"' (1942, 85), allowing for the complex system of image–sound relationships sketched in *The Film Sense*; it is there in Adorno's and Eisler's 'music ... setting itself in opposition to what is shown on the screen' (2007 [1947], 26–8); it informs Kracauer's distinction between parallelism and counterpoint (sound and images denoting the same or different ideas), perpendicular to that between synchronous and asynchronous sound (sound matching or not matching what we see; 1961, 111–15 and 128–32). (For further discussion and examples of the idea, see Gallez 1970.) Lissa uses both distinctions more flexibly: she allows for a fuzzy borderline between synchronism and asynchronism via 'loosened-up' forms of mutual sound/image motivation that pull them apart 'temporally, spatially, causally, emotionally'. Audiovisual counterpoint for her covers a range of options: music linking strands on the image track; music dynamizing static images; music commenting on images or characterizing protagonists; music adding 'its own content' to images; music anticipating a scene; music in counterpoint to speech and noises; and music in Eisensteinian montages of thesis and antithesis implying a conceptual synthesis (Lissa 1965, 102–6). The idea is still present in Hansjörg Pauli's distinction between musical 'paraphrase, polarisation and counterpoint': music matching the 'character of the images'; music imbuing images with an interpretation; and music contrasting with images (1976, 104), a division he later retracted as too simplistic (1981, 190). The problem with such systems is that they undersell the multi-layered complexities of sound film. Both sound and vision can consist of different strands, but whereas the use of split screens or layered images is rather rare, the layering of multiple auditive strands in more complex ways (that is to say, different combinations of dialogue, noises, diegetic and nondiegetic music at the same time) is not uncommon in film. When in a film 'we hear one or two simultaneous sounds, we could just as well hear ten or fifteen, because there is ... no frame for the sounds' (Chion 2009 [2003], 227). Furthermore, images, sounds or music can rarely be reduced to a single 'character', and a static model of image–sound relationships ignores the dynamic, temporal nature of both. This complexity does not preclude simplifying systems, but they need to be understood as heuristic crutches.

Another approach to ordering film music that proliferated from the 1930s onwards is to describe its functions. Lists of functions have been too many and too various to be surveyed here (early ones are discussed in Lissa 1965, 107–14; other examples include Spottiswoode 1935, 49–50 and 190–96; Schaeffer 1946; Copland 1949, elaborated in Prendergast 1992 [1977], 213–26; Manvell and Huntley 1957, 69–177, and 1975, 63–198; Kracauer 1961, 133–56; Gallez 1970, 47; La Motte-Haber and Emons 1980, 115–219; Schneider 1986, 90–1; Chion 1995a, 187–235; Kloppenburg 2000, 48–56; Larsen 2005, 202–18; Bullerjahn 2014, 53–74; for classical Hollywood film Gorbman 1987, 70–98, and Kalinak 1992, 66–110). Lissa's list can illustrate a feature of such catalogues: their synoptic nature means that they range across the realms of different theories. Lists of functions focus on their being performed by music at the expense of their place in a particular theoretical framework. Lissa distinguishes between music underlining movement, music as stylization of sounds, music as representation of space, music as representation of time, deformation of sound material, music as commentary, music in its natural role, music expressing mental experiences, music as a basis for empathy, music as symbol, music as story anticipation and music as a formally unifying factor (1965 [1964], 115–231). One of the categories, the deformation of sound material, is not a function in itself, but a range of techniques for different purposes; the others comprise aspects of the semiotics of film music, of its narratology, of its psychology and of film form.

Lists of functions are compiled not on the basis of understanding film as a super-system of formal systems – typical for neoformalist film theory associated with scholars such as David Bordwell, Kristin Thompson or Carroll (for example, see Bordwell 1985; Thompson 1988; N. Carroll 1996; Bordwell and Thompson 2010) – but with regard to the making and perception of films. If we understand the former as anticipation of the latter, the two are related (though not as mirror images, because not all intentions are realised and not all perceptions anticipated), and we may see the categorization of functions of film music as part of the poetics rather than the theory of film – part of the craft of making rather than the science of analysing film. A counterpart of such a perspective is the phenomenological approach, an analysis of the experience of film music, which is an implicit part of many analyses, but has rarely been the subject of methodological discussion (Biancorosso 2002, 5–45, is the most elaborate example).

Monument Valley: Musical Monoliths in the Desert

Although early film-music theory was born of film-sound theory and the work of film theorists rather than musicologists, for most of the twentieth century not just music but sound itself became a sideline for film theory which was 'resolutely image-bound ... sound serving as little more than a superfluous accompaniment' (Altman 1980, 3). (Anthologies such as Stam and Miller 2000 and Simpson *et al.* 2004 mention music on only 8 and 5 pages, respectively, out of total lengths of 862 and 1,487 pages.) For a long time, studies of film music were relatively few and were either practical primers (Sabaneev 1935); surveys of film music as a whole, made from historical as well as systematic perspectives, but without a specific theoretical aim, such as the studies of Kurt London (1936), Roger Manvell and John Huntley (1957), Georges Hacquard (1959), Henri Colpi (1963), François Porcile (1969) and Roy M. Prendergast (1992 [1977]); or idiosyncratic monoliths, such as Adorno's and Eisler's *Composing for the Films* (2007 [1947]) or Lissa's *Ästhetik der Filmmusik* (1965 [1964]).

The fame of Adorno and Eisler is indeed based on their idiosyncratic views more than on their work's usefulness as a textbook, which it is not. In one sense, it is an adjunct to Adorno and Max Horkheimer's *Dialectic of Enlightenment* (1947), a case study of 'the most characteristic medium of contemporary cultural industry' (Adorno and Eisler 2007 [1947], xxxv); it is a polemic of two creative minds thrown by history right into the heart of the capitalist system that had occupied their thinking for many years; it is an exploration of alternatives to the Hollywood orthodoxy (using Eisler's own film scores as counter-examples). The biting criticism of Hollywood's 'Prejudices and Bad Habits' in the first chapter may be the least interesting one because it states the obvious: that much film music does what is expected of it in terms of musical style, semiotic referencing and narrative function, but does it in an unobtrusive way that relegates it to 'a subordinate role in relation to the picture' (*ibid.*, 5). The book is also occasionally curiously retrospective: two of the bad habits, the attempt to justify music diegetically and the use of classical hits as stock music (*ibid.*, 6–7 and 9), were not really relevant anymore in the mid-1940s, and many examples of scores by Eisler refer back to the early 1930s. But the chapters on musical dramaturgy, musical resources and aesthetics (*ibid.*, 13–29 and 42–59) contain insights and ideas that show a belief in the potential of music to release 'essential meaning' from the 'realistic surface' of film (*ibid.*, 23). Many of these insights remain unredeemed, and while film music has discovered the use of many 'new resources and techniques' (*ibid.*, 21) since 1947, it has also transformed many of them into new 'bad' habits. The most important contribution of the book to film-music theory was perhaps that it widened the range of what 'theory' meant – that it need not be restricted to theorizing film music as a subsystem of the film text, but that the economic, institutional and social conditions of the making and reception of films were crucial to their structure. Even though that seems obvious, one danger of the theory-proliferation mentioned in the first part of this chapter is that theories of different aspects of film and its music do not speak to each other, and whatever one may think of Adorno's and Eisler's aesthetics, their attempt to intertwine sociology with the structure and style of films and their music was (and is) a salutary lesson.

Lissa's own idiosyncratic monolith, written two decades later, takes almost the opposite tack, perhaps consciously so. Lissa ignores Adorno's and Eisler's lesson of socio-economic contextualization and casts music as part of film not as 'mass culture', but as art: a synthetic art reliant on the 'organic cooperation of the means of different arts' (1965 [1964], 25). If Adorno and Eisler were anxious for music to become productive in film by retaining its integrity, Lissa sees its difference to the rest of the film as the potential to become an 'integrative factor' in the 'dialectic unity of the layers of sound film' (*ibid.*, 27, 65). Through historical convention, music has become integral to film because it adds a dimension: unlike most elements of a film, music does not represent a (fictional) reality, but is a reality in its own right (though this does not apply to diegetic music, which is representational), and while the images 'concretise . . . the musical structures', linking them to specific meanings, they in turn 'generalise the meaning of the images' (*ibid.*, 70). The dialectics smack of an attempt to justify music in film via an unnecessary reductive principle (there are enough films without music that work perfectly well, after all), but the idea of music as integral to a new multimedia art informs analyses of the functions of film music, of the role of form and style, of music in different genres and of its psychology that for the time were matchlessly detailed and differentiated. One idiosyncrasy of the book – at least for readers in Western countries – is that many examples are from films made in the Eastern bloc (though for the German version references to Western films were added; *ibid.*, 6). Despite that, it is a loss that the book has never been translated into English; though its interest today may be mainly historical, for that reason alone a translation would still be worthwhile.

Becoming Film Musicology: The Constitution of a Discipline

The hearing loss of film theory eventually made way for a return to the interest in sound and music that had been integral to early sound-film theory, programmatically in the 1980 'Film/Sound' special issue of *Yale French Studies* mentioned above. The quantity of film-music literature picked up as well, but widely read books such as Claudia Gorbman's *Unheard Melodies* (1987) or Royal S. Brown's *Overtones and Undertones* (1994) still show traces of the older, synoptic model (as does Helga de La Motte-Haber and Hans Emons' *Filmmusik* in 1980), though new theoretical concerns now come to the fore.

Its balancing of survey and theoretical perspectives new to film musicology made Gorbman's film-music book the first port of call for a generation: it uses ideas from semiotics, narratology and suture theory to explain the workings of underscoring in narrative fiction films, and applies its tools to classic Hollywood as well as to René Clair and Jean Vigo. The most eye- (or ear-)catching idea gave the book its title: that the melodies of film scores usually go unheard, evading conscious audience awareness. Already Arnheim in 1932 had averred that 'film music was always good if one did not notice it' (2002 [1932], 253; my translation), one of Adorno's and Eisler's bugbears. Gorbman recasts it via the concept of suture: the idea that film needs to overcome the ontological gulf between the viewer and the story on the screen, and that it has developed ways to suture that gap, to stitch the viewer into involvement with the narrative (1987, 53–69). Visual strategies were crucial to suture theory, for example shot-countershot sequences. Music offered another thread for the stitching of 'shot to shot, narrative event to meaning, spectator to narrative, spectator to audience' (*ibid.*, 55), the more so since most viewers lack the concepts to assess critically the effects of musical techniques.

Suture is just one concept from what Bordwell ironically characterized as Grand Theory (1996): the confluence of ideas from (mainly Lacanian) psychoanalysis, (post)structuralist literary theory and (post)Marxist sociology that became a major strand of film theory in the 1970s (from hereon written 'Theory' to distinguish this complex of ideas from the generic term). Different strands of Theory try to show how cinema – as an institution, as a technology, as a (prefabricated) experience, as a narrative medium – and the structuring and editing techniques of film create illusions: of realism, of continuity and coherence, of meaning, of authority, of subject identity and connection, illusions reducing the viewer to a cog in an ideological machine. Despite the tempting capacity of music to help bring about the quasi-dream state cinema engenders (Baudry 1976), music has not played a significant role in Theory, nor the latter in film musicology. (Jeff Smith [1996] criticizes the idea of 'unheard melodies' with regard to Gorbman 1987 and Flinn 1992; Buhler 2014b discusses psychoanalytically grounded theories mainly with regard to film sound overall, with few references specifically to music.) One reason may be that film musicology discovered Theory when its heyday was coming to an end; another reason may be that musicology does not have a tradition of the ideas that informed Theory (and much film musicology was done by musicologists). The cachet of Theory has waned, together with psycho-analysis as a psychological theory, and with the socio-political ideas that had entered cultural theory with the Frankfurt School of social philoso-phers, Adorno in particular. Even if 'critical theory generally understands psychoanalysis not as providing a true account of innate psychological forces … but rather as providing an accurate model for how culture shapes, channels and deforms those psychological forces' (Buhler 2014b, 383), the latter is not independent of the former, and Theory as a social theory is no less problematic than as a psychological one. But ideas about cinema as a dream-machine, and about sound and of music in it, may be partly recoverable in other theoretical frameworks, even if their original foundations have become weakened.

More durable may be the semiotic and narratological perspectives in Gorbman's book. Semiotic functions of film music had long been a strand of the literature, even *avant la lettre*: the use of commonly understood musical codes to suggest time, place, setting, characters; the provision of an experiential context by establishing mood and pace; the interpretation of story and images by underlining aspects of them – in short, the creation, reinforcement and modification of filmic signification through music. However, semiotics are more prominent in analyses of individual films and repertoires of films, often done in DIY fashion, without an explicit theoretical framework (not necessarily a bad thing); coherent theoretical or methodological models are relatively rare. The most elaborate one, Philip Tagg's 'musematic' analysis, was developed for television music (Tagg 2000; Tagg and Clarida 2003 applies the idea to a wider range of television music); other theoretical approaches to film-music semiotics can be found in Lexmann 2006 and Chattah 2006 (which distinguishes between semiotics as a focus on the relationship between signs and what they signify, and pragmatics as a focus on the relationship between signs and their users and contexts).

As with semiotics, narratological concepts had been applied to film music long before narratology came into play by name, chiefly in the distinction between 'source music' and 'scoring': music that has a source in the image (or suggested off-screen space) and music that has not, i.e. music on different levels of narration. Many different terms have been used for, more or less, this distinction (see Bullerjahn 2014, 19–24 for a list), but the most common are diegetic and nondiegetic (or extradiegetic) music (see Gorbman 1980 and 1987, 11–30). To replace old terms by new ones needs a justification, and the obvious one is that 'source music' and 'scoring' are specific to the craft of film music, while 'diegetic' and 'nondiegetic' link into a theoretical system, developed by Gérard Genette (who borrowed *diégèse* from Étienne Souriau: see Genette 1980 [1972], 27), but also common in film studies, and related to the story/discourse distinction more common in literary studies (see Heldt 2013, 19–23 and 49–51 for the terminological background). Film musicology has rarely ventured beyond the basic diegetic/nondiegetic distinction. Gorbman applied Genette's term 'metadiegetic' to music which might be interpreted as being in a character's mind (1987, 22–3), problematic because the embedded narration to which Genette applies it differs from Gorbman's usage (see Heldt 2013, 119–22); and Jerrold Levinson (1996) tried to make Wayne Booth's concept of the implied author useful for film musicology, though he misappropriates the idea (see Heldt 2013, 72–89). Systems of levels of narration extend further, however, from historical authorship via implied authorship and extra-fictional narration to nondiegetic, diegetic and metadiegetic levels, and also take in the differentiation between objective and subjective narrative perspectives, as in Genette's concept of 'focalisation'. (For examples of such systems, see Genette 1980 [1972], 227–37; Chatman 1978, 146–95; Bal 2009, 67–82; and Branigan 1992, 86–124; see Heldt 2013 for an application to film music.) How music relates to most of these concepts has not been explored, and much less other elements of film narratology, such as the relationship of music to temporal ordering with regard to aspects such as filmic rhythm, ellipses, anticipation and retrospection (see, for example, Chatman 1978, 63–79; Bordwell 1985, 74–98; Bal 2009, 77–109), to historical modes and norms of narration (Bordwell 1985, 147–55), or to the distinction between narration and monstration (Gaudreault 2009 [1988]), important for film because the relationship is very different from that in literature, and most filmic 'narration' consists in the organization of access to information rather than the literal telling of a story.

The other hitch in the relationship of film musicology and narratology has been that film musicologists have worried about the diegetic/nondiegetic distinction more than scholars in other disciplines. Some have explored how music can blur the distinction, or how it can transition between categories (for example, Neumeyer 1997, 2000 and 2009; Buhler 2001; Biancorosso 2001 and 2009; Stilwell 2007; Norden 2007; J. Smith 2009; N. Davis 2012; Yacavone 2012). Others have questioned the usefulness of the concepts as such, suggested alternatives or posited that they have been misused (for example Kassabian 2001, 42–9, and Kassabian 2013; Cecchi 2010; Winters 2010 and 2012; Merlin 2010; Holbrook 2011, 1–53). The main bones of contention have been the claims that the categories make an *a priori* distinction too rigid for the reality of film (music), and that to call music nondiegetic distances it from the diegesis and misses its part in establishing it. But the critique applies more to applications of the concepts than to their substance. Narratology has never understood them as quasi-ontological categories, but as heuristic constructs in the reader's or viewer's mind, in a process of 'diegetisation' (see Hartmann 2007 and Wulff 2007), an evolving understanding of the boundaries of the storyworld that is open to revision. The categories should also not be burdened with tasks they cannot fulfil: they say nothing about *what* music does in a film, or how realistically it tells its story. And the criticism that 'nondiegetic' falsely distances music from the storyworld (Winters 2010) misconstrues the relationship of narration and diegesis: the voice of a heterodiegetic narrator in a novel, for example, is by definition not part of the diegesis (and in that sense distanced from it), but it is crucial for creating the diegesis in the reader's mind, and so integral to it; the same applies to nondiegetic music as one of the 'voices' of filmic narration (Heldt 2013, 48–72).

Such disputes stem from a general problem of film-music theory: it gets many of its ideas – usually via film theory – from other disciplines, not least from the much larger and livelier field of literary theory. That does not make ideas inapplicable, but they need to be vetted and adapted. As a narrative medium, film is structurally quite different from, say, a novel (the quintessential form of most literary theory). With few exceptions, a novel consists of a single data stream, and the task for the reader is to imagine; a film consists of sound and vision, which can both be split into any number of data streams, and the task for the viewer is to synthesize. What this means for the applicability of narratological concepts has been considered only fitfully by film theory, and hardly at all by film musicology.

What is true of semiotics is also true of other theoretical perspectives important to film studies, such as genre or gender; in recent film musicology, these have been more often theorized in the process of analysing film-music repertoires. Outlines of a theory of genre and film music have been suggested (see Brownrigg 2003; Scheurer 2008, 7–47; Stokes 2013), and much work has been done on particular film genres. That is even truer of questions of film music and gender, necessarily linked to particular repertoires and their musical codes. The melodrama has been a field of such theorizing (for example, see Flinn 1992; Laing 2007; Bullerjahn 2008; Haworth 2012; and Franklin 2011 for a wider genre horizon), but questions of gender affect the musical practices of many other film repertoires as well.

Synthesis or Pluralism?

Trying to pinpoint the state of film-music theory is like taking a snapshot of an explosion. Film musicology has expanded so rapidly over the last generation – and is continuing to do so, and is already being subsumed into the wider field of screen-media musicology – that any summary will be outdated before it has been printed. *Plus ça change* ... Writing in 1971, Christian Metz saw a 'provisional but necessary pluralism' in film studies, but hoped for a future time when the 'diverse methods may be reconciled ... and film theory would be a real synthesis' (1971, 13–14; my translation). Not only has this synthesis yet to happen, it has not even come any closer, and the provisional pluralism seems to be here to stay. Perhaps we should simply enjoy the ride rather than worry too much about mapping its course.

7 Studying Film Scores
Working in Archives and with Living Composers

KATE DAUBNEY

The definition of a film score as musical text is now more complex, or perhaps more loose, than it has ever been. From the multiple handwritten materials of the earliest years of Hollywood scoring to the technologically generated soundscape of current scoring technique, the initial challenge facing a scholar who wishes to analyse a written score is to identify whether one even exists. While some film scores have been published in concert-hall versions (which do not necessarily reflect how the music appeared in the film), scholars seeking original manuscripts must seek out library, archive or personal holdings by composers.

However, handwritten scores – as opposed to those produced using music technology – do not always reflect clearly the individual stages in the process of composing and recording music for film, and it is often likely that the final sound of a recorded score will not mirror accurately what is notated on the page. Post-composition, the complex balancing of the score against other soundtrack elements – such as special effects or dialogue – is often micro-managed by sound editors to the extent that what seems like a striking instrumental line on the page becomes obscured in the finished screen product. To complicate this, handwritten scores, particularly those from the 1930s and 1940s, may not have references to these other soundtrack elements: classical-era Hollywood composers frequently used only dialogue as a signpost for placement and synchronization, as if suggesting that the music had little else to compete with in the soundtrack. Finally, there are the effects of the editorial process on the score: scenes added, cut, extended or reduced all place demands on the composer at the eleventh hour. Versions of a notated score may not include all the last-minute alterations, so there are often pieces of recorded music heard in a film that are apparently undocumented.

With these caveats in place, however, notated musical texts are a fascinating resource for the study of both individual pieces of film music and the compositional process. Unusual and distinctive musical textures or the exact rhythmic notation of a theme can be revealed, and it is possible to see levels of organization in a manuscript which otherwise escape the ear. The extent of the revelations is sometimes determined by the sources: notated manuscripts come in different forms, from fully orchestrated scores such as those by Bernard Herrmann, to Max

Steiner's four-stave 'pencil drafts' (see Platte 2010, 21) intended for others to orchestrate. With more recent technological developments, the definition of 'manuscript' has expanded to include MIDI files which can be studied collectively to explore structural and developmental processes in a way which is not possible even with a heavily annotated handwritten score. These can lead to a more holistic study of the sound design of a film, expanding the remit of the film musicologist.

In 2000, I established a series of Film Score Guides, designed to enable scholars to bring all the contingent factors in a score's composition together with its analysis. Though initially published by Greenwood Press, the series transferred to Scarecrow Press in 2003 and has grown from its first volume, on Steiner's 1942 score for *Now, Voyager* (Daubney 2000), to cover a contrasting range of traditional and innovative scoring techniques across a wide variety of films from the 1930s to the twenty-first century. In the research for these volumes, the authors drew on diverse academic library, studio and personal archives, and this chapter collates our experiences of this type of research. As series editor, I have had a fascinating oversight into the complexity and revelations of this process, and the authors have generously shared their experiences through personal discussion, as indicated below.

Working in an Archive

For scholars wishing to work on American or British film composers, there are a number of useful archival holdings. In the United States, these include (but are not limited to): the University of California Los Angeles Film and Television Archive; the University of Southern California; the University of California Santa Barbara; the Margaret Herrick Library at the Academy of Motion Picture Arts and Sciences in Beverly Hills; the US Library of Congress (LOC); the University of Syracuse, New York State; and Brigham Young University, Utah. Holdings in the United Kingdom are wide-ranging, though some focus more exclusively on British composers and/or British film. Thanks to the diligent and detailed investigation by Miguel Mera and Ben Winters into the holdings of film-music materials in the UK on behalf of the Music Libraries Trust, there is now a comprehensive assessment of holdings available (Mera and Winters 2009). These include university libraries such as those at Leeds, Oxford, Trinity College of Music and University College Cork; national libraries and archives such as the British Library, the BBC Music Library and the British Film Institute; and other small specialized collections.

Increasingly, contemporary composers keep their own digital archives of materials, including emails and MIDI drafts, and scholars who have the opportunity to work with such composers have the benefit of a sometimes greater range of detail than might have been sifted out in an older paper-based collection. Indeed, as the Scarecrow authors have found, the range of factors affecting the composition of a film score is both fascinating and, at times, overwhelming. The richness and diversity of materials available in an academic or personal archive enables study of a score's composition in the context of scrapbooks, notebooks, letters, emails, interviews, memoranda and studio internal documentation such as production schedules and cue sheets. Furthermore, research is often not limited to one archive: in the case of David Cooper's contextual research of Herrmann (2001 and 2005), he used The Bernard Herrmann Papers at the University of California Santa Barbara; the Library of Congress for its microfilm copies of many of the holographic scores and some original manuscripts; and the CBS collections at the New York Public Library and the Music Library Special Collections at UCLA for Herrmann's music for radio and for television, respectively.

It is easiest and most productive to visit an archive in person, if at all possible, and several days should be allowed for looking over the materials. Scholars must keep extensive and accurate records of archival research – particularly if they are able to visit only once – as it is not always possible to photocopy materials without securing a licence in advance. Most archives produce catalogues of their holdings which allow for preparation in advance and a more focused and productive visit. Building a relationship before arrival with an archive director or manager is also essential, as you are more likely to be able to access what you need if they understand what your aims are for the visit. You will also find out what limitations there are on copying or even viewing materials, due to fragility, preservation, external loan and so on.

Obtaining photocopies of original scores or from microfilm for study away from an archive can be extremely difficult, if not impossible, and often requires permission of the copyright holder as well as the archivist. A scholar intending to publish research, including transcriptions or reproductions of score material, will need to obtain copyright permission to do so, and in some cases also a licence to reproduce the score for research purposes. The archivist may be able to access the network of companies and individuals with the authority to grant copyright permissions, which can itself be a long and convoluted process: this issue is discussed in more detail later in the chapter.

During my PhD research on Steiner, content from which was later published in my Film Score Guide on *Now, Voyager*, I spent a week studying the Max Steiner Collection at Brigham Young University. The Steiner Collection is an excellent and diverse accumulation of materials, from personal letters to his four wives and his son, to the 177 volumes of bound manuscript film scores. The Academy Award statuettes for *Now, Voyager* and *Since You Went Away* (1944) sit in a vault, while three enormous scrapbooks covering the years 1930–53 chronicle the period of Steiner's greatest industry through his own choice of newspaper reviews, underlined by the composer in thick blue or orange pencil. There is also, among other materials, correspondence with Jack Warner and David O. Selznick, and a collection of copies of contracts, royalty statements and original songs and other compositions from Steiner's pre-Hollywood career in Vienna and on Broadway.

With such a range of material, it can be difficult to know where to start, and certainly it can be helpful to begin with a particular score and work outwards through the contextual material. A holograph may provide some sense of the composer's personality through style of notation, approach to editing and, perhaps most conspicuously, through marginalia and other written commentary. For example, Steiner's pencil drafts contain many ribald annotations to his orchestrators. His comments paint a vivid picture of his often scornful opinion of the films' subject matter or leading actors, giving a clearer insight into his attitude and approach to process than many other more formal documents he wrote. For example, in the score for *Dodge City* (1939) he annotates a dialogue cue, 'How d'you like these here onions?' with the remark, 'God help us!—The whole picture is like this— I am resigning!!' (Steiner 1939b, 33). Bette Davis once observed that Steiner was 'one of the great contributors to countless films with his musical scores. Many a so-so film was made better through his talents' (Stine 1974, 11), but she was doubtless unaware of how the composer judged her: in the pencil draft for *The Bride Came C.O.D.* (1941) he complained that 'She cries like a stuck pig' (1941, 28).

Steiner also demonstrates his frustrations over having to write so much music in such a short time. Against one long sustained chord in the score to *The Oklahoma Kid* (1939), he notes: 'Always good when you don't know what to write' (1939a, 163), and – lacking the time to write everything down in the pencil draft to *Dodge City* – he asks for an orchestration of 'Everything bar the kitchen stove!' (1939b, 145). His notes sometimes indicate a desire to shift responsibility for decision-making to his orchestrator, as in the pencil draft to *The Gay Sisters* (1942) where he admits to Hugo Friedhofer: 'I don't know how to orchestrate this—all I know is I hear a SORT of "sentimental" Children's TUNE' (1942, 79).

The other advantage of archival research is the discovery of circumstantial materials that build a picture of the context in which the music was composed, shedding light on a particular strategy or situation which influenced a score's construction. A studio's internal documentation such as production schedules or chains of correspondence have significance for the deduction of process that is useful in a creative context where the means of production are often invisible. But personal documentation can also reveal this, such as letters from Steiner to his third wife, Louise Klos, written on his behalf by his secretary. For example:

> He is working very hard, as you can imagine. [*Since You Went Away*] is another picture like "Gone with the Wind" [1939]; twenty one reels; changes every day; having to get approvals from Mr. Selznick for every melody he writes, etc., so you can appreciate from his former experience [*Gone with the Wind*] what he is going through.
>
> (Letter to Louise Klos Steiner, 25 May 1944; Max Steiner Collection, Box 2, Folder 1; Film Music Archives; L. Tom Perry Special Collections, Harold B. Lee Library, Brigham Young University)

This body of contextual detail often has to stand in the place of more formal documentation of the composer's art. Steiner completed an (as yet) unpublished autobiography in 1964 entitled 'Notes to You', but its value to the scholar is fairly limited, as it is full of unsubstantiated and inaccurate anecdotes about his life, and contains comparatively little discussion of scoring practice. He also did not experience the cult of celebrity which generated the television-interview opportunities and greater media coverage enjoyed by later composers.

By contrast, students of Herrmann's scores can find published interviews (as in R. S. Brown 1994, 289–93) and footage of Herrmann talking about his work, but his scores tend to be fully orchestrated (rather than the short forms of the Steiner archive) and contain very little in the way of marginalia. As Cooper observes, it can be difficult to deduce process from such a clean manuscript:

> I would be interested to know from Herrmann how many of the musical decisions were 'intuitive' and how many were rationalised, though I guess he would generally go for the latter. I would also be interested to know how he dealt with issues of timing, both in composition and performance. For example, he did record *The Ghost and Mrs. Muir* [1947], but not *Vertigo* [1958], and was renowned for his ability to work without aids.
>
> (Cooper, personal communication, 1 March 2004)

Sometimes, archival work does not make matters clearer. When Ben Winters (2007) explored the relationship between Erich Wolfgang Korngold and his orchestrator Friedfhofer during the composition of the score for *The Adventures of Robin Hood* (1938), he found that the manuscript materials threw up more questions than answers ... Evidently there was a degree of trust between them (as Friedhofer's oral history recounts), and that perhaps explains in part why there were virtually no written instructions about orchestration recorded on Korngold's short score ... [And] while pages of *Robin Hood* short score that existed only in the hand of Friedhofer suggested that boundaries between composition and orchestration may in a few cases have been less clearly defined than we might have supposed, that evidence never extended to 'proof' of authorship. In short, examining the manuscript materials opened up areas for speculation rather than serving to define the nature of the relationship.

(Winters, personal communication, 10 July 2012)

Working with a Living Composer

It might seem that working on the scores of a living composer would be easier, but there are different obstacles and restrictions to gaining access to material. Sometimes individuals are unwilling to be frank about particular situations, or about colleagues and other participants in the film business, not least because they may have to work with them again in the future. Nevertheless, with access to a composer and the opportunity to discuss his or her work, the exploration of compositional process can be fascinating. Obtaining scores can still be a lengthy process because those of living composers tend not to be archived, and are often kept anywhere from studio libraries or storage facilities to the composer's personal collection. The most effective approach is to contact the composer directly, via their agent or their personal music-production company. Approaching studios is not always useful, as staff are often unaware of what materials are held in storage, and catalogues are virtually non-existent. Cultivating and acknowledging contacts and developing networks are vital parts of the film-music research process.

Mera (2007) had the benefit of considerable access to the personal holdings of Mychael Danna while preparing his book on Danna's score for *The Ice Storm* (1997). Danna provided access to all his personal materials, including MIDI and audio files, as well as making himself available to discuss his process of composition and the finished work. Working with MIDI and audio files might seem to provide a clinical, less intimate picture of the creative process, but in practice the technology makes it possible to view process on a more precise level. MIDI sequencer files show the set-up of a composer's workstation, giving an added perspective on what equipment is used and how it contributes to the process. They also often contain an audio track with dialogue and sound effects, which, while helpful to the orchestrator and conductor, also gives an immediate picture to the analyst of how the composer accommodates the potentially competing elements in the soundtrack. This microscopic level of detail can bring a different focus to analysis, as Mera explains:

> One of the most important features of this sort of material is that it is extremely useful in showing how a composition progresses and develops. In some instances there are sixteen versions of the same cue, so it is possible to chart the composer's thought processes from initial idea to finished product. When you also know something about how the composer was influenced by the director, the producer, or even the temporary score during this process, the sequencer files become a very powerful analytical tool, which allows the musicologist to pursue analyses of intention as well as interpretation. MIDI files can be seen to be a very detailed equivalent to the traditional composer's sketch.
>
> (Mera, personal communication, 29 March 2004)

Danna's generous co-operation with Mera emphasizes the personal aspect of working with a living composer. Trust is an important element in the relationship, and the emphasis moves towards sharing and discussion, from the more objective analysis that we engage in when composers are not personally known to us. Mera agrees that the input of the composer is 'incredibly helpful', but points out that a certain balance is required when a composer does co-operate with the research process:

> The potential problem is that the composer will say something about their work that ruins your nice, neat academic argument. However, I find this debate to be one of the most interesting features of understanding a living film composer's work. Scholars have, in my opinion, been nervous to talk to film composers about their work or to draw information from interviews and so on. It depends on who the composer is, of course, but I don't understand why there is not at least the desire to try and understand a composer's intentions before applying an interpretation to what they have done.   (*Ibid.*)

Even with the composer's participation, the musicological process is not always easy. Charles Leinberger (2004) had the opportunity to interview Ennio Morricone for his book on the score for *The Good, the Bad, and the Ugly* (1966), an interview which was conducted on the composer's terms, in Italian and in his home city of Rome. The opportunity to hear the composer playing from his own score at the piano was clearly a unique experience, as it would be for any scholar, although in other respects Morricone was less keen to participate in the analytical process. He was particularly reluctant to explain certain distinctive aspects of his technique for fear of being copied by other composers, and Leinberger was faced with a decision about how he should respect Morricone's wishes and protect what the composer saw as his trade secrets.

Janet Halfyard (2004) had a completely contrasting experience when preparing her book on Danny Elfman's score for *Batman* (1989). Elfman has consistently declined to engage with academic study of his work, though he has, in contrast with his classical-era predecessors, given a huge number of press interviews which provide an account of his scoring methods. Despite approaches to participate, Elfman was unwilling to contribute anything to Halfyard's research, but she does see a specific advantage in this:

> It left me free to explore my own readings of the music without having to bow to the obvious authority of the composer's own version of events. I would love to have discussed the film with him, but the fact that he wasn't interested did give me a lot of freedom that I would potentially have lost if his readings had been very different from my own. As it is, they are my readings, everything that I have got from the score in the absence of the author's own interpretation. And I'm actually rather impressed that the score doesn't need him explaining it for all those multiple layers of meaning to come out.
>
> (Halfyard, personal communication, 2 March 2004)

Elfman's score for *Batman* sits beside Prince's soundtrack album for the same film, and for Halfyard this was another area which would have benefited from the composer's participation:

> I would like to have asked Elfman how much of Prince's soundtrack album had already been written when he started work on the score, because of the relationship between Prince's 'Scandalous' motif and the 'Bat-theme'; and how intuitive his scheme of time signatures for rationality and irrationality was.   (*Ibid.*)

Tracking down all the contributors to the musical component of the film can be complicated and time-consuming, and with older films it can also be a question of exploring other pre-composed music contemporaneous to the film's production or relevant to the period of its narrative, such as the extensive use of vernacular songs and march tunes in *Gone With the Wind* or the wartime popular hits of *Since You Went Away*. It also puts emphasis on exploring the role of other studio staff in the process. Was a temporary track used, or was there input from a music editor or even the director on scoring matters? It can be crucial to the process of analysing originally composed music to find out what form these other interventions and contributions took, so it is useful to explore whether studio papers are available.

An additional factor in Halfyard's research was that the score she used was a full orchestral score written in the hand of Elfman's orchestrator and assistant, Steve Bartek. Elfman typically composes about half the material on a sequencer, filling out the other half by hand onto the sequencer print-offs. Bartek then orchestrates in full this sixteen-stave short score. A photocopy of Bartek's score was made available by the Warner Bros. Music Library, but small sections of his notation were illegible. The challenge to certainty created by this small detail is indicative of a larger, interesting question about the ability of the scholar to examine the authorial relationship between a composer and his orchestrator when the orchestrator's score is the only one available.

Heather Laing (2004) revealed a similarly close relationship between Gabriel Yared and his orchestrator John Bell during research for her book on *The English Patient* (1996). In an interview with Laing, Yared gave an explanation of how he and Bell had collaborated on a later film score that brought a level of specificity valuable to the analyst:

> With the help of his sound engineer Georges Rodi, [Yared] creates an exact synthesizer version of each cue, which is then translated by Bell into actual instrumentation. 'But,' says Yared, there is 'not one note to add, not one harmony to change, not one counterpoint to add – it's all there and it's divided into many tracks . . . [E]verything is set and I don't want anything to be added, and anything to be subtracted, from that.' The synthesizer demo for *The Talented Mr. Ripley* [1999] is therefore, according to Yared, indistinguishable from the final instrumental tracks that appear in the film. (Laing 2004, 26)

A recurrent issue pondered by scholars is the role and nature of intuition in the compositional process, and this frequently emerges in discussion with composers. Several of the scholars mentioned above have discussed the process of compositional decision-making and its effect on analytical interpretation, and having a trusting relationship with the composer may make it possible to explore these issues. From an analytical perspective, we are often keen to pin down definitive explanations for why a particular instrument or chord or melodic motif is used, and answers from composers can appear to lend weight to the conclusions. But there is always an element of tension in the publication of research in which a composer has been involved. Laing observes, 'I was really lucky with [Yared] – I'm not at all sure how I'd be feeling had I been working with someone who wasn't as interested or supportive as he was. Nonetheless, my heart was in my mouth from the moment I sent him the draft manuscript to the moment I received his comments!' (personal communication, 23 November 2004).

Copyright and Other Considerations

In general, if a composer has been dead for more than seventy years then there is greater freedom to quote extracts from scores because they are in the public domain, but because film music is still a relatively young art, most of the materials that scholars want to use are still covered by copyright. Finding the copyright holder and obtaining permission from them remain the biggest obstacles to the citation of film scores in published material. For example, Cooper was advised that he was the first person to have been loaned a personal copy of one particular Herrmann manuscript by Paramount, and found it difficult to track down the right person in the studio from whom to secure permission, before finally resorting to help from a film-music 'insider' (personal communication, 1 March 2004). Generally, studios are still unprepared for requests to study film scores or for copyright permission for score reproductions: it took over a year for me to secure permission for extracts from Steiner's scores for *Now, Voyager* and other films, via a very circuitous route through Warner Bros. in California to IMI in the United Kingdom, who actually held the copyright.

Securing copyright permission relies primarily on making contact with the right person in the right organization. Ownership of copyright is not always clear, particularly with music from a film where the publication rights from sheet music, for example, may differ from the rights for the soundtrack recording and the video release. The composer's own company may also be involved. It is vital to begin by finding out exactly which company or individual owns the rights to reproduction of the orchestral score, and it is recommended that this should be done right at the beginning of research, because it can be extremely time consuming and frustrating to locate the copyright owner, and then to get permission. Archivists can often be helpful in this respect with a composer who has already died. Sometimes companies themselves are not certain which copyright they own, and one must be prepared to make follow-up calls to individuals until permission is granted.

Whatever agreement is reached, it is important that permissions are obtained in writing, and negotiation is often worthwhile if a rate seems excessive. Even over the decade and a half since I first sought permission for reproduction in my Film Score Guide, there has been virtually no coherence in the way that companies approach granting of these permissions, or the costs incurred. Companies often pluck a figure out of the air to judge the scholar's commitment to the project and to explore his or her potential revenue from the publication. It can also be difficult to compare different agreements and licences: some copyright holders will levy a charge per bar or per page, whilst others equate 'cues' to 'songs' in order to bring parity to other music-copyright agreements. It is always important to consider carefully what one is being asked to pay for.

International factors can also bring complications, firstly in terms of language. Laing's research into Yared's film scores necessitated working with French companies, and she recommends securing the help of a translator for all the languages in which the composer's films were originally made, as the language of copyright negotiation can be complex (personal communication, 23 November 2004).

If the research outcome is a book, the publisher will usually have a form that can be used to request permission which gives details of what rights will be required, and it is worth stressing that the research and the eventual publication are of an academic type. This is because author royalties for academic books tend to be extremely low, and the copyright holder will be reassured that you are not hoping to make a lot of money from their copyrighted property. It is useful for the author to be able to indicate to the score's copyright holder at the time of application how many musical examples he or she will want to use, and in what form. This may be a difficult decision if the research is still in its early stages, so it is worth asking for a 'rate per bar' rather than a fixed fee for usage. Scholars need to confirm whether they wish to make direct reproductions from the original manuscript or MIDI file, or whether they will be creating their own reductions to short score or single lines of notation. There may be some distinction made between these two types of usage, and if they are using a photographic or scanned reproduction of original manuscript material they will need to get permission from the archive, and possibly pay them a fee also, both for copyright and for reproduction of the image, which will often be done by the archive.

Copyright holders of scores are usually concerned that publishing the examples will deprive them of revenue from performance rights. In fact, it is more likely that published material on film music will increase an audience for recorded forms of the score, such as those on CD or DVD. Concern has arisen partly from ignorance about film musicology: copyright holders of film and popular-music scores are not accustomed to seeing analysis of their music in print, despite film musicology now being a well-established academic discipline. They are generally unaware that musicological usage does not involve large extracts of a complete score but usually just a few bars, of which public performance would be inconceivable. Film musicologists should be prepared to explain in their application for permission exactly how they are going to use the music, so that there is no doubt for the copyright holder. They should also clarify exactly how the permission will be referenced, and include that reference with every single notated example. They may also need to provide details of the quantity of the print run. However, despite scholars being as clear as possible about their requirements, attitudes have been slow to change within the industry (see Davison 2007).

Halfyard's experience with *Batman* was surprisingly easy, but she went into the process well prepared:

> The copyright of the score is held by Warner Bros., and they were happy to allow me permission once they were satisfied that it was a serious project with

a reputable company. There were some problems actually raising the licence, simply because the guy I was dealing with didn't reply to emails for a couple of months, but once he got back in touch, things went very smoothly, and they were incredibly generous, charging me a pittance for the licence, given that the cost was coming out of my own pocket. The original estimate was that it would be about £3 per bar, but in the event, I was able to cut that by over two-thirds.

(Halfyard, personal communication, 2 March 2004)

The scholar and copyright holder both need to be aware that the expenses for research are likely to come from the writer's own pocket, as academic publishers very rarely have budgets sufficiently large to pay for many copyright permissions. A formal invoice by the copyright holder and a receipt for payment are valuable commodities. Where there is any doubt at all about the content or significance of a licence, legal advice should be sought before agreeing to it.

8 Returning to *Casablanca*

PETER FRANKLIN

Directed by Michael Curtiz and premièred in New York on 26 November 1942, *Casablanca* acquired iconic status even before its national release in January 1943, at the height of the Second World War. An advertising campaign had capitalized on the coincidence of the recent allied successes in North Africa, and the subsequent taking of Casablanca. One cartoon-style advertising poster, put out by the Warner Bros. studio, read: 'Casablanca captured by the allies . . . but Hollywood got there first!' (Harmetz 2002 [1992], 275). The film's relationship to events in the war – in which the Americans were now fully involved – was fortuitous; its quality was nevertheless dependent upon the well-honed skills and operational virtuosity of Hollywood, and particularly Warner Bros., in producing films at high speed and at unpredictably varying levels of available funding (in this case relatively modest).

The emblematic role of composers as the final link in the chain of creative effort that went into such films has played a contradictory part in the critical reception of their music. The speed and intensity of the Music Department's work in 'finishing' the completed and edited movie might well have been a source of pride. A less charitable approach would have it that this involved 'packaging' the product by bathing it in music that some of its actors and critics affected to regard as redundantly lavish and over-emphatically manipulative. For others, its redundancy was practically mitigated by the fact that it was apparently barely noticed by habitual cinema-goers and in turn ignored by neutral commentators. In the case of *Casablanca*, the music most audiences would notice and remember was not even by its named composer, Max Steiner, but by a no more than moderately successful popular-song writer, Herman Hupfeld, whose 1931 song 'As Time Goes By' plays a crucial role. At first, its inclusion was famously objected to by Steiner, who would have preferred to write his own hit song (Harmetz 2002 [1992], 254).

Already we begin to see how and why it is that this particular iconic film might function also as a significant focus of questions, issues and approaches that have been addressed and utilized in more recent attempts to get to grips with classical Hollywood scores. It might be observed that *Casablanca* in fact triumphantly thematizes, as much as it demonstrates, what film musicologists have sought to understand about the character and function of such scores. Central to that project here must be the numerous recognizable popular songs of the period that are heard in Rick's Café Américain. Like 'As Time Goes By', these were neither composed nor arranged by Steiner (M. M. Marks 2000, 185, n. 15). Particularly interesting, however, is their relationship to Steiner's extensive and complex underscore that we, the audience, may hardly notice while receiving its subliminal suggestions and emphases.

Analysing the Score: The Diegetic/Nondiegetic Crossover

Like many Hollywood films addressing the European war in the early 1940s, *Casablanca* has an unashamedly American agenda beneath its evident sympathy with the 'good' Europe of the Alliance – something strikingly marked by the opening credits' musical flare for the name of the composer of the underscore. The (Austrian) Germanic appearance of his name is simultaneously acknowledged and publicly disavowed by Steiner's having insisted upon using the opening of the *Marseillaise* as his own musical marker here – one that recurs throughout the film as a signifier of the 'old' French revolutionary values of *Liberté-Égalité-Fraternité*; the words are ironically glimpsed on-screen as the Free France sympathizer, who becomes caught up in the police hunt for the killers of two German couriers, is shot dead at the entrance of the Palais de Justice at the end of the opening scene. Here the *Marseillaise* motif assumes a tonally dark, minor mode, emphasizing the underscore's sympathetic affiliations and exemplifying classical Hollywood's use of recurring figures and motifs to reinforce moments of visual or narrative significance. Their recurrence or recollection has often been associated with Wagner and the Wagnerian 'Leitmotiv', occasionally with Steiner's apparent assent (Thomas 1973, 122). But we must give more thought to the multi-faceted 'Americanism' of *Casablanca*'s agenda in relation to the music heard in Rick's Café. It would be as well to start with its proprietor.

Humphrey Bogart's Rick, deliberately unaffiliated in any obvious political sense, is 'damaged by disappointments in the past . . . [He] has left his native America for shadowy reasons; he has a track-record of supporting underdogs – in Ethiopia and Spain. It is also clear that he has a core of decency' (Reid 2000, 63). Now he is running a sort of nightclub (with behind-the-scenes gambling). This functions as a dramatically charged way-station for all those trying to escape the war, and the Nazis; securing the prized exit visas will enable them to fly to America from their limbo-like waiting-room on the margins of the European conflict, although Major Strasser's German officers keep a close watch on what is going on in this outpost of 'Vichy' France (the southern part not directly occupied by the Nazis, but politically subservient to its German masters in Paris and Berlin). Music plays a significant role throughout *Casablanca*, but particularly in the Café Américain. Its more than 'aesthetic' or merely 'entertaining' function is dramatically emphasized by the way in which the film shows the café's clientele using it as a cover for clandestine deals and bartering smuggled family jewels for that ticket out to the fabled land of peace and normality on the other side of the Atlantic. But more than this: the very songs performed by singer-pianist Sam (Dooley Wilson) and the café's band often have a textual as well as practical significance in relation to the situation and plot. It is this that generates what I would call the film's 'thematization' of how popular music works.

On one level such music clearly distracts its participants and listeners from their immediate cares and woes through humour or by invoking the pleasures of love. But Sam's launching into the audience-participation song 'Knock on Wood' (M. K. Jerome and Jack Scholl, 1942) does more than act as an aural cover for clandestine deals and furtive conversations. It also 'performs' the process of allowing musical immersion to 'take us out of ourselves', as we say, and to make life seem better:

> 'Say, who's got troubles?'
> [chorus response:] *'We got troubles!'*
> 'How much trouble?'
> *'Too much trouble!'*
> Well now don't you frown,
> Just knuckle down and
> KNOCK ON WOOD!

Subsequent verses, all followed by the café's clients 'knocking on wood' (tapping in time a three-beat figure on their tables), ask the same question with respect to being unhappy, unlucky and having 'nothin''. As if to convince everyone that through communal fellow-feeling and honesty music has indeed done its work, the last two verses ask *'Now* who's happy?' ('We are!' comes the response) and *'Now* who's lucky?' ('We are!').

Martin Marks notes that many of the songs heard diegetically (where we see the musicians or understand where the songs are being performed in the world of the characters) have a highly suggestive relationship (in terms of lyrics and titles) with ongoing events in the drama:

> Occasionally the association is ironic, as when Sam plays 'It Had to Be You' the moment Ilsa and Victor walk back into Rick's. Harder to catch is the verbal irony of the scene in which we are introduced to Rick: while he stands in the inner doorway to his casino and refuses admittance to a pompous German banker, the energetic fox-trot heard on the background piano is 'Crazy Rhythm,' [Irving Caesar *et al.*, 1928] whose chorus begins 'Crazy rhythm, here's the doorway, I'll go my way, you'll go your way.'   (M. M. Marks 2000, 173)

This sort of relationship between dramatic situation and 'source' (diegetic) popular music is one that would be utilized well beyond the era of classical Hollywood into the compilation film scores of our own period. The implications of the way in which such correspondences address the cinematic audience and its possible attentiveness to musical-referential detail also extend beyond the 1940s. They are nevertheless fundamental to the problem of 'intention' in the kind of film-scoring practice exemplified in *Casablanca*. How much musical information might its mid-1940s viewers have been expected to take in as part of their movie-going experience? One approach, as implied earlier, would relegate such correspondences to the level of a private, sub-surface game of musical reference that was being played by the composer or the studio's Music Department for his or its own amusement. In the case of *Casablanca*, the foregrounded thematization of the role played by music that is both heard and seen to be performed as part of the *mise-en-scène* might lead one to the conclusion that Curtiz and the production team were envisaging, at least in part, a more knowing and attentive audience than sceptics would have us believe. Certainly no cinema-goer could miss the musically articulated drama of the scene in which Victor Laszlo, the Czech Resistance leader (as Ilsa's husband, he is the idealistically noble third member of the central love-triangle) emerges from a tense private confrontation with Rick about the stolen letters of transit (Rick had concealed them on Sam's piano after they were left with him by the ill-fated Ugarte). He is then confronted by an even tenser scene in the main café. A group of German soldiers has commandeered the piano and launched into an inflammatory patriotic rendering of 'Die Wacht am Rhein' (Karl Wilhelm, 1854; text by Max Schneckenburger, 1840). Laszlo seizes the initiative and encourages the band to strike up the *Marseillaise*, which is powerfully sung by all the non-German café patrons, effectively drowning out the musical influence of the Germans.

The intensity of that musical/political confrontation was heightened by the fact that many of the actors participating were themselves refugees, some visibly crying as they sang (Harmetz 2002 [1992], 213). It is common to refer to the scene as one of 'duelling anthems' (Buhler *et al.* 2000, [Introduction] 6), and while this in fact overlooks what Marks has noted about the relatively neat fit 'in overlapping counterpoint' of the two ostensibly 'contesting' themes (2000, 184–5, n. 12, and 161; see also Franklin 2011, 121–2), the use of clear musical signification to make a powerful dramatic point is self-evident. Less so, perhaps, is the full significance of what the contemporary audience might or might not have known about the popular song that furnished Steiner with the main theme of his score and whose immortalization by the film's use of it, some years after its initial appearance in a Broadway show (*Everybody's Welcome*, 1931), is largely responsible for the fact that we still remember the name of its composer and lyricist, Herman Hupfeld.

'As Time Goes By ... '

The use of Hupfeld's 1931 song will take us into the heart of *Casablanca*'s underscore, which uses it and other key musical motifs (including the opening of the *Marseillaise* and *Deutschland über alles*) with both obvious and less obvious referential significance. Since it is introduced as a diegetic performance (and not anticipated in the musically rich extended title-sequence and ensuing introduction), it is worth considering it as it might have been recalled by members of the audience and as the song would subsequently be re-marketed as sheet-music, both advertising and capitalizing on the film's success. The 1940s copy shown in Figure 8.1 had a cover photo of Ingrid Bergman and described the song (beneath the title and by-line) as 'from *Casablanca* / starring / Humphrey Bogart / Ingrid Bergman / and / Paul Henreid / Directed by Michael Curtiz / A Warner Bros Picture'; it was marketed in London and Sydney by Chappell and Co. Ltd., but internally identified as copyrighted in 1931 'by Harms Inc., New York'. Its formal presentation, characteristic of the period, is worth noting.

The song as we know it (though its sheet-music accompaniment is much less improvisationally florid than that heard in the film) appears on the inside two-page spread, headed 'Refrain', but prefaced with six closely printed lines of 'Verse' text (Hupfeld n. d., 2). A boxed note directs us to 'See back page for Introduction and Verse', where we find a four-bar piano introduction followed by twelve bars of Verse, setting those six introductory lines of text in *parlando* style, and in the primary key of E♭ major, concluding on a dominant seventh in preparation for the Refrain (for which we turn back to the central spread). This consists of a two-stanza opening section and a two-stanza 'middle section', the first of the latter pair in A♭ major, the second back in E♭, in which key the song concludes after a reprise of the Refrain. The complete text, with the preliminary Verse, is as follows:

Introduction & Verse:
This day and age we're living in gives cause for apprehension,
With speed and new invention, and things like third dimension,
Yet, we get a trifle weary, with Mr Einstein's the'ry,
So we must get down to earth, at times relax, relieve the tension.
No matter what the progress, or what may yet be proved,
The simple facts of life are such they cannot be removed.

Figure 8.1 Sheet-music cover (c. 1943) of Herman Hupfeld's 1931 song 'As Time Goes By' (Chappell & Co. Ltd). Reproduced by permission of Faber Music Ltd.

Refrain:
You must remember this, a kiss is still a kiss,
A sigh is just a sigh;
The fundamental things apply,
As time goes by.

And when two lovers woo, they still say "I love you,"
On that you can rely;
No matter what the future brings,
As time goes by.

Moonlight and love songs never out of date,
Hearts full of passion, jealousy and hate;
Woman needs man and man must have his mate,
That no one can deny.

It's still the same old story, a fight for love and glory,
A case of do or die!
The world will always welcome lovers,
As time goes by.

You must ... (etc.)

The full text of Hupfeld's original song thus interestingly contextualized the part that we know (the Refrain) from its use in *Casablanca*. That song about the basic existential authenticity of romantic love, absolving us from worry about 'the future', and thus somehow transcending time, proves to be just one part of a larger whole. The first two stanzas of the Refrain are what we hear in Sam's initial performance, at Ilsa's request. The 'fundamental' truths of love are celebrated with a gently lilting tune punctuated with laid-back, improvisatory links between the phrases (more fluid and jazzy than Hupfeld's rather four-square original) from pianist Elliot Carpenter, who dubbed Sam's on-screen accompaniment (M. M. Marks 2000, 174). The full text nevertheless 'explains' the dreamy celebration of love quite explicitly as an escapist indulgence. The lyrics adopt the tone of a down-to-earth ordinary soul, troubled and perplexed by modernity as manifested in technological progress and 'Mr Einstein's the'ry [theory]'.

More curious are the last two stanzas of the Refrain, which we hear Sam play and sing only in the Paris flashback. The relaxed and happy evocation there of Rick's recalled love affair with Ilsa distracts our attention from the odd juxtaposition of 'Moonlight and love songs' with the next line's 'Hearts full of passion, jealousy and hate'. The 'man must have his mate' image seems crudely to validate and naturalize the binary, whose underlying tension is emphasized in the Refrain's last stanza, where the battle of the sexes is tendentiously masculinized as 'a fight for love and glory, / A case of do or die.' In sum, this popular love song reveals the darker side of those 'fundamental things' which seem textually blown apart by the violent imagery that precedes the conventional gesture towards containment of the emotional damage in the final *non sequitur*: 'The world will always welcome lovers' – and emotionally destroy them, perhaps, as had Ilsa's apparently inexplicable abandonment of Rick on that last train out of Paris.

The Underscore: Subjectivity and Gender

Of course popular songs don't just mean what they say. They also mean what they have come to mean in the lives and emotional experiences of their consumers. The song that had become 'their song' for Rick and Ilsa has acquired a shared nostalgic charge of the memory of their love-affair; certainly for Rick, but perhaps so too for Ilsa, although we are led to question our initial assumptions. Her apparently surprising exercise of agency in leaving him in the lurch (reversing the usual gender politics of such things in Hollywood romances) seems to carry over to the very way in which the old song had arrived in the movie's 'present' – in the world of Rick's Café, that is – at the command of Ilsa when she overcomes Sam's rational (and loyal) preference not to reawaken those particular memories of moonlight and love songs. Rick's response, revealing his vulnerability and initiating the real drama at the heart of the film, is indeed to want to stop it. He angrily approaches Sam: 'I thought I told you never . . . ' – at which point he sees her. We learn more when he subsequently collapses, the worse for drink, in the darkened café after closing time. He has been waiting for Ilsa to come back, watched over by the loyal Sam whom he finally gets to play for him what he cannot bring himself to name ('You played it for her, you can play it for me'). When he hears it, the camera becomes explicitly subjective. In the conventional way of such things in the period, it approaches closer and closer to Bogart's face until the dissolve into the flashback in which we see what we know he is thinking, remembering Paris and their love-affair. The *Marseillaise* might redundantly seek to tell us we are in front of the Arc de Triomphe, but we know we are also in Rick's mind, where the memory of it resides. The implicit 'feminization' of Bogart in this scene was attested to rather unpleasantly by Paul Henreid, the aristocratic Austrian actor who played Laszlo and is reported to have observed, shortly before he died, that 'Mr Bogie was a nobody . . . ':

> Bogart was a mediocre actor. He was so sorry for himself in *Casablanca*. Unfortunately Michael Curtiz was not a director of actors; he was a director of effects . . . [H]e could not tell Bogart that he should not play like a crybaby. It was embarrassing, I thought, when I looked at the rushes.
>
> (Quoted in Harmetz 2002 [1992], 97)

That feminization has repercussions for the underscore. Motivic and place markers aside, this now comes into its own, rather more in what we have come to think of as the conventional style of classical Hollywood. It feels as if, for the first time since the title/opening credits/introduction sequence, a genuine underscore is allowed to escape the dramatic requirements of Rick's clients for a steady stream of diegetic songs and distracting 'light' music, whose choice and placement in the level of the sound mix proves so complex and considered. The music for the opening section of the Paris flashback – a joyful stream of orchestral music that seems energetically goalless in the headlong, *schwungvoll* irresponsibility of its flight – has all the characteristics for which Hollywood film composition was mocked by critics like Theodor Adorno and Hanns Eisler, who found it regressively irrational and emotionally manipulative (2007 [1947], 14–15). It is accordingly often treated to conventionally feminizing critical description ('self-indulgent', 'sentimental', etc.), or amusedly suffered as one of the standard ways in which, as Marks puts it, Steiner 'approached his task like a composer of traditional dramatic music, constantly thinking about music's ability to interpret what is depicted on screen' (2000, 163).

In fact, Marks's essay amply demonstrates that the music does much more than redundantly 'interpret', or (to adopt another trope of popular film-music criticism) 'tell us what characters are thinking'. While it certainly, and quite specifically does that in this case, it also functions on other levels. Here is Marks on its technical role here:

> the bright music is the sole element on the soundtrack for about two minutes, and for good reason. Without it the sequence (which includes some standard process shots that appear quite crude) would be utterly unconvincing; and just as opera composers often relied upon music to accompany scene changes, so it became routine for Hollywood composers to cover lead-ins to all flashbacks.
>
> (M. M. Marks 2000, 175)

The issue of the 'lead-in' is vital here, since what actually happens is a visual dissolve (from Bogart's face to the Paris of old, through which he once happily drove with Ilsa) accompanied by a seamless musical transition from Sam's rendering of 'As Time Goes By' on the piano to the background orchestra. This continues and then expansively elaborates on the song's theme, as if telling us that this is what it 'means' to Rick: remembered joy that inspires present sorrow at its loss. We might put it that far from 'interpreting' what we see on screen, the music is in fact actively playing a significant role in constructing Rick's subjectivity (of course, the precise way in which it does that must depend upon Steiner himself having 'interpreted' the film before composing it).

If this famous flashback presents one site in *Casablanca* where Hollywood's typical mode of late-romantic underscoring is encountered, others are no less interesting, both earlier in the film and later. Leaving aside for a moment the extended introductory sequence, heavily underscored throughout, an important earlier section of underscoring – also closely linked to the complex relationship between Rick and Ilsa and similarly arising from a diegetic performance of 'As Time Goes By' – follows its already discussed first performance by Sam, at Ilsa's request. I have described its interruption by Rick, who angrily comes up to Sam to enforce his ban on it. At the moment Rick's eyes meet Ilsa's, the moment when he sees her for the first time in the film, an orchestral stinger emphasizes the melodrama of the situation before taking over the rendition of 'As Time Goes By' in a darker harmonic context that once again stresses Rick's point of view, but actually does something rather more in what follows. It suggests now a shared subjective consciousness that wordlessly links Rick and Ilsa beneath and alongside the outwardly polite conversation that ensues when Rick makes an exception to his rule of not drinking with the customers. He significantly joins the table with Ilsa, Laszlo and Captain Renault (played by Claude Rains in skittish form as the local Chief of Police who deliberately balances his pragmatically 'unspecified' sympathies with the need for judicious cultivation of the Germans – particularly the overbearing Strasser, intent upon preventing Laszlo from leaving Casablanca).

The subtlety and complexity of Steiner's underscoring is further demonstrated in the intensely 'private' conversation, or perhaps paired monologues, of the scene immediately following the Paris flashback, when Ilsa does finally appear in the darkened café, only to find Rick now decidedly the worse for wear. Her entry is marked by dramatic musical signalling. This again spells melodrama, from the viewpoint of the manipulative, virtual third-party observer and musical master-of-ceremonies of the cinematic drama, whose excesses are often assumed to be all that Hollywood underscoring does (not so much explaining the filmed drama as generically classifying or 'marking' it in ways derived from silent-era accompaniment practice and popular operatic models before that). Almost immediately, however, the music returns to its role of performatively constructing subjectivity: first, once again, that of the emotionally wounded and still uncomprehending Rick, but then, as if in a musical equivalent to a changed camera-angle, shifting its allegiances to Ilsa when she tries to tell her side of the story. Given what we assume of her past (on the basis of Rick's Paris flashback) and have so far experienced of her personality in the present (as when hypnotically coaxing Sam into playing the song she wants to hear), it comes as something of a surprise when her underscoring assumes more conventionally Hollywood-style feminine characteristics that anticipate the near-normalization of gender roles in the final sections of the film. The key passage is when she tells Rick how she had first met her heroic and clearly idolized Laszlo. Her attempt to describe him is haloed (in a distantly faded-down underscore that one has to strain to catch behind her words) by high, angelic strings and what Marks, forgetting Laszlo's Czech origins, describes as 'a warm hymnlike melody with elemental diatonic harmonies [that] sounds like the national anthem for his unidentified homeland' (2000, 173).

It is, of course, Ilsa's recalled infatuated image of Laszlo that, as I have suggested, in reality reflects perhaps more upon her than it does upon him – although its derivation is another indicator of Steiner's attention to detail. Its opening figure may be interpreted as a kind of free inversion of the melody for the last two words of the first line of 'Deutschland, Deutschland über alles'. The notes for 'über al-les' are simply realigned in pitch, and their general shape retained, but the three-note figure for 'alles' is approached from below by two portentously rising notes, rather than the two descending notes of 'über' in the original. Ilsa's idealized image of her husband is thus neatly marked as the converse of the German supremacy he seeks to overturn. If that detail was unlikely to be spotted by most cinema-goers, the revealing subjective femininity of the barely audible background music (might it ironize Laszlo's constructed nobility?) is as unavoidable as the comparatively significant absence of any subjective underscoring for either party in the closely personal conversation Ilsa subsequently has with him in The Blue Parrot bar. Here we have only the place-defining orientalism (the underscore seems to imply some unseen diegetic source) that is associated with the much more 'local' and decidedly un-American establishment owned by Signor Ferrari: in this role, Sidney Greenstreet accommodates the standard Hollywood association of English accents with decadence and dodgy dealings.

An Ending and the Beginning

It is all too easy to mock classic-era Hollywood scoring. Steiner himself often affected to mock it, and himself, in score-annotations and messages to his orchestrator, Hugo Friedhofer (Franklin 2014, 115; see also Chapter 7 of the present volume). It would nevertheless be a matter of regret if, in concentrating here on those ostensibly unconventional aspects of the *Casablanca* score that richly deserve and no less richly repay careful study, I have appeared to downplay the significance and subtlety of its 'conventional' underscoring (albeit questioning that there ever was such a thing). By this I mean the kind of underscoring that stands outside the depicted narrative world of the film and appears to utilize a powerful generic rhetoric that might distantly derive from the old-fashioned showman's cry of 'Roll up, roll up! This is the show you must not miss!'; it expresses itself in an excitedly persuasive desire to 'manage' the audience's enjoyment of the movie ('This is where you will want to cry; here is where you will shiver at what may happen next!').

Here too *Casablanca* seems more knowingly than deviously to perform such rhetorical moves – above all in the long title-sequence and ensuing introduction. Where Orson Welles's 'News on the March!' in *Citizen Kane* (1941) seems to have used genuine newsreel music that exemplified all the rhetorical manners I have referred to, to the point of caricature, Steiner's version here is in some senses more restrained and considered in its mode of address. Of course, the fanfared, drummed-up excitement is there in the *Marseillaise* flare for Steiner's name and what Marks has called the 'frenzied exotic dance' (2000, 164) that crudely places the action in a merely generic 'Moroccan' North Africa. But he knows, and we know, that that's what we pay our money for: the kind of attention-grabbing introduction we need to settle into our seats and position the popcorn.

What is interesting is how it proceeds to give ground to an actual voice-over: the nondiegetic speech of the kind that always appropriates special power in classical Hollywood movies; we are to assume that it tells a kind of Truth. Here that Truth takes the form of a complex, condensed exploration of where and why Casablanca might be the site of a peculiarly relevant form of contemporary drama, at that stage of the war. As actual newsreel footage of displaced people and refugees flickers across the screen map of the route to Casablanca, the underscore, slightly reduced in volume, assumes a manner of impassioned sympathy for the unfortunates we gaze upon. This new theme, which will recur only once (as the plane bearing Strasser and his officers flies in across the heads of longing onlookers), assumes the tone of a kind of Rachmaninovian lament that seems to allude to the opening phrase of Irving Berlin's song 'Let's Face the Music and Dance' ('There may be trouble ahead ... '), which had supported a celebrated dance sequence for Fred Astaire and Ginger Rogers in *Follow the Fleet* (1936). Perhaps it is the range of sources of meaning on which this music draws – this music that is neither 'classical' nor 'popular' but has about it something of both – that makes us feel more in shared conversation with it than cowed by its grandeur or shocked by its vulgarity.

9 Parental Guidance Advised?

Mash-Ups and Mating Penguins in *Happy Feet*

FIONA FORD

Since the industry-wide adoption of computer-generated (CG) animation in the mid-1990s – starting with Pixar's *Toy Story* in 1995 – full-length animations have been among the most commercially successful features made or financed by Hollywood in the twenty-first century (Box Office Mojo 2015). The associated merchandizing is also hugely lucrative, capable of generating vastly more income than the films themselves. (For instance, the Disney Brand Corporation generated $40.9 billion from their licensed merchandizing in 2013; see Graser 2014.) As consumers, we are constantly being encouraged to enhance our cinematic 'experience' through branded toys, clothing, food and other 'lifestyle products'. The over-abundance of merchandise aimed at very young children lulls many parents into thinking that the associated films are suitable for their offspring, yet many of these CG animations have not been designed with pre-schoolers (or even under-tens) in mind. This is because digital technology has diminished many of the traditional distinctions between live action and animation, enabling the films to be 'shot with the speed, allusiveness, and impact of movies for adults ... [making them] too noisy, dazzling, and confusing for very young brains to take in' (Kirby 2009, 128). Advances in motion-capture technologies have also made these films 'less identifiably "cartoonish" and therefore less apt to be defined automatically as juvenile entertainment' (N. Brown 2012, 295).

There are other adult enticements. Many of the scripts for CG animations rely on copious amounts of dialogue to tell the story and deliver the comedy (the latter through tongue-in-cheek humour and meta-textual references) rather than visual, non-textual means which younger children can more easily follow. Moreover, these scripts are often delivered by leading names from the movie and music industries, and some catchy pop songs are included on the soundtrack. Whilst overtly adult sexual behaviour is still strictly avoided, allusive references typically manifest themselves through this use of pop music, which has become 'the semi-sublimated packaging of adult sexuality for young children' (Kirby 2009, 134). George Miller's digitally animated feature *Happy Feet* (Animal Logic Film, 2006; a co-production for Warner Bros. and Village Roadshow Pictures) – set largely among a colony of Emperor penguins in Antarctica – is a prime example. Beneath *Happy Feet*'s surface pleasures, there are some ugly aspects concerning sex and race with which the pop songs on the soundtrack are inescapably entwined. This chapter will examine two short sequences of pop-song mash-ups which are at the core of debates regarding the film's efficacy.

Miller approached the animation as if it were a live-action movie, aiming for a photo-realistic aesthetic and simulating ambitious fast-moving camera techniques. Although the penguins are anthropomorphized, they also exhibit many traits of real penguin behaviour. The director drew much of his initial inspiration and knowledge about Emperor penguin society from the wildlife documentary series *Life in the Freezer* (BBC, 1993) and was particularly fascinated to discover that each Emperor penguin has a unique display song which it uses to attract and thereafter locate its mate within a noisy colony. From this biological fact, Miller's ideas grew into 'an accidental musical' about a colony of singing penguins, each of which had an individual 'heartsong', and a misfit hero – Mumble – who can't sing, but is compelled to tap dance (Maddox 2006). The penguins' heartsongs were culled from pre-existing pop classics about love, relationships and lonely hearts, whilst their movements – both naturalistic and choreographed – were generated by human performers wearing motion-capture body suits. A low-resolution of these digitized performances was available for viewing in real-time – like live-action shooting – before being manipulated and refined in post-production (Leadley 2006, 52). (In a similar manner to the principles of motion-capture, Disney's animators from the 1930s onwards often used live action of humans and animals as an expedient way of drawing more intricate aspects of anatomy and locomotion; see Thomas and Johnston 1981, chapter 13.) Savion Glover, considered amongst the world's greatest tap-dancers, furnished Mumble's tap dancing whilst Elijah Wood provided his voice; the other lead penguins were voiced by well-known Hollywood actors with demonstrable singing abilities (Hugh Jackman, Nicole Kidman, Robin Williams and Brittany Murphy) or by recording artists (Fat Joe, Chrissie Hynde). The British composer John Powell had executive control of the entire soundtrack: he wrote the original orchestral score and was also responsible for the arrangement and production of most of the pre-existing pop songs, adding some of his own material in an appropriate vein where necessary to piece everything together. Powell has scored or co-scored an impressive list of live-action and animated films since the late 1990s – the latter mainly for DreamWorks Pictures/DreamWorks Animations (including the *How to Train Your Dragon* franchise, since 2010) and Blue Sky Studios (for example, the *Rio* franchise, since 2011).

The plot of *Happy Feet* concerns Mumble's struggle for acceptance within the colony. Unable to develop an individual heartsong with which to woo a mate, he expresses himself through tap dancing and grows up an embarrassing misfit. The elders exile him, claiming that his offensive toe-tapping is responsible for the lean fishing season. Mumble – accompanied by a Rockhopper penguin-guru called Lovelace (Williams) and a motley crew of Adélie penguins led by the sex-crazed Ramon (also Williams) – sets off on a perilous quest to find those truly responsible for the reduction in fish: the rumoured 'aliens' (humans) at the 'Forbidden Shore'. Ultimately, Mumble returns with some humans in tow and persuades his colony to unite in a mass display of tap dancing; the subsequent TV footage of this spectacle compels mankind to stop destroying the food and habitat upon which the colony depends, restoring ecological balance.

The digital technology used in *Happy Feet* allowed for breathtakingly accurate renditions of the Antarctic landscapes, and also the flexibility to animate individual penguins independently during shots of the entire Emperor colony dancing (one scene showing half a million birds) or to animate any of Mumble's six million feathers during close-ups (Byrnes 2015). These stunning visual details led to the animation winning an Oscar and a BAFTA award in 2007 for Best Animated Feature. The actual content of the film proved more controversial than its technical artistry. On the film's release in November 2006, some right-wing media commentators in the United States roundly condemned it as subversive propaganda because of its overtly anti-religious/anti-authoritarian stance, its pro-environmental messages regarding the impact of overfishing and man-made pollution and its pro-gay subtext – the latter due to Mumble's being 'different'. (For a sample of such reports, see Dietz 2006 and Boehlert 2006.) There are also many dark aspects to the story: Mumble is attacked by a series of increasingly larger predators and other dangers (skuas, a leopard seal, killer whales and the propeller of a fishing vessel) and 'loses his mind' when captive in a zoo. Scary moments in children's animation are not a new phenomenon – for example, they occur in *Snow White and the Seven Dwarfs* (1937) and *Watership Down* (1978) – and Miller had already demonstrated in his earlier screenplays for *Babe* (1995) and *Babe: Pig in the City* (1998) that he was not afraid to incorporate challenging topics within family-oriented fare. Yet there was an obvious disparity between the cinema marketing campaign for *Happy Feet* and the film's actual content. The official trailers glossed over the excessively nightmarish aspects and completely omitted the environmental topics; the only 'warning' on film posters was 'May cause toe-tapping'. Many parents with very young children were therefore completely unprepared for the film's true content, which was understandable given the G (General) or U (Universal) ratings it received in Australia and the United Kingdom, respectively, but perhaps less so in the United States, where the film was given the stronger PG rating due to scenes of 'mild peril and rude humor'. The New Zealand film classification agency also swiftly changed the film's initial rating from G to PG after receiving complaints from the public (see New Zealand Government 2015).

Happy Feet has received little attention from academic writers. It has been included in some 'ecocritical' studies of US animations from the 1930s onwards (Murray and Heumann 2011; Pike 2012), which conclude that pro-environmental messages in 'enviro-toons' like *Happy Feet* and *The Simpsons Movie* (2007) can be a more effective way to instigate public debate than environmental journalism, but they do not result in environmental activism. Philip Hayward (2010) has written a brief survey of Powell's original score and the pop songs interspersed within it either as diegetic performance by the animated characters (singing and dancing) or as nondiegetic underscore. His concluding remarks highlight how the sonic text often undermines the 'notionally liberal [and] eco-progressive' stance of the film, easily enabling it to 'be read in terms of . . . entrenched racial stereotyping in US society', with the Emperor penguins representing the WASP mainstream and the wily Adélies as parodic Hispanics (Hayward 2010, 101). He also draws attention to the white appropriation of black culture:

> Musically, many of the featured songs originate from African American performers and/or genre traditions [soul, R&B, rap], yet the most prominent vocal performers are Euro-Americans . . . [Moreover,] Glover's tap dance routines . . . do not register in the film's copyright music credits. His work is heard but invisible, rendered incidental, unheralded and unremunerated by royalties despite its central role in the film and its soundtrack – an unfortunate endnote to a film about tolerance, inclusivity and equality of creative expression.
> (Hayward 2010, 101)

Tanine Allison has expanded upon this theme, suggesting that 'motion capture acts as a medium through which African American performance can be detached from black bodies and applied to white ones, making it akin to digital blackface' (2015, 115), and citing the conglomeration of Glover's tap dancing with Wood's voice as the prime example. (The social/racial stratification of the penguins in *Happy Feet* does have some positive elements: for example, the Adélie penguins wholeheartedly embrace Mumble as one of their own, despite his obvious differences.)

Popular song has been omnipresent in the soundtracks of animated features financed by US studios since the 1930s. Whereas Disney continues its longstanding tradition of commissioning original songs, many other animation studios have opted to raid the twentieth century's back catalogue of commercial hits from the US and UK charts.

This trend parallels the advent of fully computer-generated animations in the 1990s; DreamWorks' *Antz* (1998) and *Shrek* (2001) are early examples. As in their use in live-action film soundtracks, these songs are chosen for the appropriateness of their lyrics to the scene in question, the general cultural vibe which they evoke or the expedient way in which they can act as a surrogate for unstated sentiment; they can appear as part of the underscore or be performed directly by the characters; they often have a humorous intent; and they invoke nostalgia in those who recognize the sources (typically the older members of the audience). Such uses of pre-existing popular song were also endemic to the anarchic cartoon shorts issued by Warner Bros. from the 1930s onwards. Also in keeping with the tradition of Bugs Bunny, Daffy Duck *et al.* is the penchant for modern-day animated characters (at least one per film) who break into song mid-speech and pepper their dialogue with identifiable song lyrics and other pop-culture references (say Donkey in *Shrek* and Ramon in *Happy Feet*). *The Simpsons* (airing on television since 1989) and Pixar's *Toy Story* franchise (since 1995) have proved to be highly influential templates for re-introducing this approach, tapping into (and helping to create/propagate) the accumulating database of postmodern pop-culture.

The *Happy Feet* soundtrack is demonstrably more musically intricate and varied than those in many animated feature films, being a complex weave of forty-one (credited) pre-existing songs – a mixture of 'popular' and 'pop' spanning just over a century from 1892 to 1999 – and Powell's orchestral score. (There are also the now ubiquitous new pop-song tie-ins placed in the end credits to promote the film, namely Prince's 'Song of the Heart' and Gia Farrell's 'Hit Me Up'; other occasional song lyrics, uncredited, have influenced the dialogue.) Around half of the songs are concentrated into two mating scenes in the form of mashed-up song lyrics sung by the penguin characters, the first (in the opening sequence) showing how Mumble's parents met and the second Mumble's clumsy attempts at attracting his childhood sweetheart Gloria (Murphy). During the four-year gestation of *Happy Feet*, Miller and Powell collaborated closely over the selection of pre-existing music, which accounts for about twenty-five minutes of the soundtrack. Much time and effort was expended in choosing and re-working pop songs in order to fit the dramatic requirements and most ideas were discarded in the process – Powell estimated that their success rate was probably only five per cent (Goldwasser 2006). It can therefore be assumed that these two mating scenes, though accounting for about 11 minutes of the finished film length (108 minutes), took a disproportionate amount of Powell's time in production and development.

Introducing the 'Lullaby of Antarctica'

Happy Feet has one of the most ambitious and arresting opening sequences in a feature-length animation. It sets the scene on a cosmic scale, going from the macrocosm of outer space to the microcosm of the penguin colony. (Similar openings can be found in Miller's *Mad Max: Beyond Thunderdome* from 1985 and Pixar's *WALL-E* from 2008.) In less than four minutes, the audience is shown how Mumble's parents Norma Jean (Kidman) and Memphis (Jackman) met and created his egg. The dialogue is minimal; instead the narrative impetus is provided by a collage of four-teen song quotations, plus a fifteenth in a short coda joined by some bridging material written by Powell. For a transcript of the scene, together with the sources of the songs, see Table 9.1.

A voice-over in a trailer to *Happy Feet* made it clear that 'In the heart of the South Pole, every penguin is born with a song to sing – everyone except Mumble'. It helps to be aware of this basic premise in advance and to be acquainted with how Emperor penguins find a mate – the latter supposedly common knowledge since Luc Jacquet's documentary *March of the Penguins* (*La marche de l'empereur*) was released in 2005 – in order to understand the primary narrative function of the (sometimes disembo-died) song lyrics in the opening scene. The initial lack of action gives the soundtrack beneath the title sequence a special prominence. As the shape of a giant penguin amidst a galaxy of stars emerges from the blackness, we hear the melodies of two intertwined songs with minimal accompaniment. These are k. d. lang singing 'Golden Slumbers' (in what proves to be the role of a narrator) and a male voice singing lines from 'I Only Have Eyes for You', the latter written for *Dames* (1934). At this point it is unclear whether or not we are hearing underscore. This opening is reminiscent of the number 'Lullaby of Broadway' (Harry Warren and Al Dubin, 1935) in Busby Berkeley's *Gold Diggers of 1935*, which begins (and ends) in total blackness with the title song emanating from an invisible source. In *Happy Feet*, lang's lines 'Sleep pretty darling do not cry / And I will sing a lullaby' also suggest that what follows will be a spectacular and musical fantasy: a 'Lullaby of Antarctica'. (Miller pays homage to Berkeley's distinctive choreographic style elsewhere in the film where the penguins' underwater formations briefly make kaleidoscopic patterns typical of those in the 'By a Waterfall' routine from the 1933 backstage musical *Footlight Parade*.)

The 'camera' then hurtles us through space – past a red-hot planet emblazoned with the film title – and through Earth's atmosphere into the penguin colony. En route we hear more fragments of songs from unseen voices (mostly male) intertwined with some spoken lines from a female – soon to be revealed as Mumble's mother Norma Jean – who is

Table 9.1 *Transcript of the first mating sequence and song sources in*
Happy Feet.

Key to transcript:
Spoken text is in roman and sung lyrics are in italics. Simultaneous or overlapping lyrics are
indicated by a /.
FP = unnamed female penguin; MP = unnamed male penguin
Codes to song sources are indicated below.

Song Code & Title		Written By		Key Recordings	
A1	'Golden Slumbers'	1969	John Lennon Paul McCartney	1969	The Beatles
A2	'I Only Have Eyes For You'	1934	Harry Warren Al Dubin	1959	The Flamingos
A3	'With a Song in my Heart'	1929	Richard Rodgers Lorenz Hart	1948	Perry Como
A4	'Tell Me Something Good'	1974	Stevie Wonder	1974	Rufus and Chaka Khan
A5	'Only You and You Alone'	1954	Buck Ram	1955	The Platters
A6	'Unchained Melody'	1955	Alex North Hy Zaret	1965	The Righteous Brothers
A7	'Where is the Love?'	1972	Ralph MacDonald William Salter	1972	Roberta Flack and Donny Hathaway
A8	'Vesti la giubba' from *Pagliacci*	1892	Ruggero Leoncavallo	1907 1958	Enrico Caruso Mario Lanza
A9	'Kiss'	1986	Prince	1986 1988	Prince Tom Jones/Art of Noise
A10	'Hello'	1984	Lionel Ritchie	1984	Lionel Ritchie
A11	'Broken Wings'	1985	Richard Page Steve George John Lang	1985	Mr Mister
A12	'Let's talk about sex'	1991	Herby Azor	1991	Salt-n-Pepa
A13	'Gimme all your lovin''	1983	Billy Gibbons Dusty Hill Frank Beard	1983	ZZ Top
A14	'Heartbreak Hotel'	1956	Mae Boren Axton Thomas Durden	1956	Elvis Presley
A15	'Never Can Say Goodbye'	1971	Clifton Davis	1971 1974	The Jackson Five Gloria Gaynor
JP1	[backing material]		[John Powell]		
JP2	[backing material]		[John Powell]		

Table 9.1 (*cont.*)

		Song Code
[Deep space; a galaxy of stars.]		
Narrator:	*Once there was a way to get back homeward*	(A1)
MP #1:	*Are the stars out tonight?*	(A2)
Narrator:	*Once there was a way to get back home*	(A1)
MP #1:	*I only have eyes*	(A2)
Narrator:	*Sleep, pretty darling, do not cry*	(A1)
MP #1:	*For you*	(A2)
Narrator:	*And I will sing a lullaby*	(A1)
MP #2:	*With a song in my heart*	(A3)

[The 'camera' begins to zoom past a planet bearing the film's title to Earth and then Antarctica]

FP #1/<u>backing chorus</u>:	So *Tell me / Tell me <u>something good</u> /* *Tell me that you love me / Tell me, baby /* *<u>Tell me something good</u>*	(A4)
MP #3:	*Only you . . .*	(A5)
NORMA JEAN [unseen]:	But how can you know for sure?	
MP #3:	*. . . can make this world seem right*	(A5)
NORMA JEAN:	Is there really just one?	
MP #4:	*I need your love*	(A6)
NORMA JEAN:	So many songs, but I'm feeling so lonely.	(A14)

[Zoom shot, moving towards penguin colony; there is a cacophony of voices but few are distinguishable.]

FP #2:	*Where is the love?*	(A7)
MP #5:	*Ridi, Pagliacci*	(A8)

[The penguins are now in view. As Norma Jean wanders through the colony looking for a mate, she is pestered by many prospective male suitors.]

Table 9.1 (*cont.*)

		Song Code
NORMA JEAN [seen] and <u>MPs</u>:	*You don't have to be beautiful*	(A9)
	<u>*Ow!*</u>	(JP1)
	to turn me on	
	<u>*Ooh . . . ooh . . . ah yeah!*</u>	
	I just need your body, baby	
MP #6:	*Hello*	(A10)
NORMA JEAN:	*From dusk till dawn*	(A9)
MP #6:	*Is it me you're looking for?*	(A10)
NORMA JEAN:	*You don't need experience*	(A9)
MP #7:	*Take . . .*	(A11)
NORMA JEAN:	*To turn me out*	(A9)
MP #7:	*. . . these broken wings*	(A11)
NORMA JEAN:	*You just leave it all up to me*	(A9)
MP #8:	*Let's talk about eggs, baby*	(A12)
NORMA JEAN:	Huh?	
MP #8:	*Let's talk about you and me*	(A12)
NORMA JEAN:	Uh-uh. Huh-uh.	
NORMA JEAN& <u>MP CHORUSES</u>:	*You don't have to be rich to be my pearl /*	(A9)
	<u>*Oh Norma Jean, Norma Jean /*</u>	(JP2)
	<u>*Gimme all your lovin' . . . Come on /*</u>	(A13)
	You don't have to be cool to rule my world /	(A9)
	<u>*You're my Queen /*</u>	(JP2)
	<u>*All your hugs and kisses too /*</u>	(A13)
	Ain't no particular song	
	I'm more compatible with /	(A9)
	<u>*I wanna be your man /*</u>	(JP2)
	<u>*Gimme all your lovin' /*</u>	(A13)
	I just want your extra . . . Boys!	(A9)
	<u>*That's my plan /*</u>	(JP2)

Table 9.1 (*cont.*)

		Song Code
	All your hugs and kisses too /	(A13)

[Norma Jean turns round and asks her many admirers to leave her alone.]

NORMA JEAN: Boys! Give a chick a chance.

[Norma Jean turns back to find a male penguin on a mound in front of her; he is in an Elvis pose.]

MEMPHIS:	*Well, since my baby left me*	(A14)
	I found a new place to dwell	
	It's down at the end of Lonely Street	
	At Heartbreak Hotel	
	And I said, 'I'm feeling so lonely, baby,	
	I'm feeling so lonely . . .'	
MEMPHIS & NORMA JEAN:	*'I'm feeling so lonely . . .'*	(A14)
NORMA JEAN:	*'. . . I could die.'*	(A14)
MEMPHIS:	*Don't have to be rich to be my girl*	(A9)
NORMA JEAN:	*Don't have to be cool to rule my world*	(A9)
MEMPHIS:	*You rule my world*	(A9)
NORMA JEAN:	*You're the particular song*	
	I'm compatible with	(A9)

[The other penguins gather in a heart-shape formation around Memphis and Norma Jean; see Figure 9.1.]

MEMPHIS:	*I just want your . . .*	(A9)
NORMA JEAN & MEMPHIS:	*. . . extra time* / *And your kiss*	(A9)

[See Figure 9.2]

LOVELACE [unseen]:	His Mom and Dad met in the usual way.	
	The song became love	
	and love became the egg.	

[Norma Jean carefully passes her egg to Memphis.]

NORMA JEAN: Memphis? You got it, sugar?

Table 9.1 (*cont.*)

		Song Code
MEMPHIS:	Yeah. Oh, yeah. Safe and warm.	
NORMA JEAN:	Hold it tight, now.	
MEMPHIS:	Whoa, I think I felt a move in there.	
LOVELACE [unseen]:	And in the usual way . . . the moms left for the fishing season . . . while the dads stayed home to do egg time.	
NORMA JEAN:	You gonna be okay, Daddy?	
MEMPHIS:	Oh, sure, honey. We'll be waiting for you, right here on Lonely Street.	(A14)
NORMA JEAN:	*I love you more and more, tell me why . . .* Bye-bye, now.	(A15)
MEMPHIS:	Goodbye, Norma Jean. Don't you worry about a thing.	
NORMA JEAN:	*Don't wanna let you go.* *I never can say goodbye, boy.*	(A15)

overwhelmed at hearing 'So many songs'. The line 'Ridi, Pagliacci' from the famous tenor aria 'Vesti la giubba' ends the final cacophony with a dash of late nineteenth-century Italian opera before the penguins finally come into view. Only now does it become apparent that we have been overhearing Norma Jean as she wanders around the colony (as a real Emperor penguin would), listening to the heartsongs of various males in the hope of finding her one true love. She launches into her own heartsong, an upbeat rendition of the opening verse and chorus from 'Kiss'. The accompaniment is rendered through minimal rhythm and bass, throwing the vocal lines into sharper relief. Heartsong incipits (typically only one or two lines long) from more male suitors are expertly woven around her phrases in the manner of a Club DJ using multiple turntables. Norma Jean ignores them all until her attention is finally grabbed by Memphis and his rendition of 'Heartbreak Hotel'; their union was pre-destined in her spoken line from this song ('I'm feeling so lonely') before she even met him. As Memphis stands before her on a mound of ice, he sings his courtship call (first verse and chorus) and stretches out his wings in an obvious impersonation of Elvis Presley. In time-honoured fashion from opera, operetta and musical, the pair signify their mutual attraction and impending union by instinctively being able to sing lines from each other's songs in the manner of a love duet.

The official soundtrack recording (Warner Sunset/Atlantic 756783998–2, 2006) features a version of the 'Kiss'/'Heartbreak Hotel' duet which is different from the film soundtrack in two key aspects. First, the breadth of the film's opening has been curtailed, the track starting just before Norma Jean's first spoken line ('But how can you know for sure?'); and, second, the pre-existing pop songs interwoven with 'Kiss' have been entirely replaced by innocuous backing material supplied by Powell and his team, presumably for copyright reasons. This makes the album track anodyne in comparison with the opening of the film soundtrack.

The sophisticated beauty of the opening scene was lost on the reviewer in *Sight & Sound*, who reckoned that it 'may put some viewers off the picture, as we're thrust into the midst of CGI penguins mouthing pop and rock numbers in a kitsch parody of *Moulin Rouge* (2001)' (Osmond 2007, 56). Hayward also noted how the presence of Kidman and the 'use of disjunctured, "mashed-up" song dialogues between romantically aligned characters' has marked similarities to Baz Luhrmann's 'Elephant Love Medley' sequence in *Moulin Rouge!* when Christian (Ewan MacGregor) and Satine (Kidman) 'exchange snippets of seminal popular love songs' (2010, 95). Miller's reference to this iconic love duet is much more than a kitsch parody or a token acknowledgement of fellow Australian artistry: it is dramatically apposite for the union of Mumble's parents and constitutes a beautiful, albeit extremely brief, celebration of romantic love. Miller draws deliberate visual parallels by using Luhrmann's trademark heart shapes (Armour 2001, 9). Just as the romance between Satine and Christian is framed by a heart-shaped window and culminates in a kiss, so Norma Jean's and Memphis's courtship takes place within a heart-shaped space formed by the other penguins (see Figure 9.1) and the pair

Figure 9.1 *Happy Feet*: the penguins make a heart-shaped formation around Norma Jean and Memphis.

Figure 9.2 *Happy Feet*: Norma Jean and Memphis bring their beaks together, forming a heart shape.

mark their union in accordance with real Emperor penguins by throwing back their heads, bowing and bringing their beaks together in a heart shape (see Figure 9.2). For real Emperor penguins, this 'bowing' often precedes copulation and is also associated with egg-laying (T. Williams 1995, 157). Sure enough, as a coda to the first mating scene the narrative moves swiftly to the new parents with their egg, which Norma Jean entrusts to Memphis, singing 'Never Can Say Goodbye' as she and the other 'wives' bid farewell and leave for a fishing trip.

The essential purpose and necessity of heartsongs is only explained once the film is well underway, when a young Mumble and the other penguin chicks attend a special singing class. Here, the teacher, Miss Viola (Magda Szubanski), encourages her young charges to try out the song they can hear inside themselves, informing them that 'Without our Heartsong, we can't be truly penguin, can we?' (Thus Mumble's fate as a misfit is sealed.) The audience is given a foretaste of the second mating scene when two chicks, Gloria (Alyssa Schafer) and Seymour (Cesar Flores), attempt their heartsongs in embryonic form (the first verse of 'Boogie Wonderland' and the chorus from 'The Message', respectively; for song sources, see Table 9.2).

With the audience now fully conversant in the courtship rituals of these singing penguins, it seems entirely natural for the adult Gloria to be bombarded with lyrics from different songs when she is looking for a mate in the second mating sequence. Whilst the introduction and structure mirrors the opening sequence from the extreme-long shot of the colony onwards, in other ways this second sequence is the complete opposite of the first. It uses far fewer songs (six) yet is longer (over seven minutes) because it concludes with large quantities of dialogue and a mass dance extravaganza. Crucially, the narrative outcome is different because the anticipated union of Mumble and Gloria is thwarted. For a transcript of this scene (up to the point at which Mumble 'sings') and a list of song sources, see Table 9.2. Gloria – singing the first verse from 'Boogie Wonderland' in a slower, more soulful tempo than the

Table 9.2 *Transcript of the second mating sequence and song sources in* Happy Feet.

Key to transcript:
Spoken text is in roman and sung lyrics are in italics. Simultaneous or overlapping lyrics are indicated by a/.
FP = unnamed female penguin; MP = unnamed male penguin
Codes to song sources are indicated below.

Song Code & Title		Written By		Key Recordings
B1	'The Message'	1982	Ed Fletcher Melle Mel	1982 Grandmaster Flash & the Furious Five
B2	'No Scrubs'	1999	Kevin Briggs Kandi Burruss Tameka Cottle	1999 TLC
B3	'Boogie Wonderland'	1979	Allee Willis Jon Lind	1979 Earth, Wind & Fire
B4	'I'll Make Love to You'	1994	Kenneth Edmonds	1994 Boyz II Men
B5	'Shake your bon-bon'	1998	Rosa, Child & Noriega	1999 Ricky Martin
B6	'My Way'/'A mi manera'	1967/9	Claude François Jacques Revaux Paul Anka	1969 Frank Sinatra 1969 Paul Anka 1998 Paul Anka and Julio Iglesias
JP3	[backing vocals]		[John Powell]	

		Song Code
SEYMOUR:	*Don't push me 'cause I'm close to the edge*	(B1)
FP #3:	*I don't want no scrub*	(B2)
SEYMOUR & <u>MP CHORUS</u>:	*I'm trying not to lose my head /* *<u>G-L-O-R-I-A, Glo-ri-a</u> /* *It's like a jungle sometimes* *It makes me wonder* *How I keep from going under*	(B1) (<u>JP3</u>)
GLORIA & <u>MP CHORUS</u>:	*Midnight creeps so slowly* *Into hearts of those / <u>Glo-ri-a</u>* *Who need more than they get* *Daylight deals a bad hand to a penguin /* *<u>G-L-O-R-I-A, G-L-O-R-I-A</u>/* *Who has laid too many bets / <u>Glo-ri-a</u>*	(B3/<u>JP3</u>)

Table 9.2 (*cont.*)

		Song Code
MP #9 & **MP BOY BAND:**	*I'll make love to you / Love to you* *Like you want me to / Want me to* *And I'll hold you tight / Hold you tight*	(B4/IP3)
MP #9 & MP CHORUS:	*Baby, all . . . / Glo-ri-a*	
GLORIA **& MP CHORUS:**	*The mirror stares you in the face /* *G-L-O-R-I-A* *And says, 'Baby—'*	(B3/IP3)
MP #10:	*Shake a bon-bon, shake a –*	(B5)
GLORIA:	*'It don't work.'*	(B3)
GLORIA, **MP CHORUS & MP #10:**	*You say your prayers* *Glo-ri-a / Shake a bon-bon* *Though you don't care* *Glo-ri-a / Shake a bon-bon* *You say your prayers* *Glo-ri-a / Shake a bon-bon* *Though you don't care*	(B3) (IP3/B5)
	Glo-ri-a / Shake a bon-bon *Glo-ri-a, Glo-ri-a, Glo-ri-a, Glo-ri-a,* *Glo-ri-a, Glo-ri-a, Glo-ri-a, Glo-ri-a*	(IP3/B5)
GLORIA:	Boys! Boys! Boys!	
MUMBLE [RAMON]:	*Na-na-na!* *Na-na-na-na-na-na-na-na.* *Yo sé, se termino* [etc.].	(B6)

original recording by Earth, Wind and Fire – meanders through bands of male penguins who compete for her attention by bombarding her with their heartsong incipits. Again, the accompaniment is an embryonic rhythm and bass; the harmonies are mostly provided by the choruses of male penguins. Gloria quickly stops and turns to scold her suitors (as Norma Jean did) and then is confronted by Mumble on a mound of ice, just as his father had appeared before Norma Jean. He attempts to woo her with a rendition of 'My Way' in Spanish, backed by his Adélie friends, but she quickly realizes that he is only miming – Ramon is the real singer – and turns away in dismay. Mumble then persuades Gloria to sing to the rhythm of his tap dancing, and she reprises the verse of her heartsong at a faster tempo, leading to a rousing uptempo version of the chorus which 'featur[es] Mumble's tap patterns as a polyrhythm' (Hayward 2010, 96). Unable to resist the 'groove', their entire generation of penguins joins in the dance until the elders put a stop to the frivolities and exile the aberrant toe-tapper.

Soft-Porn Penguins?

Whilst the soundtrack consists of an eclectic mélange of songs from several decades, the majority are a mix of iconic R&B, Motown and hip-hop numbers, originally recorded by non-white solo artists and vocal groups (see song sources in Tables 9.1 and 9.2) – hence the criticism that *Happy Feet* narrates, 'however indirectly, the white appropriation of black culture' (Allison 2015, 114). Many of the animated penguins adopt the choreographed movements associated with their particular artist and the original performance context of the song, on stage or in music videos. This ranges from Memphis striking an Elvis pose before singing 'Heartbreak Hotel' in the first mating scene to a penguin 'boy band' in the second, who pester Gloria with their Boyz II Men parody ('I'll make love to you') after which a male penguin wiggles his behind like Ricky Martin and entreats her to 'Shake a bon-bon'. Certain characters carry over their musical personae into their dialogue and general demeanour: Memphis is clearly a 'Southern boy' with conservative views; and Seymour – even as a chick – has a bigger build than all the other penguins, like the American rapper Fat Joe who provides his adult voice. Such stereotyping can seem crude and offensive, but these rapid audiovisual cameos are a particularly efficient means of differentiating the main characters when the majority of penguins are indistinguishable from each other.

Miller and Powell made no attempt in these mating scenes to assign songs from one chronological period to a particular generation of penguins. Norma Jean sang 'Kiss' from the 1980s alongside Memphis's 'Heartbreak Hotel' from the 1950s, whilst the next generation, Seymour and Gloria, had classics from the early 1980s and late 1970s, respectively. Older members of the audience should easily recognize the mashed-up pop-song selections and find them comic in their juxtaposition and in the incongruity of their new context; younger viewers need only follow the basic narrative, drawn in by the novelty of cute penguins singing and dancing to a groovy beat. Powell produced the two mash-up sequences to an exceptionally high standard; they are slick and have seamless transitions between the disparate elements. Despite the confines of working with other peoples' song materials, there is still much originality evident in their combinations and production. Although all the song fragments are performances in the sense that the penguins are putting on a display to attract a mate, their function is categorically narrative and the song mash-ups are an expedient and apposite means of rendering the mating rituals musically. (The mating displays are also clear examples of how sound – particularly music – is often the catalyst driving the creation of the animated image and is at the core of its meaning and affect: see Paul Wells in Chapter 16 of this volume.) Indeed, it would be easy to re-imagine the first mating scene in the context of *Moulin Rouge!*, with Satine searching for her true love amidst a lascivious throng of men (appropriately dressed like penguins in black tie and tails) at the eponymous nightclub. However, the racy lyrics and choreography in this – and the second – mating scene are much more challenging within the context of an animation aimed at a family audience. (Christian commentators in the United States have picked up on this aspect more than mainstream reviewers: see Greydanus 2006.)

The content of some songs was rendered more innocent chiefly by avoiding the narratives in the verses, sticking instead to the more memorable hook of a catchy chorus (for example, 'I'll make love to you'; 'Gimme all your lovin''; Shake your bon-bon'). In the case of 'The Message', using only the chorus avoided its grim narrative about inner-city violence, drugs and poverty. Other songs were tweaked to fit better with penguin society (and avoid receiving a higher-rated certification): 'Let's talk about sex' became 'Let's talk about eggs'. Less easily dismissed are the heartsongs chosen for Norma Jean and Gloria ('Kiss' and 'Boogie Wonderland'), whose lyrics received only minimal changes. For example, the opening verse of 'Boogie Wonderland': 'Midnight creeps so slowly into hearts of those [men] who need more than they get, Daylight deals a bad hand to a penguin [woman] who has laid too many bets' (the original words are indicated in square brackets). Whilst the message in the chorus is straightforward and appropriate to *Happy Feet* ('Dance, Boogie Wonderland'), the opening verse seems a bizarre choice, given its narrative about a woman who is constantly searching for romance on the dance floor to dull the pain of her many loveless relationships with men; this also creates a gratuitous and unlikely backstory for Gloria.

Both female protagonists have human-like buxom, curvaceous bodies which are in stark contrast to the more penguin-like males surrounding them, and both give highly sensualized performances of their songs. Gloria, in particular, seems to be overtly aroused by Mumble's tap dancing and is inescapably drawn to his 'groove'. Norma Jean is patently cast in the mould of Marilyn Monroe by using the screen siren's real forenames and through Kidman's breathy singing style. Edward Rhymes (2007) has noted how celebrity status and artistic legitimacy have been accorded to certain white females like Monroe who are allegedly recognized more for their sexual assets than for any innate talent, yet black women (say in hip-hop videos) acting out the same behaviour are demonized for their sexual promiscuity and immodesty. It is therefore a strong statement for the ultra-white Kidman in the guise of Monroe to sing the extremely raunchy lyrics in 'Kiss', a song generally associated with male singers (Prince and Tom Jones). Rhymes would regard such a decision as having '"deified" and normalized white female explicitness and promiscuity' (*ibid.*), despite the cloak of 'digital blackface' (Allison 2015, 115) provided through the filter of an animated penguin.

The two mating sequences in *Happy Feet*, in appropriating 'sexed-up' songs and choreography from the music industry to portray lone, hyper-sensualized female penguins being pursued by groups of clamouring males, typify the soft-porn styling that is now endemic to many media forms. Concerns about the increasing 'pornification' of popular culture and the negative effects this is having on young people had already been raised by commentators in the United States prior to the release of *Happy Feet*. For example, Don Aucoin wrote in the *Boston Globe*:

> Not too long ago, pornography was a furtive profession, its products created and consumed in the shadows. But it has steadily elbowed its way into the limelight, with an impact that can be measured not just by the Internet-fed ubiquity of pornography itself but by the way aspects of the porn sensibility now inform movies, music videos, fashion, magazines, and celebrity culture . . .
>
> What is new and troubling, critics suggest, is that the porn aesthetic has become so pervasive that it now serves as a kind of sensory wallpaper, something that many people don't even notice anymore . . .
>
> But it is perhaps the world of popular music where the lines between entertainment and soft-core porn seem to have been most thoroughly blurred. It is now routine for female performers to cater to male fantasies with sex-drenched songs and videos.   (Aucoin 2006)

It is telling that *Happy Feet* received classifications for theatrical release in Europe and North America which overlooked the raciness inherent in the lyrics and choreography. Moreover, the film examiners appear to have missed (or ignored) a latent porn reference: the Rockhopper penguin guru is called Lovelace – after Linda Lovelace in *Deep Throat* (1972) – and wears a 'sacred necklace' (a set of plastic six-pack rings) which eventually begins to choke him (see Massawyrm 2006; Osmond 2007, 56). The use of (barely disguised) sexual content in *Happy Feet* is merely part of an ongoing market trend. A 2004 study by the Harvard School of Public Health, reported in the *New York Times*, highlighted how 'a movie rated PG or PG-13 today has more sexual or violent content than a similarly related movie in the past' (cited in N. Brown 2012, 278). Soft-porn styling and barely disguised racy lyrics in supposedly family-friendly fare are also present in Miller's sequel *Happy Feet Two* (2011; again scored by Powell). This begins with a grand song-and-dance medley of pop songs performed by different sections of the Emperor penguin colony, in which the next generation of male chicks, led by Seymour's son Atticus (Benjamin Flores Jr), do a break dance to the hip-hop song 'Mama said knock you out' (LL Cool J, 1990) – re-worded 'Papa said knock them out' – and the irresistible snow-covered female chicks respond with 'We're bringing fluffy back', wiggling their behinds and urging us to 'Get your fluffy on / Shake your tail' in a brief mash-up of Justin Timberlake's 'Sexyback' (2006) and Mystikal's 'Shake it Fast [Shake ya ass]' (2000).

Who, exactly, was the target audience for *Happy Feet*? Walt Disney aimed his early animated features at an undifferentiated 'child of all ages' (a child-adult amalgam later identified by the American TV industry in the early 1950s as the 'kidult'), whereas his live-action family movies gradually introduced a change in focus to an adult, middlebrow audience (N. Brown 2012, 153 and 195). Arguably, films such as *Happy Feet* and its sequel also virtually ignore the young children at whom much of the merchandizing and marketing is aimed. Instead, the main target audience comprises adolescents and youth-obsessed middle-aged adults, the latter group now forming the biggest demographic in the Western world (and hence the one with the greatest potential spending power).

The annual *Theatrical Market Statistics* for the US entertainment industry (issued by the Motion Picture Association of America) since 2001 show a marked trend towards standardization of product, with films rated PG-13 (typically the blockbuster franchises based on comic books and toys) and PG accounting for around 80 per cent of the twenty-five top grossing films each year. (PG-13 films have supplanted films rated R (Restricted), which require a parental presence for any viewers under the age of 17, as the dominant group.) Notably, the vast majority of animated features receive a PG rating in the United States; the G rating is virtually obsolete. This in itself is indicative that many films nominally suitable for young children now regularly contain more adult content. In the case of *Happy Feet*, there are obvious aspects of its script, soundtrack and visual styling which may even suggest a PG-13 rating. Robin Murray and Joseph Heumann might suggest that these aspects are ultimately counterproductive and damage Miller's heartfelt pro-environmental message, because in 'enviro-toons' such as *Happy Feet*, 'the call to [environmental] action is diluted by the ongoing call to buy' (2011, 244).

Miller strengthened his warning about impending environmental disaster in *Happy Feet Two*, urging us all to unite in our aim to stop the effects of climate change. Jacquet also returned to the Antarctic to make the documentary *Ice and the Sky* (*La glace et le ciel*; 2015) about the career of veteran French glaciologist and climate-change expert Claude Lorius. The French director was shocked to see how, since his last trip to the continent, climate change has increased temperatures, introducing unprecedented rainfall – with devastating effects on the survival of penguin chicks (MacNab 2015). The giant panda might be the best-known 'poster animal' for environmental conservation, but in the world of cinema another black and white animal, the Emperor penguin, is the one still trying to get our attention.

10 Materializing Film Music

MIGUEL MERA

In his influential book *Audio-Vision: Sound on Screen*, Michel Chion coined the phrase 'materialising sound indices' (1994, 114–17) as a means of describing aspects of a sound that draw direct attention to the physical nature of its source and the concrete conditions of its emission. Chion contrasted examples of footstep sounds that consist entirely of inconspicuous clicking with sounds that provide the feeling of texture (leather, cloth, crunching gravel). On a sliding scale, an abundance of materializing effects can pull a film scene towards the physical, or their sparsity can lead to a perception of narrative and character as abstract. Chion also argued that many Western musical traditions are defined by the absence of materializing effects:

> The musician's or singer's goal is to purify the voice or instrument sound of all noises of breathing, scratching, or any other adventitious friction or vibration linked to producing the musical tone. Even if she takes care to conserve at least an exquisite hint of materiality and noise in the release of the sound, the musician's effort lies in detaching the latter from its causality. (Chion 1994, 114)

The conceptual framework for Chion's argument can, of course, be traced back to Roland Barthes's essay 'The Grain of the Voice' (1977, 179–89), which examined the split between the voice and language. There are clear similarities between Barthes's notion of the phenosong and genosong and Chion's sliding scale of materializing sound indices. Both writers identified how technical prowess and expressive force in much musical performance irons out the workings of the physicality of production. Indeed, this seems an entirely appropriate description of the vast majority of mainstream orchestral film music where instrumental recordings strive for effortless clarity and perfect evenness; microphones are carefully placed to avoid scratchy or breathy sounds, intonation is always precise. How, then, might an audience be encouraged to feel the material conditions of a sound's source in film scores, and what could that approach bring to the cinematic experience?

Outside of mainstream Western soundtrack production there are many types of music that explore precisely these issues: certain genres of contemporary classical music or experimental electronic music such as glitch, which employs deliberate digital artefacts, immediately spring to mind. Indeed, in the digital age materiality is often foregrounded in music that is heavily technologically mediated (Demers 2010; Hainge 2013; Hegarty 2007), particularly where noise is a centralizing concept. In many non-Western cultures instrumental materiality is also often celebrated and sounds proudly reveal their physical origin. The buzzy quality that is described by the Japanese concept of *sawari* is a pertinent example (Takemitsu 1995, 64; Wierzbicki 2010, 198).

The apparent lack of materializing effects in mainstream soundtrack production is, unsurprisingly, also reflected in existing audiovisual scholarship: music and sound have been somewhat sidelined in discussions of sensuous materiality (Sobchack 1992, 2004; L. U. Marks 2000, 2002; Barker 2009). When ideas about physicality and materiality do exist they tend to be confined to discussions about sound design or electronically generated music (Coulthard 2013; Connor 2013). In this chapter I explore how musical noise in instrumental music is tied to material causality and announces its hapticity, creating an embodied connection with the audio-viewer. Some musical gestures powerfully recall the human motor actions that produce them, revealing the tactile physicality of their source. Some musical materials directly encourage sensation and enact the body. What does it mean to 'grasp' or be touched by a sound?

I will examine this issue through two examples that highlight different attitudes towards materialized film music. Jonny Greenwood's score for Paul Thomas Anderson's *There Will Be Blood* (2007) consistently draws attention to its own physical materiality with textures – like the oil at the heart of the film's narrative – that seem to issue from the very ground itself, a space that I argue is embodied by and through the music. The score celebrates haptic 'dirtiness' with the use of microtones, clusters and aleatoric and extended instrumental techniques. Greenwood is best known as the guitarist in the band Radiohead and not as a traditional film composer. I will argue that it was his position as a film-music outsider, coupled with Anderson's independent filmmaking spirit and unconventional working practices, that allowed an embodied, dirty and haptic music aesthetic to be created in *There Will Be Blood*. The incorporation of a range of pre-existing pieces, including selections from Greenwood's score for Simon Pummell's film *Bodysong* (2003), and his orchestral works *Smear* (2004) and *Popcorn Superhet Receiver* (2005), are central to this attitude. But this is not the whole story.

On Anderson's and Greenwood's next collaborative film project, *The Master* (2012), there was a softening of the connection between materiality and causality. The noisy rupture that made *There Will Be Blood* such an extraordinary visceral experience had not entirely disappeared, but it had become somewhat sanitized. It is tempting to suggest that this shift occurred because Greenwood had learned to become more of a 'film composer', resulting in greater security in both the compositional and collaborative approach. This resonates with debates about the political and ideological implications of noise as most forcefully proposed by Jacques Attali (1985). Undesired or undesirable noise is understood as politically resistant, serving to disrupt the existing normative conditions and bring about a change in the system.

The score for *There Will Be Blood*, then, arguably represented something of an emerging new direction in contemporary film scoring that was both a reaction to the tight formatting of mainstream Hollywood films and an expression of the dirty media soundscapes of modern life. The score for *The Master* could be seen to have become assimilated into the mainstream cinematic language as a less resistant version of its former aesthetic self. Of course, it is not quite as simple as this. I also argue that the difference in approach reflects a standard Cartesian separation between the mind and the body, which is tied to the central narrative concerns of each film. The scores for *There Will Be Blood* and *The Master* respectively focus more on the body and the mind, exploring the boundaries between materiality that does not think and mentality that does not have extension in physical space. They represent the fluidity of contemporary film-scoring practice, demonstrating why Chion's sliding scale of materializing sound indices is both useful and timely. By locating Chion's materializing effects within phenomenological perception, we are able to reevaluate the impact of film-scoring traditions and consider previously undervalued aspects of soundtrack production.

Haptic Music

Studies of the haptic qualities of cinema have frequently argued that touch is not just skin deep but is experienced in both the surface and depths of the body. By dismantling binary demarcations of externality and internality, phenomenologists have highlighted the intimacy of cinema's immersive connection to the human body rather than the distance created by observation. Hapticity does not refer simply to physical contact but rather to a mode of perception and expression through which the body is enacted. It describes our experience of sensation, how we feel the cinematic world we see and hear. As Vivian Sobchak argued, 'the film experience is meaningful *not to the side of our bodies, but because of our bodies*' with the result that movies can provoke in us the 'carnal thoughts that ground and inform more conscious analysis' (2004, 60; emphasis in original). For Jennifer Barker, 'tension, balance, energy, inertia, languor, velocity, rhythm' are all cinematic aspects that can be considered tactile, 'though none manifests itself solely, or even primarily, at the surface of the body' (2009, 2). Despite these broad and multivalent sensational aspirations, however, existing studies have been heavily biased towards the visual. Laura Marks's concept of 'haptic visuality' (2002, xiii) tacitly seems to write sound out of experience. The same could be said of some of the most important books in this field: *The Address of the Eye* (Sobchak 1992), *The Skin of the Film* (L. U. Marks 2000) and *The Tactile Eye* (Barker 2009). Admittedly, 'The Address of the Ears' or 'The Ears of the Film' do not make quite such punchy titles, but if we are interested in multisensory experience in order to 'see the seeing as well as the seen, hear the hearing as well as the heard, and feel the movement as well as see the moved' (Sobchak 1992, 10), then there appears to have been a curiously superficial engagement with the sonic. As if to acknowledge this lack, Sobchak has more recently explored concepts of 'ultra-hearing' and 'ultra-seeing' (2005, 2) in Dolby Digital promotional trailers, although this does remain a rather isolated study.

The central claim I hope to advance is that in haptic film music the ears function like the organs of touch. In fact, more than this, I do not hear solely with my ears, I hear with my whole body. The ears are the main organs of hearing, but not the only ones. Total deafness does not occur since some hearing is achieved through bone conduction. Certain kinds of film music, particularly where there is a high degree of materialized sound, encourage or even demand a more embodied relationship with the audio-viewer. This is partly because of a mimetic connection to what is heard, a coupling of the body with the physical means of production of the sound itself. It is particularly true where instrumental music approximates noise, where materializing sound indices are more apparent. A clear definition of the ontology of noise is, of course, challenging, but here I adopt Greg Hainge's five-point conception which ultimately suggests that 'noise makes us attend to how things come to *exist*, how they come to stand or be (*sistere*) outside of themselves (*ex-*)' (2013, 23; emphasis in original). Hainge argued that noise resists, subsists, coexists, persists and obsists. He moved beyond the conception of noise as a subjective term by highlighting the ways in which it draws attention to its status as noise through material reconfiguration. Most usefully, he argued that there need not be a split between the operations of noise as a philosophical concept and its manifestations in expression; in other words, it is not necessary to separate the ontological from the phenomenological (Hainge 2013, 22).

Existing research has focused on how loud and/or low-frequency sounds permeate or even invade the body. In these cases, specific frequencies and amplitudes deliberately exploit the boundaries between hearing and feeling. Don Ihde explained that when listening to loud rock music, 'the bass notes reverberate in my stomach' (2007, 44). Julian Henriques, likewise, demonstrated how low frequencies and extreme volume are deployed in the reggae dancehall sound system. Henriques argued that, in this musical culture, the visceral quality of the sound results in a hierarchical organization of the senses where sound blocks out rational processes. He described this process as sonic dominance, which

> occurs when and where the sonic medium displaces the usual or normal dominance of the visual medium. With sonic dominance sound has the near monopoly of attention. The aural sensory modality becomes *the* sensory modality rather than one among others of seeing, smelling, touching and tasting.
>
> (Henriques 2003, 452; emphasis in original)

Does sound need to be dominant for it to be experienced haptically? I would argue that haptic perception is still evident in works whose recourse to volume and amplitude is less clearly marked. My focus here is on something more subtle; music does not need to make my whole body shake or beat on my chest for me to feel it. Furthermore, in cinema the interconnecting relationships between sound and visuals do not typically rely on the obliteration of one medium by another: there is unity in the symbiotic creation of the haptic.

Lisa Coulthard's exploration of haptic sound in European new extremism, which is in many ways a close relative of this study, explores low-frequency hums and drones in relation to silence. I wholeheartedly agree with Coulthard's celebration of the corporeal: 'The blurring of noise and music works to construct cinematic bodies that move beyond their filmic confines to settle in shadowed, resounding form in the body of the spectator' (2013, 121). She perceives 'dirtiness' in the sonic imperfections offered by the expanded low-frequency ranges provided by digital exhibition technologies. I share the interest in the blurred boundaries between noise and music, but whereas Coulthard shows how sound both relies on and frustrates the quiet technologies of the digital, I explore how musical noise is tied to material causality and announces its hapticity. My aim, therefore, is partially to rehabilitate instrumental music within recent phenomenological discussions, which I see as an increasingly relevant and important aspect of soundtrack production. I also see this phenomenon as part of a broader aesthetic film-music tradition that reflects an inherent conflict between materialized and de-materialized music and, by extension, between the body and the mind. In seeking to reconcile these concepts, I want to move away from the most obvious physical experiences of loud and low-frequency music, to explore the caress as well as the slap, and to locate gradations of materialized sound.

Sound Affects: *There Will Be Blood*

There Will Be Blood is rich in haptic, visceral experiences. The oil we see and hear bubbling in the ground is like the blood coursing through the veins of the film, ready to erupt at any moment. In an early scene, following the first oil discovery, the camera lens is spattered with the black, viscous substance, threatening to splash through the membrane between the screen and audio-viewer. In celebration of the discovery a worker meta-phorically baptizes his child by rubbing oil on his forehead. These two-dimensional visuals cannot break through the screen, but sound can. The adopted son of protagonist Daniel Plainview, H.W., loses his hearing following an explosion and the audience is sonically placed inside his body, experiencing the muffled and phased sound. We are literally invited to perceive the sound phenomenologically, not just hearing but feeling it in the body. We sense interiority and exteriority simultaneously, the envir-onment within the experience of an other, but also outside it as an experience mediated by an other.

Additionally, Daniel Day Lewis's vocal representation of Plainview is so rough and grainy that it almost seems as if there is sandpaper in his throat. One cannot hear this without a tightening of one's own vocal cords. In a scene where the dubious church pastor, Eli Sunday, exorcizes a parishi-oner's arthritis, he explains that God's breath entered his body 'and my stomach spoke in a whisper, not a shout'. The ensuing guttural appeal, 'get out of here, ghost', repeated by the entire congregation and becoming increasingly more strained, is chilling in the physical immediacy of its impact. Barthes's phenosong is invoked in these vocalizations. The film constantly revels in aural textures that remind us of our own bodily existence and experience. There is much more that could be said about these and other sonic aspects of the film, but my focus here is on the music, which works on a more abstract, but nonetheless potent, level.

Matthew McDonald noted that Greenwood's score is 'exceptional for the overwhelming intensity established during the opening frames and returned to frequently throughout the film' (2012, 215). The music used is extracted from Part One of Greenwood's *Popcorn Superhet Receiver* for string orchestra. The score explores clusters and quarter-tones in the manner of Polish composer Krzysztof Penderecki, an enormous influ-ence on Greenwood. The initial idea was to explore the concept of white noise created by two octaves of quarter-tones and to generate rhythmic material based on clusters, but the non-conformity of the individual players became more important to the composer as the piece developed:

> I started to enjoy these 'mistakes': the small, individual variations amongst players that can make the same cluster sound different every time it's played. So, much of the cluster-heavy material here is very quiet and relies on the individual player's bow changes, or their slight inconsistencies in dynamics, to vary the colour of the chords – and so make illusionary melodies in amongst the fog of white noise.
>
> (Preface to Greenwood 2005)

Example 10.1 Score reduction/representation, *Popcorn Superhet Receiver*, bars 37–9. Music by Jonny Greenwood © 2005. Rights administered worldwide by Faber Music Ltd, London WC1B 3DA. Reproduced by permission of the publishers. All rights reserved.

pp ff pp

Indeed, a single stave is allocated to each of the violins (eighteen), violas (six) and cellos (six) throughout the piece. The four double-basses are divided across two staves. The individual variations or 'mistakes' exploited in the score celebrate the lack of uniformity in an orchestra. Following Alex Ross (see below), McDonald identified a string cluster becoming a contrary-motion glissando and moving towards and away from the pitch F♯ as a distinctive moment in the score (Example 10.1). This glissando is synchronized first with an exterior shot of mountains, subsequently with Plainview crawling out of a mine shaft having broken his leg, and much later in the film with shots of Plainview burying the body of an imposter he has murdered. McDonald argued that the music's connotative function shifts 'from the realm of setting to the realm of character' and he moved towards the idea that the landscape and the individual are connected and inseparable, 'a demonstration that the nature of the westerner is shaped by the nature of the West' (2012, 218).

I want to take this idea a stage further and suggest that it is the connection made between the film's landscape – the metaphorical body of the film – the central character, Plainview, and our own embodied experience that are substantially shaped by the score and constitutes its extraordinary power. That fruitful tension has only been realized subconsciously by some commentators, who have, perhaps understandably, struggled to identify the elusive impact of the music that they find caught in a liminal space between the representation of landscape and the representation of character.

The recurrent glissando passage highlights friction. We feel the massed weight of bows on strings and left-hand tension on the fingerboard as the instrumentalists slide towards and away from the F♯ pitch centre. The sound moves from a 'noisy' state towards pitched 'purity' and then back again, bringing about the reconfiguration of matter that Hainge describes in his ontology of noise. Through this process we become aware of the physical nature of the sound source shifting between materialized and de-materialized effects. The materialized sound, the noisy, dirty music, makes its presence known, keeping us in a state of heightened tension. Friction and vibration are enacted in our bodies and embodied musical listening plays a significant role in our connection to both character and landscape in the film.

In his insightful review in the *New Yorker* (2008), Ross seems partially aware of his own bodily experience but is not fully prepared to make the connection. He argues that the glissandi 'suggest liquid welling up from underground, the accompanying dissonances communicate a kind of interior, inanimate pain'. Whose pain, though? For Ross, this seems to be tied exclusively to character so that the 'monomaniacal unison' tells us about the 'crushed soul of the future tycoon Daniel Plainview'. I suggest that this is also 'pain' that the audience is encouraged to feel through the soundtrack and it belongs as much to them as to environment or character. Ross's presentation of a series of unresolved binary oppositions is most forcefully expressed in his understanding of the music as both 'unearthly' and the 'music of the injured earth'. He gets closest to what I argue when he suggests that filmgoers might find themselves 'falling into a claustrophobic trance' when experiencing these sequences. All of this goes towards, but does not quite enunciate, the audience's embodied connection. The simultaneous interiority and exteriority explains why the music is at once 'terrifying and enrapturing, alien and intimate'.

As I have been suggesting, the landscape in *There Will Be Blood* could be said to be metaphorically alive: the ground bleeds when it is ruptured, it groans and pulses through the use of sound design and music. Equally, Plainview could be seen to be emotionally dead, a walking cadaver, reduced to a series of bodily functions, motivated only by greed. Unsurprisingly, then, notions of burial, emergence, death and rebirth are central to the connection between the body and the land. In a scene in Little Boston, a worker in a mine shaft is accidentally killed by a drill bit that strikes him from above. As his mud-, oil- and blood-spattered body is removed from the shaft, the opening of Greenwood's score for *Smear* (2004) is heard. Here the music emphasizes the space between pitches. The three-line staves in the graphic score (Example 10.2) represent a single whole-tone between concert G and A. Two ondes martenots, a clarinet, horn and string ensemble generate a constantly variable, insecure yet narrowly constrained texture. The fluctuating material is always in a state of becoming, never resting and never locating the pure tone. It is music in the cracks that highlights resistance to fixity, drawing attention to its own internal apparatus.

The cue 'Proven Lands', which is derived from Part 2b of *Popcorn Superhet Receiver*, is heard when Plainview attempts to purchase William Bandy's land in order to allow smooth passage for a pipeline. (The cue's title, and those given below, are as they appear on the soundtrack album, Nonesuch 7559-79957-8.) Travelling with his imposter brother, Plainview undertakes a levelling survey and we are shown a series of breathtakingly beautiful landscape shots. The music, however, has a kinetic energy that belies the purely functional nature of the surveying task. The upper strings are required to strum

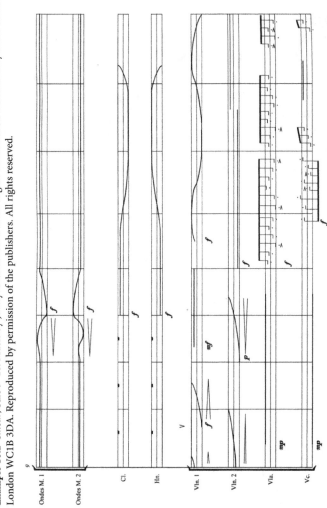

Example 10.2 *Smear*, bars 9–16. Music by Jonny Greenwood © 2004. Rights administered worldwide by Faber Music Ltd, London WC1B 3DA. Reproduced by permission of the publishers. All rights reserved.

rapid and relentless muted quaver pizzicati using guitar plectra, enhancing the clipped and percussive nature of the sound. The double-basses repeatedly slap the fingerboard and play pizzicato glissandi. The primary characteristic of this music is the dynamic exposure of the physicality of its source, the focus on human motor action. When we hear it, I suggest, the neuromuscular system is activated sympathetically. It generates motion, or the simulation of motion, within us. This concept reflects current research within neuroscience, particularly in relation to mirror neurones (for example, Mukamel *et al.* 2010), which suggests that neurones are fired in the brain not only when humans act but also when they experience the same action performed by others. It is primarily an empathetic mode that may help us understand or make connections to others. An embodied mode of film scoring may, in turn, help us to engage directly with characters and/or narrative.

One of the film's most striking cues follows a gusher blowout where a derrick is consumed in flames. The subsequent attempt to put out the fire, intercut with H. W.'s hearing loss ('I can't hear my voice'), is accompanied by a relentlessly visceral five-minute cue. The music is adapted from Greenwood's track 'Convergence', which was originally composed for the film *Bodysong*. This documentary about human life, from birth to death, was constructed from clips of archive footage taken from more than one hundred years of film history. Given the direction of my argument, it hardly seems surprising that a film about the human body would generate music for use in *There Will Be Blood*. The piece is dominated by a recurrent anacrustic-downbeat combination played by the bass, a repetitive, punchy 'boom boom … boom boom' pattern. Over this, using the same simple rhythmic cell, various untuned percussion instruments generate polyrhythmic, chaotic clutter that constantly shifts in and out of phase. The recurrent patterns here, obviously, resemble a heartbeat, or multiple heartbeats, or perhaps also the mechanism of the drill in an emphatic organic/inorganic axis. Ben Winters (2008) noted the recurrent trope and importance of the heartbeat in film soundtracks, which he perceived as effective at helping us experience fictional fear in the context of own fear-inducing corporeality. In this sequence the score sets the heart racing and generates heightened and enacted excitement.

The intensity of the cue is further enhanced by some significant additions and modifications to the original 'Convergence' music. Greenwood superimposes the string orchestra, playing nervous, rapid figurations, clusters, and 'noisy' and 'dirty' textures. The low strings are especially materialized, generating growling glissandi, with aggressive bow strokes that slice, razor-like, through the frenzied texture. The bass pattern is enhanced digitally with beefed-up and distorted low frequencies enhancing the mimetic thumping, but as the camera tracks into a close-up of Plainview's face towards the end of the sequence, the music is gradually filtered, reducing the high frequencies and making a more internal sound, the rhythm as felt inside the body. The relentless rhythmic drive in the scene is, therefore, narratively subsumed into Plainview's body, but it is also by extension subsumed into our bodies as it mimetically regulates the heartbeat, another form of embodied interiority and connection. The incorporeal of Plainview's screen body is enacted through the music in our bodies. This could partially explain the curious fascination with the odious character: when we observe Plainview we also experience a tiny part of ourselves.

The examples derived from Greenwood's pre-existing scores demonstrate the importance of the role of the director and the music editor in the selection and use of aural materials. Greenwood also composed music specifically for the film, but did not write music directly to picture and instead provided a range of pieces that were spotted, edited and re-configured: 'Only a couple of the parts were written for specific scenes. I was happier writing lots of music for the film/story, and having PTA [Paul Thomas Anderson] fit some of it to the film' (Nonesuch Records 2007). Unlike most soundtrack composers, Greenwood found that he 'had real luxury' (Nialler9 2011) in not being expected to hit specific cue points or to write around dialogue. He was given free rein to write large amounts of music with specific scenes only vaguely in mind. This working approach seems to have resulted in several striking combinations of music and image. It is noteworthy, however, that the purely 'original' music for the film is much less materialized and more traditional in its construction (for example, cues such as 'Open Spaces' and 'Prospector Arrives').

The materiality in *There Will Be Blood* reflects the fluidity of the collaborative method, the clear directorial selection of musical materials and the relative inexperience of the composer, a potent mixture resulting in the disregard for certain scoring conventions and 'rules'. The choices made by the director, editor and composer, especially in the use of pre-existing music and modified pre-existing music, contribute to a striking embodied experience. Writing in *Rolling Stone*, Peter Travis explained that the first time he saw the film he 'felt gut-punched' (2008). The instrumental music is fundamental in generating much of the hapticity that is a marker of the profound impact of the film and its score.

Incorporeality Regained: *The Master*

There are many surface similarities between *There Will Be Blood* and *The Master*. The films are both about pioneers, dysfunctional families, the roots of American modernity, manifestations of nihilism and conflicts between the evangelical and the entrepreneurial. They are both astonishing and detailed character studies. In *The Master*, the frontier landscape of *There Will Be Blood* is partially replaced by the sea. Musically, however, we appear to be in the same territory, but this is only initially the case. Greenwood's pre-existing orchestral music is once again employed, and we hear two movements, 'Baton Sparks' and 'Overtones', from *48 Responses to Polymorphia* (2011). This piece is a homage to Penderecki's *Polymorphia* (1961), composed during his so-called sonoristic period, where the focus on textural sound masses and timbral morphology provided a new means of expression (Mirka 1997, 2000). It is prophetic that the composer of *Threnody for the Victims of Hiroshima* (1960) is a shadowed presence in a film that opens on an island in the South Pacific on V-J Day 1945. We might, therefore, expect materiality to be centralized in the score for *The Master*. Yet, despite several initial glimpses of a visceral mode of scoring, this music soon gives way to something more 'refined'.

The opening shot of the sea is accompanied by an aggressive, if brief, Bartókian string passage – the initial gestures from 'Baton Sparks' – but this soon recedes into a series of slow suspended harmonies reminiscent of Barber's *Adagio for Strings* (1936). Images of demob-happy naval officers wrestling on a beach and the inappropriate actions of the sex-obsessed protagonist, Freddie Quell, contain the strongest indication of the embodied musical potential in the score. *Col legno* low strings and a jazz-inspired bass spring around a solo violin playing jerky and scratchy gestures. The score for *The Master* begins where *There Will Be Blood* left off, promising a materialized aesthetic, but this is not what is ultimately delivered.

As the story progresses, particularly after we have been introduced to Lancaster Dodd, the leader of a movement known as The Cause, the music takes on a bittersweet, ironic quality. For example, the music derived from 'Overtones', which is first heard at a wedding on board a boat, contains lush string movement based around white-note clusters and artificial harmonics. It is almost too sweet and cloying, perhaps suggesting that Dodd is not to be trusted. There is clearly still a degree of materiality in the construction of the score, with a characteristic use of indeterminacy (Example 10.3). Greenwood employs I.R.I. tremolos, which he describes as 'Independent, Random and Intermittent notes added to a held pitch – like a fingered tremolo but with only occasional use of the second note' (2011, 15). However, the music does not emphasize noise, rather it generates a beautiful, gossamer-like harmonic texture revolving around C major, which could easily float away in the sea air. In Hainge's ontological taxonomy, the potentially 'noisy' elements in this construction do not challenge: they coexist harmoniously and centralize musicality rather than critiquing it. The potential 'noise' is not a by-product of expression but central to the expressive harmonic content. To be sure, this is not standard mainstream

Example 10.3 'Overtones' from *48 Responses to Polymorphia*, bars 22–9, fluttery textures and bitter-sweet harmonies. Music by Jonny Greenwood © 2011. Rights administered worldwide by Faber Music Ltd, London WC1B 3DA. Reproduced by permission of the publishers. All rights reserved.

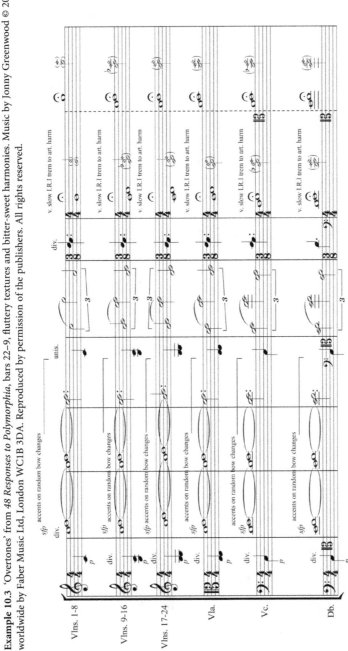

film-music fare either, but equally it does not focus the audio-viewer's attention on material sensation as was the case in *There Will Be Blood*.

Significantly, the more heavily materialized sound-mass sections from *48 Responses to Polymorphia* – such as the first half of 'Overtones' – the moments that resonate most closely with Pendercki's sonoristic musical language, have not been deployed in *The Master*. It is the sections with fewer materializing effects, the pitch-biased and harmonically rich music, that are used to support narrative representation. The choices made by the director, editor and composer in the use of pre-existing music function in this score much more like traditional film music.

The same is true of a good deal of the music Greenwood composed specially for the film. In a scene where Freddie Quell finds himself on board the Master's boat and begins to learn the methods of The Cause, the music employs impressionistic gestures and patterns as a reflection of the journey ('Alethia' on the soundtrack album, Nonesuch 532292–2). Quell is adrift metaphorically and physically: he listens to a recording of Dodd explaining how man is 'not an animal'; he observes a regression therapy session; he attempts to attract the attention of a woman to whom he has never spoken by writing 'do you want to fuck' on a piece of paper and presenting it to her. The cue is entitled 'Back Beyond' and the chamber ensemble, featuring clarinet and harp, bears some resemblance in harmonic structure and orchestration to Ravel's *Introduction and Allegro* (1905). The modal vacil-lation, blurred and layered harmony, and consistent use of arpeggios reflect the unpredictability of the sea and the aimless drifting of the protagonist. This music is concerned less with materiality than a series of harmonic extensions built above the D♭ home pitch. It leads to the moment when Dodd begins a series of disquieting psychological questions designed to unearth Quell's past traumas.

Later, when Quell supports Dodd in promoting his new book, *The Split Saber*, the score features a series of suspended F♯ diminished-seventh chords resolving onto C♯ major. The homophonic yearning created by the intimate chamber ensemble could easily be located within the rich panoply of film music's harmonic heritage. Towards the end of the film, Quell takes another boat journey, this time across the Atlantic, in order to be reunited briefly with Dodd. Here the E minor harmonies generate a traditional tonal hier-archy, with particular prominence given to the dominant seventh and its tonic resolution. This suggests greater clarity, perhaps some degree of finality on Quell's part – an effective way to indicate character progression through harmonic development. It is music rich in expressive harmonic potential, but not rich in its use of materializing sound indices.

One way of reading this softening of the connection between materiality and causality is that Greenwood had learned to become a 'proper' film composer by the time he worked on *The Master*, following his experiences on *Norwegian Wood* (2010) and *We Need to Talk About Kevin* (2011). The experiments undertaken in *There Will Be Blood* became more refined, less resistant and thus assimilated into a mainstream system. If it takes an outsider to question the normative model, the successful outsider also eventually becomes part of the formatting of the new system. Tempting though it is to pursue this interpretation, it is only partially true. We have already seen how the decision to focus on materialized sound is frequently encapsulated in the pre-existing music of *There Will Be Blood* and is, therefore, closely tied to the decisions of the director and music editor. *The Master*'s pre-existent music is much less materialized. Indeed, voices from the past in the form of Ella Fitzgerald's 'Get thee Behind Me Satan' (Irving Berlin, 1936), Helen Forrest's 'Changing Partners' (Larry Coleman and Joe Darion, 1953) and Jo Stafford's 'No Other Love' (Paul Weston and Bob Russell, 1950) suggest an important role for nostalgic reverie, rather than materialized sensation.

The distinction I attempt to articulate here may simply say as much about the narrative and aesthetic differences between the two films as anything else. This in turn affects the function and purpose of both scores. Whereas *There Will Be Blood* worked hard to make the audience feel each moment, *The Master* focuses on internal memory. Dodd's methods centralize the idea of past-life regression, recalling memories from before birth, as a beneficial and healing process. Freddie is a veteran suffering from nostalgia. The film constantly delves into the past and into the recesses of the mind. Anderson has suggested that Quell could be understood as 'a ghost' (Hogan 2012), a man who is both dead and alive. Indeed, it could be argued that the soundtrack, much like Quell himself, is an apparition, an intangible construct of the mind. In *There Will Be Blood*, Plainview is also dead, in a way, but the music brings him purposefully to life through landscape. Conversely, in *The Master* Quell's impulsive and animalistic acts of violence (such as strangling a customer in a department store or smashing a toilet in a jail cell) are never accompanied by any musical score.

If we accept the conceptual framework of Cartesian dualism, then the aesthetic positioning of the two scores reflects a shift of focus from the body to the mind. In *Principles of Philosophy* (1644), René Descartes gave the first systematic account of the interaction between the mind and body. He discriminated between mental and material 'substances', arguing that they were distinctive and excluded each other, but he also suggested that the body causally affected the mind and the mind causally affected the body. The two films centralize material substance and mental substance respectively, a move away from texture, form, location and weight towards images, emotions, beliefs and desires. Whereas the representation of the land and Plainview in *There Will Be Blood* emphasized material embodiment, Quell and Dodd in *The Master* reflect the ethereal workings of memory.

I do not wish to suggest for one moment that *The Master* does not contain effective film music, or that it lacks narrative engagement, simply that its materiality is not as foregrounded as in *There Will Be Blood*. Some hapticity in *The Master* may be located, as Claudia Gorbman has suggested (2015), in Philip Seymour Hoffman's varied and virtuosic vocal representation of Lancaster Dodd. In any case, there is a clear difference in the material nature of the two film scores, which invites us to identify and understand distinct approaches to the use of materializing effects.

Conclusions

Chion's materializing sound indices, though previously considered solely in relation to sound design, could be used to describe the aesthetic and embodied differences between the instrumental scores for *There Will Be Blood* and *The Master*. *There Will Be Blood* attempts to engage the audio-viewer by infiltrating the body as a means of reaching the mind. *The Master*, instead, focuses primarily on the mind as the main narrative space of the film, and constantly scrutinizes memory.

By aligning Chion's theory with phenomenology, we are able to understand the contents of aural cinematic experience as they are lived, not as we have typically learned to conceive and describe them. Indeed, a sliding scale of materiality could be a useful tool in exploring a range of film scores. Within this context, we could argue that Greenwood is a more 'material' composer than many others. Yet, there are also distinctions in his methods and approaches based on narrative context, collaborative relationships, interactions with pre-existing music and so on.

This chapter has attempted to re-establish a connection between the haptic and the aural, so that our understanding of instrumental film scoring is no longer unnecessarily disembodied. A phenomenological approach could usefully re-materialize our objects of perception. Indeed, if we were to re-evaluate some significant moments in film-music history using this conceptual framework and sliding scale, we might more fully understand the extraordinary visceral impact of Bernard Herrmann's score for *Psycho* (1960) or of John Williams's for *Jaws* (1975). This is film music that remains powerful to this day, in no small part because of its embodied qualities. Noise need not be understood as a by-product of the filmmaking process, or as a danger to the integrity of the body, or as a force to be attenuated. Some film scores feature prominent materialized elements that directly attempt to stimulate the material layers of the human being. There are modes of instrumental scoring where there is an abundance of materializing sound indices and we can simultaneously feel as much as we hear.

PART THREE

Genre and Idiom

11 Film Noir and Music

DAVID BUTLER

Film noir is one of the most potent and influential cultural categories to emerge in the twentieth century, following its initial appearance in the Hollywood cinema of the 1940s and 1950s. That influence has reached far beyond film; and the noir 'mediascape', as James Naremore (2008, 254–77) has termed it, now takes in television, photography, painting, fashion, literature, comic books, video games and, especially, music. Charlie Haden's ensemble Quartet West, John Zorn's *Naked City* (1990), Sandra Lawrence's *Noiresque* project, the singer Laura Ellis (the 'Femme Fatale of Jazz'), Pumajaw's *Song Noir* (2014), Guy Barker's 2002 work *Sounds in Black and White* ('a film noir for jazz ensemble') and John Adams's thirty-minute symphony *City Noir* (2009) are only some of the musical manifestations of film noir as a source of inspiration. These latter-day responses to film noir are less concerned with a faithful recreation of the kind of music that was featured in the original films noirs of the 1940s and 1950s and engage more with the idea of film noir and what that sounds (or sounded) like. As Adams has commented,

> *City Noir* was first suggested by my reading the so-called 'Dream' books by Kevin Starr, a brilliantly imagined, multi-volume cultural and social history of California . . . Starr chronicles the tenor and milieu of the late '40s and early '50s as it was expressed in the sensational journalism of the era and in the dark, eerie chiaroscuro of the Hollywood films that have come to define the period sensibility for us . . . Those images and their surrounding aura whetted my appetite for an orchestral work that, while not necessarily referring to the soundtracks of those films, might nevertheless evoke a similar mood and feeling tone of the era. I was also stimulated by the notion that there indeed exists a bona fide genre of jazz-inflected symphonic music, a fundamentally American orchestral style and tradition that goes back as far as the early 1920s (although, truth to tell, it was a Frenchman, Darius Milhaud, who was the first to realize its potential with his 1923 ballet *La création du monde*).   (Adams 2009, 2)

Adams's comments underline the fact that the cultural memory and idea of film noir (or jazz-inflected symphonic music, for that matter) is not necessarily in keeping with the actuality of the films and their music.

   None of this haziness around the 'facts' of film noir should be surprising given that film noir is one of the most contentious terms in film to define. Studies of film noir have referred to it variously as a genre, a mood, a cycle or a movement, ranging from a body of films responding to a specific socio-historical moment (the United States in the 1940s and 1950s) to something more culturally, temporally and geographically diffuse, with Naremore (2013, xix) advocating the word 'category' as the most appropriate to encapsulate these differing stances. The term 'film noir' was first applied by French critics such as Nino Frank to a wave of Hollywood movies which arrived in France following the end of the Second World War. These films were typically urban crime dramas with an emphasis on murder and seduction, featuring the quintessential noir figures of the vulnerable male protagonist (often an investigator) and the sexualized femme fatale, with a dark tone often characterized by cynicism and fatalism. The first major study of film noir was Raymond Borde's and Etienne Chaumeton's 1955 book *Panorama du Film Noir Américain*; and, following in their footsteps, later scholarship would seek to pin down, control and define the parameters of film noir and its formal properties. Alain Silver asserts that 'if observers of *film noir* agree on anything, it is on the boundaries of the classic period, which begins in 1941 with *The Maltese Falcon* and ends less than a score of years later with *Touch of Evil* [1958]' (1996, 11). Yet that agreement is no longer so assured (if it ever was). Although there is much to be said for the parameters Silver mentions, they would exclude a late entry like *Odds Against Tomorrow* (1959), which has impeccable noir credentials, not least in terms of its music.

More recent work on film noir and the concept of genre has complicated the earlier claims of clear-cut boundaries and definitions (see, for example, Bould 2013), with Sheri Chinen Biesen (2014) discussing how the noir ethos spread beyond the black and white crime dramas of the 1940s and informed colour musicals such as *Words and Music* (1948), with Gene Kelly choreographing and featuring in the 'Slaughter on Tenth Avenue' jazz-inflected ballet sequence scored by Richard Rodgers; *The Band Wagon* (1953) and its 'Girl Hunt Ballet – A Murder Mystery in Jazz'; or *A Star is Born* (1954). But this awareness of noir's porousness and seepage into disparate genres has not deterred some academics from attempting to identify, as Richard Ness does, a 'specific sound' for film noir – a musical equivalent to what might be considered the essential or trademark visual, thematic and narrative traits of film noir. For Ness (2008, 52–4), these features include: a defiance of the tonal tradition of classical Hollywood scoring through the use of dissonance and atonality; an avoidance of European-influenced, neo-romantic music in favour of a more modernistic, 'urban' American sound using contemporary techniques and popular musical idioms; the breakdown of traditional diegetic/nondiegetic distinctions; the use of unusual instrumentation and experimental recording techniques; a decrease in the amount of music and a move towards smaller ensembles and selective instrumentation rather than a full orchestra; and the use of musical fragments rather than fully developed melodies.

There is no denying the presence of these traits in a number of noir scores from the 'classic' era of the 1940s and 1950s: for example, Johnny Mandel's music for *I Want to Live!* (1958), Jerry Goldsmith's for *City of Fear* (1959) and John Lewis's for *Odds Against Tomorrow* all exemplify Ness's claims about the noir 'sound'. But they were far from exclusive to film noir. High levels of dissonance are prominent in Bernard Herrmann's score for the Victorian gothic chiller *Hangover Square* (1945), and all of the traits identified by Ness, apart from the use of popular idioms, are in Herrmann's innovative score for the science-fiction film *The Day the Earth Stood Still* (1951). Similarly, there are instances of noir scores from the classic era which do not correspond with the majority of Ness's features. Max Steiner's score for *The Big Sleep* (1946), steeped in the principles of late nineteenth-century orchestral romanticism, and Perry Botkin's for *Murder by Contract* (1958), which is a showcase for Botkin's pop-based solo multi-tracked electric guitar, are two examples from opposite ends of the classic era of film noir which embrace conventional tonality and extended melody. From the more conventional orchestral work of Steiner to the jarring dissonances of Miklós Rózsa and the jazz-inflected scores of the 1950s, there was no one uniform approach to the use of music in film noir, and some of the varying approaches would result in fresh directions in mainstream film music.

Early Noir Scores and Orchestral Innovations

The search for origins in a category as contested and amorphous as film noir is far from straightforward. Alain Silver's and Elizabeth Ward's encyclopaedic guide to film noir (1992) identifies *Stranger on the Third Floor* (1940) as 'the first true film noir' (Porfirio 1992, 269) in terms of its stylistic and thematic content, with its emphasis on crime and a critique of American institutions (the criminal justice system) as well as sequences that display the influence of German expressionism. This visual expressionism is paralleled by Roy Webb's score which, as Roger Hickman summarizes, employs 'angular melodies, strident harmonies, and colorful orchestration, including a harp and wavers produced by a vibraphone and electric organ' (2009, 166) for the film's vivid nightmare sequence. *Stranger on the Third Floor* thus underlines two of the ways in which film noir was deemed to be distinct from the dominant tendencies in Hollywood cinema at that time. David Bordwell, Janet Staiger and Kristin Thompson identify four traits of film noir at odds with mainstream Hollywood practice, including an 'attack on the motivated happy ending' and a 'criticism of classical technique' (1985, 76). By 1940, classical technique in Hollywood film scoring favoured extensive orchestral music informed by late nineteenth-century romanticism, prominent character motifs and a commitment to ensuring narrative comprehension and emotional engagement with the protagonist(s) and the dramatic situation. If Webb's score for *Stranger on the Third Floor* pointed anxiously to different approaches to Hollywood film music (which he would continue to explore throughout the 1940s in both film noir and horror), the following year would see the release of a film with a much more overt rejection of classical technique, taking in all aspects of its audio-visual style, including its score by Herrmann: Orson Welles's *Citizen Kane* (1941).

The influence of Welles's first movie on film noir is something of a given in contemporary noir criticism. Robert Porfirio acknowledges that, although it stands outside the noir cycle, '*Citizen Kane* remains the key proto-noir in so far as it signaled a break with the classic studio film which opened the way for the film noir', and that the film 'provided a virtual palimpsest of film noir's intertext' (2013, 22–3). Herrmann's score – his first for film – ushered in not just *Citizen Kane* but an approach to starting a film which would be taken up by numerous films noirs of the classic era. Classical Hollywood films of the 1930s and 1940s tended to begin with the respective studio's fanfare followed by lush upbeat title music designed to welcome the audience into the film (sometimes irrespective of the narrative's actual content), and there was little if any visual embellishment beyond the title cards for the cast and crew. *Citizen Kane* dispensed with this standard approach, jettisoning the studio fanfare and title sequence in favour of an enigmatic and brooding prelude, evocative of a gothic fairytale and reinforced by Herrmann's sombre and *misterioso* scoring for low-register brass, woodwind and vibraphone as we are drawn slowly but surely towards Kane's deathbed in the mansion of Xanadu.

Citizen Kane's influence is evident in the title sequence for Edward Dmytryk's *Murder, My Sweet* (UK title *Farewell, My Lovely*; 1944), like *Kane*, also made at RKO. An overhead, high-angle camera cranes inexorably down (reminiscent of the slow pull into the world of *Kane*) towards a table around which are sat several men whose faces we cannot make out: the protagonist Philip Marlowe is under interrogation by the police. Following an initial fanfare for the RKO logo, Webb's score accompanies this visual intrigue (who are the men round the table?) with a taut cue featuring anxious writing for orchestra as various motifs strive to develop then subside. An early orchestral statement of what will become Marlowe's motif falls away and the music appears to lose a sense of progression before a three-note phrase, which will soon be revealed as belonging to the giant ex-con Moose Malloy, is repeated insistently, growing louder and louder until it segues into a stronger statement of Marlowe's theme. The musical flow dissipates again, however, and Marlowe's interrogation becomes audible. Throughout this sequence there has been one musical constant: a sustained high-pitched wavering tone which invests the film from the start with an uneasy tension, not always foregrounded but ever-present on the edge of perception. For Roger Hickman (2009, 173), the prominent use of wavers would become one of the 'most distinctive characteristics' of the noir musical style, despite acknowledging that the diversity of film noir makes a precise definition of that style extremely difficult. The insistent repetition of Malloy's motif also establishes the character's obsessive search for his lost sweetheart with the three-note motif paralleling the three syllables which form his driving concern, 'Where's Velma?' This combination of psychological insight and anxiety in the title sequence of *Murder, My Sweet* would become one of the features of the composer who has been described as 'the voice of film noir' (Horton 1995, 2), Miklós Rózsa.

Rózsa's first noir score, for Billy Wilder's *Double Indemnity* (1944), opens with a doom-laden dirge and features a level of dissonance which was rare in Hollywood film music at that time, a decision justified by Rózsa because of the unpleasant nature of the film and its characters, but one that did not meet with the approval of Paramount's musical director, Louis Lipstone. Rózsa's noir credentials were assured, however, through a series of films in which his aggressive title cues for staccato brass and timpani would provide unusually brutal openings. *The Killers* (1946), *Brute Force* (1947) and *The Asphalt Jungle* (1950) all receive violent title cues in keeping with the fate of their respective protagonists. In *The Killers*, Rózsa's cue as the Swede waits implacably in bed at the start of the film for the eponymous assassins to burst into his dingy apartment and end his life is one of the most characteristic of noir's fatalistic ethos. Stripped of any hints of romanticism, the score is reduced to a bleak drone for brass that is only broken when the door opens and the bullets fly. Rózsa's noir phase ran from 1944 to 1950 and included less typical pictures such as the rural noir *The Red House* (1947), which offered him even more scope for psychological scoring through Edward G. Robinson's guilt-ridden character, Pete Morgan. Lyrical pastoral cues offset Rózsa's more characteristic noir brass dissonances (with tritones employed in the motif for the Red House, the site of Pete's guilt and shame) and a combination of theremin – which Rózsa had brought to prominence in Hollywood with his earlier scores for Wilder's *The Lost Weekend* (1945) and Hitchcock's *Spellbound* (1945) – and female choir convey the 'screams in the night' that haunt Pete and, ultimately, drive him to self-destruction. If *The Red House* underlines Rózsa's and film noir's versatility, three of his more representative noir projects – *The Killers, Brute Force* and *The Naked City* (1948), all for producer Mark Hellinger – would, following Hellinger's untimely death in late 1947, be brought together by Rózsa into a twenty-minute concert work, titled *The Mark Hellinger Suite* (1948) and otherwise known as 'Background to Murder', demonstrating a recognition on Rózsa's part of the importance of these films to his career.

Composers like Rózsa and Webb provided the edgy scores that one would expect to be a feature of film noir, but it would be wrong to suggest that these were the only approaches to scoring film noir in the 1940s. Steiner's roots in romanticism and preference for tonal scoring are very much to the fore in his work for *Mildred Pierce* (1945) and *The Big Sleep*, with a jaunty motif in the latter seemingly at odds with Humphrey Bogart's cynical Marlowe, and bursts of mickey-mousing (such as the harp glissando as Carmen falls into Marlowe's arms, or the xylophone glissando as a henchman leaps over a hedge before the film's climactic shootout) doing much, whether intentionally or not, to lighten the film's noir atmosphere. More characteristic of film noir was Herrmann, whose preferred dramatic themes of 'romantic obsession, isolation and the ultimate release of death' (S. C. Smith 1991, 219) would seem to have made him the perfect composer for the idiom. In the event, Herrmann provided only one score for a 'genuine' film noir during the classic era, *On Dangerous Ground* (1952), but it does not disappoint. Herrmann's willingness to employ unusual instrumentation is reflected in the score's use of a viola d'amore and steel plate, representing the film's duality of love and hate. The cold, hard and percussive steel emphasizes the pent-up rage and self-hate within Robert Ryan's character, Sergeant Jim Wilson, and in one instance provides the sound of off-screen police brutality, suggesting that Wilson has assaulted a suspect, an act which the Production Code Administration would not have allowed to be shown directly. Elsewhere, Herrmann excels in conveying Wilson's isolation within the city, scoring the scene in Wilson's spartan flat for solo muted trumpet with a suggestion of jazz phrasing, backed by restrained mid-register strings and harp. In a similar vein, David Raksin concludes *Force of Evil* (1948) with hints of jazz saxophone as the main character descends to the bottom of New York City to find the dead brother he had failed to support washed up on the shore. Both of these moments gesture towards jazz and the mythology of the jazz soloist as an alienated social outsider, but it would not be until the later 1950s that changes in American society, jazz and the Hollywood studio system would enable those gestures to become fully-fledged noir scores.

Jazz and Film Noir

The presence of jazz in film noir has become something of a given for many accounts of the essential or iconic elements of these films, informing both

academic studies and popular memory. Fred Pfeil (1993, 229) includes
'lurid jazzy bars' among the 'constitutive features' of film noir, a view
echoed by Biesen's claim that 'film noir was noted for its smoky jazz
bars' and 'embraced jazz' (2014, 2). Jon Tuska identifies the presence of
a jazz band as one of the 'traditional characteristics of visual noir' (1984,
214) and James Ursini makes a similar observation that jazz and blues are
'traditional signifiers in noir' (1996, 281). Yet these accounts of the presence of jazz in film noir are complicated by John Orr's reminder that
'African-American music has been conspicuously missing from the soundtrack of noir movies' (1993, 179). Racism and the segregated nature of
much of the United States at the time meant that the status of jazz as
a music of predominantly black origin would make it ideologically uncomfortable for it to be featured prominently by the major Hollywood studios
during the 1940s, especially the emerging idiom of bebop with its intellec-
tualism, before the Civil Rights movement had gained momentum in the
mid-1950s. Even in a film like the noir-inflected melodrama *Young Man
with a Horn* (1950), which features (for the era) a relatively progressive
portrayal of a black jazz musician – in the form of Art Hazzard (Juano
Hernandez) teaching his white mentee, Rick Martin (Kirk Douglas), how
to improve as a jazz trumpeter – racial concerns would shape the film's use
and portrayal of jazz. An internal Warner Bros. memo from 1947 advised
that a nightclub scene be staged 'so that Rick does not sit in and play with
the colored musicians. He might play from the floor or the colored boys
can leave the stand and he play solo on the stand. You understand the
reason for this and we must make the change now so that it does not creep
into the script' (quoted in D. Butler 2002, 46). Orr's reminder thus cuts
through the cultural memory and idea of what film noir sounded like,
raising the question of what kind of jazz (if any) was actually featured in
these films from the 1940s and 1950s and underlining the crucial factor of
race, which would do so much to determine both how and what kind of
jazz was used in film noir. There is a clear tension between the memory or
fantasy of film noir and the reality of the films, a fact that Robert Miklitsch
is careful to acknowledge when he refers to the 'lone saxophone soaring
into the night' as being part of the 'real and phantasmatic' imaginary of
film noir (2009, 28).

That imaginary has been stimulated further by a discursive surround
and related cultural texts such as the 'crime jazz', which flourished in the
private-eye shows that proliferated on American television in the late
1950s as the classic era of noir in cinema drew to a close. Henry
Mancini's music for *Peter Gunn* (NBC, 1958–61), featuring leading jazz
musicians like Shelly Manne, was the most prominent example of a model
of walking bass and hi-hat-backed big-band scores that was taken up by

other crime shows such as *Richard Diamond: Private Detective* (CBS, 1957–60), *M Squad* (NBC, 1957–60), *Mickey Spillane's Mike Hammer* (syndicated, 1957–60), *Naked City* (ABC, 1958–63) and *Johnny Staccato* (NBC, 1959–60), the last starring John Cassavetes as a jazz pianist and private eye with a rousing title theme by Elmer Bernstein, and with Manne, the quintessential drummer in the noir television shows and films of the 1950s, at the drums once again. The jazz-noir cultural connection could be traced even earlier, however, to examples like the 1948 black and white jazz photography of Herman Leonard, featuring prominent jazz musicians such as Dizzy Gillespie, Charlie Parker and Dexter Gordon in a visual style shared with the low-key, high-contrast cinematography that was a trademark of many of the films noirs being released at the time. Indeed, some of the most celebrated jazz films of the era, such as *Jammin' the Blues* (1944) and *Jazz Dance* (1954), incorporated a visual style which would not have been out of place in a film noir. As the co-director of *Jazz Dance*, Roger Tilton, noted, 'certain technical choices were instantly recognized to be most suitable for the pictorialization of jazz music. Black and white film ... Low key, high contrast lighting ... sharp staccato cuts' (1956, 19). Tilton's summary corresponds perfectly with Janey Place and Lowell Peterson's seminal essay on the 'anti-traditional' visual motifs of film noir used to convey the noir worldview of 'claustrophobia, paranoia, despair and nihilism' (1996 [1974], 65).

How, then, was jazz used in film noir of the classic era? It is certainly true that there are significant uses of jazz in classic film noir and that jazz was integrated into film noir far more extensively than in other films of the era. Yet it would not be accurate to say that jazz dominated the soundtracks of these films and was a constant of film noir. Jazz musicians are on screen or audible in the soundtrack in only 30 of the 302 films listed in Silver's and Ward's fulsome encyclopedia of film noir (1992), a mere 10 per cent of classic noir (see D. Butler 2002, 20–4). During the 1940s, jazz was only hinted at in a film's score – a touch of muted brass, bluesy saxophone or suggestion of rhythmic swing but little that was developed or sustained. Instead, jazz features in 1940s noir as source music via a band playing in a club or on a jukebox or record player. In many of these instances, jazz is linked in some way with the demise of an on-screen character and is frequently a metaphor for sex or violence. Drawing on well-established associations between jazz, sex and violence informed by racist beliefs about African-American culture which connected the rhythms of jazz with notions of primitivism – 'jazz originally was the accompaniment of the voodoo dancer, stimulating the half-crazed barbarian to the vilest deeds' (Anne Shaw Faulkner, quoted in *ibid.*, 38) – jazz was often used in film noir to bypass the restrictions of the Production Code Administration.

Memorable uses of jazz as source music include the sexualized after-hours jam-session drum solo in *Phantom Lady* (1944); the boxer Stoker Thompson having his fighting hand beaten to a pulp in an alleyway as a jazz drum solo from a nearby club provides the sound of the assault in *The Set-Up* (1949); Rick Martin accompanying Doris Day's pop vocals on the trumpet at the climax of *Young Man with a Horn*, and confirming his death as a creative jazz musician no longer committed to his art; criminal mastermind Doc Riedenschneider being mesmerized by a teenage girl dancing in a diner to a boppish big-band number by André Previn as the cops close in to arrest him in *The Asphalt Jungle*; and a bebop drum solo by Manne being turned into a torture device in *The Big Combo* (1955). Other musical idioms featured in striking instances of source music – nowhere more so than the erotic perversity generated by the use of the 'Venusberg' sequence from Wagner's *Tannhaüser* (1845), its libretto emphasizing the sequence's sexual delirium, playing on a record as the fascistic prison captain in *Brute Force* attacks a Jewish prisoner in his office; but it was jazz rather than classical music that would most frequently take on this metaphorical role as the sound of off-screen sex and violence.

A number of factors contributed to the greater use of jazz in the film scores of the 1950s: the growing status of jazz as an art music; white musicians, composers and arrangers becoming more active in modern jazz; the decline of the Hollywood studio system and the emergence of more independent production companies; and financial concerns over the cost of larger orchestras fuelled by falling audience numbers in the face of the spread of television. The breakthrough of Alex North's jazz-inflected music for *A Streetcar Named Desire* (1951) – with jazz-based cues such as 'Lust' reinforcing the sexual connotations of jazz in Hollywood film music – was followed by jazz-inflected films like *Private Hell 36* (1954) with its modernist score by Leith Stevens, *The Big Combo* with a score by David Raksin, and the Elmer Bernstein-scored *Sweet Smell of Success* (1957), which featured the Chico Hamilton Quintet, all of which furthered the connection between jazz and film noir. These scores tended to have a limited use (if any) of improvisation: as jazz musician and film composer Johnny Mandel put it in 1967, 'if you let a man improvise . . . he may build a climax in his solo at a point where you don't want it for dramatic reasons' (Lees 2011 [1967], 325). But a clutch of crime-based films from France with scores by US jazz musicians like Art Blakey, Miles Davis and John Lewis would prove that improvisation could be incorporated effectively into a film's score. Although Mandel's score for *I Want to Live!* made a greater use of jazz idioms than earlier Hollywood film scores, it was Lewis's 'Third Stream' score for *Odds Against Tomorrow* that really pushed the boundaries for the use of jazz in Hollywood film scoring. Lewis's score avoids the clichés of Hollywood's prevailing use of jazz, which is all the more remarkable given that the film includes a seduction scene and a crime milieu that might have encouraged such stereotypes. There is no saxophone section (preventing the typical sexual connotations of the jazz saxophone in Hollywood from taking root in the film), no use of jazz rhythms for the gang's planning and execution of a bank raid, and the score is more concerned with providing psychological insights into the principal characters. Most radically, in one scene, an extended vibraphone solo by Milt Jackson underscores the thoughts and feelings of a white character. It's a remarkable moment – the use of black jazz to score the psychology of a white character and all the more significant when one considers Quincy Jones's 1975 account of how a producer was concerned that as a black musician he would not be able to relate 'to a love scene between Gregory Peck and Diane Baker' (Lees 1975, 21). This racial mixing in the audio-visual relationship furthers the cultural fusion of Cuban big band, dinner jazz and rock'n'roll in Mancini's music for Welles's *Touch of Evil* (1958), which plays on white conservative fears about miscegenation through the central relationship between a Mexican man and a white American woman, ensuring that the classic noir era ended with genuine innovations and ideologically daring moments in its scores.

Neo-Noir, Nostalgia and Noir to Come

After the conclusion of the classic noir era in the late 1950s, noir would resurface in the 1970s and 1980s as 'neo-noir' with films that were much more (self-)aware of what film noir was and what it should include to qualify as noir. Helen Hanson (2009) divides these films into two categories: paranoid neo-noirs, such as *Klute* (1971) and *The Conversation* (1974), and nostalgic neo-noirs, such as *Chinatown* (1974) and *Body Heat* (1981). *Body Heat* (a more sexually explicit updating of *Double Indemnity*, scored by John Barry with prominent writing for Ronny Lang's alto saxophone) is the film that Fredric Jameson specifies in his influential critique of the nostalgia culture which he identified as emerging in the 1970s and 1980s. For Jameson, nostalgia culture was evidence of a regressive, socio-cultural malaise that was endemic to the capitalist societies of the late twentieth century: nostalgia culture 'approaches the "past" through stylistic connotation, conveying "pastness" by the glossy qualities of the image, and "1930s-ness" or "1950s-ness" by the attributes of fashion', and is the product of 'a situation in which we seem increasingly incapable of fashioning representations of our own current experience'

(1991, 19–21). As Philip Drake (2003, 189) states, according to Jameson history is emptied of politics and reduced to a recombination of stereotypes of the past. That might be true of a neo-noir like the remake of *Farewell, My Lovely* (1975), whose 'sinuous jazz score', as Kim Newman describes it, contributes to 'a veneer of nostalgia' that diminishes the film's noir ethos (quoted in D. Butler 2002, 154). Yet there is something more complex going on in *Chinatown*, which is concerned with politics and institutional corruption in 1930s Los Angeles. The film's score, by Jerry Goldsmith, is crucial in this complication of what might seem on the surface like a nostalgic recreation of the period with the original Paramount logo, sepia title sequence and retro font. The score begins with an upward glissando strummed along the strings of a piano, a ghostly sound complemented by high-register upward ethereal slides in the violins – Goldsmith's title cue effectively acknowledges that the spirits of the past are being summoned into being and this musical séance is complete with the bluesy melancholy of Uan Rasey's trumpet solo further evoking the swing era. As the score develops, however, Goldsmith offsets the opening bittersweet nostalgia of his memorable main-title cue with piano dissonances and experimental techniques, which owe much to the innovations of George Crumb in the 1960s, alongside passages of uneasy tonality in the strings featuring pitch clusters, harmonics and non-pitched percussion such as the guiro. This tension between the past and present within Goldsmith's score helps guard against the film's slipping into a nostalgic reverie and ensures that a sentimental fantasy of the 1930s is kept at bay and called into question.

   L.A. Confidential (1997) is far less successful in this respect in its account of early 1950s Los Angeles. *Chinatown* is a clear reference point for the film, underlined by Goldsmith being hired to provide the score, including a closing cue for solo trumpet and strings which sounds uncannily like the main theme from *Chinatown* – as if the composer had been asked by the director to pastiche his own back catalogue (perhaps not so out of step for a film set in the 1950s which features a high-class call-girl agency where female escorts are made up to look like earlier noir icons from the 1940s, such as Veronica Lake). There is a greater emphasis on incorporating 1950s source music and the overall effect, for Naremore, is a film which turns 'history into a fashion show' and allows 'good to triumph over evil', shifting away from noir into 'crowd-pleasing melodrama' and more in keeping with Jameson's thesis (Naremore 2008, 275). Nostalgia, then, is not in line with the sensibility of film noir. Characters are often on the run from the past rather than desiring to return to it – for example, the Swede in *The Killers* or Jeff in *Out of the Past* (1947) – or if they do yearn to get back to a perceived former idyll those efforts prove futile (as Dix Handley discovers in *The Asphalt Jungle*). Music is often the trigger which sets off unwanted memories: 'That tune! Why was it always that rotten tune?' bemoans Al Roberts in *Detour* (1945) as 'I Can't Believe That You're In Love With Me' (Jimmy McHugh and Clarence Gaskill, 1926) plays on a jukebox and the nightmare of his past begins again in flashback.

Where contemporary cinema is concerned, the noir ethos is more audible in those films which do not seek to recreate the sounds of noirs past. In 1955, Borde and Chaumeton identified the aim of film noir as being (depending on the translation) the creation of a 'specific alienation' (1996, 25) or 'sense of malaise' (2002, 13). That alienation has been generated in the music of film noir in a variety of ways: Ness identifies the avoidance of a 'dominant home tone' in the tonally ambiguous scores of many noirs as being analogous to those films' destabilizing of the 'security of home and family' (2008, 52), but it is also evident through the lyrics of a song like 'Put the Blame on Mame' (Allan Roberts and Doris Fisher, 1946), where Rita Hayworth's Gilda reveals, in an introspective after-hours rendition of the song, her awareness of how men have perceived women throughout society and made assumptions about her own character and behaviour, undermining the male protagonist's view of her as a destructive femme fatale. Similarly, the Italian pop motif for Vince Edwards's contract killer in *Murder by Contract* emphasizes his detachment from his victims and the 'wholesome' values of American society. The musical expression of estrangement, anxiety and social alienation is not just the preserve of non-mainstream music. As noir evolves, new forms of music and ways of articulating that fundamental alienation, such as the mix of dissonant electronica, sonic elements transforming and warping restlessly, samples divorced from their original context and aggressive drum'n' bass rhythms in Darren Aronofsky's π (1998), will emerge and problematize further the difficulty in characterizing noir through a 'unified body of stylistics' (Krutnik 1991, 19). But that is a problematic to be celebrated, and one that has enabled noir to endure.

12 Another Other History of Jazz in the Movies

KRIN GABBARD

When I was writing *Jammin' at the Margins* (1996) in the early 1990s, I thought of the book as the 'Other History' of jazz, a catalogue of myths that were constructed primarily in Hollywood which serious jazz writers should be devoted to correcting. Consequently, I had a great deal to say about a film such as *The Benny Goodman Story* (1956) because it invoked so many stupid myths about jazz. For example, in one sequence the young Benny is about to have his first date with a young woman, but he walks away when she laughs at him for wearing short pants. Within moments he hears a group of black and Creole musicians led by the legendary trombonist Kid Ory playing New Orleans jazz, a music Benny does not know. But presumably because he has just suffered his first sexual humiliation, he picks up a clarinet and begins improvising bluesy countermelodies as well as if not better than the veterans he has just joined. The entire film is naïve and racist, as it shows Benny learning from and then surpassing his black and Creole predecessors, even though they played a very different kind of music. Later in the film, Benny re-encounters Ory, who tells him that he has 'the best band I ever heard any place'.

But I am no longer so certain that movies about jazz are simple repositories of myth. Perhaps Hollywood (and other places where films are made) can tell us a great deal about jazz history, especially the music's reception. There are innumerable films where people are playing jazz, dancing to it, drinking to it, making love to it and of course talking over it. And each of these films responds to the changing practices and attitudes of the moment. So long as we construct jazz as a stack of recordings by esteemed jazz auteurs, we are likely to miss out on how it was actually experienced. This essay is essentially another 'Other History of Jazz'. It moves chronologically through the last ninety years of film history and touches on movies from diverse genres made in the United States and Europe.

Sissle and Blake (1923)

Most scholars agree that the first true jazz recordings were made in 1923 when Louis Armstrong, King Oliver and Jelly Roll Morton were all in

sound studios for the first time. In that same year Noble Sissle sang while
Eubie Blake played the piano in a short film, Lee de Forest's *Noble Sissle
and Eubie Blake Sing Snappy Songs* (1923). An experiment in synchronizing sound with the moving image, this six-minute showcase anticipated
The Jazz Singer by four years. It can be regarded not just as the beginnings
of black performance in sound cinema but also as an index for how
African-Americans were allowed to be represented in the early 1920s, as
well as for how they themselves wished to be represented. It was, after all,
the Harlem Renaissance, and both musicians appear relaxed and debonair
in their carefully pressed tuxedos. But by no means are they hypermascu-
line entertainers. Sissle's gestures even border on the effeminate.

   Sissle and Blake perform, however, with confidence, wit and enthusiasm. This confidence was bolstered by their recent hit *Shuffle Along*
(1921), the first successful Broadway musical with an all-black cast, for
which they wrote all the songs as well as the script. A black presence was
asserting itself in American popular music, in Broadway shows and even in
early experiments in sound cinema. Audiences who watched *Noble Sissle
and Eubie Blake Sing Snappy Songs* were probably most intrigued by the
synchronization of sound and image, but they definitely took pleasure in
the music of two performers who were bringing an accessible version of
black music to a mostly white audience.

Louis Armstrong (1933)

By the early 1930s, Americans could hear jazz everywhere. Armstrong had
been selling records briskly at least since 1926, when his Hot Five had a hit
with 'Muskrat Ramble'. He would appear in several films from a hybrid
genre that offered a few helpings of jazz. In the 1930s and 1940s, these films
were usually released with terms like 'Parade', 'Broadcast', 'Canteen' and
'Sensations' in their titles. Slight plots were built around attractive couples,
but the stories were regularly interrupted to feature popular entertainers.
Because they had nothing to do with the plot, black entertainers could be
kept separate from the action and indeed excised in locales where whites
were unnerved by the presence of blacks, even on celluloid.

   When Armstrong was touring Europe in 1933, the Danish film industry
cast him in one of the first of these compilation films, *København,
Kalundborg og – ?* ('Copenhagen, Kalundborg and – ?', 1934). Filmed in
a studio in Sweden in 1933 and re-edited to give the impression that a live
audience was present, the film features an elegantly dressed Armstrong
performing in front of the French orchestra with whom he was touring.
Like Sissle and Blake ten years earlier, Armstrong is elegant and debonair,

but he introduces a variety of vernacular gestures we now associate with authentic jazz, especially his verbal and musical asides. When he sings 'Dinah' (Harry Akst, Sam M. Lewis and Joe Young, 1925), he effectively rewrites the melody. He does in fact use the lyrics written for the tune, but he throws in a handful of scat phrases and several exclamations such as 'Oh, Baby'.

When Armstrong takes a trumpet solo on 'Dinah', he quotes from the song 'Exactly Like You' (Jimmy McHugh and Dorothy Fields, 1930) as well as a melody usually called 'The Hoochie Coochie Dance' (credited to Sol Bloom, 1893; see Scott 2001, 106) or 'The Snake-Charmer's Dance' before authoritatively bringing the song to an end with a high C. Although Armstrong had appeared in a few films as well as a Betty Boop cartoon in 1932, audiences at the cinema were getting the full force of his talent when they saw *København, Kalundborg og – ?*. More than virtually any other black entertainer of his day, Armstrong had found a global audience and he knew exactly how to appeal to it.

What Price Jazz (1934)

Black performers make a brief appearance in the short film *What Price Jazz* (1934), but the cast is otherwise entirely white. Dressed in nineteenth-century minstrel outfits, African-American dancers briefly appear in a survey of music and nightlife. One black female dancer in the sequence makes suggestive gyrations with her hips, provoking the allegorical figure, 'Mr. Blue Laws'.

After the montage of scenes from white and black performances, we see Mr. Blue Laws denouncing the music under a sign reading 'Society for the Prevention of Jazz'. An elderly man with a stove-pipe hat, Mr. Blue Laws is able to persuade another elderly person, Mr. Public Opinion, to join him on a raid of a night club. Mr. Public Opinion accepts a shotgun from Mr. Blue Laws, who wields an axe. They soon arrive at a club where scantily clad white women dance to the music of Ted Fio Rito and his Orchestra, one of the forgotten swing bands of the 1930s. At one point Rito himself makes the case for jazz, speaking in rhymed verse like everyone else in the film. (The source for the story is probably the medieval allegory, *Everyman*.) Mr. Public Opinion is soon seduced by the music and the dancing girls, eventually joining in and playing his gun like a clarinet. As Mr. Blue Laws angrily gives up his crusade, white women dance ineptly to Rito's all-white band as it plays music that recalls the recordings of Paul Whiteman.

In *What Price Jazz*, 'jazz' is about dancing and night life. Similarly, when F. Scott Fitzgerald coined the term 'Jazz Age' in 1922, he was not describing the music of Oliver, Morton, Armstrong and the other artists of the time who have since been canonized. Scrupulously ignoring black artists like these, *What Price Jazz* reassures audiences that it's OK to like the music they already like. The two people in the film who do not agree are made to look ridiculous. Cinema and music were part of the same entertainment industry, and they were already in the business of promoting each other.

Clean Pastures (1937)

In the 1930s and 1940s, at the same time that Warner Bros. was introducing audiences to Porky Pig, Bugs Bunny and Daffy Duck, the studio was also producing cartoons without these stock characters. Directors Chuck Jones, Tex Avery and especially Friz Freleng were responsible for the unmistakable style of the cartoons from Warners, especially the way in which, as Barry Putterman phrased it, the cartoons could 'swing' (1998, 32). Music director Carl Stalling was just as essential, consistently finding quirky, jazzy music to suit the action of the films.

At least since the early 1960s, Warner Bros. cartoons have been shown in regular rotation on American television and throughout the world. In 1968, however, several cartoons, eventually known as 'The Censored Eleven', were taken out of distribution because of their offensive depictions of black people (K. F. Cohen 1997, 54). One of these was Freleng's *Clean Pastures* (1937), a parody of Warner Bros.'s *The Green Pastures* (1936), a feature film with an all-black cast. *The Green Pastures* did not rely on the most grotesque traditions of minstrelsy, but it did portray black Americans as mildly ridiculous, devoted to fish fries and ten-cent cigars and likely to slip into indolence if not appropriately disciplined. At one point, an African-American God decides to wipe out all of humanity when he is disrespected by a young woman playing jazz-like music on her ukulele.

In *Clean Pastures*, a black patriarchal God also ruefully watches his people being seduced away from salvation by syncopated music. Early on we hear 'Sweet Georgia Brown' (Ben Bernie, Maceo Pinkard and Kenneth Casey, 1925) on the soundtrack while animated women perform in the style of Cotton Club dancers. We also see a martini shaker, a glass with an olive on a toothpick and a black hand that snaps its fingers after it lets go of two dice at a gaming table. The view then rapidly pulls back from Harlem until the earth becomes a tiny dot with stars and planets whizzing by. A path of white bottles (The Milky Way) leads us to an African-American heaven with the title 'Pair-O-Dice' over the pearly gates.

The black God sends a Stepin Fetchit-like Gabriel down to Harlem to bring souls to Pair-O-Dice. Once he has arrived in Harlem to begin the process of claiming souls for Pair-O-Dice, Gabriel encounters Bill 'Bojangles' Robinson, dressed as always in the most elegant style and dancing to 'Old Folks at Home' (1851), a minstrel tune written by Stephen Foster. A blacked-up Al Jolson then appears on the street, singing Harold Arlen's 'I Love to Singa' (1936). When he takes his trademark stance with one knee on the sidewalk, a child-sized puppet drops out of the sky and inspires Jolson to shed a tear as he briefly alludes to 'Sonny Boy' (Ray Henderson, Bud De Sylva and Lew Brown, 1928), the maudlin song that provided the tear-jerking finale to Jolson's mega-hit, *The Singing Fool* (1928). The several songs in this one brief sequence are united most prominently by their shared Warner Bros. copyright. But they also reveal the wide range of musical traditions that could represent Harlem and black America in 1937.

Neither Robinson, Jolson nor anyone else on the Harlem street pays any attention to Gabriel's ineffectual imprecations that they renounce dance halls and taverns. But then several show-business personalities appear looking down on this scene from the black heaven and offer their advice to God. Although they are wearing wings, the advisors can easily be identified as Fats Waller, Louis Armstrong, Cab Calloway and Herb Jeffries, all of them very much alive in 1937. Each of the four insists that 'rhythm' is the way to bring souls to Pair-O-Dice.

Calloway subsequently brings his orchestra to Harlem where they play a hot version of 'Swing for Sale' (Sammy Cahn and Saul Chaplin, 1936) on a street corner. Soon the celebrity musicians are leading a parade of Harlemites to Pair-O-Dice, but the song that accompanies them upwards is no longer contemporary. Instead, we hear a big-band version of another minstrel tune, 'Oh, Dem Golden Slippers' (James A. Bland, 1879). The new, jazzed-up Pair-O-Dice appears to be indistinguishable from Harlem except that people wear halos and there are apparently no cabarets or dice games. In the film's punch line, even the devil wants to live in Pair-O-Dice. Although he walks in holding his hands in prayerful fashion, Satan winks at the audience as the cartoon ends. The wink strongly suggests that Pair-O-Dice may not be a holy place much longer.

The moral of *Clean Pastures* seems to be that swing music has become so popular that it might as well be a tool for saving souls. At least the souls of black people. A simpler interpretation would be that the cartoon is having fun with familiar figures such as Robinson, Waller, Armstrong, Calloway and Jolson, all of whom were a source of great fascination for American audiences, white as well as black. Not surprisingly, the cartoon makes no real distinction between minstrelsy and jazz. In the Warner Bros. world, and in much of the popular imagination, 'Swing for Sale', 'I Love to Singa' and 'Oh, Dem Golden Slippers' are all part of black music regardless of whether or not the songs were written by African-Americans. And all of it could contain a white performer like Jolson along with a wide range of black artists, including Armstrong and Waller, now regarded as jazz geniuses.

Phantom Lady (1944)

By the mid-1940s, bebop was becoming the hippest music in the United States, even if ultimately it had little staying power with audiences. This was true at least in part because the boppers did not want their music to slip harmlessly into the mainstream like the jazz of previous generations. In the words of Amiri Baraka, bebop was 'harshly anti-assimilationist' (1963, 181). When told that their music sounded crazy, bebop musicians and their fans embraced the word: 'Crazy, man' became a term of praise. For the large movie audience, it made perfect sense that many of the boppers (as well as many pre-boppers) were hard drinkers and drug addicts.

In fact, any musician who played loud, aggressively rhythmic music could be lumped in with the new breed of jazzers. You did not have to play like Dizzy Gillespie or Thelonious Monk to speak the argot and strike the pose. In *Phantom Lady* (1944), a group of white musicians raises the roof playing music that has much more in common with the New Orleans revival than with bebop. Nevertheless, the music and the musicians were made to appear 'crazy'.

In *Phantom Lady*, Ella Raines plays the part of Kansas, the secretary of a man she knows to be innocent even after he is convicted of killing his wife. In pursuit of clues to prove her boss's innocence, Kansas dresses as a floozy in order to extract information from Cliff, a jazz drummer played by Elisha Cook Jr. In what is surely the most memorable scene in the film (and perhaps the only time in film history when Cook was allowed to kiss a woman), Kansas goads Cliff into playing an intense drum solo with the other hopped-up musicians. The camera shows her standing over him and controlling him like a puppet with her gestures. 'It is a powerful sequence, with its sexual undertones barely hidden, and it remains one of the most striking metaphors for sexual desire in film' (D. Butler 2002, 64). Even though – or perhaps because – it was played exclusively by whites in *Phantom Lady*, jazz was beginning to mean sex to a large segment of the population. The association goes back to the 'professors' playing ragtime piano in brothels in the early twentieth century and continues today with recordings by Miles Davis still providing young people with the best music for seduction.

It's a Wonderful Life (1946) and *Young Man with a Horn* (1950)

Bebop continued to be absent from the cinema of the 1940s and 1950s, even in *Young Man With a Horn* (1950), in which the trumpeter/protagonist Rick (Kirk Douglas) is said to have taken his music as far as it can go and is searching for a new sound. We see the young Rick playing in New Orleans style and eventually the sweet and showy big-band style we associate with Harry James, who in fact dubbed in the trumpet solos when Douglas pantomimes playing. If Rick was indeed after a new sound, bebop should have been inevitable in a film made just when the music was at its apex and even Goodman was leading a bebop band. But bebop was much too closely associated with blacks and with drug abuse to find a place in Hollywood's world of reassuringly wholesome (and white) family entertainment.

Black jazz musicians could, however, be put to use when that world needed to be contrasted with something sordid and corrupt. No one was more responsible for Hollywood's reassurances than director Frank Capra, especially in a film that has become a quasi-sacred Christmas ritual, *It's a Wonderful Life* (1946). Early in the film, when George (James Stewart) and Mary (Donna Reed) are falling in love, they dance enthusiastically to the music of a white swing band. But when George is allowed to see what his hometown would be like without him, he briefly visits Pottersville, the town invented by the robber baron Potter (Lionel Barrymore). When George stops into Martini's bar, a once comfortable refuge has become a sleazy saloon. In Pottersville, Martini's even has a stout black pianist wearing a derby and holding a cigar between his lips. There is no bebop in *It's a Wonderful Life*. In fact, the black man is playing an archaic style of music while whites play contemporaneous dance music. The boogie-woogie we hear in Martini's is not intrinsically sordid, but the blackness of the pianist was clearly intended to play upon the audience's bigotry and to add an extra level of depravity to Pottersville.

Ascenseur pour l'échafaud (1958)

The most successful blending of jazz and film may be the 'night walk' sequence in French director Louis Malle's film *Ascenseur pour l'échafaud* (*Elevator to the Gallows*, 1958). While Davis and his group improvise on the soundtrack, Florence (Jeanne Moreau) wanders the streets of Paris wondering what has become of her lover Julien. The novel by Noël Calef on which the film is based had only a small role for Florence, the wife of the industrialist killed by Julien. Making Florence a central character was the most brilliant aspect of Malle's adaptation, and it made Moreau a star.

Throughout most of *Ascenseur pour l'échafaud*, Julien is trapped in an elevator after killing Florence's husband. The night walk on the Champs-Elysées is beautifully shot by cinematographer Henri Decaë, and it also offers Moreau an opportunity to develop her character. Unlike the femmes fatales of American film noir, such as Barbara Stanwyck in *Double Indemnity* (1944) or Jane Greer in *Out of the Past* (1947), Florence is not greedy or manipulative. She genuinely loves Julien, and when he does not appear at the arranged time, she is a lost soul.

Malle had filmed Moreau's night walk and several other scenes without knowing who would provide the music. Only after principal shooting was over did Malle learn that Davis was in Paris for a gig at the Club St. Germain. He realized that Davis's music would fit perfectly with the action of the film. Significantly, Malle chose a jazz artist not because the film was about murder but because he knew that Davis's music could enhance the love plot. As it turned out, Davis did not have quite as much work as he had anticipated when he arrived in Paris, and he was happy to work with Malle (Szwed 2002, 152).

Jazz critic Gary Giddins has said that Malle had 'nerves of steel' to put his film into the hands of improvising jazz artists (Giddins 2006). But Davis quickly became deeply invested in the project. With the French and expatriate musicians who were his sidemen in Paris, he spent four hours playing along with scenes that Malle put into loops so that the musicians could watch them repeatedly and play along. The CD re-issue of the soundtrack includes multiple takes for each scene in the film that has music (M. Davis 1988).

As he watched Moreau's character walk through the night streets, Davis was effectively reading her mind, creating musical gestures to complement her facial expressions and body language. In one moment in this sequence, Moreau cries out 'Julien' when she sees a car that looks exactly like the one her lover owns. Davis lays out, allowing the audience to sort out what is happening as Moreau sees a bourgeois family emerge from the car. Then, as Moreau continues her stroll, his trumpet kicks back in. Otherwise, there is nothing to interrupt the communication between Moreau the actress and Davis the improvising musician. Just as Armstrong was shown at his best in the Danish film *København, Kalundborg og – ?*, Davis was given licence to make a brilliant contribution to a French film.

When the Boys Meet the Girls (1965)

Long after Armstrong appeared in the Danish film, he was in another compilation film of sorts, *When the Boys Meet the Girls* (1965). The film is an odd remake of *Girl Crazy* (1943), a George Gershwin musical starring Judy Garland and Mickey Rooney. *When the Boys Meet the Girls* is also a sequel to *Where the Boys Are* (1960), a vehicle for the country-inflected pop singer Connie Francis, who had a juke-box hit with a song of the same title. Even more bizarrely, several singers and pop groups with no relationship to Gershwin were dropped in at various moments, including Sam the Sham and the Pharaohs, Herman's Hermits, Liberace, and Armstrong and his All Stars. The film came out shortly after Armstrong suddenly appeared on the pop charts in 1964 with 'Hello Dolly' (Jerry Herman), a record that sold well enough to knock the Beatles out of *Billboard*'s number one slot, a place they had held for fourteen weeks. At roughly the same time, Herman's Hermits had a hit with 'Mrs. Brown, You've Got a Lovely Daughter' (Trevor Peacock, 1963) and Sam the Sham struck it rich with 'Wooly Bully' (Domingo Samudio, 1965). The producers were awkwardly matching up popular groups with Francis and the music of Gershwin.

In 1965, America had no PG13, R and X ratings for films. Virtually all American films were made for the entire family. There had been a rash of teenpics in the 1950s with the rise of rock'n'roll, but Hollywood was still trying to make films – especially musicals and Biblical epics – that appealed to everyone. With his infectious grin and exuberance, Armstrong fitted the bill even better than Herman and Sam the Sham. In the last shot of the film, after the characters have been sorted into pairs of lovers, Armstrong appears alone on screen and exclaims, 'Oh, yeah'.

Save the Tiger (1973)

By the 1970s, jazz no longer had a large audience, but many enthusiasts were still following a substantial number of the music's artists. In the most egregious moment of Ken Burns's ten-part documentary *Jazz* (PBS, 2001), we are told that jazz effectively died along with Armstrong and Duke Ellington, who both passed away in the early 1970s, and that it did not come back to life until Wynton Marsalis began recording in the 1980s. After that, according to Burns and his team, the narrative of jazz changed with musicians supposedly looking backwards towards honoured predecessors rather than chasing the next new thing in the future. Jazz musicians such as Dexter Gordon, Kenny Barron, Woody Shaw, Bill Evans, Betty Carter, Art Pepper and Ornette Coleman, to name only a few, had important careers in the 1970s. And geniuses like Charles Mingus, Rahsaan Roland Kirk, Jaki Byard and the members of the Art Ensemble of Chicago were making great jazz that simultaneously looked backwards *and* forwards.

The movies, however, appear to have agreed with Burns *avant la lettre*. Except for splashy star vehicles like *Lady Sings the Blues* (1972) and *New York, New York* (1977), the American cinema had little use for jazz unless it could be connected with artists such as Diana Ross and Liza Minnelli, who still had mainstream appeal. If jazz did turn up, it had much more to do with nostalgia, as in *Save the Tiger* (1973). In that film, Harry Stoner (Jack Lemmon) is a businessman striving to protect his innocent youth from the fallen world in which he lives. The soundtrack regularly features recordings from the 1930s and 1940s such as 'Air Mail Special' (Benny Goodman, James Mundy and Charlie Christian, 1941), 'Flying Home' (Benny Goodman, Eddie De Lange *et al.* 1939), and 'Stompin' at the Savoy' (Edgar Sampson, 1934), always as signifiers of a cherished past. When Harry's garment business is on the verge of bankruptcy, he hires an arsonist to burn down the factory while making it look like an accident. Unlike his business partner (Jack Gilford), Harry is prepared to undertake dangerous and illegal action in the hope that he will be able to collect a substantial insurance cheque. The film climaxes with the factory success-fully disposed of and Harry lost in reverie as he and the audience listen to the 1939 recording of 'I Can't Get Started' (Ira Gershwin and Vernon Duke, 1936) by Bunny Berigan, the white trumpeter/singer whom Armstrong once identified as his favourite among the many musicians who imitated his trumpet style (Schuller 1989, 464). The pale white jazz of Berigan may not have much cachet today, but it does give solace to an ageing character in a film from 1973.

Jerry Maguire (1996)

There is a long list of American films in which white people fall in love on the screen while audiences hear the voices of invisible black singers (Gabbard 2004). In *Jerry Maguire* (1996), directed by Cameron Crowe, the white couple played by Tom Cruise and Renée Zellweger do in fact make love while black music plays in the background. The lovers are listening to Mingus's 1957 recording of 'Haitian Fight Song'. But this scene should not be confused with the moment in *Groundhog Day* (1993) when Bill Murray and Andie McDowell fall in love while Ray Charles (nondiegetically) sings 'You Don't Know Me' (Eddy Arnold and Cindy Walker, 1955). Or with *Before Sunset* (2004), when Ethan Hawke and Julie Delpy decide they are made for each other as they listen to Nina Simone sing 'Just in Time' (Jule Styne, Betty Comden and Adolph Green, 1956). Or with any number of other films that appropriate invisible black voices for white romance.

The crucial scene in *Jerry Maguire* takes place when Jerry (Cruise) and Dorothy (Zellweger) are about to consummate their relationship. Dorothy is a single mother who has entrusted her child to Chad the Nanny (Todd Luiso), who has served long enough almost to be part of the family. Chad meets Jerry at the door on the evening when he knows that Jerry is about to make love to Dorothy for the first time. Before Jerry can enter, Chad hands him a cassette tape. Along with a great deal of oratory about the value of jazz, Chad suggests that Jerry and Dorothy listen to Davis while they make love. As Chad hands the tape to Jerry, he can be heard off-camera saying, 'I put a little Mingus on there too'. In a 1997 interview with Chris Willman of *Entertainment Weekly*, Crowe said that he originally intended to have Jerry and Dorothy make love to 'So What' (Davis, 1959) from a 1960 Stockholm concert with Davis and John Coltrane, 'But when I put it on that day, it was too languid and wasn't as good as Mingus's "Haitian Fight Song", which sounded like a herd of elephants mating. We'd already filmed the nanny saying the music was on a tape of "Miles and Coltrane" – so we later dubbed [the nanny] saying "And I put some Mingus on there too"' (Willman 1997, 25).

In *Jerry Maguire*, after Chad hands the tape to Jerry, the film jumps to a close-up of Dorothy in her bathroom preparing to join Jerry in the bedroom. At this point the audience can hear the bass solo with which Mingus opens 'Haitian Fight Song'. Anyone who cannot connect Chad's line about putting 'some Mingus' on the tape to what is on the soundtrack may assume that the music is nondiegetic, especially because Jerry and Dorothy do not acknowledge the music in any way. But then Jimmy Knepper's amazing trombone solo on the recording becomes even more amazing when he breaks into double time. At this moment Jerry gives Dorothy an incredulous look and says, 'What *is* this music?' Jerry and Dorothy both begin laughing, even more united now that they share a complete inability to understand what Mingus and Knepper have achieved.

Did Crowe know how profoundly he was revising, perhaps even ridiculing, the standard use of black music in Hollywood films? And did he know that 'Haitian Fight Song' celebrates the slave rebellions led by Toussaint Louverture in the late eighteenth century? And if so, was he associating the song with the relationship in *Jerry Maguire* between Jerry and the black football player Rod Tidwell (Cuba Gooding Jr), whom he manages? In an early scene Rod demands that Jerry repeatedly shout 'Show me the money' into the telephone so that he can continue as Rod's agent. When a black athlete demands this kind of a performance from a representative of the white power structure that controls his career, it almost suggests a slave rebellion.

Clueless white people like the fictional Jerry and Dorothy may not understand Mingus and the politics that he regularly brought into his performances. But in the late twentieth century, when jazz had definitively become an insider music, there is a strong possibility that Crowe, who worked as a music journalist before becoming a filmmaker, was communicating with fellow aficionados.

The Terminal (2004)

Steven Spielberg, who turns out to be something of a fan, made a film that turned to jazz in its final moments. In *The Terminal* (2004), Tom Hanks plays an immigrant from a fictional European country who finds himself marooned in New York's Kennedy airport because of political changes that took place in his country while he was still in the air. Only at the end do we discover that he has come to America to get the signature of saxophonist Benny Golson, the only musician in the famous 'Great Day in Harlem' photograph of 1958 who has not signed a sheet of paper passed on to Hanks by his father. When Hanks finally manages to escape from the airport, he goes straight to a hotel where Golson and his band are briefly heard playing Golson's composition 'Killer Joe' (1954).

Once again, nostalgia is what puts jazz into the film, especially because of the aura attached to the 1958 photograph of fifty-seven musicians posing in front of a Harlem brownstone. Since so many of the artists in the austere black and white photo were elderly, nostalgia was built into the photograph from the beginning, and it structures the excellent documentary film about the image, Jean Bach's *A Great Day in Harlem* (1994). To add pathos to Spielberg's film, Golson is, as of this writing, one of the two surviving musicians who appear in the photograph (the other is tenor saxophonist Sonny Rollins). There were at least a dozen survivors when *The Terminal* was released in 2004, but Spielberg surely knew that not all of them would be around for much longer and that his hero's project of tracking down one survivor would be all the more affecting.

Spielberg, who has said that he is a lifelong admirer of Golson (Saunders 2005), filmed the saxophonist when he was still in his prime and playing in typically relaxed but exuberant fashion. In *The Terminal*, a European is the only devoted jazz fan, and he has sought out Golson in honour of his father, a man from a time when jazz was still popular entertainment. But Golson plays a timeless music, not at all the fading flower of a better time, like 'I Can't Get Started' in *Save the Tiger*.

Whiplash (2014)

In Damien Chazelle's *Whiplash* (2014), jazz is not relaxed. The film presents the music as an extremely demanding art form exacting drastic life choices from those who hope to succeed. A young drummer, Andrew (Miles Teller), who wants to play like Buddy Rich, is taken under the less-than-protective wing of Fletcher (J. K. Simmons) at a music school that is clearly based on Juilliard. Fletcher drives Andrew relentlessly, even slapping him in the face to make a point about rhythm. Only at the end do we discover that Fletcher is not a sadistic sociopath but a dedicated mentor who knows that Andrew can become a great drummer only after gruelling practice sessions and a life-changing commitment. Because Chazelle has ratcheted up the intensity of his story, viewers can be caught up in it. But as Richard Brody has pointed out (2014), who would want to risk physical and mental well-being in order to play like Buddy Rich? To be fair, Rich was capable of playing with a certain level of sensitivity, but mostly he was an egomaniacal show-off. And when *Whiplash* climaxes with Andrew performing Rich's tired old trick of tapping two sticks on a snare drum gradually slower and then gradually faster, one wonders what the filmmakers think the art of jazz is all about.

Whiplash recalls any number of sports films in which mentors unrelentingly drive talented young athletes to extremes in order to ensure their success. But *Whiplash* also recalls movies about 'high art' such as the ballet films *The Red Shoes* (1948) and *Black Swan* (2010). I suppose that we have come a long way since jazz was portrayed as the music of primitive black people or pop ephemera for whites. But *Whiplash* emphasizes only the most exhibitionistic aspects of jazz as it is currently practised. There is nothing in the film about the crucial process of musicians *listening* to each other.

Nevertheless, *Whiplash* is almost reverential in its treatment of jazz as an art form, one of very few films in recent decades to make this claim.

What's next?

13 Horror and Science Fiction

STAN LINK

Narrative and Musical Convergence

During my first experiment, a kind of enthusiastic frenzy had blinded me to the horror of my
employment; my mind was intently fixed on the sequel of my labour, and my eyes were shut to the
horror of my proceedings. But now I went to it in cold blood, and my heart often sickened at the work
of my hands. MARY SHELLEY, *FRANKENSTEIN, OR THE MODERN PROMETHEUS*

In 1818, Mary Shelley had already stitched horror and science fiction
together in *Frankenstein* well before the birth of cinema. By the end of
the century, silents like Georges Méliès's *Les Rayons Roentgen* (*A Novice at
X-Rays*; 1898) – featuring skeletal images from fantastical X-ray experiments – brought this intermingling to early film (Kinnard 1995). And by
placing elements like monsters, the supernatural and psycho-killers in
contexts such as space exploration and post-apocalyptic futures, *Alien*
(1979), *Hellraiser: Bloodline* (1996), *Jason X* (2001) and *The Walking
Dead* (2010–) carry this amalgamation forwards. Woven from overlapping
narrative threads including mystery, fantasy, action-adventure, inexplicable menace, ecological disaster, social dystopia and so on, the distinction
between horror and science fiction is often located in specific scenes,
images and musical strategies rather than throughout a film's entirety
(Sobchack 2001, 17–63).

Musical treatments suggested by similar narrative palettes often overlap
as well. For example, the atmospherics of sustained, densely layered string
dissonances opening the 'slasher' film *Angustia* (1986), scored by
J. M. Pagan, or featured in *Insidious* (2010), with music by Joseph
Bishara, are stylistically similar to the outset of John Williams's score for
Close Encounters of the Third Kind (1977), a film solidly rooted in science
fiction. Physical, psychological and metaphysical unknowns, and the construction and exploration of extended natural, interior and supernatural
worlds, are all cousins in a family of related musical and sonic means even
when they are employed to varying ends.

The music-stylistic wellsprings of horror and science fiction run
deep, emerging and solidifying before film itself. Tremolos, startling dissonances and insistently ratcheting intensity were common features of the
eighteenth- and nineteenth-century melodramas that became the direct

precursors of film-scoring practices in the silent era. Drawn more directly to the irrational and fantastic, nineteenth-century musical romanticism in particular heard its share of fantasy and grotesquerie in settings such as the 'Wolf's Glen' scene in Weber's opera *Der Freischütz* (1821), Mussorgsky's tone poem *Night on Bald Mountain* (best known through Rimsky-Korsakov's orchestral arrangement from 1886) and Saint-Saëns's tone poem *Danse macabre* (1874). In these and other such works, melodic distortions, unusually chromatic or dissonant harmonies and timbral novelty evoked the supernatural.

Extant contemporaneous musical-accompaniment guides for silent film dwelled less on genre than on appropriate music for specific situations and emotions. In his *Musical Presentation of Motion Pictures* (1921), George Beynon, an experienced 'music synchronizer' in the United States, assigns horror to the 'adagio music' category of emotions that comprises 'Grief, Horror, Distress, deep Meditation and smoldering Anger'. In turn, horror quite specifically 'calls for a number that beginning softly, with an undercurrent of *tremolo* in the bass, passes into a crashing of dissonant chords, ever rising in pitch and intensity' (Beynon 1921, 16–17). Horror may have further implied particular pieces. Beynon suggests that 'the best examples of the kind are to be found in Verdi's "Otello"; while "Mefistofele" by Boito, and "Le Villi" by Puccini will give forceful excerpts admirably adaptable to scenes of Horror' (*ibid.*).

Many of cinema's earliest enduring works featured fanciful or grotesque subjects – *The Cabinet of Dr. Caligari* (1920), *The Golem* (1920), *Nosferatu* (1922), *The Phantom of the Opera* (1925) and *Metropolis* (1926) – but before horror or science fiction had solidified into cinematic genres *per se*, the prominence of more traditional elements like romantic love essentially made dramas of these films, with concomitant musical treatment. Alison Peirse notes that even *Dracula* (1931) was still characterized by contemporaneous sources as a 'mystery picture', and that 'there is no single moment in the 1930's at which horror becomes acknowledged either as a specific cycle, or a stable generic category' (2013, 6 and 8). Thus William Rosar's detailed history of the music for *Dracula* observes that Tchaikovsky's *Swan Lake* – heard in its main-title sequence – 'appears to have had a history of usage in silent films as a misterioso, and may have been chosen for *Dracula* for this reason'. He sees some of the film's other scant music in similar terms, suggesting of Wagner's *Meistersinger* and Schubert's *Unfinished Symphony* during the concert-hall sequence that '[t]he illogical order in which the excerpts are heard . . . suggests that they were chosen and arranged in this sequence for dramatic effect' (Rosar 1983, 393–4). And Peter Hutchings has noted that, within three years, *Dracula*, *The Mummy* (1932) and *Secret of the Blue Room* (1933) each used Tchaikovsky's *Swan Lake* as a kind of 'doomed romanticism' (2004, 141).

As such, the descendants of even the earliest musical horror techniques can live on in modern thriller scores like Howard Shore's for *Seven* (1995), in which athematic, slowly climbing chromatic bass movement under-scores a gruesome murder-scene investigation. Cues in Christopher Young's music for *Hellraiser* (1987) or Wojciech Kilar's for *Bram Stoker's Dracula* (1992) supply moments of late-romantic lushness such that an aesthetic of musical beauty might still overpower the implications of horror (see Deaville 2010). Moreover, indulging in a very specific nine-teenth-century technique exemplified by Berlioz's *Symphonie fantastique* (1831) and Liszt's *Totentanz* (1849), scores for films such as Jerry Goldsmith's for *The Omen* (1976), Hans Zimmer's for *The Ring* (2002), Wendy Carlos's for *The Shining* (1980) and even the stop-motion horror-musical *The Nightmare Before Christmas* (1993; music by Danny Elfman) refer to the 'Dies Irae', a medieval chant melody that came to signify doom and death. Thus the music for horror cinema can be said to have a tradition that is, to no small extent, musical tradition itself.

The Shock of the New

Beyond romanticism, twentieth-century musical explorations in expres-sionism, primitivism and modernism in the concert hall were also breed-ing grounds for many of the musical techniques doing regular service in horror and science-fiction film scores. Already by 1947, Theodor Adorno and Hanns Eisler had noted of a rampage in *King Kong* that 'the traditional music written for such scenes has never been remotely adequate to them, whereas the shocks of modern music ... could meet their requirements' (2007 [1947], 24), suggesting that the development of horror and science fiction as film genres also demanded musical development. Williams's familiar shark cue from *Jaws* (1975) echoes the watershed brutality of 'The Dance of the Adolescents' in Stravinsky's *Rite of Spring* (1913). The atonal string styles in *Angustia, Insidious, Close Encounters of the Third Kind* and *Alien* (the last scored by Goldsmith) have roots in works like György Ligeti's *Atmosphères* (1961), Krzysztof Penderecki's *Polymorphia* (1961) and George Crumb's *Black Angels* (1971). Goldsmith's score for *Planet of the Apes* (1968) is wonderfully adventurous in combining modernist serial techniques and electronic sounds with a 'primal' emphasis on percussion and animal horns as resources (see Miller 2010). Even while it was still a growing trend in contemporaneous concert music by composers like Philip Glass, the extract from Mike Oldfield's iconic *Tubular Bells* (1972) used in William Friedkin's *The Exorcist* (1973) presciently brought to the horror genre a newly emerging musical minimalism: 'A music of stasis and fragmentation, which disavows interest in progress or moving on' that 'enacts the traumatic crisis of subjectivity' (King 2010, 120). Likewise, director John Carpenter's own synthesizer scores for his *Halloween* (1978) and *The Fog* (1980) become 'the synthetic sonic embodiment of the supernatural, killing machines, which appear to be highly efficient (perhaps like the machines of the synthesizers)' (Donnelly 2010, 157).

Horror has a seemingly insatiable hunger for new sounds, and fluid relationships with eclectic sources can make even the most traditional horror and science-fiction cinema feel aesthetically progressive relative to other genres and to the larger situation of music in culture. While audiences for radio, the concert hall and recordings were able to remain largely ambivalent or even hostile towards modernist explorations, the horror genre in particular is a place where contemporary musical styles are welcomed by spectator and industry alike.

Several factors account for this embrace of the new. First, there are differences in listening modes. The concert hall implies direct attention to music, while cinema synergizes music, image and narrative in a larger, emergent context. Ligeti's *Atmosphères*, for example, popularized as accompaniment to the psychedelic 'star gate' sequence in Stanley Kubrick's *2001: A Space Odyssey* (1968), remains challenging in the concert hall. Second, the more liberal suspension of disbelief demanded by science fiction and horror engenders acceptance of the unfamiliar. Extraordinary narratives naturally imply less traditional musical characterization. Third, as with the often socially, sexually and politically progressive content in entertainments from eighteenth-century comic opera to 'B' movies and television sitcoms in the 1970s, secondary, popular, or lower social status can be liberating. In theorizing science fiction's 'popular avant-garde', Lisa M. Schmidt notes how 'a sound that is ugly or incomprehensible in many contexts ... became beautiful, profound or at least interesting in the context of film. Music which has virtually no popular audience, once adapted by soundtrack composers, has become the love object of many an aficionado and collector' (2010, 37). For Adorno and Eisler, the 'sensationalism' of cinema like *King Kong* was at issue: 'To the extent that the motion picture in its sensationalism is the heir of the popular horror story and dime novel and remains below the established standards of middle-class art, it is in a position to shatter those standards, precisely through the use of sensation, and to gain access to collective energies that are inaccessible to sophisticated literature and painting' (2007 [1947], 24). In all, the 'lower' status of science fiction and horror combine with their higher degree of sensationalism to create fertile ground for new aesthetics.

Shock, Wonder, Image and Affect

Along with their common traits, many interesting differences also emerge among the soundtrack strategies for science fiction and horror. Even where musical similarities abound, the fundamental affective goals differ markedly. Traditionally, the science-fiction soundtrack amplifies that genre's salient displacements, be they historical, spatial or geographical. More so than its characterization of looming threats in *Forbidden Planet* (1956), the imaginatively conceived synthetic music by Bebe and Louis Barron intensifies the narrative's cultural, technological and historical detachment (Leydon 2004). Described as 'electronic tonalities' in the credits, the Barrons' music detaches from musical traditions anchoring us in the here and now. Traces of orientalism in Vangelis's score to *Blade Runner* (1982) combine with pyramidal architectural imagery in evoking a futuristic and foreign Los Angeles. Similarly, James Horner's cues for *Avatar* (2009) contain drums and voices implying what Ralph P. Locke refers to as 'exotic' binarisms such as 'then/now, self/other, near/far, real/fictive' (2009, 64–71).

For horror, however, the affective goal primarily becomes negative emotions such as shock, suspense, isolation, alienation and fear. Subjectively, the traditional horror soundtrack frequently positions the viewer as victim. The menacing repetitiveness of the shark cue in *Jaws* not only cognitively describes the danger to on-screen victims, but also transfers that threat directly to spectators who experience it emotively as their own (see J. Smith 1999). Bernard Herrmann's stabbing string music encoding both the screaming victim and enraged killer during the shower murder in *Psycho* (1960) also violently punctures the composure of the spectator. As in much of horror, the soundtrack to *It Follows* (2014; music by Disasterpeace) sometimes threatens to blur distinctions between music and noise, giving shear amplitude and raw auditory overstimulation the power to become physically and emotionally assaultive. In short, by constructing binarisms and displacement, the science-fiction cue can function as a kind of musical tourism travelling outwards to exterior times and places, while by enacting emotional extremes horror music frequently plunges inwards towards psychological interiority.

Affective differences become particularly evident in musical attitudes towards imagery. Science fiction frequently involves a positive sense of spectacle with concomitant musical evocations of curiosity, awe, heroic action and so on. *2001: A Space Odyssey* exemplifies visual pleasure for its own sake: the sunrise to Richard Strauss's tone poem *Thus Spake Zarathustra* (1896), space docking to Johann Strauss's waltz *The Blue Danube* (1866) and the 'star gate' with Ligeti's *Atmosphères*.

The effect aims at sensorial immersion in which the sheer appreciation of imagery supersedes narrative progress. *Close Encounters of the Third Kind* distils science fiction's synthesis of music and spectacle to its essence by mapping coloured lights onto musical pitches for alien communication. On a more compact scale, in *Star Trek: First Contact* (1996) Goldsmith's opening texture of amorphous strings – woven together with various non-musical sounds and voices – comes into focus with an imposing brass fanfare for images of the voluminous interior of an enemy spaceship, momentarily accentuating visual grandeur over threat.

Conversely, while science fiction may treat the hostile as spectacular, horror can paint even the mundane as menacing. James Newton Howard's anxious opening music in *The Sixth Sense* (1999) builds to a close-up image of a mere light bulb. On a larger scale, the critiques of suburban life in *Poltergeist* (1982), scored by Goldsmith, and *It Follows* exemplify the horror soundtrack's strategy of estranging ordinary images such as televisions and swimming pools from the fabric of everyday life – as though the 'ordinary' itself is the horror. Visual display in horror is rooted in aversion, repulsion and perversion. Accompanying close-ups of a human embryo, the opening of Herrmann's score to *Sisters* (1972) combines jagged figurations from orchestral instruments and synthesizers, rendering the beginning of human life as an alien monstrosity. Conversely, recapitulating Strauss's *Thus Spake Zarathustra* for the revelation of the 'star child' in *2001* makes its foetal imagery an object of wonder. Science-fiction scores may emphasize spectacular physical action even over their often compellingly alien locations and futuristic technologies. The development of musical characterization in the *Star Trek* franchise offers a valuable comparison. Alexander Courage's theme for the original television series, first aired in 1966–9, featured a wordless female vocal line and bongo drums emphasizing the potential for exotic (and by implication erotic) alien encounters. The theme for the series of *Star Trek* films, however, beginning with *Star Trek – The Motion Picture* (1979), scored by Horner, became a march topic, setting a military tone (Lerner 2013, 52–71). Likewise, Williams's opening theme for *Star Wars* (Episode IV: *A New Hope*; 1977) promises nineteenth-century romantic heroism entirely akin to the composer's untroubled masculinist themes for the eponymous *Superman* (1978) and Indiana Jones in *Raiders of the Lost Ark* (1981).

Science fiction and horror may well sound differently even when presenting similar images. The non-human diva's seductive performance of the beautiful aria 'Il dolce suono' from Donizetti's opera *Lucia di Lammermoor* (1835) in *The Fifth Element* (1997) exemplifies how the musical treatment can inject sexuality into our perception of an alien who, were she to appear in the context of horror, might as easily have become an apprehension-provoking 'it', morphologically similar to the creature in *Alien*. Likewise, the jazzy syncopations in the cantina scene in *Star Wars* place its alien figures under an umbrella of mirthful curiosity rather than repulsion. *E.T. The Extra-Terrestrial* (1982), also scored by Williams, further demonstrates that in our filmic perception of an alien being, musical characterization can be the difference between a 'monster' and sympathetic appellations like 'extraterrestrial'. The score sustains clear musical distinctions between the benevolence of the children caring for the title character and the adult world whose attitudes are both threatened and threatening. Music therefore actively feeds into defining and reinforcing the generic dispositions of science fiction and horror, rather than passively emerging from them.

Musical Strategies of Horror

Most vivid among horror's musical hues are its direct evocations of negative visual, emotional and narrative elements like physical ugliness, emotional terror, sinister atmosphere, unpredictable or inexorable motion and so on. Along with contributing to a general sense of tension and the larger dramatic arc of the scene, the rhythms and dissonances during the opening of *Night of the Living Dead* (1968; music by Scott Vladimir Licina) generically amplify the deathly appearance and rigor-mortis gait of the zombie along with his victim's panic and flight. Scores for 'creature features', such as the iconic, growling brass shock motive in *Creature from the Black Lagoon* (1954), exemplify horror's baseline of dissonant musical interjection, shocks, reaction and commentary. Music's effects in this regard are simultaneously representational and immediate, as K. J. Donnelly notes: 'there is an experiential level that we can perceive *before* cognition of cinema's representational elements' (2005, 95).

Another strategy especially appropriate to the psychological effect of horror resides in the score's structural relation to narrative when offering misleading rather than reliable musical narration. In *Jaws*, the shark cue can be present with the creature, but the music won't appear when it is not an actual threat. So, when some mischievous boys create a hoax involving a fake fin, the motive does not sound. Musical narration thus remains an accurate indicator of reality even as the camera teasingly misleads the spectator with underwater perspectives. By contrast, the soundtrack at the outset of *Friday the 13th Part 2* (1981) gives a momentarily false implication of imminent danger, revealed as just a domestic cat, and then refuses to deliver advance warning as the protagonist opens her refrigerator and discovers a severed head just as she herself is attacked. Both the music (by Harry Manfredi) and its absence were misleading, heightening the masochistic pleasures of horror spectatorship by trading strategic suspense for tactical shock. Music as reliable commentary, an alliance in place since the accompaniments of the silent era (in theory, if not always in practice, as musicians were sometimes reported as drunk, incompetent or even satirizing the film), is broken, and trust becomes a field of musical play. This is a stylistic rather than a historical difference, however. The final scenes in the original *Carrie* (1976, scored by Pino Donaggio) and its remake (2013, scored by Marco Beltrami) exemplify the difference. Framed as a post-traumatic dream sequence complete with white picket fences and a virginal white dress, the original shows a surviving classmate's sunny-day visit to Carrie's burial site to place flowers. A sweet, idyllic flute tune accompanies her to the site until she's suddenly grabbed by the dead girl's blackened, bloody hand clawing up through the ground. Only at the moment of contact does the score change instantly into an unrelenting musical assault that stays with her even as she awakens. The remake is far more mundane in its thunderstorm and brooding music at the parallel scene. Even as the classmate places the flower, a heavy-metal cue gives away the impending reveal, with the music unchanging as Carrie's tombstone begins to crack. The music is not only predictable but predictive, taking the spectator ahead of the drama.

Some horror amplifies its subject by perverting traditional musical types. *The Omen*, for example, centres on an Antichrist figure drawn from the Book of Revelation. The soundtrack features choral music (by Goldsmith), the general sound of which is associated with sacred text settings. The sacrosanct tone, however, becomes ironic as the sinister twists of this pseudo-liturgical 'Ave Satani' also register the film's eschatological evil. *Rosemary's Baby* (1968; music by Christopher [Krzysztof] Komeda) opens with a wordless lullaby summoning an image of the pregnancy appropriated by a coven of devil worshippers. Indeed, the corruption of childhood innocence constitutes a musical horror strategy all its own (Link 2010). The supernatural threat to a small girl in *Poltergeist* is polarized by the appearance of a pure lullaby theme alongside the score's more amorphous and threatening cues. In *Sisters*, the forcefully reiterated four-note idea in the opening titles evokes a grotesquely distended version of childhood taunting – 'nyeah-nyeah, nyeah-nyeah' – made all the more ominous for being orchestrated with knell-evoking chimes.

In a further subversive strategy, music whose emotional implications run directly contrary to those explicit in a horrific scene has become a commonplace. In *The Omen*, a nanny jumps from a rooftop and hangs herself in front of children at a birthday party to the undaunted accompaniment of the carousel music playing below. In *The Silence of the Lambs* (1991), the narcissistic serial cannibal, Dr Hannibal Lecter, commits some of his most brutal on-screen violence to the elegant but ironic accompaniment of J. S. Bach's *Goldberg Variations* on a tape recorder. In its sequel, *Hannibal* (2001, scored by Hans Zimmer), the flowing strains of Strauss's *The Blue Danube* accompany Lecter's coy persuading of a drug-addled victim to slice off his own face with a shard of mirror. Dazed cannibalistic zombies stumble through a shopping mall in *Dawn of the Dead* (1978) satirically accompanied by abjectly banal, Muzak-like ambience. Michel Chion identifies such ironic effects that intensify emotion by 'inscribing it on a cosmic background' of indifference as 'anempathy' (1994, 8–9).

There is also a substantial body of films in which music itself becomes an explicit vehicle for the supernatural, bizarre or grotesque. As an enduring musical icon of the silent era, *The Phantom of the Opera* featured the *locus classicus* of the pipe organ at the hands of a solitary, ghoulish character. As Julie Brown observes, 'watch a horror movie and there is a good chance you'll hear an organ, probably a pipe organ. Screenwriters and directors even add organs to stories whose literary sources have none' (2010, 1). That trope is later reflected in films as diverse as *The Abominable Dr. Phibes* (1971) and the comedy-horror of *The Ghost and Mr. Chicken* (1966). Even the futuristic science-fiction mystery *Minority Report* (2002) echoes the Phantom's reclusive, enigmatic musician at the keyboard. Other keyboards such as the harpsichord make evocative on-screen appearances as a favourite symbol of antiquated, decedent aristocracy, as in *The Fearless Vampire Killers* (1967). With the harpsichord prominent in its nondiegetic score, *Interview with the Vampire* (1994, scored by Elliot Goldenthal) has vampires playing the fortepiano and piano (historically more accurate to the times of the narrative) as a means of further distancing themselves from humanity. Conversely, Bach's *Goldberg Variations*, 'the monster's signature tune' from *Silence of the Lambs*, develops into one of its sequel's '"trans-generic" elements of romance' as it moves from being mechanically reproduced to Lecter's own piano playing in *Hannibal* (Cenciarelli 2012, 127). And *The Others* (2001, scored by its director, Alejandro Amenábar) and *Insidious: Chapter 2* (2013, scored by Bishara) both exemplify a tradition of haunted pianos played by unseen forces. Indeed, 'The Haunted Piano' episode of the television series *Paranormal State* (season 1, episode 13, 2008) cuts directly to the heart of horror's seemingly consistent ambivalence towards music-making itself as a piano serves as the host for some unknown evil – exorcized only by violently demolishing the instrument.

Beyond the tradition of the keyboard, horror narratives frequently pivot around other on-screen musical sources. The power of vampiric violin virtuosity, for example, acts as a plot catalyst in *Queen of the Damned* (2002, scored by Jonathan Davis and Richard Gibbs). During the 'Asylum' season of *American Horror Story* (season 2, 2012–13), a sadistic nun maintains order among psychiatric patients with whips and a 45 rpm record of 'Dominique' (1961) by Jeanine Deckers ('The Singing Nun'), which then becomes the mocking ambience when she herself becomes a patient. In *Christine* (1983), a collection of 1950s-era popular music issues from the dashboard radio of a haunted 1958 Plymouth Fury as a token of the car's nostalgic intelligence while it kills. In *World War Z* (2013), a young girl's song of hope ironically drives a massive zombie horde to breach the wall of what was until then a safe refuge. In all, the narratively explicit use of music in horror would seem inevitable, as it often exploits or reflects larger fantasies about music itself. Music is invisible yet real, forceful without being directly physical (though see Chapter 10 for a strikingly visceral example), surrounding us here and yet emanating from elsewhere; the 'powers' of music describe the naked mechanisms of horror simply waiting to clothe themselves in its skin.

Functions of Popular Music

Like most other genres, horror and science fiction have extended their musical strategies to include popular music. During the rise of the popular soundtrack in the 1960s, some film critics and composers dismissed the use of popular music as motivated by little more than budgetary expediency and commercialism (Kalinak 1992, 186–7). Certainly the success of Ray Parker Jr's title song from the horror-comedy *Ghostbusters* (1984) exemplifies an effective means of extending the film's profitability outside the theatre. On the other hand, the rock and techno styles of the original cues for the zombie film *28 Days Later* (2002, scored by John Murphy) amplify basic filmic aspects of tempo and mood much as any other score might. This differs also from the ironic textual commentary of popular music in *An American Werewolf in London* (1981), comprising lunar-related songs as wry asides on lycanthropy: 'Blue Moon', 'Moondance' and 'Bad Moon Rising'. For the 'teenagers in danger' sub-genre of horror films like *Freddy's Dead: The Final Nightmare* (1991), *Halloween: Resurrection* (2002) and the television series *Buffy the Vampire Slayer* (1997–2003), pop-laden soundtracks deepen the *mise-en-scène* of youthful characters (see V. Knights 2010). Still, such effects can be observed throughout cinematic genres, and might be read simply as horror 'catching up' with the proliferation of popular music in cinema as a whole.

The parody of 'classic' horror in *Young Frankenstein* (1974, scored by John Morris) lies in having its monster singing and dancing to Irving Berlin's 'Puttin' on the Ritz' (1927). Likewise, the horror-comedy *Beetlejuice* (1988) uses the calypso music of Harry Belafonte as a possessing spirit taking control of a roomful of dinner guests. In a far more serious vein, so to speak, Janet K. Halfyard notes that 'rock music ensures that the primarily American audience is more encouraged to view vampires as being "like us" rather than as Other. By the end of the 1980s, therefore, a significantly new model for scoring vampire films had emerged, one that combined synthesizer scoring with rock music' (2009, 175–6).

Perhaps the apotheosis of this shift comes in casting actual pop musicians as vampires, such as David Bowie in *The Hunger* (1983) and Aaliyah in *Queen of the Damned*, but the rock, goth and club *milieux* of *Queen of the Damned* and *Only Lovers Left Alive* (2013) follow more concretely in this new tradition, as does Jace Everett's fusion of country, rock and blues in 'Bad Things', his theme song for the series *True Blood* (2008–14). However, this categorical shift of the vampire from 'them' to 'us' (or perhaps simply to a different 'Other') had already happened in the blaxploitation genre's *Blacula* (1972, scored by Gene Page) when the European harpsichord accompanying the pre-credits backstory gives way to African-American funk during the opening titles. In each example, popular music becomes a means to extend and subvert fundamental traditions and codes of horror by changing its tune.

Perhaps horror's most internally adaptive use for popular music lies in the realm of the anempathetic possibilities defined by Chion. In *American Psycho* (2000), a serial murderer uses an axe on a victim while Huey Lewis's pop tune 'Hip to Be Square' (1986) floats ironically from a stereo. The sentimental yodel of Slim Whitman's 'I Remember You' (1966) puts a velvet carpet under images of bloodied, tortured women and mercilessly executed policemen in *House of 1000 Corpses* (2003). The virgin protagonist of *Cabin in the Woods* (2012) struggles for her life against the sardonically anempathetic 'cosmic background' of REO Speedwagon's 'Roll with the Changes' (c. 1978). By disconnecting violence from pain and death and reconnecting it with pleasure, life and nostalgia, popular music can be particularly effective in reconstructing the disassociation from inflicting harm that characterizes psychopathological characters and actions. Moreover, spectators can easily find themselves in the horrific subjective position of experiencing their own transformation from victim into accomplice (Link 2004). Popular music has the power to invert the traditional masochistic pleasure of horror into spectacular sadism.

And here too we can observe a broad distinction in strategies between horror and science fiction. While horror's native deployment of popular music is traditionally in terms of its emotional signification, science fiction's usage can more naturally emphasize music's relationship to history. In *Star Trek: First Contact*, Steppenwolf's 'Magic Carpet Ride' from 1968 appears at a historically significant moment in 2063 as an anachronistic artefact of an earlier century. 'It's not that rock has no future, but that we usually imagine a future that does not rock', write Cynthia J. Miller and A. Bowdoin Van Riper (2010, 118). As such, popular music can function as a means of creating alliances between film spectators and the inhabitants of distant futures. On a much larger scale, the saga of television's *Battlestar Galactica* (2004–9) is ultimately driven by Bob Dylan's 'All Along the Watchtower', written in 1967 and further popularized by Jimi Hendrix in 1968. Used as a 'guide' to finding a long-sought new world that ends up being our own Earth from 150,000 years ago, the tune becomes a pivotal note in turning what seemed like the technologically distant future into a paradoxically prehistoric history. Conversely, *Back to the Future* (1985) turns the past into the future when its teenage protagonist from the 1980s performs Chuck Berry's 1958 classic 'Johnny B. Goode' for a high-school prom in 1955. The performance amplifies the paradoxes of time travel in a problematic way by awarding the innovations and authorship of black music to a white character who now becomes their origin. The moment unwittingly trips over the social and political ramifications of popular music by being deaf to them, and yet also lays bare popular music's allure for both horror and science fiction, genres that are ultimately about reflecting and shaping social and political ramifications.

The Expressivity of Sound

Horror and science fiction soundtracks regularly trade in blurring the distinction between music, sound and noise. As Donnelly has noted, 'When rock star Marilyn Manson was asked to provide the music for *Resident Evil* (2002), he assumed that he would also be providing diegetic sounds and atmospheres, understanding how the horror film is often seen as a coherent atmospheric package that embraces both music and sound effects' (2005, 94). To that extent, horror and science-fiction films enact an aesthetic transformation that had been going on independently within music itself, most explicitly in the work of avant-garde experimental composers like John Cage. Nevertheless, as 'the low stifled sound that arises from the bottom of the soul' in Edgar Allan Poe's 'The Tell-Tale Heart' (1843) and 'that morbid condition of the auditory nerve' in 'The Fall

of the House of Usher' (1839) testify, sounds and noises have long held
sway over the fantastic imagination on their own terms. The enigmatic,
cursed video collage of disturbing images at the centre of *The Ring* provides
its own soundtrack of equally disjointed and disconcerting noises.
The soundtrack to the avant-garde horror of *Eraserhead* (1977) contains
less dialogue than noise as the bleak ambience of its dark industrial vision,
while the 'Lonely Souls' episode of television's *Twin Peaks* (season 2,
episode 7, 1990; scored by Angelo Badalamenti) embeds a chilling use of
sound – all the more effective for its simplicity – as a turntable needle
relentlessly and rhythmically scratches away on a vinyl record while
a demonically possessed uncle brutally murders his beloved niece.

Even in the face of horror's rich musical resources, shifting the
focus from music towards sound can also become uniquely effective.
In transplanting horror from the domain of expressionism to realism,
the documentary, home video and 'found footage' styles of films like
Paranormal Activity (2007) and *The Last Exorcism* (2010) eschew musical
commentary in favour of silences, sound and noise to intensify their
illusions of immediacy and authenticity. In *The Blair Witch Project*
(1999), the spectator even receives constant assurance from low recording
quality that the film's escalating panic is genuine (Coyle 2009b). In short,
where a musical score ultimately constructs a film's fictionality, sound *qua*
sound persistently asserts its reality, however unrealistic that may be.

And yet, to the extent that we are tempted to consign sound to the task
of deepening the diegetic world, this conception is also immediately
problematized for genres rooted in the unreal: what noise can a thing
make that never existed to begin with? In science fiction, the placement of
sound to enact the operation of futuristic technological devices and
machinery enhances an illusion of functionality that the image alone
induces far more weakly. Vivian Sobchack describes what amounts to
a paradox for science-fiction sound in its 'innate desire for authenticity'
and 'necessary obsession for documenting the incredible' (2001, 216).
Watching someone press the red button is less convincing than seeing
and hearing them press the red button. Likewise, betraying the silent
reality of outer space, films like *The Fifth Element* and the *Star Wars* and
Star Trek franchises traditionally attach sounds to images of spaceships to
create perceptions of motion, speed and size. While objectively real, as an
opening intertitle feels compelled to explain, the shocking, sudden silence
of space that launches *Gravity* (2013) is rare.

Further, sound often evokes significantly more than aural information
itself. 'What is rendered', writes Chion, 'is a clump of sensations' (1994,
112). Thus, hearing the red button being pressed can amount to feeling it
being pressed. In *Alien*, hyper-realistically represented sounds from gooey

bodily fluids and soft tissue become a mechanism of horror that intensifies the intimate proximity of repulsion by rendering it tactile and not just auditory. Feeling through sound that which cannot be touched forces the spectator to experience, and not simply witness, the abjection of the 'monstrous feminine' birth of a creature tearing its way out of a man's stomach (see Creed 1986).

Conversely, sounds emanating at a distance, from off-screen space, can also become tightly woven into the psychological fabric of horror. To a degree inherent in no other genre, horror's narrative and camera work often evolve out of an invisible or hidden threat and its ultimate revelation. The ability of sound to arrive before an image has clear psychological potential for intensifying and prolonging dread. In horror, vision often chases hearing, so to speak, mirroring the accompanying sense of curiosity, danger or pursuit. The 'unseen offscreen', writes Tom Sutcliffe, 'is a place in which we cannot be touched (which is why the terror is bearable), but also a place in which we are powerless to be vigilant on our own behalf (which is one of the reasons we feel the fear personally, rather than vicariously, in sympathy with those on screen)' (2000, 107–8). With noises, music and other sounds consistently beyond the frame and eluding the eye in a huge, eerie mansion, *The Others* offers a classic example of the sonic construction of off-screen haunting. It becomes the space into which the spectator's imagination projects its own unlimited visions, provoked into supplying much of what might have been overt in visual effects. In *Poltergeist*, sound makes palpable the extra dimension into which a child has been transported. For *Rosemary's Baby*, sounds bleeding through the wall of a neighbouring apartment intensify the proximity of a Satanic coven's conspiracy to appropriate Rosemary's pregnancy. While these films boast excellent musical scores, their narratives also depend on the construction and exploitation of off-screen space.

The Voice

The soundtrack's climactic moment in *Invasion of the Body Snatchers* (1978) comes not in the music, but in the voice. An inhuman shriek issuing from the contorted face of the protagonist reveals that he too has been replaced by an alien facsimile of himself. From the signature trumpeting of Godzilla to the hair-raising bellowing of the 'smoke monster' in the television series *Lost* (2004–10), the identity and threat of a monster can be as effectively rooted in its voice as in its image. For a masked figure like Darth Vader in the *Star Wars* franchise, the voice provides vital expressive substitutes for a hidden face. In *Friday the 13th* (1980), whispered syllables appearing repeatedly in the soundtrack create the impression of a malevolent agency, the identity of which remains concealed until the film's gory climax. The dubbing of a masculine adult voice in place of a young girl's not only embodies the central illusion of demonic possession in *The Exorcist*, but also creates a sense of shock and revulsion rivalling the images of the child's invaded, tortured body. The fact that the human voice is intimately tied to identity turns its alienation, disembodiment or manipulation into physical, psychological or metaphysical disfigurement. The disrupted or destabilized voice is a horror all its own.

In *Psycho*, observes Ross J. Fenimore, 'the audience is unable to fully place Mrs. Bates's voice with her body until we learn that we have always been looking in the wrong place' (2010, 81). The disembodied voice is therefore particularly marked: 'When this voice has not yet been visualized – that is, when we cannot yet connect it to a face – we get a special being, a kind of talking and acting shadow to which we attach the name *acousmêtre*' (Chion 1999, 21). Even when heard by way of some familiar technological means, the *acousmêtre* can become an intensely unsettling presence. *Session 9* (2001) and *The Fourth Kind* (2009) hinge on the voices of severely disturbed psychiatric patients heard in tape recordings. A babysitter in the remake of *When a Stranger Calls* (2006; original version 1979) is terrorized by an anonymous telephone call asking, 'Have you checked the children?' Likewise, *The Mothman Prophecies* (2002) and *The Ring* use the telephone to conjure fear from an unidentified caller. And one of the most starkly hair-raising voices on film issues from a baby monitor in both *Insidious* and *Insidious: Chapter 2*. 'But what is there to fear from the *acousmêtre*? And what are his powers?', asks Chion; 'The powers are four: the ability to be everywhere, to see all, to know all, and to have complete power' (1999, 24). Almost god-like, then, a baleful voice from a CB radio stalks three highway travellers in *Joy Ride* (2001), seemingly both in front of and behind his prey, always able to know their location and control events at will.

The sound of the *acousmêtre* is the quintessence of horror: a power derived from disembodiment, invisibility, ambiguity, immateriality and authority. It is raw presence and, like all monstrosities, its very existence is the first thing that must be grappled with: 'Being in the screen and not, wandering the surface of the screen without entering it, the *acousmêtre* brings disequilibrium and tension. He invites the spectator to *go see*, and he can be an *invitation to the loss of the self, to desire and fascination*' (Chion 1999, 24; emphases in original). Chion's characterization of the faceless voice is thus equally evocative not only of horror, but of music itself, pointing us again to its heightened role in the imaginary landscapes of science fiction and horror. Combining fantastical subject matter with escapist desires and an absolute necessity to suspend disbelief can only intensify the creative and spectatorial investment in any means to those ends. The wager these genres place on their soundtracks is more than a merely heightened form of presentation, instead becoming existential in making horror and science fiction dramatically and cinematically viable. Relying less on the common than the uncanny – and often less on textual narrative than on image, action, effect, affect, mood and extremes of emotion – positions them to draw directly from psychological and embodied experiences, along with codes, symbols and significations. The imaginary realm of science fiction is a fact of its music, voices and sounds, just as horror lies in the beauty of their sway.

14 The Western

ROBYNN J. STILWELL

The western is perhaps *the* distinctive American storytelling genre, rivalled in cinema only by the musical. Both are spectacular and are rooted in the American drive for both individual exploration/expression (the frontier, the performance) and the formation and celebration of family and community ties (civilization, the ensemble theatrical production). They are also both marked by their 'American' musical style – although exactly what that entails varies over time.

Any genre is a loose collection of elements from character types to narrative tropes and symbolic repertoires. For the western, many of these elements were established before film arrived, in theatrical melodrama, Wild West shows and popular novels. Once captured on film, the narratives shifted emphasis from the action-adventure of the early western films to something more complex and symbolic at mid-century, as the American West became a backdrop to questions of nationhood, masculinity and Cold War ideological conflicts. The genre successfully crossed over to television, where narrative tropes about masculinity shifted from an emphasis on independence towards community and family, as befitted the living room. Although the western apparently faded from screens in the late 1960s and 1970s, that period was one in which many of its narrative tropes – and some of its musical gestures – were transplanted to the new frontier of outer space. When the western re-emerged in the 1980s, it confronted issues long suppressed in its heyday, particularly the treatment of indigenous populations that had been either demonized or erased from the landscape – that spectacular backdrop against which the new nation had mythologized itself.

Coincident with the fading of the western from Hollywood was the rise of the so-called spaghetti western (considered in detail in Chapter 17). The term was originally disparaging but has come to represent not just an industrial structure (westerns made by European – primarily Italian – artists and institutions, and shot mostly in Italy, Spain and North Africa) but a wide range of generic signifiers, including the idiosyncratic musical language innovated by Ennio Morricone.

Given the sprawl of the genre, this essay will touch upon the major trends, both narrative and musical, in the western in Hollywood, the spaghetti western, postmodernism and outer space. In the broadest historical terms, the dominant musical style shifted from folk-based at its origins, to an epic Americana symphonism at mid-century, to a studio-mediated pop-based idiom in the 1960s, with a return to symphonism in the 1980s that was both part of a wider cinematic-industrial movement and a nostalgic/revisionist look back from within the genre. The changes were gradual, shifting emphasis from certain elements to others, often affecting the choice of musical style.

While the title sequence in any film functions as an advertisement for the film – showcasing images, sounds and a graphic style that tells the audience roughly what to expect – the western title sequence seems particularly iconic, as it must accomplish not only scene-setting but time-shifting. Westerns are period pieces and, like science fiction, particularly vulnerable to the concerns of the contemporary audience. Title sequences are also usually the most extended period of foregrounded music, with the exception of another element typically featured in the western – the spectacular landscape. The scene of a lone rider or a wagon train traversing the frame against the backdrop of the prairie, a mountain pass or John Ford's all-purpose Monument Valley is an iconic, even defining, feature of the genre. It often appears in the title sequence, the bridge from the title sequence into the body of the film, a contemplative moment within the narrative, or all of the above. These emblematic moments provide a useful point of comparison when covering a wide range of films, and thus will dominate much of this discussion.

Folksong

Edwin S. Porter's *The Great Train Robbery* (1903) is usually cited as the first narrative film, giving the western primacy among cinematic genres. Output was steady throughout the silent-film era – genuine historical western figures like Wyatt Earp, Buffalo Bill Cody and Pancho Villa appeared on screen – and silent-film cowboys like William S. Hart and Tom Mix were stars. D. W. Griffith's pioneering film technique was honed in two-reelers, culminating in *The Battle at Elderbush Gulch* (1913); the staging, photography, editing and, unfortunately, the racist narrative of a white woman – petite, fair Lillian Gish in both instances – menaced by the non-white 'other' all find full flower just over a year later in *The Birth of a Nation* (1915).

The accompaniment of silent film, particularly for more modest productions, is a complex topic, one that is difficult to generalize with any certainty, but the use of cowboy songs to accompany these films would have seemed natural, as these songs – along with such portable

Example 14.1 Opening 'Indian' theme from *Cimarron*.

accompaniment instruments as the guitar, harmonica and accordion/concertina – were already a part of western lore, through actual practice as well as pulp novels, theatrical productions and Tin Pan Alley tunes. Cowboy songs included working songs that referred to the cowboys' direct experience ('Get Along Little Dogies', 'Old Paint'), sentimental parlour ballads that emphasized a nostalgia for the domestic and the 'girl left behind' ('Jeannie with the Light Brown Hair' [Stephen Foster, 1854]), dance songs ('Cotton-Eye Joe') and minstrel songs ('Oh, Susanna!' [1848], 'Camptown Races' [1850], 'Ring de Banjo' [1851]; all by Foster) that could provide toe-tapping entertainment around the campfire.

Silent-film accompanists used these songs to help score the films, reinforcing the 'rightness' of their style upon the coming of sound. The songs might well be mixed in with more broadly generic cues for suspense or romance, for instance, but also included the stereotypical 'Indian' tropes that developed during the early years of the twentieth century (see especially Pisani 2005, 241–329; also Pisani 1998; Gorbman 2000, 2001; Kalinak 2007, 2012). Early films, both silent and sound, normalize these gestures, helping to dissolve a variety of commercial songs – like those of Foster – into a 'folk' genre.

RKO's film adaptation of Edna Ferber's Oklahoma-set generational saga *Cimarron* (1931) was scored by Max Steiner, who is credited by many with developing the principles of classical Hollywood film scoring. *Cimarron* opens with an art deco sunrise/sunset card (the ambiguity of the graphic black-and-white image works to emphasize both the West of sunset with the potential and promise of sunrise) and a distinctly ominous 'Indian' theme: a modal tune in low brass that accents the flat seventh and a melodic span of a fourth, punctuated by pounding tom-tom in an asymmetrical phrasing that increases the evoked unease: see Example 14.1.

This gesture blends the heraldic function of a fanfare with the suspense of a recognizable threat (matriarch Sabra Cravat's virulent racism is eventually eased by her Osage daughter-in-law). Once past this opening gesture, however, the underscore of *Cimarron* is not distinctively 'western' or even American (although the French march style of the subsequent part of the overture had become American through adoption via John Philip Sousa around the turn of the century). In the body of the film, source music dominates, though a couple of moments hint at later practice. The '1907' caption appears over a street view, and a saloon-style piano can be heard distantly; the music's presence is roughly justified, but it also serves a transitional function. Similarly, the final extended sequence is a banquet honouring Sabra's new position as Congresswoman. A small cadre of musicians at the extreme left of the screen (not always visible in some prints and broadcast versions) justifies a few dances and marches as we see various characters interacting for the last time. A slow, hymn-like march first heard in the opening titles returns as the matriarch is reminded of her absent husband – a man who is never able to settle into domesticity and continually seeks the excitement of the westward-pushing frontier, and who will be killed in an oilfield accident in the following scene. The film then closes with the dedication of a statue to the 'Oklahoma Pioneer' (a substitute memorial); the march returns and could possibly, plausibly have been played at this event, but it climaxes with the final title card. A similar transition from frame to diegesis occurs at the beginning: a trumpet fanfare ends the orchestral overture, handing off to a cavalry bugle call that creates a bridge from the credit sequence, matching more by gestural than thematic similarity.

Another film that avails itself of that surprisingly common suturing device, John Ford's *Stagecoach* (1939) heralds a new generation of prestige western features, blending high production values and weightier narratives with the action and generic tropes in an 'A' version of what had been primarily a 'B' genre, produced in a steady stream throughout the decade. *Stagecoach* star John Wayne had established his career in such films for Monogram and Mascot Pictures. These low-budget, high-output 'B' westerns appeared as both stand-alones and serials. Musically, they were heavily reliant on source music, with underscore largely confined to the titles. Tremendously popular (in aggregate), these 'B' movies would reinforce the western's generic blending of cowboy, parlour and minstrel songs.

An important subgenre of 'B' westerns often excluded from discussion is the singing cowboy film. Republic Pictures produced many with stars Gene Autry and Roy Rogers, and their popularity should not be discounted. These films were successful enough to have a productive run from the 1930s to the early 1950s, and the stars are still household names. Rogers had begun his career as a singer with the Sons of the Pioneers, a smooth, six-part harmony group that performed in a style not unlike the swing bands of the era. They continued to perform together as Rogers became a star (a 1942 film directed by Joseph Kane was actually called *Sons of the Pioneers*), and they sang in several Ford films, including *Rio Grande* (1950) and *The Searchers* (1956). Most scholarly examinations of the western tend to start with *Stagecoach* and the arrival of the western as a prestige feature (or follow a star or auteur like Wayne or Ford); and these films have a degree of song performance that shunts the genre identification towards the musical. Whilst genre can be a useful organizing principle, it can also force divisions that are questionable (see Altman 1987; Neumeyer 2004).

Stagecoach displays its indebtedness to song with its 'Musical score based on American Folk Songs' credit, and no fewer than six listed music personnel, none of whom contributed significantly to the score; according to Michael Pisani, the most substantial scoring was by Gerard Carbonara, who is not even credited (2005, 300). This blurring of authorship arguably strengthens the primacy of the folksongs. The cueing of familiar songs (including 'western' favourites like 'Jeannie with the Light Brown Hair') as underscore is smoother, perhaps, than in earlier films, but still within traditions begun in the silent era. As Kathryn Kalinak (2007) has amply shown, Ford's westerns are full of songs, often stressing communal singing, dancing or church service. In this strain of the western, the song is a form of domesticity (both of 'home' and of 'taming') and is often used to symbolize the narrative tension between the individualism of the frontiersman and the pull towards family and community.

Although the musical style started to shift towards something more mythic and expansive in the early 1950s, song was still crucial to several classic westerns in a Fordian manner. Not surprisingly, these scores were written by melodists: *Red River* (1948) and *High Noon* (1952) by Dimitri Tiomkin, and *Shane* (1953) by Victor Young.

Shane's conjunct, flowing melodies are matched by the narrative theme and the landscape in George Stevens's film. Unlike the wide open spaces of Ford, or the widescreen spectacles of the latter 1950s, *Shane* is set on a farm nestled in encircling mountains. The domesticity of the family unit is threatened from outside, even by the (anti)hero Shane, who comes to help but poses a threat to the nuclear family by offering a more active, individualistic male figure for the son and implicit competition with the father for the mother. Young's thickly orchestrated but simply voiced title music follows the tiny image of Shane on his horse over vast scrublands into the sheltered valley. Shane's image increases in the frame, and close-ups of a deer and the little boy bring us nearer to the story. As we approach the farm, the mother's singing of a Scots-Irish folksong winds through the thinning orchestral strains in perhaps the most complex counterpoint of the score.

Tiomkin's scores for *Red River* and *High Noon* are quite different. Howard Hawks's *Red River* is more like a Ford western, though the male chorus singing 'Settle Down' in the opening credits is unseen. In its lyrical sentiment and homophonic singing, it calls for domesticity and community, but the vigorous performance preserves the requisite, rough-hewn masculinity of the traditional western. Yet this film is one of the earliest and most explicit in confronting the postwar shifts in American masculinity. Wayne had gone from the rebellious 'kid' Ringo in *Stagecoach* to the hard-nosed, individualistic father figure Tom Dunson, now pitted against the 'new man' in his thoughtful adopted son Matt (Montgomery Clift), willing to talk before drawing his gun – a new model of bravery (see Cohan 1997). Tiomkin's extensive score quotes folksongs, such as the fiddle tune 'Turkey in the Straw'; and Dunson's theme is diatonic, arching, with a straightforward quaver-quaver-crotchet rhythm, none of which would be out of place in a Ford film. However, the chromatic, romantic violins for Fen (Colleen Gray), whom Dunson loves at the start of the film, approach melodrama in their depiction of eroticism and emotion.

Red River also uses a visual trope that seems particularly prevalent in the immediate postwar period: the use of a storybook or diary to frame the film explicitly as storytelling. This may be simply an adaptation of the increasingly ornate title cards of films of the period, but it may also be a function of the generational shift. By the late 1940s, the 'West' was no longer within the living memory of most audiences; it was now 'once upon a time'.

This storytelling trope is transferred to the nondiegetic underscore in Fred Zinnemann's *High Noon*. Tiomkin's song-based score is exceptionally flexible within what seems to be such strict limitations: almost all the musical material is derived from the title song, a standard 32-bar song form with a short coda ('wait along'). The lyrics sketch out most of the important plot points, but they are frozen in time at the crux of the narrative – when Amy (Grace Kelly) leaves her husband Will Kane (Gary Cooper), who is torn ' 'twixt love and duty'. Tiomkin's deployment of this theme draws constantly on the audience's primed knowledge of Tex Ritter's hit version, released before the film. The striking opening phrase 'Do not forsake me' takes on various meanings: Will's plea to Amy and Amy's pleas to Will; and similarly for both Will and the townspeople. The orchestration is lush and romantic for the love scenes, hymnic for the wedding, minor and chromatic for scenes of conflict or spare guitar and harmonica for an isolated Will alone; when Amy leaves, Ritter's voice comes in on the line 'You made that promise when we wed', as if we move into Will's thoughts at that moment, shifting the conceptual placement of the music from diegetic to metadiegetic. Even the mix of the soundtrack is brought to bear, with isolated shots of Kane to heighten his sense of isolation: the beginning of Ritter's recording is not just low in volume, but also miked at a distance, an effect repeated as Will grows smaller and smaller in the frame upon approaching the church in fruitless search for assistance from the townsfolk (see also Lerner 2005).

The bridge of the song, that which speaks of conflict, is rhythmic and disjunct in comparison to the broad-ranging, flowing A melody. While this theme is used extensively for Miller and his henchmen, it also functions as a leitmotif for discord between Will and Amy. The one character who stands outside the musical framework of the song is Helen Ramírez (Katy Jurado), who by virtue of her ethnicity and open sexuality stands outside the community; a stereotypical *paso doble* is distressingly imprecise and vague for a character so strong and distinctive.

Tiomkin used the theme-song strategy in later westerns, such as John Sturges's *Gunfight at the O.K. Corral* (1957) and *The Alamo* (1960), directed by John Wayne; but he was never again able to be so concise, perhaps because of the very limitations of the 'real time' strategy in *High Noon*. After the Second World War, the western was moving in a different direction, away from the direct and communal implied by the folksong and towards the epic and spectacular.

Manifest Destiny

The opening musical gesture of *Stagecoach* is the future of the western score in chrysalis. While the film's credits, as well as its score, give primacy to folksong, the opening fanfare combines familiar western tropes with hints of things to come. A clip-clop rhythm is haloed by medium-high strings circling like the spin of wagon wheels, and a brass fanfare rings out in angular, uplifting perfect intervals and assertively striding rhythms.

The source of the fanfare's tune is a melody associated with the cowboy song 'Bury Me Not on the Lone Prairie'; however, this melody only appears to have become attached to the song in a 1932 collection (Studwell 1994, 66). This version was quickly 'answered' by a very similar tune from western singer-songwriter Carson Robison and his Buckaroos with 'Carry Me Back to the Lone Prairie', on the premise that a cowboy could not conceivably want to be buried anywhere else

Example 14.2a Opening melody from *Stagecoach*.

Example 14.2b 'Bury Me Not on the Lone Prairie'.

Example 14.2c 'I'm an Old Cowhand from the Rio Grande' from *Rhythm on the Range*.

(Catherine A. Robison n.d.). Compounding the signification, the melody also shares some structural traits with the tune of Johnny Mercer's 'I'm an Old Cowhand from the Rio Grande' for the singing cowboy film *Rhythm on the Range* (1936) starring Bing Crosby. (Roy Rogers and the Sons of the Pioneers would also have a hit with the song.) Thus, within a seven-year span, we can observe the formation of a small family of tunes functioning across the folk and the commercial realms, and as the orchestration in *Stagecoach* realizes, they share with such traditional songs as spirituals and work songs a phrasing that encourages call-and-response performance, embedding communality in the structure (see Examples 14.2a–c). The song(s) would have been fresh in the ears of a 1939 audience, although an audience today will probably hear the seeds of epic westerns of the 1950s and 1960s. Ford's visual emphasis on movement of people on horseback or in wagon trains through a spectacular landscape (often diagonally across the screen to create perspective) fuses the music with the image of westward movement in a trope that bespeaks 'Manifest Destiny'.

In the postwar era, the United States was taking its position as a superpower, envisioning itself as one nation *under God* (the words were added to the Pledge of Allegiance in 1954 explicitly to contrast America with the 'godless Communists'). While debates about American masculinity were often finding expression in the subtext, American nationality and nationalism were emblematized in these title sequences.

The 'outside' threat of the Indians (without a trace of irony, alas) that had made a brief, intrusive appearance, both visually and musically, in *Stagecoach* was eventually erased in favour of the unbroken majesty of the landscape and the music. This musical trope is not unrelated to the centuries-old European pastoral, but altered to fit the more rugged landscape of the American West: the undulating arched melodies over smooth, rolling rhythms are transformed into soaring, angular melodies constructed of perfect intervals and gapped modal scales over agitated, urgent rhythms, often wreathed with the spinning strings that impart forward motion. The gentler pastoral, often couched in warm woodwinds, still appears in domestic moments, or more intimate stories, such as *Shane*.

The musical language of the Manifest Destiny trope can be, and usually is, traced back to the American art music of the 1930s, particularly that of composers Virgil Thomson and Aaron Copland. Thomson's scores for two documentaries directed by Pare Lorentz, *The Plow that Broke the Plains* (1936) and *The River* (1938), use a simple, straightforward, mostly modal musical language based on American folksongs, hymnody and popular dance music – the same sources as for many western scores. Copland was inspired by the directness of expression in Thomson's handling of his musical materials and simplified his own compositional voice for both musical and political reasons. Copland felt that at a time of such societal stress (the Depression and the trajectory towards war in Europe), it was important to speak to, not over, his audiences (of course, that also would have financial benefit), and as a composer, he searched for a distinctly 'American' voice. During his studies in Paris in the 1920s, he had thought that might include jazz; a trip to Mexico in the early 1930s inspired the symphonic composition *El Salón México* and heralded an influx of additive rhythms (the piece strongly influenced Bronislau Kaper's 1953 score to *Ride, Vaquero!*); and Lincoln Kirstein's commission of *Billy the Kid* (premiered in 1938) for Ballet Caravan was accompanied by a volume of cowboy tunes for inspiration. Copland also scored the documentary *The City* (1939) and cinematic adaptations of *Of Mice and Men* (1939) and *Our Town* (1940), as well as the ballets *Appalachian Spring* (1942) and *Rodeo* (1943), developing a distinctive language that melded Anglo-Irish melodic patterns, quartal harmony, asymmetrical rhythms and metric modulations – and, perhaps most significantly, a spacious orchestration founded on a strong bass, a largely empty mid-range and a sharp, clear upper register (see also Lerner 2001).

Copland's style clearly struck a chord with audiences, and the connection with distinctly American themes in his ballets and films, as much as any specific musical gestures, helped reinforce his position as an American composer. He did not score a film that might be considered squarely a western until Lewis Milestone's adaptation of Steinbeck's *The Red Pony* (1949). Despite the essentially domestic nature of the story and a de-emphasis of the landscape in favour of medium-close shots, the score is a full-blown manifestation of those features of Copland's style most associated with Americanness and specifically 'the West'. Still, while some Hollywood scores might show incidental influence, it was not until 1958 and Jerome Moross's score for William Wyler's *The Big Country* that the Copland-esque Americana style really became stamped on the Hollywood western (see also Whitmer, 2012).

The title sequence of *The Big Country* was designed by Saul Bass, the graphic designer most noted for his stunning, minimalist movie posters and Hitchcock title sequences; although the typeface is the only obvious graphic element, the eye of the advertising designer is evident throughout, as the camera focuses on both the large-scale movement of the stagecoach sweeping through the amber-grained prairie (the sequence is in colour, but the colour palette makes it appear sepia-toned) and close-up detail of the horses' heads, their hooves and the spinning wheels of the stagecoach. Moross's sweeping title theme is composed of three basic gestures: busy, circling high strings and winds; a wide-ranging angular landscape-line melody in strings and brass; and a driving bassline in an asymmetrical rumba rhythm – 3+3(+2) – the last beat of which is silent, but felt. Pulses in the brass punchily subdivide the rhythm.

It is not that Moross and Bass created something new with this title sequence – in fact, quite the opposite. All the pieces that had been building come together in a hugely effective apotheosis. In Sturges's *The Magnificent Seven* (1960), Elmer Bernstein goes even further by adding more active rhythmic pulses in the mid-range. One notable element of the *Magnificent Seven* title sequence is that the landscape itself is frozen in a still image: the music provides more than enough motion. Bernstein would compose many similar, driving-soaring scores during the 1960s and 1970s for westerns, many of them starring Wayne in the last gasp of Manifest Destiny as a (relatively) uncomplicated concept. Even in Wayne's latter films, from as early as *The Searchers* to his final *The Shootist* (1976), the mythic/epic tended to turn from the triumphantly heroic to the tragic.

In this late, arguably mannerist period of the classic Hollywood western, comedy also came more to the fore. Bernstein's distinctive style can also be heard in Johnny Williams's score for *The Rare Breed* (1966), a comic western in which the asymmetrical, driving rhythms and soaring landscape line come together not in the title sequence but in the birth of the distinctly American calf of a Longhorn cow and Jersey bull. Jack Elliott's and Allyn Ferguson's raucous, fiddle tune-based theme for Burt Kennedy's

Support Your Local Gunfighter (1971) pushes and pulls expectations through wildly asymmetrical rhythms as the camera follows a train through the mountainous landscape – a visual pun on the classical opening for a film in which the 'hero' is afraid of horses. One must know the conventions in order to play with them, as is so brilliantly parodied by the Sheriff riding past the Count Basie Orchestra in Mel Brooks's *Blazing Saddles* (1974), running roughshod over accepted conventions of musical style, historical period, urban/rural and diegetic/nondiegetic. (This striking image is depicted on the cover of the present book.) Brooks would toy with audience expectations of music's placement again by stashing a cellist in the closet in *High Anxiety* (1977), but the presence of the Basie Orchestra also plays into the running jokes surrounding 'Black Bart' (Cleavon Little). The Sheriff reinserts African-American presence into the American landscape in a tightrope parody that plays on racial stereotypes in order to satirize them. The 'justified' musical accompaniment also recalls the singing cowboy films of the 1930s, primarily the series of all-black musical cowboy films starring jazz singer Herb Jeffries including *Two-Gun Man from Harlem* (1938) and *The Bronze Buckaroo* (1939).

The one arena where the heroic elements of Manifest Destiny may have followed unproblematically is to the 'final frontier' of outer space. Whilst the theme to the *Star Trek* television series (1966–9) used quartal harmonies, its soaring 'landscape' line was performed by an otherworldly female voice in an unorthodox studio mix (though an episode that recapitulates the gunfight at the O.K. Corral has a score reminiscent of Copland). Even as late as 1983, *The Right Stuff* was essentially scored as a western; it was cast with such actors as Sam Shepard, Ed Harris, Fred Ward, Scott Glenn and Lance Henriksen, all of whom made a number of westerns in an era when few were being made. The parallel between cowboys and astronauts permeates the film, which treads the fine line of admiring the Mercury astronauts while underlining their flaws with comedic flair.

The Spaghetti Western

The Hollywood western diminished in importance during the 1960s, particularly as American society began to confront some of its political divisions. At the same time, European filmmakers, led by Sergio Leone, took on the quintessentially American genre and reshaped it; and Morricone, Leone's frequent collaborator, radically rewrote its musical language. While the imagery was often similar to Hollywood's (even if shot in South Europe or North Africa), spaghetti westerns were simultaneously more morally ambiguous and more self-conscious about the iconic imagery. Morricone, while obviously skilled in orchestral composition, was also adept at popular-music styles and the use of the recording studio.

The opening of *For a Few Dollars More* (*Per qualche dollaro in più*; 1965) is at once homage, subversion and reinvention. A tiny figure on horseback wends its way through the desert landscape, but instead of a magnificent Manifest Destiny cue, or even a folksong, we hear only sound effects: the jingling of harness, the slap of leather, the strike of a match. The sounds are extremely closely miked, as if they are coming from right beside the listener, yet the only person we can see is that figure in the distance. We could interpret this as contorted aural perspective, until a gunshot rings out 'beside' the listener's ear, and the figure falls from his horse like a target in a shooting gallery; the bullet reinforces the distance from audience to image, making us realize we have been at the shooter's point of audition all along. The iconic image is skewered, and when the title cards come up, the graphics jump around on screen to avoid the gunshots that punctuate the main-title cue (most of the cards are 'shot', but Morricone's escapes). The music is primarily composed of a Tiomkin-like male chorus, reduced to rhythmic grunts, surf-style electric guitar and a twangy mouth harp. The studio manipulation required in order to balance these elements, vastly different in volume, is significant, and the spectator is cued to sonic deceptions from the beginning.

The crossover between sound effect and music reaches its apotheosis in *Once Upon a Time in the West* (*C'era una volta il West*; 1968). The squeak of a tin windmill, the creak of a door or floorboard, the whistling of the wind, the crow of a rooster, even the taunting chatter of a character to a caged bird are among the elements that are arranged rhythmically and dramatically to score the opening scene. The blend of sound effect, sparse musical utterances, expectant silences and static staging, such as in the final three-way shootout in *The Good, the Bad, and the Ugly* (*Il buono, il brutto, il cattivo*; 1966), have become emblematic of the spaghetti western.

The sparse, gritty look and feel of the spaghetti western crossed back to Hollywood at the end of the 1960s. *Butch Cassidy and the Sundance Kid* (1969), scored by songwriter Burt Bacharach, took the contemporary studio approach to scoring in an era when Hollywood films were eschewing orchestral scores, in part for financial reasons given the breakup of the studio system, and in part because the aesthetic choices for 'realism' tended more towards source scoring. Sam Peckinpah's *The Wild Bunch* (1969) had self-consciously marked an end of an era. The archaic brutal, destructive masculinity of the characters is symbolized by the opening sequence: the bunch rides into a Mexican town past children gleefully watching a swarm of ants devour a scorpion. Jerry Fielding's score layers militaristic snare-drum rhythms, guitar flourishes, warm woodwind choirs in the foreground and distantly miked muted trumpet-calls. The terse but elegiac tone presages the echoing trumpet calls of Jerry Goldsmith's score for *Patton* (1970), another period film in which traditional American masculinity is challenged against the contemporary backdrop of Vietnam.

Postmodernism and Revisionism

Although the term 'postmodern' has been endlessly debated, one feature generally agreed upon is the self-conscious assemblage of iconic elements in ways that highlight their constructedness, comment upon or undermine their coherence. While this is most often couched in 'postmodern cool', Lawrence Kasdan's *Silverado* (1985) offers a warm, wry nostalgia. An affectionate homage to the western movies and television of Kasdan's childhood, *Silverado* still manages to comment on some of the things that had been erased from those westerns, such as the African-American experience in the West. The claustrophobic opening, with a shootout inside a small shack, is almost pure spaghetti western visually and in its *musique concrète* construction of the sound-effect-as-music track; but then Emmett (Scott Glenn), having vanquished his many attackers, opens the door and passes through, like Dorothy into the land of Oz: the darkness turns to light, the claustrophobic shack expands to a widescreen vista of the Rockies and Bruce Broughton's main-title cue captures the magnificence of Bernstein's Manifest Destiny idiom.

The debate on how far back to place the 'revisionist' western is complex, and some revisionist themes can be found in the 1950s, but certainly the American western is firmly in a revisionist period by the 1980s. By the 1960s, the treatment of Native Americans was the generic elephant in the room, confronted head-on by a few films like Ralph Nelson's *Soldier Blue* (1970), but otherwise avoided, even in *Silverado*. The issue was at the centre of two revisionist westerns from 1990: Kevin Costner's famous but problematic *Dances with Wolves* and Australian director Simon Wincer's comedic but arguably more convincing *Quigley Down Under*.

One of the ironies of John Barry's score for *Dances with Wolves* is that the racial difference between the white men and the Lakota is unmarked: both are scored by the same post-romantic European-style music (Scheurer 2008; Gorbman 2001). Only the aggressive Pawnee have more stereotypical 'bad Indian' music. Although Wincer's *Quigley Down Under* is a comedy, it still manages to be more trenchant on race and gender than *Dances with Wolves*. Wincer and composer Basil Poledouris had been responsible for the hugely successful television miniseries *Lonesome*

Dove (1989), based on Larry McMurtry's western novel. The displacement of the western to Australia in *Quigley Down Under* sets the racial conflict into relief. American sharpshooter Matt Quigley (Tom Selleck) is hired by English rancher Elliott Marston (Alan Rickman) to rid his station of vermin. Upon his arrival, Quigley discovers that the 'vermin' is a tribe of aborigines that Marston wants removed from 'his' land, and Quigley teams up to defeat him with Crazy Cora (Laura San Giacomo), whom Marston has essentially bought to service his men. The title sequence is filled with iconic images of boots, rifles, bullets, spurs and so on, and a cheeky transposition of the 'travelling through the landscape' to a sailing ship on the ocean. Poledouris's score is a pastiche of the Manifest Destiny trope, but with nautical flair.

Walter Hill's *Geronimo: An American Legend* (1993) is, like *Dances with Wolves*, an attempt to see the Indian experience through the eyes of sympathetic white men (this story actually has two nested narrative frames: an army officer who engages Geronimo and the army officer's aide, who narrates the film), when the story rightfully belongs to Wes Studi's eponymous hero. Ry Cooder's score attempts to provide a voice for the Native Americans, but – however beautiful – the synthesis of various kinds of Native American music (mostly Yaqui, which is not only the wrong tribe, but the wrong geographical region) is carefully constructed exoticism. By contrast, Cooder's folk, minstrel and war song-based score for Hill's *The Long Riders* (1980) is, despite the occasional presence of the oud, far more historically representative.

Based on a turn-of-the-century *corrido* (a popular narrative song), Robert M. Young's *The Ballad of Gregorio Cortez* (1982) is about a real-life manhunt that resulted from a linguistic misunderstanding. The film follows both the white lawmen, through the eyes of a reporter (a device allowing a critical distance within the narrative common to a number of revisionist westerns), and the Mexican-American fugitive Cortez, whom we encounter seemingly without mediation. Reflecting the narrative crux of the story, the Spanish in the film is untranslated, creating the same linguistic barriers in the film that the characters encountered. The *corrido* itself, at times with male vocals, forms the basis for the synthesizer score, a choice possibly determined by budget but also focusing the temporal distance of the film's point of view.

As the revisionist western sharpens awareness of genre history and narrative tropes, the musical style becomes more flexible, highlighting pertinent aspects of the genre's history in telling the stories now consciously placed in a more knowing frame. In films like Clint Eastwood's *Unforgiven* (1992) and Ang Lee's *Brokeback Mountain* (2005), the intimate, personal nature of the stories returns to the folksong aesthetic of an earlier time, in surprisingly delicate, acoustic guitar-based scores, even when set against larger-than-life landscapes. The Manifest Destiny trope still exists, but is now found primarily in baseball films, such as Barry Levinson's *The Natural* (1984), scored by Randy Newman, and Young's *Talent for the Game* (1991), scored by Randy's cousin David Newman.

The Morricone–Leone aesthetic had a profound impact on a younger generation of filmmakers beginning in the 1980s, just as Morricone and Leone themselves went to Hollywood. Alex Cox is most noted for his punk-themed films *Repo Man* (1984) and *Sid & Nancy* (1986), but he also directed *Straight to Hell* (1987), an hallucinatory fantasia on a western, and *Walker* (1987), a purposefully anachronistic biopic of American mercenary William Walker, who led a coup in nineteenth-century Nicaragua, as a commentary on 1980s American foreign policy. In both cases, the music by the Clash's Joe Strummer seems initially anachronistic; but that, of course, is the point. In contrast, punk band Chumbawamba's Morriconian score highlights the spaghetti-western elements of vengeance and redemption in Cox's futuristic version of the Jacobean *Revengers Tragedy* (2002). South African director Richard Stanley uses western imagery extensively in both the post-apocalyptic *Hardware* (1990) and the fantastical *Dust Devil* (1993); Simon Boswell's spare musical scores recall both Morricone and Cooder, and the added compilation of heavy metal, industrial disco-punk and Rossini's *Stabat Mater* (1841) works remarkably well to highlight the Biblical subtext of *Hardware*.

The detour into science fiction for elements of the western genre followed the trajectory of Manifest Destiny from the Pacific Ocean to outer space, but with the shifting – and fragmenting – concepts of what it is to be American, the western has changed. Sensitivity to the complexity of American experience, along racial/ethnic, class, sexuality and gender lines has challenged the core principle of white masculinity, opening up new tributaries of musical expression. The genre presently offers fewer overall trends, and more individual takes on, revisions of and even rejections of the long and changing history of the genre. As with any successful critique, however, most of these films are highly aware of the conventions and their rhetorical and symbolic baggage, using them to comment upon the past of the genre as well as contributing to its continued salience.

15 The Music of Screen Musicals

CARYL FLINN

I

Whether on stage or screen, musicals have always been rather complex objects of study, with their mixed parentage of music halls; opera and operetta; regional, ethnic and national folk tunes; and the mass-produced hits of star songwriters and performers. Even today, the genre resurrects dusty oppositions between low and high aesthetic practices – the purported crassness of 'show business' against esteemed creative work – garnering either adoration or disdain from audiences in the process. Screen musicals add even more queries to the mix: does, for instance, the presence of performance numbers make films like Rainer Werner Fassbinder's *Lili Marleen* (1981) or Todd Haynes's *Superstar: The Karen Carpenter Story* (1988) musicals? What is specific to musical style, or to its narrative? When soundtracks tend to dominate their films, as in *Easy Rider* (1969), does that make the films musicals? Why are singers in top hats more iconic than those in cowboy hats? What of filmed adaptations that appear 'less musical' than their stage shows, as with *Rent* (2005), with its reduced continuous singing and recitative? How should we situate early twenty-first-century television shows like *Glee* (Fox, 2009–15) and the various 'Idol' competitions within the genre? Why are *Repo! The Genetic Opera* (2008) and *The Rocky Horror Picture Show* (1975) rarely considered musicals when approached as cult films? And what does one do with Robert Altman's *Popeye* (1980) or the porno musical *New Wave Hookers* (1985)? What, in short, is a musical?

Genre films continually remind us how limited – and permutable – the critical category of genre actually is, and that's what makes them so interesting. You teach the concept to deconstruct it, knowing full well that it is indestructible, whether as a critical concept or a form of industrial practice and marketing. Curiously, while musicals may have a fuller array of issues to consider than other film genres, scholars have come nowhere near to exhausting or even pursuing them, and only recently have begun to explore some of the more pressing questions, not the least of which is the role played by music and song.

This chapter aims, then, to provide a brief overview of film-musical scholarship and to explore its impact on conceptions of the genre in addition to our understandings of its music. Those trends – actually, concepts and categories – have enjoyed a certain hegemony that scholars are only now starting to dispute in reopening the conversation about what constitutes a musical, much less a 'classical' one. My focus in this chapter takes aim at that classical paradigm not to dismiss it – for it continues to exert great influence – but to show its inability to account for many film musicals that are typically considered part of it, much less the thousands circulating outside of that paradigm. Musicals have always generated a flurry of publications and commentary, but the first wave of serious academic study didn't begin until the 1980s, led by scholars such as Rick Altman (1987), Jane Feuer (1993 [1982]) and Richard Dyer (1985). Before, assessments typically took the form of historical overviews and popular appreciations – useful, but lacking the analytical and historical rigour of this new scholarship. In the 1960s, when scholars began treating film genres as legitimate objects of study, they turned overwhelmingly away from musicals in favour of westerns and film noir, leading the feminist and cultural-studies scholars of the ensuing decades to note how easily academia sustained longstanding, popular biases of musicals as disreputable, feminized diversions.

In attacking that paradigm, Altman, Feuer, Dyer *et al.* gave the musical a seat at the academic table. There, film scholars treated the genre first and foremost as an aesthetic artefact, flocking to questions of form, a focal point that was powered by the post-structuralism and semiotics pervading cultural studies, and film and literary studies, at the time. Keen on identifying narrative structures and patterns, scholars focused on the contrast between musical numbers and narratives or the genre's overall, often exaggerated use of form in order to consider their ideological impact. (Musical-theatre scholars, by contrast, typically explored aspects beyond musical texts such as their production and financial components or their relationships with critics and audiences, a difference partially explained by the fact that it was often within the grasp of musical-theatre readers to produce stage musicals – at schools, regional theatres, etc. – whereas producing 35 mm and 70 mm film musicals was more out of bounds.)

The 1990s gave way to a second wave of film-musical scholarship. Buoyed by advances in lesbian, gay and queer (LGBTQ) scholarship that exposed how musicals (and often musicals criticism) codified various aspects of sexuality and gender, film-musical scholars turned away from generic concerns to focus on wider socio-historical issues, contexts and audiences. Consequently, the understanding of musicals also shifted. Instead of starting from the binary structures of narrative/spectacle, or of serious/frivolous from inside the films (including the gendered and racia-lized dimensions that characterized these oppositions), scholars challenged them. Three of the many prominent scholars informed by LGBTQ con-cerns helped guide these shifts. Steven Cohan has elaborated queer and proto-queer traces in film musicals over different historical eras (for example, see Cohan 1997 on masculinity in movies from the 1950s); Matthew Tinkcom has turned to MGM's Freed Unit to exemplify what he maintains is a gay/queer form of labour (1996); and Brett Farmer has considered gay reception and fandom (2000). Others have explored the genre's rich relationship with camp, and more recently, with related affective economies such as shame and pride (Robertson 1996; Dyer 2001; Flinn 2013). In short, instead of approaching film musicals as autonomous texts, scholars started to position them as phenomena that always interacted with outside forces.

But of course not everything shifts when academic trends do. Indeed, this second wave has emerged as musicals are still widely regarded as unworthy, feminine 'fluff'. Today's queer approach to the film musical doesn't shirk away from the scorn heaped on it but rather examines, and occasionally celebrates, its ostensibly 'cheaper' features in light of its intimate pleasures and impacts, particularly for marginalized audiences. Consider the relatively recent cinematic cliché of gay men swooning to musical numbers, as Kevin Kline's closeted character does in *In and Out* (1997); or the underexplored treasure trove of musicals that emerged from the New Queer Cinema in the mid-1990s, such as *Zero Patience* (1993), *I'm Not There* (2007) and *Velvet Goldmine* (1998).

In shifting the paradigm, musical scholars obviously did not, nor could not, overturn all problematic assumptions swirling around 'the musical'. Indeed, the singularizing term of 'the' musical itself merits interrogation, as it implies that one type, one model, of musical cinema rules the roost – and most of you reading this can imagine what that model is. For like their predecessors, the majority of Anglophone scholars hold to the conception of musicals as high-budget flights of fancy, in the process leaving other kinds of musicals to the side. A more inclusive notion of musical style, for instance, would take into account those made in the former German Democratic Republic (GDR), such as *My Wife Wants to Sing* (*Meine Frau macht Musik*; 1958); or documentary-styled musicals such as *The Sound of Mumbai: A Musical* (2010), which dramatizes the story of ghetto children in India auditioning to perform songs from *The Sound of Music* (1965) for a lavish one-night show in Mumbai; or Wim Wenders's popular *The Buena Vista Social Club* (1999), which promoted recordings and performances of the Cuban musicians it chronicled.

Many Anglophone scholars still tend to approach 'the' musical as an American phenomenon, with forays into Australian and British musicals and, of course, the endlessly – if deservedly – cited *Les parapluies de Cherbourg* (*The Umbrellas of Cherbourg*; 1964), directed by Jacques Demy. In publications and academic courses, Hollywood musicals are taken as the point of departure, the point of origin, before 'other' alternative film-musical practices are explored – typically to be contrasted to that primary practice. Writes Adrian Martin:

> A true history of the musical . . . would have to recognize that the model taken as the 'dominant paradigm' of the genre (those Hollywood musicals made in the forties and fifties, mainly associated with MGM), is far from being an absolute and determining reference point. It is only our myopia, and our easy acquiescence to American domination of popular cinema, which has made it so.
>
> (A. Martin 2001, 70)

Small matter that the years of that 'dominant paradigm' remain contested, or that the ostensible Golden Era it absorbs doesn't conform to actual industrial practice. For instance, Hollywood studios actually produced more musicals in the early sound period than during the mid-1950s – logically enough, given the novelty of film sound in the former era and the ballooning budgets of the second. Consider also that the number of musicals produced in India has long outstripped Hollywood's. Already, we see that the 'classical' Hollywood musical doesn't have much stable authority. But that hasn't stopped the myth that it has.

Any cultural hegemony requires multiple supports from a variety of sources. Some are very pragmatic. Martin, for instance, considers sound recording and dubbing practices and technologies. Any movie or genre that relies heavily on its soundtrack – such as musicals, screwball comedies or texts with elaborate multi-track dialogue – is more difficult to translate and thus more difficult to export. The impact of dubbed or even subtitled musical numbers, observes Martin, can be quite diminished, less immersive or comprehensible – although it can also lead to some enjoyable camp. Exceptions exist, to be sure, often in big-budget films such as *The Sound of Music*, for which European and Latin American audiences heard numbers re-recorded with lyrics in German, Italian, Spanish and French.

Obviously, Hollywood's elephantine reach around the globe elevates a US-centric conception of film musicals. It does so through its movies (or actual product) and through their markets of distribution and exhibition. But its reach is also cultural and ideological, taking the form of 'big star' personalities, of spectacular budgets and special effects, of opulent, white notions of glamour and so on. An efficient system, it seems to supply US musicals with the cultural, conceptual and economic muscle to squelch the many musicals made differently and made elsewhere – that is, in the majority of the world.

The bias does far more than centralize and privilege Hollywood musicals. It also privileges, or at least standardizes, particular representations of gender, class, regional and ethnic identity in what Martin rightly describes as a financial and ideological colonializing process. For instance, one of the so-called non-classical musicals mentioned earlier, *The Buena Vista Social Club*, asserts its white, male, Western dominance through the conspicuous presence of US musician Ry Cooder and, especially, German director Wenders, the ethnographer/discoverer who 'rescues' the aging Cuban musicians from oblivion.

To be sure, North Atlantic film-musical scholars are becoming increasingly aware of these trends. Anthologies such as *Musicals: Hollywood and Beyond* (Marshall and Stilwell 2000) and *The International Film Musical* (Creekmur and Mokdad 2013) explore a variety of global case studies, with the latter organized into chapters based on national and regional traditions almost unheard of by many Western scholars, such as those of Greece, Japan, Turkey and Germany. Scholars have exposed racial and regional biases within Hollywood musical culture by tackling issues such as racial integration (Knight 2002); local and community theatre (Wolf 2015); musicals and television screens (Stilwell 2011); musicals in relation to sound-recording technologies (Altman 2013); and reception patterns among under-represented audiences (Garcia 2014).

Not all of the post-1990s musicals (and their scholars) push conceptions of musicals into unexplored new terrain, and in fact some rely on scaffolding that closely parallels that of the trends they're trying to upset. Rather than contrasting oppositions between narrative and spectacle, for instance, newer practices often contrast the fictionally stable classical paradigm against the fluctuating, abundant alternatives they assume to be working outside of it. To be sure, this happens at the hands of practitioners and critics eager to chip away at that classical dominance. For them, non-majoritarian musical cultures tend to offer quaint or colourful spice to perk up white Hollywood, as Baz Luhrmann may be said to have done in the Bollywood moments of *Moulin Rouge!* (2001) – on which more later. At other times, 'non-classical' musical practices get treated as loci of authenticity, folk- rather than industry-driven, for instance, or somehow more directly expressive, authentic and less commercial, such as *Bran Nue Dae* (2009) from Aboriginal Australia. This process occurs in major commercial projects as well, as in a string of UK musicals starting in the 1990s that were devoted to working-class characters, including *The Full Monty* (1997) and *Kinky Boots* (2005), both adapted later into monster hits on Broadway. In other words, to contrast the diverse, open multiplicity of musicals beyond Hollywood – including those tagged as 'post-classical' or 'anti-classical' – against the 'classical' ones, is simply to flip the earlier terms, now ascribing a wide-open, healthy heterogeneity to one group that's positioned against an ostensibly ossified bad guy. Feminist film-maker and theorist Trinh T. Minh-ha acknowledged that kind of mapping in another context and advocated a different way out that takes 'margin-ality as a starting point rather than an ending point' (quoted in Keating 1998, 25).

With musicals – and the music therein – we might begin that process by considering the multi-directional global paths of their influences. For instance, *The Sound of Music* – in many ways the monarch of classical Hollywood musicals – reverberates in an array of global practices such as the Australian musicals *Moulin Rouge!* and *Mental* (2012). But neither of these films presents their predecessor as an originary text; and Lars von Trier's *Dancer in the Dark* (2000) goes even further. Like *The Sound of Mumbai*, *Dancer in the Dark* references the 1965 classic to make searing contrasts between the wealthy, upbeat world of the Trapp children and the grinding, inescapable poverty of the others.

'Bollywood' musicals – on which more below – offer a strong example of a musical tradition that shares Hollywood's love of lush spectacle and upbeat feelings, but is scarcely concerned about seamlessly integrating songs into storylines or logic. The result? These songs move into the foreground, with enough emphasis to outstrip that of the prominence numbers receive in revue-style musicals, the narratives of which are ske-letal at best.

Despite conceptions to the contrary, then, the classical and non-classical – or Hollywood and non-Hollywood – are not Manichean opposites. They are intermingled and messy. And as movies like *The Sound of Mumbai* demonstrate, influences are never a one-way street. In the film's brilliant opening, a voice-over intones: 'It would be easy to say, "if they [the children] believe in their dreams, they will do it." That would be the American way. But this isn't America, this is India.' Musical practices feed off other musical practices: consider how the Swedish pop group ABBA migrated via Australian musicals to the British stage as *Mamma Mia!* (1999) and then to its bizarrely cast US screen adaptation (2008), both directed by Phyllida Lloyd. Or how Sixto Rodriguez, an enigmatic 1970s US pop/folk singer, zigzagged from Detroit to South Africa and back, his movements tracked by Swedish director Malik Bendjelloul in his award-winning 2012 documentary *Searching for Sugar Man*. In the 1930s and 1940s, Soviet 'tractor' and 'factory' musicals showed the unquestionable influence of Busby Berkeley's opulent work at Warner Bros., despite having been produced during the reign of Zhdanov's mandated socialist realism. Half a century later, von Trier's *Dancer in the Dark* paid homage to those Soviet musicals every bit as much as it did to *Les parapluies de Cherbourg, Cabaret* (1972), *The Sound of Music* and *Pennies from Heaven* (1981).

Many of today's scholars are unpacking the category of the film musical, noting its contradictions, complexities and the endless non-cinematic forces that work alongside it. At its best, that scholarship expands our awareness of musicals in the purported Golden Era of the 1940s and 1950s every bit as much as the examples cast out from it. Sean Griffin (2014) has worked on swing musicals from B studios pitched for teen audiences; Jennifer Fleeger (2014b, 106–36) has written on Disney musicals as musicals for children (rather than as Disney films); Laura Gutiérrez (2010) has explored how Mexicanness was constructed through musical performances; and Desirée Garcia, in *The Migration of Musical Film* (2014), has reshaped the familiar themes of community and home by focusing on musicals made in the US classical era for African-American, Latino and Yiddish audiences. US-made musicals that followed on the heels of that classical era, however, remain extraordinarily under-studied, indeed, avoided like the plague – *Xanadu* (1980), anyone? As of this writing, only a few intrepid scholars have tackled this era, such as Kelly Kessler in her book on 1970s and 1980s musicals, *Destabilizing the Hollywood Musical* (2010); and Dyer in essays such as 'Is *Car Wash* [1976] A Musical?' (2011, 145–55).

Not surprisingly, academia's renewed interest in the genre began as musicals started enjoying their own revival in the 1990s. Less an old person's genre, the films migrated from the silver screen to online venues ('Dr. Horrible's Sing A-Long Blog', postings of miniaturized musicals, etc.) and to television, in which numerous non-musical series offered one-off musical episodes, such as 'The Bitter Suite' in *Xena: Warrior Princess* (Renaissance Pictures; season 3, episode 12, 1998), and 'Once More with Feeling' in *Buffy the Vampire Slayer* (Mutant Enemy Productions; season 6, episode 7, 2001). There's a caveat to the television trend, however, for musicals were not at all new to US television, having appeared in the 1950s in abridged forms of Broadway hits, or even, as in the case of *Cinderella* (1957), premiering on the small screen.

In the early twenty-first century, television has full-out musical shows like *Glee* and reality shows and/or song and dance competitions in varied global productions, including the British series *Pop Idol* (ITV, 2001–3) and *Strictly Come Dancing* (BBC, since 2004) and *The Voice of Holland* in the Netherlands (RTL4, since 2010). That resurgence has enriched our conception of the musical, notably because these new iterations are no longer film musicals so much as screen musicals. The foundations of that shift – arguably laid by music video of the 1980s – have left a significant impact, namely steering our collective focus towards the musical content of screen musical culture. And so, at last, we turn to those songs.

II

Despite the long list of issues raised around screen musicals, few scholars have tackled the role played by their songs and their music. Part of this omission may stem from simple oversight, with scholars taking the music for granted; or perhaps it comes from being discouraged by their lack of credentials in musicology – certainly a contentious point for many film-music scholars. In that vein, it's perhaps not shocking that scholarship on musical songs tends to be written by those trained in musicology rather than in film, and that cinema scholars largely avoid the topic, despite notable exceptions such as Dyer and, especially, Altman. Many of these English-language scholars are and were Hollywood-weaned, and perhaps were simply accustomed, almost unconsciously, to associate a certain type of music with film musicals. Despite that connection being more imagined than real, it is so deeply ingrained that scholars haven't risen to contest it with the zeal with which they have challenged other aspects of the genre, shadowing Claudia Gorbman's reference to narrative cinema's music as its 'unheard' melodies (1987).

The master song pattern associated with both film and stage musicals is a 32-bar form, stemming from Tin Pan Alley. A 32-bar song typically subdivides into an AABA phrase structure in which the B portion serves as a bridge (providing harmonic as well as melodic contrast to the A phrases), or an AABC pattern in which the C portion introduces a final phrase different from the first two. Other patterns, such as ABAC or ABAB, are also common. A self-contained structure of this kind frequently functions as a refrain (also known as a chorus) following an introductory verse section, in the manner described by Paul Laird:

> A verse is often rendered in speech rhythms, often over a simple, chordal accompaniment, somewhat like operatic recitative. It is not commonly the verse that communicates stylistic information about the music. That comes in the chorus, which might range from a fast dance tempo to a slow ballad. It is also the chorus that a listener remembers; there are many famous songs for musical theater for which only the most rabid of fans know the verse. (Laird 2011, 34)

Laird discusses classic stage musicals, but his observations are no less appropriate for screen musicals. Not surprisingly, the song's hook tends to be located in the chorus, that part of the song which leaves audiences humming after the show has ended. The strong beat and dynamic rhythmic patterns of many song choruses lead Laird (2011, 42) and Lehman Engel (1975, 106) to argue that 'rhythm songs' (not all of which are based on the 32-bar form) are behind some of the more successful Broadway musicals; these songs, they maintain, with their 'propulsive' beat, boast choruses that are not only easy to remember but spur you to tap your feet or even dance: for example, Marvin Hamlisch's 'One (Singular Sensation)' (*A Chorus Line*, 1975; filmed in 1985) and Richard Rodgers's (AABA) 'I'm Gonna Wash That Man Right Outa My Hair' (*South Pacific*, 1949; filmed in 1958). But refrains needn't be propulsive and energetic to be memorable, of course, as we know from Jerome Kern's powerful 'Ol' Man River' (*Show Boat*, 1927; filmed in 1929, 1936 and 1951).

The classical musical paradigm also positions its songs in particular, if not always predictable, places along story lines to serve certain functions. Introductory numbers set the proverbial stage; dance or novelty numbers give audiences a respite from dialogue or plot; other songs establish thematic issues and tensions, such as the 'Jet Song' from *West Side Story* (Leonard Bernstein and Stephen Sondheim, 1957; filmed in 1961), or the emotional rumblings of characters, as in 'If I Loved You' from *Carousel* (Richard Rodgers and Oscar Hammerstein II, 1945; filmed in 1956).

To label this 'classical' understanding of songs as a fiction is not to diminish the dominance its conventions have had across hundreds, if not thousands, of screen musicals. The seeming ubiquity of all those essentially simple 32-bar song forms has compelled scholars, critics and audiences alike to take them to be the only type of song at work in the genre, a perception compounded by the fact that the same structure shapes many jazz standards and pop tunes. Indeed, the form has long been around us, in TV theme songs, elevator music, and so on, since the 1960s.

The term Tin Pan Alley identifies a location in lower Manhattan as well as an early form of mass song production. A machine of endlessly varied musical influences, that laboratory was home to and reflected the diverse musical traditions of immigrants newly landed on US soil. Influences came from Irish ballads, African-American slave songs, blues, Yiddish music, Viennese operetta, American vernacular music, English burlesque and marching and military tunes. True, much of Tin Pan Alley's output followed the 32-bar format, but we should heed critics and scholars who caution against affixing a monolithic song form or structure to all of Tin Pan Alley, or to all of Hollywood musicals. (That Tin Pan Alley music prevailed during the 'Jazz Age' suggests the stylistic cross-pollination actually at work.)

Here, that tendency to unify 'classical' practice also gave shape to early film-music studies, as Jennifer Fleeger (2014a) has noted in challenging the all-but-monolithic conception of neo-romantic scoring that I, along with many others, attributed to scores from Hollywood film music's own Golden Era. Fleeger, who focuses on Hollywood cinema during its transition to sound, stresses the popularity of operetta and jazz, along with the hopes of moguls to produce filmed 'jazz opera' during this time. We can follow Fleeger's lead by turning to the actual diversity working in the classical era of Hollywood musicals: operetta was popular in the early and mid-1930s, swing in the 1940s, cowboy and early country and western music in both, rock'n'roll in the 1950s and jazz and blues across decades. In the 1950s, classically infused 'ballet suites' appeared in US musicals: for example, Gershwin's symphonic poem *An American in Paris* (1928) was reworked in MGM's eponymous musical, directed by Vincente Minnelli in 1951, along with some of the composer's own Tin Pan Alley songs.

That the basic AABA pattern has so many variants hardly revolutionizes the fundamental song structure, but, as Raymond Knapp and Mitchell Morris argue, it demonstrates that it is 'not a singular form but an array of conventions' (2011, 91). Even the most conventional song requires variation: Knapp and Morris note how the famous classic 'Oklahoma!' (Rodgers and Hammerstein, 1943), for instance, contains 16-bar phrases, instead of the usual 8. Chromatic elements inflect show songs, as do atypical accentuation patterns and pentatonic modalities, as we hear in standards such as 'Nearly So' in *The King and I* (Rodgers and Hammerstein, 1951; filmed in 1956), often making blatant attempts to exoticize music, setting and the ethnic 'others' affiliated with both. Moreover, if the 'classical' musical tune was easily singable, plenty were not, as shown by Ethel Merman, who held the note on 'I' in Gershwin's 'I Got Rhythm' for 32 (some say 64) bars on the opening night of *Girl Crazy* (1930; filmed in 1932 and 1943).

Like the films in which they appear, these tunes were born in an era of mass production, leading scholars to note how film genres and film songs both adhere to the shifting patterns of standardization (for efficiency) and difference (for originality). As Knapp and Morris (2011, 92) maintain, the standard conventions of songs in musicals help stabilize – or ward off – what they call their 'disruptive elements', an action that provides the comfort of familiarity, even when unconsciously recognized, with the excitement of novelty.

Film musicals vary from their stage counterparts for a number of reasons, and those reasons affect the music – and vice versa. With film musicals being typically more expensive and thus deemed 'riskier', Hollywood studios had considerable financial incentives to keep song styles simple enough to be repeatable and enhance the memorability of the film-going experience. A song's catchiness or novelty could help it, even in the Sherman Brothers' tongue-twister 'Supercalifragilisticexpialidocious' from *Mary Poppins* (1964). Having good song material shored up not just the success of the musical on screen, but of ancillary products such as original soundtracks – not to mention the off-screen lives of songs in stage and club performances, recordings, or on radio, television and, later, online.

While not the focus of the present essay, it is worth mentioning the need for further study of other musical components of musicals. Not everything is song. Many musicals, for instance – particularly those given big budgets – open with instrumental music taking the form of overtures to introduce audiences to upcoming songs and narrative movements (much as opening titles of non-musical films will announce musical themes and motifs). More recently, film musicals will close out with a single rock, pop or hip-hop piece, sometimes taken from the show, sometimes not; sometimes sung by someone in the show, sometimes not, a practice also characterizing non-musical texts such as *The Sopranos* (HBO, 1999–2007). The majority of the instrumental music in musicals, though, appears as underscoring that, with equal if not greater intensity than the overtures, borrows portions of the show's songs to make varia-tions of them. In *The Sound of Music*, for instance, Rodgers put one of the children's most juvenile numbers, 'The Lonely Goatherd', into waltz time during the Captain's party for the sophisticated Baroness.

The *performance* of songs in musicals also deserves additional study, whether in terms of vocal delivery or bodily and kinetic performance more generally. While it would be difficult, and undesirable, to identify a dominant vocal style over the course of screen musicals (classical and otherwise), many have been popular: belters like Barbra Streisand, croon-ers like Bing Crosby, the rockers of *Hedwig and the Angry Inch* (2001), the balladeers of *Once* (2006). Some trends come and go, some return, others don't, some never leave. (My hunch here is that stage musicals exhibit more loyalty to a stable group of vocalists and vocal trends than their cinematic counterparts, as in the trend of male 'speak-singing' during the 1950s and 1960s, or the female pop-diva belters of the late twentieth and early twenty-first centuries.)

Differences between stage and screen musicals arguably depend less on their formal traits so much as on the technology behind their production and reproduction. It's impossible to overstate the importance of recording, miking and sound-mixing technologies in that regard. In addition to creating an almost physical sense of space, they also affect the kinds of songs and singing styles that appear in the film. For instance, once early microphone technology was able to record nearby sounds free of ambient noise, crooning took off. By contrast, the Italian tradition of syncing voices in post-production made it difficult for film musicals to gain much traction there. Miking and recording technologies have also furthered the ability of screen songs to convey directness or intimacy, features that cameras could easily reinforce, whether by position, duration or distance. The effect didn't even have to rely on close-ups, the usual example given when differentiating stage from screen musicals. The camera in Dudley Murphy's 1929 short *St. Louis Blues*, for instance, in which Bessie Smith twice performs the eponymous song (W. C. Handy, 1914), focuses sometimes on her, sometimes her listeners, but remains in medium shot, capturing the singer in profile. But Smith's doleful facial expression and posture convey a sense of intimacy and emotional veracity regardless.

Like many popular songs, those in screen musicals are fiercely, and not unreasonably, understood as expressions of the characters or of performers – such as Bessie Smith or Judy Garland – who sing them. This applies to many forms of popular music in the West: I recall as a child my confusion listening to Joan Baez singing in the first person in 'The Night They Burned Old Dixie Down' (Robbie Robertson, 1969) in lines such as 'I'm a working man'. On screens, the synchronization between the voice we hear and the performer we see effortlessly activates these default settings: we read faces for the expressive content we assume is being generated by the songs. This is one reason that obvious lip syncing is so jarring – and especially when the synchronization is done to a voice that could not possibly be the singer's own, as elaborated in musicals such as *Pennies From Heaven* (see below) or in the musical-like practices of films such as Hans-Jürgen Syberberg's adaptation of *Parsifal* (1982) or Werner Schroeter's *The Death of Maria Malibran* (*Der Tod der Maria Malibran*; 1972), films whose on-screen performers mouth recordings of other singers who are differently gendered, differently raced, emerging from scratched discs, etc. Westerners have been so conditioned to find emotional expression – and veracity – in songs that we almost demand that they 'speak' to us or otherwise invite us in, consciously or unconsciously, emotionally or physically.

Like the original UK television series by Dennis Potter on which it was based (BBC, 1978), Ross's *Pennies From Heaven* showcases songs that exemplify, almost literally, the song type linked to 'the' classical musical. The movie is stuffed with Tin Pan Alley songs which Walter, the lead character, a sheet-song salesman, is having difficulty peddling. It is the Depression, and, if the songs are not helping Walter out financially, they do enable him to slip into elaborate flights of fancy – largely of his financial and sexual prowess. Audiences hear the songs in un-enhanced recordings from the 1930s and 1940s by earlier performers such as Helen Kane or Bing Crosby, but view them as Steve Martin and his co-stars exaggeratedly lip sync to them. The musical's brilliance is in working within the very Hollywood model it exposes, choreographing numbers à la Busby Berkeley, screening footage of Fred Astaire and Ginger Rogers performing Irving Berlin's 'Let's Face the Music and Dance' from *Follow the Fleet* (1936) in front of a transfixed Walter.

In many ways, *Pennies From Heaven* ought to be considered a classical musical, with its extravagant production numbers, its utopian touches, its A-list stars and its director – who was also responsible for *Funny Lady* (1975) and *Footloose* (1984). But it isn't. For *Pennies* shows the *inability* of musicals (and songs) to uplift in any real sense and instead articulates the descent of those who lose themselves to the mass-made hopes and fantasies made and voiced by others. (When the film was released, professors taught it to exemplify the kinds of film-music practices that Bertolt Brecht or Theodor Adorno and Max Horkheimer might endorse.) Presenting recordings without updating or enhancing them, *Pennies From Heaven* makes its songs show signs of their own weariness, demonstrating not simply their age but their inappropriateness to Walter's (and our own) circumstances. After all, how many studio musicals end with the hanging of the lead character? (Less than twenty years later, Trier's 'hundred-camera musical' *Dancer in the Dark* mounted a similar critique of the musical, and it too hanged its lead character at the end.)

In that regard, it is impossible to overstate the influence of Dyer's assessment of the film musical's 'utopian' possibilities – generated by sensual rather than representational signs and impressions – on first-wave Anglophone scholars (1985, 206). Thematically, the musical seems to provide the ideal model, and Hollywood's proclivity for happy endings, particularly in the studio musicals on which Dyer focuses, lends itself readily to the concept. (But then so do the musicals of the former GDR and Soviet Union.) Years later, Dyer argued for the special impact made by songs, which, he claimed, could 'dissolve the boundaries between the self and others' (2011, 3). Songs in musicals don't always take up that function, of course, whether it's Tim Curry's anthemic 'I'm Just a Sweet Transvestite' (Richard O'Brien, 1973) from *Rocky Horror*, *Hustle & Flow*'s 'It's Hard Out Here for a Pimp' (2005; song by Three 6 Mafia and Cedric Coleman), or almost anything by Stephen Sondheim. Indeed, countless songs run roughshod over that and other functions scholars ascribe to them. Their emotional expressivity, for instance, is certainly not the aim of most musical novelty numbers, even in the most classical of musicals. Cole Porter's 'Be a Clown' as performed by Garland and Gene Kelly at the end of

Minnelli's *The Pirate* (1948) offers an example in which songs don't always line up with narrative, character or emotional expectations.

Whether traditional or experimental, many film-musical production practices – be they from India, Japan or Italy – make no push whatsoever towards visual or even emotional verisimilitude. Sometimes, recorded voices aren't matched or attached to the actors we see performing them, in which case the song becomes more (or less) than the mere expression of character psychology. Even musicals within that expressive tradition strain it by using songs for collective expression, which often occurs in politically motivated musicals, such as Marc Blitzstein's US stage show *The Cradle will Rock* (1937) or Luis Valdez's movie *Zoot Suit* (1981), with music by Daniel Valdez and Lalo Guerrero. The movie musicalized the backdrop of the US 'Zoot Suit Riots' during the Second World War, in which white sailors and police attacked men of colour, mainly Chicanos, for whom the zoot suit was an expression of ethnic pride and masculinity. This film, like the stage show from which it came, 'unrealistically' uses visuals and songs to bring Anglo-American stereotypes of Chicanos to life, exposing them for their hyperbolic departures from the lived realities of Chicanos. Both story and song covered issues dealing with class, family life, assimilation into Anglo-American culture and police harassment, depicting them in intensely stylized, often clichéd ways. The same technique characterizes other musicals pitched to specific group formations with vested interests in activism. There are 'AIDS musicals' such as *Jeanne et le garçon formidable* (*Jeanne and the Perfect Guy*; 1998) from France and *Zero Patience* from Canada. Spike Lee's *School Daze* (1988) stages the politics of African-American hair and skin tone in a face-off at a high school gym in 'Straight and Nappy', a number evocative of the 'Jet Song' but with humour thrown into the mix.

India's musicals work within a tradition of saturated spectacle and romance that easily rivals that of MGM, but they also reflect diverse and specifically Indian customs, with references to different forms of folk music and to traditional and contemporary popular and art songs. Most scholars use the term 'Bollywood' as a shorthand to identify this musical tradition, which has the benefits of recognition to readers but the pitfalls of short-changing non-Hindi Indian film and musical production, including, for instance, the Tamil film industry, Telugu-language Tollywood, *et al.* Still, a few features are worth noting: musical numbers will invoke religious deities, temple dances – such as *bharatanatyam*, which British colonial rulers had outlawed for the connection they thought it had to prostitution – and utilize influences derived from Western and Occidental modernisms. For our purposes here, however, the place and prominence of Indian musical songs deserve our fullest attention. For in contrast to the golden classical model linked to US studios, the songs of these regional traditions take precedence over much of their logic and storylines, joyously standing back from verisimilitude and forcing dialogue to take a back seat as well. Unlike viewers across the United Kingdom, North America and Australia who will often 'binge' watch films and shows, audiences in India tradition-ally return to musicals for the purpose of re-experiencing the songs, with the movies functioning as a sort of visualized iTunes or radio. So firmly is the singing tied to star vocalists (some of whom do not appear on the screens themselves) that the musicals tend to function as a medium of song delivery, not unlike physical and online recordings. As Corey Creekmur and Linda Mokdad state in their introduction to *The International Film Musical*, 'popular music *is* film music; the hit song that does not derive from a film . . . is rare' (2013, 1).

These examples, along with those that dramatize the complex pathways of global influences, reveal how diverse musical production actually is. The array of musicals – and the growing focus on that variety – challenges the notion of old Hollywood as the gold standard for movie musicals. In the same vein, I hope to have shown that even the gold standard aligned by Martin with 'those Hollywood musicals made in the forties and fifties, mainly associated with MGM' is similarly open-ended. Despite its grip on our collective imaginary, that category is, and never was, unified or stable, despite assumptions to the contrary. In the same way, although the hege-monic conceptions of music and song within musicals retain an equally firm hold, they too proceed from conflicting and divergent influences, forms and practices. To take the focus of this essay, for instance, songs are not always hog-tied to emotional intensity – particularly as an expres-sion grounded in sincerity – and many post-1990s musicals have banked on audiences' over-familiarity with that convention, replacing sincerity with satire, as in *Cannibal! The Musical* (1993) and *South Park: Bigger, Longer & Uncut* (1999), both by Matt Stone and Trey Parker, the creators of television's lewd animated series *South Park* (Comedy Central, since 1997). In their films, a few spare, single piano notes played under plaintive emotional moments are all it takes to expose the convention while stabbing it hilariously through the heart.

Just as we can challenge the obsessive singularity given to 'the' musical, so too can we argue that even the Hollywood dominant wasn't beholden to a particular type or style of music. But we need to be clear: there is no shortage of marketing and cultural institutions that still enforce that conception, and the success of the formula enforces its enduring staying power. Many US and US-influenced film musicals still gravitate to simple story lines and to simple tunes. We could say that's the American way; but it's not the only American way, nor, of course, the only way at all.

Here we can re-introduce the question 'What is a musical?' that started this chapter with the cover of a recent anthology, *Film's Musical Moments* (Conrich and Tincknell 2006). It features the familiar image of John Travolta and Uma Thurman dancing in Quentin Tarantino's *Pulp Fiction* (1994), a film whose compilation soundtrack is as iconic as the movie itself. Why can't we consider *Pulp Fiction* a film musical, instead of – or in addition to – a movie filled with 'musical moments'? Do musicals require that songs and music emerge from the lips of the players or the instruments that we see on screens in front of us (sounds that are usually recorded elsewhere and often by others)?

Simply by posing these sorts of questions, scholars, producers and consumers alike are expanding the parameters of the musical genre. (Some, like Martin, have proposed doing away with the term 'musical' altogether.) Still, and despite the relative neglect of the songs and music of screen musicals, they are easily their most crucial feature. More than narrative structure, more than energetic spectacle, the songs are at the heart of the wobbly category we understand to be a 'musical'. In all of their diversity, these songs make the question 'What is a musical?' so critical, and remain the key to the genre's financial successes and emotional resonance. But it remains a question in flux, one we cannot answer by finding ossified classic patterns on the screens through which we encounter so many varieties of music, song and dance.

16 'Britannia – The Musical'

Scores, Songs and Soundtracks in British Animation

PAUL WELLS

It is almost customary to begin essays about animation with some qualifying remarks about its marginalization as a film form, or its supposed status as a predominantly children's entertainment. Recent developments in animation studies have served as a corrective to this assumption, however, and proven the validity of animation as a distinctive mode of expression and art-making of long standing world-wide (see Beckman 2014; Buchan 2013; Cholodenko 1991 and 2007; Furniss 1998; N. Klein 1993; Leslie 2002; Wells 1998, 2002 and 2009). There is now much greater recognition of significant practice in anima-tion of high seriousness and work of incisive social and cultural insight (see Furniss 2008; Selby 2009 and 2010; Wells and Hardstaff 2008; Wells 2014). Nonetheless, the address of the relationship between the animated image and sound – arguably, fundamental in its distinctiveness – has been relatively under-explored (see Coyle 2009a and 2010; Goldmark 2005). Moreover, the specificity of the music used in animated films has been examined even less, a neglect which also extends to the particular influence of national contexts and cultures in determining aspects of the relationship between sound and image, which has gone almost unnoticed or is tacitly taken for granted. The following essay, then, will explore the specific case of the soundtrack in British animation, with a particular focus on the use of music.

It is important to note at the outset that this neglect is not only endemic in animation studies, but also in the analysis of film music. While some histories of film music do acknowledge the cartoon sound-track (for example, Prendergast 1992 [1977]; Cooke 2008), it is quite often ignored. In what is otherwise a comprehensive engagement, Lack (1997), for example, employs terms like 'mickey-mousing' but fails prop-erly to acknowledge cartoons or the work of composers Carl Stalling and Scott Bradley; he does, however, suggest that the more experimental work of Norman McLaren and Oscar Fischinger is a pertinent contribution to film scoring. Similarly, Romney and Wootton (1995), though providing a useful overview of the relationship between popular music and film since the 1950s, don't turn their eyes to animation, failing to mention *Yellow Submarine* (1968) while noting other Beatles films, and including *Cool World* (1992) but not addressing any other animated feature – or, indeed, short-form animation. This raises a number of other issues relevant to this discussion. For example, the overwhelming attention paid to mainstream live-action cinema soundtracks has largely developed theoretical analyses that have absented an engagement with animation. This might not be quite so significant if animation did not operate in a different way in relation to the construction of its soundtracks, even though film sound design *per se* has become a more complex phenomenon in the contemporary era. Crucially, then, as well as privileging British animation – not mentioned even in studies of British film scores – it is important not only to look at the ways in which animation shares the core traits and applied principles of traditional film scores and soundtracks, but also how it potentially differs from them.

Music and sound in animation share all the functions which have become traditional in film soundtracks, but crucially music occurs not as a consequence of the action, but as its catalyst. A vocal performance is most often the stimulus to animation, and not merely the aural evidence of the actor's presence in a material context. Music is frequently the vehicle by which any motion in the animated image is timed and executed, with sound effects being the chief articulation of an action's meaning and affect. Sound in animation does not merely anchor and illustrate aspects of the image but is highly instrumental in the very creation of the image itself.

So profoundly influential is the American animated cartoon in the whole history of animation, it is often concluded that the products of the major studios – Disney, Warner Bros., Fleischer, MGM and UPA (United Productions of America), among others – constitute a canon of work that defines animation as a form. Unsurprisingly, therefore, although animation is still under-written about in general, its literature is dominated by the Hollywood cartoon, and while the recovery and re-evaluation of this work is welcome, it has the effect of marginalizing animation from other countries that have extensive histories of production and achievement in their own right. Providing a useful analytical template, Goldmark has sought to situate the fragmented sound collages created by Stalling and dynamic scores by Bradley within broader musical traditions, arguing that 'the natural complement to the study of jazz is a study of classical music. If we are to believe the oppositions set up in the cartoons and films of the 1930s,

'40s, and '50s, these two genres are cultural and aesthetic antagonists, constantly jockeying for social preeminence' (2005, 8). This observation places the cartoon soundtrack as a site evidencing tensions between high and popular culture. In the American tradition, the manner in which vaudevillian tropes and the vernacular energy of jazz and swing mixed freely with opera and classical music in the soundtrack helped to define the medium of the cartoon. By contrast, the tensions between high and popular culture in the British context were made more pronounced by an obvious class consciousness, and there were very clear demarcations, for example, between the classicism of the concert hall and the idioms of the music hall, between art and entertainment.

While British cinema practice had experimented with primitive models of sound synchronization since the early 1900s, silent animation, like its live-action counterpart, enjoyed the accompaniment of live music, singers and crude sound recordings. As Lack notes, though,

> The enduring symbol of the silent era, the lone piano player seated in front of the cinema screen, was something akin to a lightning conductor. His performances were close to acts of quotation as diverse musical sources and inspirations were sandwiched together often via improvised abridgements.
> In live performance the status of the source works was changed forever.
> An accompanist was not merely playing a piece derived from Mozart or Grieg, he was 'instancing' it, changing it, intentionally summoning up some part of those works whose emotional impact could work towards the greater impact of the image.   (Lack 1997, 39)

In this description, it is possible to recognize some elements which became particularly pertinent in relation to animation: first, the idea of the 'lightning conductor' supporting the work of the 'lightning cartoonist', both apparently creating the image or sound 'in the moment'; and second, the concept of selective and emotive 'instancing' in choosing pertinent images and sounds. This sense of 'in the moment' situations and specific 'instancing' of gestures and actions was to characterize British cartoons most particularly, because they were not based on the dominant idiosyncrasies of the main characters, such as those typical of the iconic Disney and Warner Bros. productions.

The popularity of British animation increased considerably during the First World War through the films of Lancelot Speed and Dudley Buxton, and the early post-war period realized its first, and sadly forgotten, star, Bonzo the dog, created by G. E. Studdy. (Bonzo was so popular that he had his own mechanically animated advertisement in London's

Figure 16.1 'Private Bonzo', about to escape from jail in *Tanked*, c. 1925.

Piccadilly Circus.) In October 1924, producer Gordon Craig at New Era Films engaged the American producer, director and animator William A. Ward to collaborate with Studdy and ten assistant artists to produce the first of twenty-six films featuring Bonzo, 'the Studdy dog'. Bonzo immediately became a popular character (see Figure 16.1), his cartoons representing the first real advances in character animation and comic narrative in British animated cartoons, and a development of visual gags that emerged out of situations, rather than singular satirical observations that were the primary focus of animated political caricature (see Babb and Owen 1988). Significantly, they became influential in the emergence of the first British sound cartoons, featuring 'Orace the 'Armonious 'Ound, animated by Joe Noble. (The *h*-dropping is a feature of London's Cockney dialect.) The first, *The Jazz Stringer* (1928), premiered at the Tivoli Cinema in The Strand, London, in December 1928. The recently rediscovered '*Orace in The First Talking Cartoon in the World; or Music Hath Charms* (1929) is a particularly notable example of an early soundtrack on a British cartoon as it is clearly experimenting with the possibilities of sound. Noble himself introduces the cartoon, indicating that it is the second featuring 'Orace, and a further endorsement of Britain's love of dogs. Noble peels back the paper on his easel to reveal a blank page, noting that 'Orace has gone and that he 'will have to draw him all over again'. 'Orace volunteers to draw himself, however, eventually hitting Noble over the head with his brush. Noble then suggests that having drawn himself, he can now amuse the audience. At this point, the film cuts from Noble's studio to a full cartoon space, much of its design and choreography, thereafter, reminiscent of Felix the Cat (1919–32).

Sounds are largely introduced in a singular way, and match particular actions. A gypsy approaches the public house, 'Ye Brazen Konk', and begins to play his hurdy-gurdy. Music plays but is not acknowledged by anyone in the bar, and the gypsy walks away lamenting 'trade is slow today'. 'Orace then appears, first noticing a billboard advertising 'the Tropics', and then the gypsy's abandoned hurdy-gurdy – 'Orace actually mistaking the crank-handled box for a movie camera. He then steps into the billboard to go to 'the Tropics' to make a film, seeing some monkeys playing and a sleeping lion on his arrival. 'Orace then speaks directly to the audience: 'Shhhh, don't breathe'. In what becomes a staple of cartoon gags as the form develops, visual puns also invite aural rhymes – in a 'think bubble' we see the lion is dreaming of a tree trunk being sawn: a literal depiction of the phrase 'sleeping like a log' but using the sound of the sawing to represent the lion's snoring. This apparently simple though highly condensed image is an indicator of the multiple layers of meaning achieved through sound synchronization in the cartoon. 'Orace begins to 'film' the lion using the hurdy-gurdy but the music awakens him, and he pursues 'Orace, roaring loudly. Here the music and sound effects are literal, but when the lion pounces on 'Orace, loud noises are used to indicate an explosion. 'Orace is transported to heaven and in Felix-style jumps up and down on a cloud as if it were a trampoline and leans upon another cloud as if it were a wall. Only then does he realize that the whole incident has been caused by 'pesky music', but just when he thinks he might be at peace, a conductor – speaking with an unpersuasive American accent – strikes up a three-piece 'Angel Chorus', featuring one blackface minstrel and two white musicians, to play an up-tempo jazz piece. Crashing to Hades in despair, 'Orace is comforted by the fact that there is a sign saying 'no circulars or street musicians', entering into hell with words from Charles Dickens's *A Tale of Two Cities* (1859) – 'It is a far, far better thing . . . ' Spoken idioms in British cartoons often attempt to mine the musicality imbued in dialects and local sayings – 'lord lumme' (Lord, love me) – and in well-known literary forms. It is a marker of a key aspect of British cartoons in general, and particularly in relation to the use of sound and music, that they are informed by 'wit' – something which is self-consciously amusing *and* clever, and if possible indigenous yet somehow universal.

The film demonstrates the early trademarks of British cartoon sound, some aspects borrowed from the American shorts and some already committed to a singularly British approach. The sound is for

the most part diegetic and with an indexical referent, but of course –
more than anything else at this stage – the sound itself was a novelty:
a novelty made even greater by the fact that an animated dog
appeared to talk and angels could seemingly play music. So swift
were the technical developments in the cartoon in the United States,
however, that British cartoons were soon left in their wake. Disney
made *Steamboat Willie* in 1928 and by 1933 the studio had made
Flowers and Trees in Technicolor; it perfected 'squash'n'stretch' per-
sonality-driven character animation in *Three Little Pigs* (1933), also
featuring Frank Churchill's memorable ditty 'Who's Afraid of the Big
Bad Wolf'; and by 1937 the studio had advanced the spatial depth of
the cartoon by using a multi-plane camera in *The Old Mill* (1937).
Crucially, these *Silly Symphonies* were advancing the relationship
between music and motion, a process continued in other cartoons
with extraordinary sequences like the tornado drawing up Mickey
Mouse's barnyard orchestra while the music plays on in *The Band
Concert* (1935). The cartoon implicitly plays out the tension between
the cultural ambition to play classical music, initially Rossini's
William Tell Overture, set against the more reactionary and retrograde
folk idioms epitomized in Donald Duck's rendition of 'Turkey in the
Straw', already enjoying homespun popularity, of course, by being the
tune whistled by Mickey in *Steamboat Willie*. Disney's ambition to
bring animation together with classical music was ultimately fulfilled
in *Fantasia* (1940). These radical developments in the cartoon over
less than a decade – echoed too, in shorts made at Warner Bros. and
the Fleischer brothers' studio – prompted two key responses in
Britain, both closely related to music.

The Disney cartoons enjoyed widespread distribution, and proved
very popular in Britain. This created a number of problems for British
production companies, who essentially had to create something different
in order to compete. Anson Dyer and Archibald Nettlefold formed
Anglia Films Ltd in 1935, embarking on two approaches designed to
reach British audiences already won over by the *Silly Symphonies*.
The first was to create a series of operatic burlesques, parodying popular
operas; the second, to make a series of eighteen cartoons based on Stanley
Holloway's already highly successful 'Sam Small' and 'Albert' monologues, which he had honed on radio, and which featured singularly British
characters that might find purchase in a different way to Hollywood's
cartoon animals.

The first opera burlesque (1936) was based on Bizet's *Carmen*, clearly
chosen not for its initially radical depiction of doomed tragic-comic love

and lawlessness, but for its well-known arias, 'Habanera' and 'Toreador Song'. The story, too, omits the more adult crimes of passion, casting Don José as an inept soldier, initially seduced by the gypsy Carmen, in order to aid the skullduggery of Remendado and his smugglers, and later to compete with Escamillo, the toreador, for Carmen's affections, by impressing in a bullfight. Don José, despite his name, is essentially a typically English hero, characterized by his inherent sense of impending failure and defeat, unremitting embarrassment and unlikely triumph. Though humiliated by the smugglers and hung from a yardarm – castigated and punished, too, by Zuniga, the Lieutenant of the Dragoons – Don José, manacled with a ball and chain, manages to knock out all the bulls in a comically inventive sequence, winning the Betty Boop-like Carmen's affection ahead of the bemused Escamillo. It is the music, though, and mainly the 'Toreador Song' that brings pace and emotion to the piece, even given its exaggerated comic tone.

Sam Small, in films like *Sam and His Musket* (1935) and *'Alt, Who Goes Theer?* (1936), finds himself at odds with his supposed superiors, and often in dialogue with the Duke of Wellington himself. When Sam's musket is knocked to the floor in the first film, he refuses to pick it up, even when ordered to do so by all the ranks in the army, until the Duke himself requests it; the Duke also picks up Sam's abandoned musket when Sam finds himself unexpectedly having tea with the king and queen. The slow rhyming couplets that advance the stories in the 'Sam Small' and 'Albert' monologues are amusing, and clearly work on stage and on the air, but in the cartoons they serve to over-elaborate and inhibit the action. While the monologues epitomized a popular literary tradition in a vernacular form, their indigenous qualities in wordplay did not service the image-making in a persuasive way. Holloway's delivery and the limits of the piano accompaniment resulted in the pacing of the cartoons being too slow, and the comic action predictable – and, by comparison with Disney's inventive sight gags, banal. This ultimately led to the comparative failure of the series. Several further 'Sam' shorts were produced, and *The Lion and Albert* (1937) was made but not exhibited, and there were no further opera burlesques; both series proved uneconomical, and unable to challenge the Disney stronghold.

At the same time, the more experimental tradition in Britain was finding a foothold. Len Lye and Norman McLaren emerged as key figures in creating abstract works of high invention, working closely on the relationship between image and sound, seeking to create a model of visual music. Pavel Tager in Moscow had considered the idea of creating graphical or drawn sound directly on film as early as 1926, and animator Mikhail Tsekhanovsky had worked on a project in 1929 with the composer Arseny Avraamov, but the experiments by László Moholy-Nagy, Rudolf Pfenninger and Oskar Fischinger in Berlin in the early 1930s are better known. In Britain, Lye made three outstanding shorts for the GPO Film Unit: *A Colour Box* (1935), *Rainbow Dance* (1936) and *Trade Tattoo* (1937). *A Colour Box* was the first film with drawn sound exhibited to a public audience, though Sid Griffiths, who made the *Jerry the Troublesome Tyke* series in the 1920s, had drawn some sound effects on the 'Sam Small' films. Lye's film had the novelty of using Dufaycolor and combined highly textured colourful imagery with dance music by Don Baretto and his Cuban Orchestra. *Rainbow Dance*, made on Gasparcolor stock with Visatone-Marconi sound, overlayed footage with colour effects, and though a quasi-surreal narrative, was made more figurative by the use of a repeating motif of the dancer Rupert Doone as a man with an umbrella, a guitarist, a hiker and a tennis player. The music, by Burton Lane, was played by Rico's Creole Band, again providing an up-tempo rhythm and a celebratory tone before the stentorian tones of the narrator concluded the film with the words, 'The Post Office Savings Bank puts a pot of gold at the end of the rainbow for you. No deposit too small for the Post Office Savings Bank.' *Trade Tattoo* takes this concept further by seeking to align the rhythms of a working day with the idea of a celebratory pageant in the style of a military tattoo. It was influenced by Walter Ruttmann's *Berlin: Symphony of a Great City* (1927), and sought to apprehend the 'musicality' imbued in everyday activities. Though an intrinsically romantic idea, the film once more combines optical effects with live-action documentary footage, and uses five pieces of music played by the Lecuona Cuban Band, employing their percussive and pulsating rhythms to complement Jack Ellitt's precise editing.

McLaren advanced sound experiments of this kind much further after his relocation to Canada in 1941. As Lack has noted, in *Blinkity Blank* (1955) McLaren used fragments of music and sound

> to produce a dazzlingly kaleidoscopic freeze, as literal an animation (if not quite as sensational) as Yves Klein's 'paint-wrestling' experiments with naked debutants in Paris around the same time. McLaren took sound animation to an astonishing level of sophistication. He was able by minute visual refinements to produce variations as slight as one tenth of a tone and sound duration of as little as one-fiftieth of a second with over one hundred different dynamic shadings.
>
> (Lack 1997, 110–11)

McLaren is much discussed in relation to his visual achievements, but less so for his responsiveness to sound. It was always his stated intention to have the same proximity to film itself as the painter has to a canvas, and it is clear that his engagement with music is one attuned to the immediacy of the musicianship in the songs and soundtracks he deployed. One need only compare the rapid painted and scratched dynamics of his response to pianist Oscar Peterson's jazz playing in *Begone Dull Care* (1949) to the slow metamorphoses of pastel drawing illustrating a French lullaby, performed by Anna Malenfant, in *La Poulette Grise* (1947) in this regard. The culmination of McLaren's sound work came in *Synchromy* (1971), where he photographed sound-card patterns on to the soundtrack area, using and multiplying them for the visual representation, so that in essence, the viewer sees what they are hearing. 'Music' for animation, then, could be rendered in numerous different ways, and was an intrinsic component in defining the distinctiveness of any one animated film.

This was especially important to Hungarian émigré John Halas, who established the British studio Halas & Batchelor with his English wife, Joy Batchelor, initially making *The Music Man* (1938) before embarking on a fifty-year career in animation production (see V. Halas and Wells 2006). Halas, as well as being an accomplished designer and animator, was an entrepreneur and global advocate of animation as a form of expression that could speak to utopian ideals of education and communication. He also had a deep belief in animation as art, and, though he admired Disney cartoons, believed that Hollywood had cast animation only as a medium for comedy and distraction, and that it possessed much greater potential as a creative medium. This had already been significantly proven in the European tradition, but had received little recognition, something Halas was determined to change both through the work of the Halas & Batchelor studio, and also in his work for the Association Internationale du Film d'Animation (ASIFA), the international body representing animators worldwide. Halas theorized animation in order to define it for those outside the field, particularly those in business and industry, and tried to produce films in a British context that resisted the dominant traits of the Hollywood cartoon. He wished to embrace sound in a way that moved beyond imitation and counterpoint into greater degrees of evocation and accentuation. Interestingly, this proved to be a strategy counter to that taking place in live action, where the Second World War provoked a greater investment in romantic and patriotic scores for film by composers like Ralph Vaughan Williams, William Walton and Allan Gray. Halas essentially turned to more contemporary modernist stylings in the music deployed in wartime shorts like *Dustbin Parade* (1942), and later in films like *The Magic Canvas* (1948), which declares 'Here is something different from the ordinary cartoon film' and pointedly advises the audience to 'Relax and let your eyes and ears enjoy it'. Mátyás Seiber, the composer of the score and another expatriate from Hungary, comments that the film was

> an abstract project: consequently, I considered that a similarly 'abstract'
> chamber music piece would be the most appropriate musical equivalent.
> I chose the rather odd combination of one flute, one horn and a string quartet.
> The form of the piece is that of a rather free 'phantasy', consisting of several
> sections. A slow contrapuntal piece covers the first section. At the dramatic
> moment of the human shape breaking into two the horn enters for the first
> time. The speed increases, and at the moment when the bird breaks away the
> flute takes over. Now follows an 'allegro' moment which covers the storm
> sequence. The next section, the revival of nature, is expressed by a 'pastorale' in
> the music. This is followed by a 'scherzo', covering the play with the waves.
> Then a bridge section leads back to the recapitulation of the slow, first
> movement, as the bird returns to the human shape. But the slow movement
> returns transformed: instead of a low-pitched brooding mood as it appeared
> originally, it comes back now in a higher register, and a solo violin ends the
> piece as the bird disappears in the distance.
>
> (Quoted in J. Halas and Manvell 1958, 249)

Halas had the deliberate intention to bring the visual elements closer to the condition of music, arguing that animation had the greater liberty to create images so synchronous to music that the viewer might lose their orientation in delineating one from the other. Halas, a long-time student of animation, learned quickly from how sound and image coalesced in other films and, when using Holloway to deliver Thomas Dibden's 'The Sailor's Consolation' in the second of his *Painter and Poet* series (1951), he decided against the full animation and slow pacing that had been deployed in the 'Sam Small' films, preferring instead to 'animate' John Minton's drawing by rapidly moving a rostrum camera. Seiber's score for *The Magic Canvas* was one of many he was to write for the studio, alongside Halas & Batchelor's similarly long-standing collaborator, Francis Chagrin. Halas argued:

> the composer is, in fact, frequently more essential to the animator than is the
> writer ... For the cartoon the composer must be able to respond exactly to the
> continuous movement which carries its own accents and responses in
> every second of the score. And yet he must develop an unfettered melody which
> will captivate an audience and rouse it through its atmosphere as well as through
> its wit.
>
> (*ibid.*, 69–70)

In this he drew attention to the key issue of whether the soundtrack should be written before the animation or created and synchronized afterwards. There are many cases of films, of course, which do both, and – more regularly – the soundtrack is developed along with the storyboards and animatics advanced for any one film. Sometimes, sound works as the provocateur of the image; at others, sound literally underpins or enhances it. Seiber (whose style was influenced by Bartók, Bach and Schoenberg) was convinced that each aspect of the music in film should perform a narrative or emotive function, so this was particularly suited to the 'instancing' of many animation scenarios. Equally pertinent was Chagrin's eclectic output of orchestral music and popular songs, which provided him with a wide vocabulary from which to choose when scoring animated films. By using these composers, Halas sought to offer a corrective to some of what he perceived as the crassness and vulgarity of the American cartoon, by employing a 'wit' that signalled a conscious desire to be both sophisticated and satirical. In *The Cultured Ape* (1960), a jungle ape turns out to be a virtuoso musician (see Figure 16.2), who, like King Kong, is captured and brought back to 'civilization'. Ironically, civilization proves too uncouth for the cultured ape who finds his art and ability rejected by three strata of British society: the upper class, who are both jealous and resentful of his musical talents; the middle class, who merely prefer his musical efforts 'in the background' of their chatter; and the working class, who prefer more popular, 'street' music like skiffle. Music here, then, is a barometer of social identity, habitus and taste,

Figure 16.2 *The Cultured Ape*: the simian who likes to play minuets and jigs on his flute. (Score by Mátyás Seiber.)

but as the final line suggests – 'when the arts go out of fashion the artist must retire and wait' – the arts tend to be cyclic, and curators, sponsors, critics, viewers and listeners sometimes fickle.

Seiber delivered an affecting score for Halas & Batchelor's landmark feature, *Animal* Farm (1954; see J. Halas and Batchelor 1954), while Chagrin was to create a virtuoso variation on the Stalling-style bricolage of the American cartoon soundtrack in his work for the same studio's *Tales of Hoffnung* (1964). Adapting Gerard Hoffnung's amusing caricatures of classical-music culture in Europe, the cartoons targeted the elitism and pomp of classical musicians and the ineptitude of those attempting to play an instrument. If the 'fragments' in Stalling's cartoon soundtrack serviced the narrative and principally the gag, or provided motifs for characters, Chagrin's Hoffnung cartoon soundtracks playfully engaged with the music itself, and were unambiguously about the orchestra, the conductor, the musician and their audiences. The music is 'composed, re-composed, arranged, disarranged and conducted by Francis Chagrin', and the credits include the coda, 'with acknowledgment and apologies to ... ' before listing the composers used in the film's music track. This demonstrates the sustained respect for the culture being parodied; but it signals, too, that even if the graphic puns and exaggerated caricature appealed to children, there was also an intention to reach and engage with an adult viewer familiar with classical music. Chagrin uses Chopin, for example – yet not his famous funeral march – and Mozart, Wagner and Tchaikovsky, but his musical palette is much wider in its inclusion of more extended pieces by Boccherini, Borodin, Auber, Rimsky-Korsakov, Grieg, Gounod, Delibes and Gruber. In many ways, Chagrin's versatility and knowledge matched the broader aims and cultural reach of the studio, which embraced everything from Gilbert and Sullivan's *Ruddigore*, directed by Batchelor in 1967, to the Roger Glover/Alan Aldridge collaboration *The Butterfly Ball* (1974) and Kraftwerk's Beach Boys parody, *Autobahn* (1979) – 'Fahr'n, Fahr'n, Fahr'n on the Autobahn'. The latter marked the beginning of the video era in Britain, and pointed to a key development in realigning animation with the popular song, though – in Halas's mind – without sacrificing its engagement with art.

Indeed, this had been an important aspect of the way in which GB Animation, led by ex-Disney director and animator David Hand, had used popular songs in their *Musical Paintbox* series in the immediate post-war period. Simply, the songs helped to define geographical areas and historical principles, operating as a touchstone for folk idiom, a nostalgic engagement with tradition and a resistance to the modernity completely embraced in the work of the Halas & Batchelor studio. In *Yorkshire Ditty* (1949), a lady reacts to a modern artist's abstract interpretation of the landscape by breaking the canvas over his head. This incident is couched within a story of local romance, and initially played out to the local ditty 'On Ilkla Moor Baht'at' (Yorkshire dialect for 'On Ilkley Moor without a hat') when the community go to the village hall to watch a magic-lantern show – a convenient way to introduce montage-style animation – and embrace the entertainment as 'A Reet Gradely Show' ('a really excellent show'). This is a highly localized and deter-minedly backward-looking fairytale, where the literally homespun wool is spun direct from a sheep into a household blanket, and the natural appeal of the Yorkshire moor – a bleak snow-laden landscape or a green and pleasant land – is preferred to the sophisticated and contemporary in the material world. *Devon Whey!* (1949) implies that 'Devon, Glorious Devon' (suggested here on the soundtrack by Sir Edward German's popular Edwardian drawing-room song, written in 1905) is another Eden; the epic grandeur of the landscape is imbued with history and represents the backdrop to progress, here epitomized in the voyages of Sir Francis Drake. Folk ditties like 'The Green Grass Grew All Around' and 'Uncle Tom Cobleigh' are modernized through the use of animation – the line-drawn grey mare on its way to Widdecombe Fair inexplicably pumped up and exploded by its riders for a comic effect. In *Cornwall* (1949), a tale of smuggling and piracy is played out to 'Blow the Man Down', the sunset across the rocky shoreline another reminder of endur-ance and continuity.

Music in this instance is used to recall time and place, a process redolent of a broader theme in British animation to identify its legacy and to celebrate its heritage. This has been absorbed into the vernacular idioms of Oliver Postgate's SmallFilms productions for British television, including the folksongs in *Bagpuss* (1974), the Vernon Eliot scores and the musical 'gibberish' spoken in *The Clangers* (1969–72), the latter discussed by Philip Hayward (2013). British heritage has also been celebrated through the presence of popular cultural icons like The Beatles in *Yellow Submarine*; the animation sequences in The Sex Pistols' *The Great Rock'n'Roll Swindle* (1979); Gerald Scarfe's coruscating Gilray-styled illustrations for *Pink Floyd: The Wall* (1982); Paul McCartney's composition for *Rupert and the Frog Song* (1984), a musical adaptation based on the Mary Tourtel and Alfred Bestall stories; and Howard Blake's score for *The Snowman* (1982), based on Raymond Briggs's book, and featuring the most famous song in British animation, Blake's 'Walking in the Air'.

British heritage, too, is a fundamental aspect of the films of Bob Godfrey, whose musicals, like *GREAT* (1975) and *Millennium – The Musical* (1999), perhaps best summarize the relationship between animation, sound and 'Britishness'. Colin Pearson's script for Godfrey's *Know Your Europeans: The United Kingdom* (1994) includes some satirical lyrics, set to the tune of Gilbert and Sullivan's 'I Am the Very Model of a Modern Major-General' from *The Pirates of Penzance* (1879), which make some fundamental observations about British identity, and help to conclude this discussion:

> The British are a nation of considerable antiquity,
> Who colonised the globe with quite remarkable ubiquity.
> They turn up everywhere from Abu Dabi to Nigeria,
> And quickly tell the natives what it is to be superior.
> The British are a multi-coloured polyglot society,
> Descended from invaders of most dubious variety,
> Their pedigree is Viking, Anglo-Saxon, Jute and Arian,
> With bits of Hun and Huguenot, but basically barbarian.
> The British are devoted to the arts and intellectual,
> At sports enthusiastic, but entirely ineffectual,
> They patented inventions of amazing ingenuity,
> Their efforts gastronomical are viewed with ambiguity.
> The British are a monarchy in love with ceremonial,
> Impressed by pomp and circumstance and palaces baronial.
> The Royals all conduct themselves with dignified sobriety,
> And so the British tabloids always treat them with propriety ... !?!
> The British are eccentric, unreserved and unconventional,
> Stiff-upper lipped, and buttoned-up, hidebound and condescentional,
> Permissive and profane and positively puritanical,
> Bohemian, and Bloomsbury, bucolic and botanical.

These observations are preceded by images of Sir Henry Wood conducting one of his Promenade concerts, a cricketer, a deer-stalkered huntsman, a fat man exercising, spectators watching a tennis match, a barmaid pulling a pint, a van driver in the rain, a farmer milking a cow, choir boys, Morris dancers, a soccer player and some rowers; the sequence ends with two women asking, ' 'Ere, what about us ladies?' They are reassured that women will be represented by Emily Brontë, Florence Nightingale and Vera Lynn later in the film. The combination of the 'Englishness' of Gilbert and Sullivan, the delineation of a British typology and some wholly recognizable icons sums up how music, indigenous concerns and animated imagery have come together in highly distinctive forms. British animated films and the musical idioms that underpin them have helped to represent the embedded contradictions of British culture and alternative perspectives, while speaking directly and inventively to a knowing and informed audience embracing irony and wit. 'Britannia – The Animated Musical' remains invariably in tune.

PART FOUR

Music in World Cinemas

17 Leone, Morricone and the Italian Way to Revisionist Westerns

SERGIO MICELI

The accidental first meeting between director Sergio Leone and composer Ennio Morricone at school (Miceli 1994, 104) and the fact that one of Leone's collaborators later made him listen to Morricone's 1962 arrangement of Woody Guthrie's 'Pastures of Plenty' (1941), as sung by Peter Tevis, are just two of the many varied and sometimes contradictory elements from which the movie project *Per un pugno di dollari* (*A Fistful of Dollars*; 1964) originated. In this chapter, I will discuss some of the more significant incidents.

Although it is important to bear in mind that Morricone's first movie with Leone was one of his earliest 'official' cinematic undertakings – the very first being Luciano Salce's *Il federale* (US title *The Fascist*; 1961) – on the one hand *Per un pugno di dollari* was supposed to be a 'B' movie in which nobody seemed to have faith (Miceli 1994, 107). Notoriously, Leone took the screen name Bob Robertson, a pun on 'Robert, son of Robert' (a homage to his father, Roberto Roberti – born Vincenzo Leone, 1879–1959 – a celebrated director of silent movies), while Morricone was credited as 'Dan Savio', a pseudonym he had already employed in some variants for certain pop-music works, and a choice hinting at his ongoing work in both spheres. On the other hand, perhaps because of this very shaky beginning, the authors took otherwise inconceivable liberties. The movie was also the first collaboration between two men who shared a similarly obsessive care for their work, with Leone being unusually attentive to the sound components in the film. This led Leone to make requests that were in one sense specific, but also quite vague from a strictly musical point of view – optimally for Morricone, who never had much regard for musically literate directors. In Leone's case, in other words, one should speak neither of a general music education nor, more simply, of any musical practice, but rather of an exceptional sensitivity towards the mutual interaction between *all* the constitutive elements of a movie, including the acoustic components made up of sounds with a musical quality and also noises with a musical quality, both pragmatically employed on the same level of efficacy. Leone's movies are indeed among the most noteworthy in post–Second World War Italian

This chapter was translated from Italian by Claudio Vellutini.

cinema for the polymorphism of their expressive means. Their frequently cited 'operatic' imprint is a descendent of a pre-existing conception of spectacle that is independent from historical models. The fact that Leone served as assistant director to Carmine Gallone, one of the masters of film-opera, for *Il trovatore* and *La forza del destino* (both from 1949) should not be regarded as prophetic. As for Leone's alleged consistency of style and tone – both somewhat incoherent in my opinion – this is a subject to which we will return in a brief analysis of the so-called Dollars Trilogy.

Morricone adheres to the same trajectory of refinement and expansion that characterizes the director's entire output up to his 'swan song' in 1984, *Once Upon a Time in America* (Morricone and Miceli 2013 [2001], 56–7 and 181–2). From their second movie – *Per qualche dollaro in più (For a Few Dollars More*; 1965) – onwards, and to an increasingly greater extent as their partnership consolidated, Morricone would compose in advance some of the music that Leone would then use during the shooting (*ibid.*, 188; Garofalo 1999, 133). Although such a process was very unusual by production standards, Morricone's compositions have always main-tained – with both Leone and others, therefore independently from the needs of any single director – a fruition identity (a high degree of stand-alone musical quality), which in some ways has little to do with music's traditional function as a commentary to the images on screen (De Melis 1989, 12). Already in *Per un pugno di dollari*, closed numbers prevail; their marked stylistic profiles allow them to be musically self-sufficient. This trait cannot yet be regarded as an instance of market-oriented clairvoy-ance, since nobody foretold the resounding success that the movie and its music would enjoy from the Florence premiere onwards. It is easier to assume – and the pre-production circumstances seem to confirm – that because of his lack of ambition the director was content with an adaptation of some melodies functioning as frames. Morricone, meanwhile, seems to have done nothing more than to follow his instinct as an arranger, aiming not so much for music that would be functional to the movie as that which would be immediately recognizable, as he was certain that this would help both the film and the music. Contrary to what is generally theorized about film music and spectatorship, the spectator would leave the cinema with a conscious memory of the music's presence. Paradoxically, one could argue that Morricone has built his reputation as a film-music composer only through a 'partial' faithfulness to the movie – although such faithful-ness might have appeared complete to many directors. Depending on the goals of the movie and its supposed place in the market, Morricone's palette ranged (and still ranges) from easy-listening to experimental music. Whatever the case, nothing could be more untenable than the assumption that the cinema industry exploited and wasted the composer's talent. With some exceptions, rather, it could be argued that it was Morricone who exploited the cinema industry, ingraining it into his productive and speculative network that has involved every aspect of his activity. But let us now look closer at the first movie of the trilogy. (The discussions which follow are based on the DVDs included in the box set *C'era una volta Sergio Leone*, issued in Italy by CVC. Please note that these may differ in some details from DVD releases of the films currently available in Anglophone countries.)

For a Fistful of Dollars

Out of a total duration of 100 minutes, the music of *Per un pugno di dollari* amounts to a considerable 38. Only twelve minutes present non-thematic musical materials. Two cues, instead, have a recognizable thematic function: 'Titoli' ('Titles') and 'Per un pugno di dollari' ('For a fistful of dollars'). They function as main themes and recurrent motifs. They substantially differ in structure and processing: while being both monothematic, the first can be defined as segmented but dynamic and the second as articulated but static; the first is mostly contrapuntal, the second mostly monophonic; and 'Titoli' has a shifting multi-purpose quality whilst 'Per un pugno di dollari' has a fixed and clear-cut one.

Seen from its horizontal layout, 'Titoli' is characterized by a propulsive urgency and an assertive eloquence that belong to Morricone's signature style. Typical is the anacrusis that opens the human whistling as a launching pad for the energetic leap of the ascending fourth, and the overarching breadth of the entire phrase – bound together and rhythmically unified by the prevailing series of crotchets – which unfolds in a regular stepwise motion. With its spontaneous, transparent lyricism, this melody conveys an 'optimistic' mood that can nonetheless become ironic and taunting through the techniques that will be described below.

Let us now turn to segmentation. This is a significant stylistic technique and a fundamental compositional process in Morricone's film music. There are three forms of the long melodic cell, A, plus another one in the reprise: A'''. Each of them is enclosed in a phrase mark: see Example 17.1. A ends on the tonic, and therefore is self-contained. A' instead takes on a dialogic function with A''. A simple rhythmic figuration (R) precedes the resulting unit, which fulfils several functions: it introduces and supports the entire piece, and also serves as an anticipation/recollection of the musical passage, depending on the use within the movie. A beautiful tripartite coda follows (C, 1–2–3), which is increasingly emphatic and almost lied-like, in the ways it brings back the melodic cell and highlights it by expanding the opening

Example 17.1 'Titoli' melody from *Per un pugno di dollari* (*A Fistful of Dollars*).

interval (C–A–A–F ... D–A–A–F). The sense of drama thus created culminates with the gesturing towards the semibreve with the unexpected and pre-resolving leap from D to G: see two bars before ③.

Example 17.2 Electric-guitar variant of 'Titoli' material.

Example 17.3 Chorus bridge in 'Titoli'.

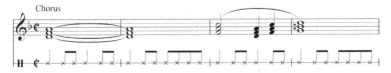

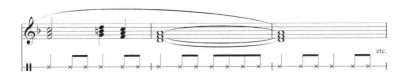

The variant played by the electric guitar (Example 17.2) constitutes an alternative version of the entire block (A–A'–A'') and its repetition (A–A'–A'''). It is a re-reading of the original material in a deliberately more nuanced and up-to-date sound. The interval A–D undergoes a process of rhythmic contraction through repetitions of the inverted mordent A–D–C#–D, which are also separated by crotchet rests. Such contraction adds a character of cheeky concision. I will explain later why we should define this segment as 'pseudo-rock': think of the use of the electric guitar in 'L'uomo dell'armonica' from *C'era una volta il West* (*Once Upon a Time in the West*; 1968) to discern the difference between a 'domesticated' rock passage and a 'non-domesticated' one.

This almost unambiguous identification with the electric guitar and the overt allusion to the rhythm of equestrian galloping are perhaps the most prosaic elements of the entire piece. One last large-scale and important component should be pointed out: the bridge sung by the chorus (Example 17.3). This is the only chordal episode with an expressly rhetorical function – one that was derived, upon Leone's explicit request, from the arrangement of 'Pastures of Plenty'.

The macro-element that builds the piece we have just segmented can be combined in a variety of ways (as indeed happens in the movie), including the insertion of new materials that are similar in function to medieval tropes. Although it is impossible to take all these materials into account here, one observation on the definition of a 'closed piece' is in order – a definition that, in my opinion, is useful only to a certain extent. This is a compositional technique that, because of its polyvalent and interchangeable nature, is paradigmatic of film music. We will come back to this point, as it is fundamental to this analysis.

Let us return to our initial description of 'Titoli' as a contrapuntal piece and focus on its smaller-scale elements. The most important is a simple descending scale covering the range of a perfect fifth – a series of five semiquavers that 'slide' down to the tonic, as if to evoke the glissando effect of the five-pipe Pan flute that Morricone would employ later in his career (Example 17.4). As the piece unfolds, this minimal element comes out as another essential and characterizing feature. Placed at the beginning of the bar, the recorder initiates a lively contrapuntal proliferation marked by the intervention first of the whip on the strong beat of every other bar, then of the anvil on the other strong beat, and finally of a bell playing on the tonic on the first weak beat. This continuous stumbling and the resulting irregular pulse create a spirited and imaginative effect which is further enriched by the diversity of harmonics in the percussion, which conveys an imperfect intonation congruent with the overall outcome.

Later, strings and vocalizing singers are added to a rhythmic background reinforced by more conventionally used percussion. The result is deliberately redundant. The most interesting passage, however, is the light attack of the acoustic guitar (R in Example 17.1) and the whistling. They establish the first and most convincing expressive layer to which the other sounds, also combined in a similarly natural way, contribute shortly thereafter. In addition to the previously noted rhythmic pulse – which is musical in its own right but also suggestive of trotting horses (Tagg 1990) – the aim here is to create a sound world which takes life from 'primordial' elements of extreme simplicity and archaic purity, fluctuating between the epic and the playful (Carpitella 1985). On the other hand, the following electric-guitar variant updates the subtle pre-existing materials, toning down and annihilating their nuanced 'philological' allusions. The electric guitar's urban sound hints quite explicitly at the idioms of rock, though duly domesticated. Thus comes to the fore a range of possible identifications between types of

Example 17.4 Contrapuntal texture in 'Titoli'.

products and types of audiences, this time with a generational orientation that reveals more prominently its market-oriented implications. Finally, the triumphalism and magniloquence emerging from the choral bridge, which proceeds from an accumulation of triads – the crudest section – to the

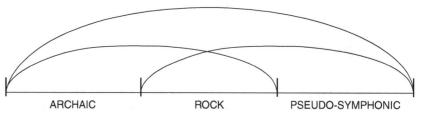

Figure 17.1 Stylistic tripartion in the music of Ennio Morricone.

following *tutti* reprise of the theme, featuring full musical forces, are too ostentatious to be taken seriously. Yet one may suspect that large sections of the audience misunderstood this point, seeing, albeit unconsciously, a serious tone in the third section of the piece. One can rely on the mini-mizing effects of irony and take for granted a shared critical threshold that recognizes hyperboles and the rhetorical value of antiphrasis; or one can interpret the whole piece in a completely different way. To simplify some-what roughly, 'Titoli' may reproduce – or slyly suggest – a tripartite model of social development corresponding to the ideological goal of bourgeois integration. The human whistling, the sounds of simple instruments, often derived from animals, refer to a remote civilization that lives close to nature, which is characterized by a diverse but coherent set of values, the prevailing one being individualism, with a foundational sense of free anarchy. By turning the guitar, a poor and elemental instrument, into an electric instrument and thus updating its sound, the rock idiom suddenly creates a technological, present-day context, wherein, by common assumption, social gathering and transgression proceed hand in hand. (As an instance of relocation of the West in an industrialized context, think of *The Asphalt Jungle*, directed by John Huston, in 1950.) Finally, the classical orchestra and chorus stand in for a disciplined society, celebrating itself in an inevitably rhetorical fashion and content with its fear of innovation.

Figure 17.1 provides a representation of the stylistic tripartition that can be found in 'Titoli', in other pieces of the trilogy, as well as outside the movies in the western genre from the same period scored by Morricone (Morricone and Miceli 2013 [2001], 170).

We should now examine whether this music can speak to spectators from a variety of social classes at the same time, even though it originates in popular entertainment, which amounts to a sort of 'squaring the circle'. As for the dilemma of the historical truthfulness of the musical score, for a western movie this is not a real problem, especially in Leone's output. Morricone avoided falling into the trap of writing music *à la manière de . . .*; this was noticed even by some film critics, who nevertheless did not com-pletely resign themselves to the fact (De Fornari 1984, 43). This was at times due to the necessity of complying with a director's requests, which were sometimes pragmatic, and other times even coarse; on the other hand, Morricone found the slavish recreation of someone else's idiom uninteresting, while, because of both his nature and his professional experience in the recording industry, he had clearly in mind the need to provide a product that the people (more than the audience) could discern from among others.

It would surely be interesting to dedicate a few pages to analysis of the second theme that provides the movie with its title. A prototypical gunfight piece, 'Per un pugno di dollari' lends itself to audio-visual analysis. It also originates from a compromise and from the composer's secret and innocuous 'revenge' on the director. But both for an analytical discussion and for other savoury anecdotes that include Dimitri Tiomkin, Eugene O'Neill and Franco Zeffirelli, I will have to refer the reader to other texts: Frayling 2008 [2005], 92; Miceli 1994, 117–21; Morricone and Miceli 2013 [2001], 188.

We should also mention briefly one peculiar function fulfilled by the most incisive micro-element of the theme of 'Titoli': the descending semiquaver scale moving from dominant to tonic, and played by the recorder. We can call this a 'leitmotivic function' (but this is not a leitmotiv, since this definition applies only to Wagner and his followers). Several times throughout the film the elementary whistling intervenes in an unexpected (and therefore even more effective) manner, almost mockingly, without any instrumental support. Yet it is associated with the actions of the Man with No Name (Clint Eastwood), sometimes simply to mark his appearance, or it underlines one of his ironic lines. Because of its position, we should consider it a clear instance of *mediated level*, a sort of alternative language the protagonist thinks about, or resorts to. (The first formulation of the theory of levels dates back to the 1970s. In synthesis, the *internal level* (diegetic) indicates musical events belonging to the scene of the movie: the musical source is visible or its site can be imagined; sometimes it corresponds to playback, and it shows no artistic intention of the director. The *external level* (nondiegetic) – undetermined musical source, indexing function, ubiquity – can be typical accompaniment/commentary, even with a leitmotivic function. When it reaches the limits of expressive neutrality, it can be a generic background. The *mediated level* (metadiegetic) is an internalized musical source, which can be identified with the memories and the emotions of a character, as a kind of mimetic or subjective point of listening. It can acquire any function from the other levels, especially the leitmotivic function. It does not reveal the artistic intentions of the author. For more on this subject, see Miceli 2011 and 2013; Morricone and Miceli 2013 [2001].) While the leitmotivic function may seem plausible due to the continuous identification between the character and the sonic event, the thematic inconsistency of the musical object may also make it seem inadequate. Nonetheless, if we think about the gradual process of reduction of generative cells towards which Morricone was already hinting, it would not be out of the question to suppose that this figuration is one of the smallest recurrent themes in the history of film music – as taciturn as the character to whom it belongs.

For a Few Dollars More

Per qualche dollaro in più (*For a Few Dollars More*; 1965) came out in the wake of the first movie's success – a good example of maximal output for minimal effort. Implicitly, it was intended to follow the example of its successful model, but it could also count on a more substantial financial backing. The movie was more ambitious and undoubtedly less crude than its predecessor – which is already noticeable in the opening credits before the music – if only because of Leone's attempt to provide the main characters with some psychological depth (something which he always achieved with character actors). *Per qualche dollaro in più* is more expansive in every direction as a consequence of the greater availability of money alluded to in the title. It lasts two hours and ten minutes (compared to the one hour and forty minutes of the earlier movie). The main characters increase from two to three: Il Monco (El Manco, 'the one-handed', Clint Eastwood), Colonel Mortimer (Lee Van Cleef) and El Indio (Gian Maria Volonté), the *vilain*. Finally, the amount of music also increases. Once again, there are two main themes: 'Per qualche dollaro in più' corresponds to 'Titoli' in the previous movie, while 'La resa dei conti' ('The big gun-down') corresponds to 'Per un pugno di dollari' (both gunfight pieces are in D minor). The additional 'Il vizio di uccidere' ('The vice of killing') and 'Addio colonnello' ('Farewell, Colonel') bring the music to a total of forty-eight minutes, thirty of which present thematic features. The remaining eighteen minutes are functional insertions, somewhat in line with the underscore technique.

The gunfights in the movie, of course, are numerous and involve a variety of characters. Yet the music provides a narrative guide that establishes a reliable hierarchy indicating which gunfights are too insignificant for a musical theme (for instance, the one between Mortimer and the Hunchback, Klaus Kinski), or others that are simply symbolic, like the amusing first skirmish between El Manco and Mortimer – practically a courtship between two men.

While Leone's output in the western genre may be summarized by the well-known, and still current, Latin motto '*Homo homini lupus*' ('a man is a wolf to his fellow man'), the second movie features an unusual character in Colonel Mortimer. A bounty killer out of necessity, rather than by vocation, he leaves his share of the reward to Il Monco at the end of the movie, satisfied with having avenged himself on El Indio for the rape of his sister and the murder of her husband (Frayling 2000, 196). In this respect, the piece 'Addio colonnello' – characterized by an orchestral and choral writing that is too different from the rest of the score not to stand out – finds its justification. The character of Mortimer is a pretext, or an opportunity, to establish a new style, neither as understated as it used to be (guitars, Jew's harps, recorders, Pan flutes, percussion, whips, anvils, bells – by far the most interesting features) nor as over the top (trumpets at the limit of their register, choral textures sung by somewhat silly male voices). Here Morricone exercises a touch of class: the velvety strings, the well-blended brass section, the crucial and dazzling soloistic function of the woodwinds and a more refined choral ensemble – with the spiritual presence of female voices – achieve a typical mainstream popular-music sound, one that will reappear in *C'era una volta il West*. It was a concession to the international market, from which the Italian cinema industry was almost absent due to its provincial – or even parochial – aspirations (with hindsight, however, this was not necessarily a shortcoming). Within the context of the movie, though, this atmosphere was a rather out-of-place solution; the only exception is the quotation of a carillon-like tune associated with a chiming pocket watch that was consistent with the goals of the production and the recording company. It was a successful move, however, since it satisfied the taste of that *cultivé* group of spectators otherwise barely impressed by the vocal and instrumental solutions of the concluding sections of the leading themes; these spectators were looking for a sort of musical *bon ton*, something Morricone would include in his soundtracks with increasing frequency from the 1970s, independently from the genre of the movie. This testifies to what I have already called a 'partial' faithfulness to each movie. Incidentally, there is a noteworthy development. In the most dramatic moments of the movie, the score relies on musical techniques typical of contemporary art music: dissonant and unsettling clusters of string harmonics, and timpani glissandi.

One of the most notable features in *Per qualche dollaro in più* is the use of music as an essential dramaturgical, or narrative, element, starting from musical micro-elements that can be identified with characters (*mediated level*): the flute for Il Monco, the Jew's harp for Mortimer and the chiming pocket watch for El Indio. The segmented yet linked structure of the theme 'Per qualche dollaro in più' follows that of 'Titoli' from the previous movie, featuring a similar stylistic division. Yet the overall result aims at a process of accumulation, with the three segments overlapping to a greater extent than in the first movie. In addition to the human whistling – which at the time had already become a trademark that would accompany Morricone up to the present day, despite himself – the use of the Jew's harp to produce quite unusual sonic textures and ambiguous intonation is the composer's most farsighted appropriation, one which set a benchmark for a crowd of imitators. (I use the term 'appropriation' rather than 'invention' because the first innovator among Italian composers specializing in film music was Mario Nascimbene, whose scores first featured a Jew's harp, a harmonica, a bicycle bell, the ticking of a clock and the clicking of a typewriter. See, for instance, *Roma, ore 11* (1952), directed by Giuseppe De Santis.) But while we have thus far considered the musical features of the instrument, one cannot overlook that the Jew's harp also creates a semantic short-circuit because of its seemingly foreign nature in relation to the context of the movie. Seemingly, indeed, because the Jew's harp acquires a transgressive connotation from being associated – albeit obliquely – with a herding community of coarse individuals living in isolation, a community that, moreover, produced the phenomenon of banditry. Several of the following movies confirmed both the unequivocal meaning of this *topos* and the composer's inclination to follow his own musical direction, no matter the genre of the movie.

The Sicilian Jew's harp player Salvatore Schilirò performs the elementary rhythmic beat by loosely diminishing the crotchets. In so doing, he supports a melody that sets up a contraposition between two linear opening segments and a nervous and dynamic development. During two bars, on the long notes, the recorder adds a small cell made up of a run of semiquavers ending with a quaver (see antepenultimate bar in Example 17.5) – a micro-element that is similar, even in its being played by the recorder, to the one we have already discussed in 'Titoli' from *Un pugno di dollari*. The other parts of the theme follow the pre-existing pattern: the electric guitar enters by presenting a cell that develops the one previously played by the recorder. This time the guitar is paired with rock drums, an addition more noticeable and stylistically consistent with the atmosphere that the solo instrument brings about (i.e. less 'classically' percussive than in the previous movie). The guitar solo is followed by male voices – this time in unison and not in triads, hence even more elemental in sound – and the orchestra. These may appear as secondary differences; yet they can be related to the stylistic choices in 'Addio colonnello' or to the modernist-sounding athematic pieces. The features of each segment seem to express strongly diverging tendencies of the typical stylistic traits on which each segment is based, by an opposite emphasis.

As was mentioned above, in this chapter it is impossible to examine each main theme of the trilogy in detail. Our choice is dictated by the presence of the previously noted stylistic tripartition targeted on an audience *sui generis*, one that cuts across generations and classes. This said, let us consider more closely the duel pieces. First, one general consideration:

Example 17.5 Jew's harp passage from *Per qualche dollaro in più* (*For a Few Dollars More*).

the definition 'gunfight piece' refers to film-music genres that date back to Tiomkin's score for *High Noon* (1952), well over half a century ago, and that concern the western genre, which can encompass either tragic or Italian comedy elements. It goes without saying that the western is a genre that runs through the entire history of cinema, from *The Great Train Robbery* (attributed to Edwin S. Porter, 1903), to *Django Unchained* (directed by Quentin Tarantino, 2012), via *Dances with Wolves* (directed by Kevin Costner, 1990).

Very extroverted, and in its own way innovative, the gunfight cue 'La resa dei conti' from *Per qualche dollar in più* features richly contrasting expressive techniques (Example 17.6). While this cue is also based upon conjoined segments that are at once autonomous and yet easily distinguishable, the piece also has a nucleus upon which the other two segments depend in either a preparatory or summarizing function. This nucleus is based upon the much-abused opening inverted mordent from Johann Sebastian Bach's Toccata and Fugue in D minor for organ (BWV 565).

Example 17.6 'La resa dei conti' ('The big gundown') from *Per qualche dollaro in più.*

Moderato

etc.

Example 17.7 Pocket-watch chime from *Per qualche dollaro in più.*

As for the other segments, the first one, very suggestive and ever-present throughout the movie, is associated with a chiming pocket watch (Example 17.7). It consists of an undulating figuration based on a mechanical counterpoint between an ostinato of dotted quavers and an equivalent but more regular figuration. It features a celesta sustained by a light layer of strings and delicate percussion. Aside from the theme, 'La resa dei conti' is presented either as a miniature, with its chimes and lack of instrumental support – a realistic reference to the object, the pocket watch, which produces the sound (*internal level*) – or it is presented in a distorted liquefied rendition through an electroacoustic re-elaboration during the flashback sequences of El Indio's marijuana reveries (*mediated level*). The character recalls one key episode of the movie: how he took possession of the pocket watch after killing a young man and raping his partner, who, in turn, committed suicide afterwards.

The second segment has no motivic potential. It is constituted by a paroxysmal sequence of demisemiquavers in alternation with the carillon (chimes) and castanets. The resulting effect recalls a bullfighting ritual, but for the first time in the soundtrack of a Leone movie the harmonic substance is no mere support: it here takes on a modulating, and therefore dynamic, function. This happens thanks to the electric guitar, which in its repetitions begins with the tonic and, after each alternation with the carillon and castanets, presents the same ostinato but each time with varying timbres. At the point of giving way to the third segment, trumpet solos, choir and orchestra introduce the moment of the duel.

Because 'La resa dei conti' is tightly bound to a more elaborate narration, it presents different features from those of the previous movie. As much as the theme of *Per un pugno di dollari* was tortuous, homogeneous and in its own way complex (yet it must be remembered that its basis was pre-existent), this one, instead, is extroverted and segmented. As a result of such segmentation, it also displays that stylistic differentiation that we have thus far encountered only in the multifunctional pieces associated with the opening credits and other main scenes.

The tripartition is similar: the initial scene features a downsized and deliberately unassertive orchestration, here represented only by the carillon (chimes and celesta); the middle section – rock – is assigned again to the electric guitar, irreplaceable in this context; finally, the last section, whose magniloquent and ritualistic forces are supposed to bring the message to a universal level, presents here the rich sonorities of a grand organ (whose flimsy narrative motivation will be discussed later) or, in the final gunfight, a solo trumpet with an emphatic orchestral accompaniment. Since the narrative goes back to the chiming pocket watch, the music follows suit. As for the relations and interferences between visual and sonic components, not only does the conception of the piece work in an excellent manner, but it also communicates a rather singular sense of empathy that merits description.

In the sequence set in a deconsecrated church that now shelters a group of outlaws, El Indio takes barbaric revenge on the man who made his arrest possible. The man is forced to listen to two shots, with which a member of the gang of El Indio stealthily kills his little son and his wife. Then El Indio challenges him to a gunfight paced by the chiming pocket watch – the same watch El Indio stole from Colonel Mortimer's sister – which will signal the beginning of gun play when its mechanism comes to a stop, a ritual that will be repeated in the movie's finale. Interestingly, on the one hand the ritual established by the outlaw reintroduces a phatic function of the handover from the music to the sound of the gunshots that had already emerged in the previous movie; on the other, here it brings both the characters' and the spectators' aural focus to an extreme point of intensification. The succession of the segments is: carillon – (strings) – electric guitar – organ – carillon slowing down, and finally the gunshots. Even the central segments belonging to the rhetorical and artificial *external level* – a sign of the authors' will to bare their narratorial presence through their own commentary – all become sounds that the characters can perceive through a sort of psycho-perceptive 'blackmail': a typical instance of *internal level* or similar definitions (Lissa 1965 [1964], 427ff).

The duellists examine themselves with their ears open, and it is as if the *external level*, despite its abnormality, becomes *internal*. Furthermore, because of this mechanism, spectators experience those segments in a reduced detachment. Whether one likes it or not, it is as if everybody, both within and outside the movie, is depending on the music.

Some observations on the organ and the Bach quotation are in order, not so much in relation to the movie but to Morricone as a composer *tout court*. The general features of the Italian renewal of the western – with its many tributes to the American masterpieces, from John Ford onwards – involve redundant, overstated and perhaps even arrogant musical solutions (without hindering the composer from producing sophisticated solutions in terms of timbre and small-scale themes). These hyperbolic solutions are conducive to unusual aural experiences, from the carillon to the organ – from the micro-mechanic to the macro-mechanic; from an instrument symbolic of profanation to an instrument symbolic of untouchable sanctity; from an immanent to a transcendent dimension. All these interpretations could be further developed, but suffice it here to mention them only in passing.

The composer has repeatedly justified to me his choice of the organ as a narrative cue prompted by the deconsecrated church where the first gunfight takes place. This explanation, however, seems hardly convincing. To begin with, it is only a small church turned into a pigsty. Furthermore, on several occasions Morricone has manifested his indifference to realistic motivations and it is thanks to such indifference that he has come up with his most unexpected and savoury solutions. It is therefore hard to establish what led the composer to quote Bach – perhaps the shared key of D minor led to the idea of the organ, whereas the small church might have at most accommodated nothing more than a run-down harmonium. In any case, for a classically trained musician such a glaring reference to one of the most hackneyed commonplaces of Western art music – certainly the most hackneyed within Bach's output (although its authorship has long been disputed) – clashes with the alleged intention of paying homage to the Eisenach maestro. I mean no offence by claiming that this would be a singular homage. It would be as if a similarly academically trained painter were to manifest his admiration for, say, Leonardo da Vinci by choosing the *Mona Lisa*, maybe in a Duchamp version (with moustache and beard); or as if a writer trained in the study of the classics and indebted to Shakespeare were to choose the line 'To be or not to be, that is the question' as an epigraph for one of his works, and then insert it into a Gilbert and Sullivan operetta.

In addition to such a banal choice, it is surprising that Morricone chose to identify himself with such a double vulgarization. One may argue that this line of reasoning does not take into account the context of the scene, and that, for this reason, another Bach toccata would not have achieved the same effect. Once we agree that this choice reached its scope and even overdid it to become a textbook instance of *kitsch* (embraced by Federico Fellini in *La dolce vita*, 1960), this unnegotiated concession to the bad taste of the audience is symptomatic of a weakening of those ideals that had spurred and influenced the composer. Shortly afterwards, he would again resort to Bach, and in utterly commercial movies – for instance, in Henri Verneuil's *Le clan des Siciliens* (*The Sicilian Clan*; 1969). But he would do so without going too far, in a disguised way, while the instance of *Per qualche dollaro in più* seems to be the case of a self-punishing instinct, of a masochistic 'the worse, the better'. It is not my aim here to indulge in pseudo-psychology, yet several objective biographical data point this way, along with other similar musical output by the composer.

The final gunfight is of a completely different nature. Here, both Leone and Morricone give a demonstration of their individual and collaborative ability. The piece therefore deserves analysis in greater depth: see Table 17.1, which lays out the most relevant musical events of the final sequence (which is followed by a coda – sentimental at first, and then comic – of which we cannot give a full account here). Following the antecedent/consequent principle, well known in music, a thorough examination of the background is in order. This will help clarify the context, and 'reconstruct', at least in part, how the sequence under consideration was perceived. In other words, we must approach this scene by gradual steps.

The Good, the Bad, and the Ugly

The third movie with Leone, *Il buono, il brutto, il cattivo* (*The Good, the Bad, and the Ugly*; 1966), constitutes partial, yet eloquent enough, proof that in Morricone evolutionary processes take place through carefully engineered connections. First, let us briefly discuss the movie.

More ambitious than its predecessor, this work is also more pretentious and discontinuous. The plot holds together less coherently, the relationship between duration and intensity of the episodes is not always well balanced – and the episodes themselves not always resolved – and above all the tone of the movie ranges from the crudest of infanticides to belly-laugh comedy sketches, encompassing several weak sentimental and rhetorical moments. This is where, in my opinion, Leone's output reaches its lowest point, since such dubious incoherence may jeopardize the apologetic discourse that constitutes the backbone of his movies. It also creates several problems with the music, besides the objective one of sustaining a

Table 17.1 *Analysis of final gunfight from* Per qualche dollaro in più (For a Few Dollars More).

BACKGROUND EVENTS

No.	Running Time	Event	Visuals	Dialogue Sounds Music	Notes
01		Exterior Day Monco and Colonel Mortimer kill the members of El Indio's gang.			**Background Event 5**
02		Interior Day El Indio and the last member of his gang, Groggy (Luigi Pistilli), speak about their enemies. El Indio becomes pensive as he pulls the chiming pocket watch towards himself. El Indio opens the pocket watch. Groggy asks for the meaning of the object. El Indio does not answer, but...	Camera tracks in on the Extreme Close Up of El Indio. Detail Shot of the pocket watch, then gradually out of focus.	Sound effect of a metal object pulled on the table: *explicit sync point*. Chimes: *internal level – explicit sync point* at the opening of the watch. Chimes ostinato (repeated five times); then:	**Background event 4** There are no short-cuts or compressions in the time dimension. Story time corresponds to film time. This certainty is essentially established by the music.
03		... a flashback begins. El Indio recalls the whole episode of the killing of the man, and the rape and suicide of the woman. Red flash of light and end of the flashback.		*Mediated level* Special acoustic effect: string harmonics mixed electronically with fragments of the chimes motif.	**Background event 3**
04		A voice from outside overlaps with the chiming pocket watch. It is Colonel Mortimer who, revealing his own identity, asks El Indio to come out. Gradually El Indio comes back to reality and closes the pocket watch.	Similar to no. 2. Extreme Close Up of El Indio. Camera tracks out.	*Internal level* Chimes, 2½ repetitions in *rallentando...* ... suddenly interrupted. *Explicit sync point*	**Background event 2**
05		Suddenly El Indio stands up. He and Groggy take their weapons. Groggy leaves in a different direction from El Indio. El Indio follows him with his eyes.		Wind effect.	**Background event 1**

Table 17.1 (cont.)

DUEL PART I

No.	Running Time	Event	Visuals	Dialogue Sounds Music	Notes
01	01:55:09	**Exterior Day** Mortimer observes the farmer's house.	Establishing Shot for a fraction of a second. Immediately, from the left, Mortimer enters the frame in a Close Up of his profile. Both planes are kept in focus.	As above. **First partition – archaic** (already present in other moments).	A remarkable instance of a double point of view, typical of Leone, and of which he was a master. An Extreme Long Shot, generally experienced as contemplative and not emotionally engaging (or hardly engaging, even if an ambush is about to take place in this case), is partially juxtaposed with a Close Up having the opposite effect, a personalized and unexpectedly dramatic one.
		Mortimer's attention is drawn by a creaking door. El Indio leans out of it for a moment. Mortimer gets ready to shoot. Groggy comes out of another small door. Although he is running, he is shot and falls behind a wall. The following cutting is very fast and brisk: Mortimer comes out into the open to see the face of the man he shot, but El Indio opens another door, shoots at Mortimer and disarms him. El Indio steps down, holding the gun in his right hand and the pocket watch in his left hand. He approaches Mortimer, puts the gun in the holster, and enacts his favourite ritual:	Reverse Shot – Medium Long Shot of Mortimer. Tele-Photo. Reverse Shot – Medium Long Shot of Mortimer.	As above. Creak effect. Gun-shot effect. Wind effect. Gun-shot effect. Steps and spurs effects. *Explicit sync point* Wind effect. EL INDIO (to Mortimer): 'When the chimes end, pick up your gun… Try and shoot me, Colonel … *just try.*'	This is the beginning of the actual duel scene, led by music at *internal*, *mediated* and *external* levels.
		El Indio opens the pocket watch. Mortimer looks at his gun on the ground. El Indio takes a few steps towards Mortimer. El Indio loses the aggressiveness he has expressed up to this point and looks at the pocket watch intensely.	Close Up/Detail Shot of the gun lying on the ground (presumably a Point of View Shot). Close Up.	*Internal level:* celesta/chimes. *Explicit sync point* Chimes motif (4 repetitions). *Internal level* *Mediated level* *Implicit sync point* Light background of strings from the 5th repetition with key changes.	
		As the mechanism of the watch's chimes slows down, El Indio once again takes control.	Wide-Angle Close Up from behind of El Indio holding the pocket watch. The portrait of Mortimer's sister is visible. On the background, much further away than the previous shots had suggested, is the Colonel. Reverse Shot. Close Ups of the faces of the two, then followed by Extreme Close Ups.	8 repetitions: the first two are varied in the harmonic backing of the strings, the other 6 follow the original model. Gradual *rallentando* of the ostinato; strings from *p* to *pppp*.	Note the shift from *internal* to *mediated level*: El Indio 'hears' something beyond the mere ostinato. He is fixated on the fact that the woman could have killed him, but instead committed suicide. In so doing, she rebuked him completely…
		El Indio is about to draw his gun and shoot.	Extreme Close Up of Mortimer looking at the gun on the ground (Point of View Shot). Detail Shot of El Indio's right hand, slowly reaching for the gun.	Solo chimes, *rallentando.*	
	01:57:26				

Table 17.1 (*cont.*)

DUEL PART II

No.	Running Time	Event	Visuals	Dialogue Sounds Music	Notes
02		El Indio turns towards the source of an indistinct sound, at his far left. Mortimer, who has been looking at El Indio, slightly turns his head to the right.	Reaction Shots of both characters.	**First partition – archaic** (already heard). *Internal/external level* The chiming of a second pocket watch is vigorously juxtaposed with the first one.	The sound precedes the image by a fraction of a second. At least in part, this is the beginning of a process similar to the one described at the beginning of Duel Part I.
		A third man's arm is revealed, its hand holding a second pocket watch, twin to the first. Mortimer realizes that he no longer has the twin watch in the pocket of his waistcoat.	Establishing Shot of Courtyard Rapid intercutting of Close Ups and Detail Shots of facial expressions and the two different watches.	*Implicit sync point:* A light tap on the body of a guitar can be heard as the arm reaches a stable position. This is rhythmically synchronized with the celesta, which, while repeating the ostinato, foreshadows a melodic development. The strings do not only produce chordal layers, but are engaged in an internal counterpoint with the other instrumental parts.	Each acoustic (here, musical) element contributes to enlivening the scene.
			Close Up of the hand to a Medium Shot revealing Monco's face.	*Implicit sync point* on the Medium Shot of Monco's face. He looks resentfully at El Indio, while strings play a *crescendo* on the sustained chord. The melodic development is delayed, but at the same time it is made impending by the beginning of the	Leone edited the entire sequence of the duel following pre-composed music. Explicit/implicit sync points are not the only pieces of evidence of this. Monco now utters a succession of sentences/statements, all intertwined with the guitar's repetitions of a single note on predictable harmonies.
			Monco (seen from rear) walks into a return of the courtyard Establishing Shot.	**Second partition – rock** (already heard).	
		Monco directs his rifle at El Indio, deterring him from reacting.	Alternation of Medium Shots and Close Ups of all three characters.	The electric guitar is restricted to a series of repeated notes, modulating on the harmonic backing of the strings. The chimes keep playing; castanets are added (for this reason I have referred to the 'bullfight' in the essay).	7 repetitions of the chimes only, because the 8th is sung by the chorus. The chorus serves as an introduction to the last section, where the main melody of the trumpet finally emerges against a robust choral background.

Table 17.1 (*cont.*)

No.	Running Time	Event	Visuals	Dialogue Sounds Music	Notes
		Monco approaches Mortimer and passes his belt and gun to him.		3 repetitions of the ostinato; then between the 3rd and 4th: MONCO (to Mortimer): 'Very careless of you, old man.' 4th ostinato. Between the 6th and 7th ostinatos: MONCO (to Mortimer): 'Try this!' (he unties his gun belt and passes it to Mortimer). 8th repetition. Vocalizing mixed chorus. MONCO (turning to El Indio): 'Now we start...'	The ways in which Monco addresses Mortimer are significant: confidentially at first in his benevolent reproach, then becoming more peremptory as he elevates him to a role equal to that of El Indio.
				Third partition – pseudo-symphonic (already heard).	
		Monco sits on the wall that demarcates the place of the duel, and waits for the guns to be drawn. This will happen when the chiming of 'his' pocket watch has wound down.	Long Shot of courtyard. Camera tracks in to Close Up of Monco's face; alternating Medium Shots and Close Ups of the two duellists and Monco's face.	After the trumpet has presented its melody (see Ex. 17.6), boldly backed by the mixed chorus, the instrumentation is reduced.	The 'triumph' in the duel as *topos* of the eternal battle between good and evil, but also as *topos* of the choice between survival and death.
			Detail Shot of Monco's hand, gun and pocket watch (open to reveal portrait of Mortimer's sister).	The chimes return to the foreground, supported only by the lower strings. The castanets are still playing, and an effective figuration played by the timpani can be heard, which reproduces a short version of the coda from the guitar's ostinato.	
			Rapid cutting between Extreme Close Ups of all three characters' faces.	Wind effect.	
		El Indio is about to shoot first...	Close Up of El Indio's moving gun hand, intercut with Medium Shot of Mortimer.	Chimes almost winding down, with percussion.	
		... but Mortimer pulls out his gun more quickly. El Indio falls, but it looks as if he can still shoot. After an attempt, he finally collapses.	Long Shot of courtyard; Close Up of Monco; Medium Shot of El Indio on ground.	Gun-shot effect.	
		Mortimer is ready to shoot again, but El Indio dies.	Cutting between Close Ups of Monco and Medium Shots of Mortimer.	Gun-reload effect. *Explicit sync points* MONCO (after spitting out a piece of cigar): 'Bravo!'	

Table 17.1 (*cont.*)

No.	Running Time	Event	Visuals	Dialogue Sounds Music	Notes
		Monco expects his gun belt to be returned, but Mortimer has forgotten it. He approaches El Indio's corpse and retrieves the pocket watch he had given to his sister.	Detail Shot of open pocketwatch in Mortimer's hand.	Elegiac cor anglais solo based on trumpet melody.	Mortimer looks at Monco sideways, but betrays no emotion: his appeal lies in the fact that his expression can be interpreted in many ways.
			Medium Shot of Monco and Mortimer, side by side.	MONCO (looking down at portrait): 'There seems to be a family resemblance.'	
	2:02:07				

three-hour movie – problems of characterization, tone, incisiveness and endurance. We can say from the outset that Morricone followed the movie too faithfully (but would it have been possible to do otherwise?), as he mirrored its few qualities and many shortcomings, but also introduced some innovative and remarkable elements.

The first and most noticeable consequence of this is the higher number of themes along with their more problematic hierarchic organization. The piece 'Il buono, il brutto, il cattivo' ('The good, the bad, the ugly') is the typical opening credit piece (I will call it 'Il buono' for the sake of brevity). Similarly, 'Il triello' ('The trio') is the essential gunfight piece – the neologism of the title, suggested by Leone, refers to a combat between three people. Yet in these pieces one would look in vain for the expressive prominence and quantitative relevance (both in terms of the duration of each piece and of their cumulative pervasiveness) that characterized those from the previous movies.

'Il buono' follows the same principles as the two previous pieces, yet its structure is even more fragmented (Example 17.8). Its generative cell is one of the happiest ideas in Morricone's film music; once again, it testifies to the composer's unmatched skills at investing raw sonic material with plausible musical meaning, while at the same time preserving its primordial features. Here, the composer probably takes his cue from the howl of a coyote. After the usually bare, rhythmic and tribal opening, a fourfold and disarmingly simple leap of a fourth opens semi-phrase A, which is provided with a condensed yet ineluctable micro-motivic potential – a jingle that has not

Example 17.8 'Il buono' (opening titles) from *Il buono, il brutto, il cattivo* (*The Good, the Bad, and the Ugly*).

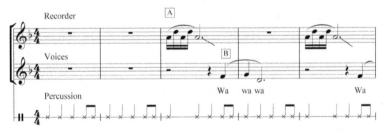

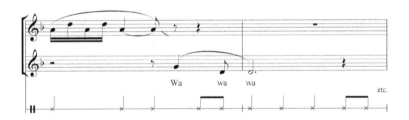

yet developed into a full melodic design. Noteworthy is the juxtaposition between the contraction of four semiquavers and expansion of one minim, marked by an important pitch fall (not a real portamento, since the fall arrives on no clear pitch). In contrast to this element, semi-phrase B – more appropriately, an 'answer' – features a much simpler outline. Such an outline would have neither melodic nor rhythmic meaning on its own, but acquires significance by virtue of the relation between the two parts, of which the first has a more marked character, since it condenses two contrasting tendencies – contraction versus expansion.

As happened in the similar pieces in the previous movies, the micro-motivic characterization of each previous piece is exposed and completed by the end of the opening nucleus – the semi-phrase B, indeed, regularly ends on the tonic. This technique is repeated four times, but with the function of each section gradually shifting: when the semi-phrase B occurs the second time, it moves towards chord VII (C major), thus heightening the harmonic tension. (Although this is arguably a modal piece, here it is treated as if it were in the key of D – an approach which reflects Morricone's own thinking.) Then the contraction of semi-phrase A is left unexpectedly unresolved by a tie binding the last semiquaver to the following dotted minim. This is worth noting because it results in a contradictory aural effect: on the one hand, a feeling of unexpected suspension seems to neutralize the familiar rhythmic pattern; on the other, this effect happens on the tonic, the ultimate place of harmonic stasis. The integration between the two semi-phrases is even more emphasized when it occurs for the last time, since A yields a quaver to B, and the latter immediately turns into a codetta.

A substantial difference with respect to musical cells from the previous movies is the thematic concentration with which this process is charged. In other words, in both *Per un pugno di dollari* and *Per qualche dollaro in più* the small cells combined with pre-existing materials by means of contrapuntal integration, while here the micro-thematic cell constitutes *the theme itself*. This works to the advantage of the following section, which as usual features the electric guitar, more foregrounded in this case. Let us consider 'Il buono' even further and discuss its timbral component, without which the compositional process would be deprived of its most inventive element. The micro-motive of the coyote aligns itself with the previous ideas, and brings back once more 'folkloric' instruments: semi-phrase A is played by a soprano recorder, and then by two vocalizing male voices processed electronically with subtle modifications of the pitch and the substantial addition of reverberation. This instrumentation also appears in other versions: one features a bass ocarina, a terracotta instrument with a timbre poor in overtones and, in this case, with a slight flutter (an effect typical of certain wind instruments that makes them sound like a turtle-dove). As the portamento further accentuates, the outcome is that of a sardonic and uncanny animality, produced by the anthropomorphic disguise and by its reiteration. With regards to the anthropomorphic disguise, the most traditional insult addressed by Tuco to Blondie's mother turns into the musical cell on the vowel 'ah'. As for the reiteration, it confers on the whole piece a totemic significance typical of ostinati, whether musical or non-musical (Bologna 1992, 89–100).

The answer B is performed by another, much less processed, male voice. Its timbre is metallic and cutting, highlighting the derisive character of the music. Alternatively, recourse is made to human whistling – which keeps up with the tradition of the previous movies – and a constellation of soft and enticing murmurs which have a degree of relation with an area of experimentation in contemporaneous art music: the Gruppo Improvvisazione Nuova Consonanza (New Consonance Improvisation

Example 17.9 Electric-guitar segment from 'Il buono'.

Group), which Morricone joined around 1964 at Franco Evangelisti's invitation. Going back to the general features of 'Il buono', the gradual growth and conceptual separation of each section undergo an important process of integration: indeed, each entrance alternates or overlaps with the others. Consequently, the identification of a segment with its target audience, previously more clear-cut, also weakens, although it is still present in principle. Better to illustrate this point, consider how the rock-music aficionado has to detect the electric guitar from within an impressive instrumental and vocal ensemble of a considerably different aesthetic pedigree (Example 17.9). Each section yields something of its own to the others, creating a stylistic osmosis that is also an important sign of the composer's type of career trajectory.

From the first portion of the rock segment, one notices that the features of the musical writing are further away from those fitting an electric guitar than earlier pieces. Indeed, if one were to remove the original instrument and substitute it with a female voice or violin, the writing would remain plausible.

Here I have avoided an in-depth analysis of 'Triello', even though it constitutes a piece of considerable interest. It appears 170 minutes into the movie, reflecting the movie's unusual length: the piece, indeed, lasts 4′27″. Consider that the first thematic unit, performed by the trumpet, enters after 1′36″ of exhausting introduction. Rather than leading to the drawing out of the guns, it yields to a series of athematic fragments, then to portions of the introduction, and then even to echoes of the carillon from the previous movie (is this instance of self-quotation a meta-musical equiva-lent of the director's meta-filmic choices or more simply a concession to the audience?). A full recapitulation only occurs at 3'25"; in short, this is a case of musical *coitus interruptus* of the most atrocious kind. Irony aside, the piece fulfils an obvious function within the movie, while, from a musical point of view, it confirms Morricone's exceptional – and uni-versally acknowledged – qualities as an orchestrator.

A special case is the piece 'L'estasi dell'oro' ('The ecstasy of gold'), due to its very effective – even memorable – relationship with the images, and to its compositional features. This is the last piece I will discuss; I will dedicate only a few lines to it, although it deserves an entire essay. 'L'estasi dell'oro' was conceived as an ambitious audio-visual project: Morricone was asked to compose a self-sufficient and structurally unified piece while using implicit sync points (*sincroni impliciti*) to bind it to the movie images. (An explicit sync point is the exact and unambiguous correspon-dence between a filmic and a sonic/musical event: at times, the music 'doubles' the sound by superimposition, and imitates it. An implicit sync point is a more subtle conjunction: this category comprises changes in timbre, harmony, rhythm, dynamics, the beginning or conclusion of a melodic fragment and any musical event/parameter as long as it is linked to something as nuanced happening on screen. For the distinction between implicit and explicit sync points in the context of the theory of levels, see Miceli 2013, 481–567.) On the occasion of our classes at the Accademia Musicale Chigiana in Siena, held between 1991 and 1996, a high-spirited Morricone listed all the sync points and commented upon them during the projection of the sequence.

In the movie, Il Brutto fills the space of a vast circular cemetery, searching restlessly for a name on a tomb. Leone 'fills' the same space by alternating dolly shots, close-ups, telephoto shots and point-of-view shots at a gradually increasing pace. But, above all, it is Morricone who 'fills' the space with this piece specifically conceived for this sequence (Example 17.10). Today, the 'angelic orgasms' vocalized by Edda Dell'Orso are among the least syrupy ones of Morricone's entire output; the piece's beautiful melody – possessing a remarkably compelling com-municative drive – is repeated in a loop. The stretto before the concluding repetition, in particular, is of excellent, almost contemporary, art-music compositional quality.

An experiment I often conducted in the classroom (at both the con-servatory and the university) consisted of projecting the cemetery sequence without its music. The outcome was an obvious demonstration of how fundamental Morricone's presence has been for a particular way of conceiving film music.

At this point, it is possible to go back briefly to the implicit question behind the title of this chapter, namely 'what is the Italian way to revisionist westerns?' Firstly, I accepted with relief a title that did not contain the expression 'spaghetti western'. Of course, given my interlocutors, I was not surprised. In my first study on Morricone, published more than a quarter of a century ago (Miceli 1988), I deliberately avoided that slightly derogatory label, although it was commonly used. As for Leone, I leave the last

Example 17.10 Cemetery music from *Il buono, il brutto, il cattivo.*

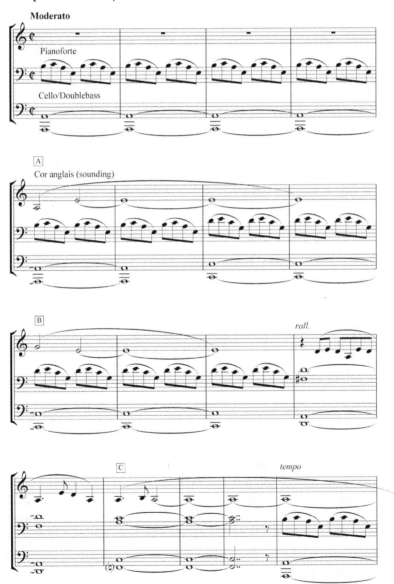

Example 17.10 (*cont.*)

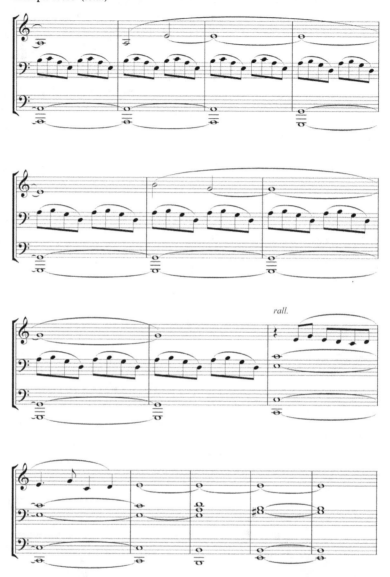

word to film historians, although my ideas on the director can be inferred in several passages of this text. Frayling wrote: 'With *For a Few Dollars More*, Leone would definitively distance his work from the vast bulk of popular Italian film-making' (2000, 200). As to Morricone, I don't think he was aware of the ideological potential implicit in his stylistic tripartition. In other words, I believe that the tripartite division into (1) archaic (the most refined to refined people); (2) pseudo-rock (pseudo-transgressive, with urbanization and actualization of the present); and (3) pseudo-symphonic, ignoring the rules of (1) and contesting those of (2), is a reality of which the composer was unaware. But it can explain his music's tremendous success in appealing across boundaries of generation and class. Morricone, however, does not seem to have been very happy with this theory of mine. The western genre fulfilled the composer's epic and rhetorical tendencies, his need to be transgressive and his desire for the free invention of new timbral combinations and melodic dilatations, as well as for micro-thematic solutions that had an enormous influence in the film industry between 1960 and 1990.

I believe that the implicit question of the title has already been given several answers. The Italian way to the western has been by and large the result of Morricone's revision. Leone looked on, approved because it was in his interest to do so, and did not feel his own valuable contribution was thereby diminished.

In this respect, it is necessary to conclude that Morricone was indeed interested in Leone's choices, but without feeling bound to them. For the composer, this was only part of the journey. Morricone, indeed, had already launched an Italian way to the renewal of film music.

18 Music, Noise and Silence in the Late Cinema of Jean-Luc Godard

DANAE STEFANOU

With a vast and ever-increasing filmography and an equally large corpus of genre-defying theoretical work, the output of Jean-Luc Godard's long career (1960–) appears, at best, labyrinthine. Unsurprisingly, several comprehensive presentations and explications of Godard's cinema have been attempted, mostly in the form of monographs or edited volumes re-evaluating his entire filmic oeuvre (for example, Sterritt 1999; Temple *et al.* 2004; Conley and Kline 2014). Among other things, these attempts problematize the political and ideological repercussions of Godard's early output (MacCabe *et al.* 1980), consider Godard as historiographer and theorist (Neer 2007; Witt 2013) and contextualize the idiosyncratic aesthetics of his later work within a broader spectrum of philosophical references (D. Morgan 2012). However, aside from some sporadic reference to sound in Godard's films since the 1980s, visuality and the predominance of the image as an affective and narrative medium remain central to most endeavours.

The ensuing chapter attempts a predominantly sound-based (rather than image-biased) navigation through the complex universe of Godard's later films. It makes a critical case for recontextualizing his notoriously eclectic approach to the soundtrack by drawing on more experimental aural art forms, such as *musique concrète*, noise music and sound art. Exploring such paradigms in connection with Godard's fragmentary aesthetic, as epitomized in his monumental eight-part *Histoire(s) du cinéma* (1988–98) and his more recent feature-length films, particularly *Film socialisme* (2010) and *Adieu au langage* (*Goodbye to Language*; 2014), the relationship between music, noise and silence emerges as a significant, albeit critically underexplored, framework for the assessment of Godard's unique contribution to contemporary non-narrative cinema.

Musical Metaphors for Sonic Objects

Music is a living element. Just like a street, or cars. It is something I describe, something pre-existent to the film. (GODARD IN NARBONI AND MILNE 1972, 234)

In his monograph on *Histoire(s) du cinéma*, Michael Witt (2013) devotes a short section to the examination of Godard as a sound artist in his own right. Witt's proposition is not without its precedents; in fact, it could be seen more as an encouragement to reconsider, perhaps more consistently, a series of fragmentary attempts to grapple with the sonic aspect of Godard's output. These include a few isolated but notably detailed analyses of sound editing, voice-overs and musical cues by Alan Williams (1982) and Royal S. Brown (1980) respectively, as well as an evaluation of sound as a gendered medium (Sinclair 2003). They also comprise hints at Godard's influence in the sphere of modern composition rather than on cinema alone (for example Jousse 1990; Griffiths 2000), astute examinations of his employment of particular compositional styles (Sheer 2001; Jullier 2004; Gorbman 2007; Stenzl 2010) and theoretical considerations of musical aesthetics within broader studies of his non-fiction films (Emmelhainz 2009; Alter 2012).

Witt's account, if only a brief sub-section in a book exclusively dedicated to *Histoire(s)*, is one of the most comprehensive attempts to date to synthesize previous literature in one cohesive, inclusive statement on Godard's sonic aesthetics. However, its vocabulary is also quite indicative of the lack of a given, terminologically consistent framework for discussing these aesthetics without recourse to visual tropes and genres. References to sound art, soundscapes and *musique concrète* are interchangeable with analogies of composition, harmony, counterpoint and orchestration. Arguably, the examination of Godard's practice as sound art is primarily contingent upon a generalized metaphor of music, rather than a specific consideration of what a composer does, and how that may differ across different spectrums of engagement with sound – including, say, post-renaissance harmonic composition, electronic soundscape design or free improvisation with everyday objects.

Godard himself seems to have played up or at least contributed to this vague characterization, and in several ways. As a director deeply interested in the processes by which meaning is assigned, transposed and displaced between stimuli, he has keenly explored various levels of metaphor through which music acquires symbolic meaning. This is best illustrated in broad-stroke gestures: in his decision, for instance, to subtitle *Film socialisme* 'a symphony in three movements', when the film has very little to do either with the conventions of symphonic composition *per se* or with the attempts of historic 'film symphony' genres to emulate symphonic textures and forms.

A further indication that composition is only a loose metaphor for Godard is found in his numerous references to the practice, aptly cited in theoretical analyses of sound in his films (for example, R. S. Brown 1980 and 1994; Witt 2013). His mention of working 'like a composer' when describing his involvement with sound editing in *Histoire(s)* is little more than a lip-service reference. A closer reading suggests a rather more complex, if not downright heretical approach to music and sound, quite divorced from any traditional compositional considerations, such as the practice of 'orchestration' being evoked in the extract below:

> Then for instance, I'll replace the dialogue with the sound of a dog barking. Or I'll try it with a sonata. I'll fiddle around with it until I'm satisfied . . . like a composer . . . I have the whole orchestra in my head while I'm editing. And when I've chosen one particular sound, then I cut the scene accordingly, and throw the rest in the bin. (Cited in Witt 2013, 199)

From the onset of the editing for *Histoire(s)*, Godard personally worked on the soundtrack, sitting at a twenty-four-track mixing board and editing all channels simultaneously. This was thanks to his sound mixer and loyal collaborator, François Musy, who essentially set up a personal studio for the director so he could record, edit and mix audio himself during film editing. Perhaps unsurprisingly, although the director's sound producers have always collaborated closely with him during the entire film-making process, this has hardly been the case with his musical associates. If anything, Godard's reluctance to collaborate with composers during production and editing may be an indication as to the rather more unmediated, openly materialist nature of his involvement with sound. After all, to 'fiddle around' with sounds, choose one in particular, then 'throw the rest in the bin' is hardly compatible with the kind of work expected from filmic composers or composers of any kind, much less so Godard's own collaborators in some of his best-known films – a long list of accomplished artists including Martial Solal, Michel Legrand, Ketil Bjornstad and David Darling, who contributed original music to *A bout de souffle* (*Breathless*; 1960), *Une femme est une femme* (*A Woman is a Woman*; 1961), *For Ever Mozart* (1996), *Éloge de l'amour* (*In Praise of Love*; 2001) and *Notre musique* (*Our Music*; 2004), among others. These very composers have often confirmed the director's own admission that he has no knowledge whatsoever about 'the technical end of music' (R. S. Brown 1994, 189), and this can perhaps help explain why Godard never really worked in conjunction with any one of them, choosing instead to discard hours of meticulously composed music with little consideration for its intrinsic structure or form. His work with Legrand on *Vivre sa vie* (*My Life to Live*; 1962) is a typical case in point: only a tiny fragment of the theme and variations that Godard had originally requested ended up being used; the rest was, quite literally, thrown in the bin (Roustom 2014). For Brown, this attests to a consideration of 'music as a material variable' rather than as 'variable material'. Indeed, even in Godard's earliest films, there is evidence that music is no longer treated as a coherent, self-standing entity, composed of organically evolving material; rather, it is often 'limited to a fragment obsessively repeated in different contexts' (R. S. Brown 1994, 190).

Under this light, Godard's gradual move away from original soundtracks and his increasing reliance on personally processed segments of pre-recorded music in his later films imply a dismissal of self-contained aesthetic objects, and a deeper problematization of formalism. On a more elementary level, it becomes increasingly clear that his references to composition and orchestration, just like his tendency to reference musical forms as titles, should be taken less literally. Trying pre-recorded sounds out in the studio, cutting and pasting them and discarding whole sections in favour of a few fragments may not be common or acceptable practice for a composer in the modernist, formalist sense of the term. It is, however, the kind of work associated with more experimental, postmodern definitions of sound art, and particularly with branches of the practice that emerged during the second half of the twentieth century, manifested in the work of composers like John Cage, and drawing on a wide body of contemporary and earlier developments, including tape-music aesthetics, ecological approaches to listening, Surrealist découpage and collage techniques, and Dadaist and Futurist conceptions of noise as poetic medium (Kahn 1999; Hamilton 2007; Licht 2007). In all its varied expressions, sound art fundamentally challenges the conception of music as an immaterial art form that is primarily concerned with tonal organization. In so doing, it often adopts an expressly non-musical approach to aural aesthetics, substituting idealistic musical preoccupations with more pragmatic considerations of 'sound as sound' (Hamilton 2007, 47).

As a materialist sound artist, Godard seems to prefer working with everything at once, having all sounds at his disposal at all times, throwing them together by force, chopping them up at random, and scrapping them altogether if necessary, quite regardless of the implicitly musical syntax that may underlie many of his chosen samples. '[L]ike another picture which isn't a picture' (Godard 1968, 79), sound is assigned the same 'value' as images. But what exactly is this value when it comes to musical sounds? Godard compares the role of music in his films to the role assigned to black colour in Impressionist painting (Godard in

Narboni and Milne 1972, 233). If we are to follow this metaphor closely, it leads to the deeply cynical suggestion that music's main value and function in Godard's cinema lies in its absence. This impression is further enforced during the lecture scene in *Notre musique*, where the film title is cited: 'The principle of cinema: to go towards the light, and shine it onto our darkness; our music'.

And yet music is omnipresent in Godard, and much more enigmatically so in his later films. It is not merely that he prefers to work with pre-recorded as opposed to originally composed music, or that, as an *auteur mélomane* (Gorbman 2007) he chooses to use powerfully evocative musical fragments as a montage element, juxtaposing them with 'neutral' sounds or arbitrary images. His practice, and his way of engaging with the musical aspects of the soundtrack, is far more concerned with sampling and processing entire musical compositions as sounds than with handling them as music. In interviews he has demonstrated little short of a complete disinterest in music as an autonomous art form, proclaiming Bach 'the perfect music for the elevator' because 'his music can be matched to any situation ... like Muzak' (Sterritt 1998, 171) or suggesting that, to an original background score by Stravinsky, he would personally prefer 'bad Stravinsky. Because if what I use is good, everything I have shot becomes worthless ... ' (Narboni and Milne 1972, 233). Godard has no qualms in extending this remark to living composers, including the composers of original music for numerous of his later films who were associated with the record label ECM (Edition of Contemporary Music). Speaking to Thierry Jousse, for instance, he referred to ECM composer David Darling – whose music had appeared in *Nouvelle vague* (1990) and who would later contribute pieces to *Éloge de l'amour* and *Notre musique* – as 'a minor Bernard Herrmann' (Jousse 2000, cited in Jullier 2004). As Laurent Jullier rightly notes, the terms of this analogy are hardly evident as the two composers share very little if anything in terms of style or technique. However, as on many other occasions, Godard discourages any attempts at a closer reading; in the same interview, he confesses to knowing 'nothing about music' anyway.

Throughout his career, Godard has advocated a decontextualized, pragmatic use of musical materials. Consequently, his musical borrowings are represented not as signifying entities, complete in themselves, but as 'sonic shards' (Bordwell 1985; Alter 2012), often brutally cut up, coarsely reassembled 'in different degrees of rawness' (Bordwell 1985, 331), and starkly juxtaposed against each other in time, resulting in an impression of multiple, simultaneous and competing soundtracks, or at least 'incompatible renderings of the acoustic environment' (A. Williams 1982, 201). Each of these renderings, however, is in itself more than an attempt to document or emulate a set of realistic acoustic situations. Every channel of audio often carries with it its own soundworld, a kind of soundtrack within a soundtrack.

Even more topical than a metaphor of Godard as composer, sound artist or even a 'virtuoso' (as critics all so frequently suggest), then, is perhaps one of Godard as listener. Aside from being a cinematic *auteur*, he is also a keen archivist of sounds and images, who finds equal (if not more) value in found objects and assemblages. This combined focus on sonic objects and listening subjects suggests a deeply rooted affinity with the electroacoustic heritage of Pierre Schaeffer, and with the very core of *concrète* composition. One of the fundamentals of *musique concrète* is the emphasis on a kind of listening that takes place when we do not seek meaning and associations in sounds, but rather attend only to their material characteristics and the ways in which we come to experience them. This mode of listening is a quintessentially phenomenological kind of process, one that Schaeffer's emphasis on acousmatic sounds and Michel Chion's notion of reduced listening have sought to clarify and distinguish from semantic or causal listening (Chion 1994, 25–9). In the latter, the focus is on deciphering meaning, or discerning source informa-tion. Similarly, reduced listening is equally distinct from background listening, where the faculty of attentive listening is suspended altogether. Other theories have sought to clarify Chion's tripartite model even further, and can certainly prove useful for exploring Godard's aural experiments in greater detail. See, for instance, Barry Truax's tripartite distinction between listening-in-search, listening-in-readiness and back-ground listening (2001), or even Huron's tentative list of listening styles and strategies, comprising over twenty different modes (2002).

Godard's own fascination with the act of listening *per se* is reflected on various fronts, but perhaps most overtly in his longstanding collaboration with ECM director Manfred Eicher (who founded the record label in Germany in 1969) and their decision to release the entire soundtrack of *Histoire(s)* as a CD box set (1999), just as, a little earlier, *Nouvelle vague* had been released as an audio recording (1997). Jullier (2004, 283–7) considers both of these audio releases as autonomous *concrète* works in their own right, while also being critical of the CD medium and its implications for listening. Witt (2013, 208) sees the audio release of *Histoire(s)* as the ultimate realization of Godard's cinematic aesthetics and implicitly acknowledges the director's debt to *musique concrète*. In the case of *Nouvelle vague*, the Schaefferian idea of acousmatic conditions as the optimal means of engagement with *concrète* aesthetics is central to the presentation of the disc as a private cinema for the ear. The CD sleeve notes present a text by Claire Bartoli, a blind storyteller/narrator, who provides an extended phenomenological account of listening to the film, without access to its visual content:

> Godard dices the sounds, the words, their echoes . . . Jostled along the paths of my listening, I am thrown off course. He identifies the opposite poles; acknowledges them in our reality but clashes them so violently that we pass beyond these polar tensions to rediscover unity.　　　　　　(Bartoli 1997, 92–3)

Little as Godard may have actually incorporated the techniques of instrumental composition in his work, his own cross-media techniques of décollage, montage, fragmentation and distortion have proved increasingly influential among composers across high and low ends of contemporary instrumental and electronic music, and not only those incorporating *concrète* elements in their practices. Aside from endeavours like the *Godard ça vous chante?* LP (1986), featuring prominent musicians responding to Godard 'as musician' through free improvisation, art-rock or tape-music idioms, there are cases like Pascal Dusapin, for instance, who cites Godard as a major influence in his opera *Faustus, The Last Night* (2003–4). Dusapin composed the words and music simultaneously on the basis of 'cut-ups' from a large amount of quoted material, so much so that it is difficult to distinguish so-called 'original' segments of the composition from borrowed ones (Dusapin 2006; see also Campbell 2013).

Cases like this bring to mind a plausible, but as yet unexplored, affinity between Godard's fragmentary sound-object aesthetic and John Oswald's notion of 'plunderphonics'. In the mid- to late-1980s, Oswald, a media artist and electronic musician, provided one of the chief theoretical frameworks for original composition from pre-existing copyrighted material. What he was essentially advocating was both an aesthetic and a political stance *vis-à-vis* quotation and borrowing, in the light of changing conceptions of creativity and musical consumption. A 'plunderphone', according to Oswald, is 'a recognizable sonic quote, using the actual sound of something familiar which has already been recorded . . . Taking Madonna singing "Like a Virgin" and rerecording it backwards or slower is plunderphonics, as long as you can reasonably recognize the source' (Igma 1988). While verbal language has such symbols as quotation marks, music possesses no such symbolism, and consequently there is no clear way of sonically denoting the extent or nature of cross-reference between different musical pieces (Oswald 1985). With the advent of digital sound, a whole new spectrum of possibilities opened up with regards to mixing and sampling, and with them, a series of ethical and legal conflicts surfaced, bringing terms such as 'audio piracy' to the forefront of discourses on recorded music. While press and theoretical attention has primarily focused on the legal controversies and/or activist implications of practices like Oswald's, the impact and resonance of his ideas on an aesthetic and technical level should not be overlooked.

Coincidentally or not, the year 1988, when Oswald's *Plunderphonics* EP was released on CD, also saw the release of *Histoire(s) du cinéma: Toutes les histoires*, the first instalment (1A) in what was to be Godard's magnum opus in a subjective historiography of cinema: an eight-part, 266-minute essay film, constructed entirely out of pre-existent filmic material. Oswald's work engages more overtly with the medium of digital-audio reproduction and focuses on temporal manipulation; it thus operates on a much more compressed timescale than Godard's monumental projects. For instance, Oswald's own take at historiography was a history of CD music (1982–92), compressed into a twenty-minute-long composition entitled *Plexure* (1993). Plunderphonics are also a more explicitly humorous approach to recorded music, and much less at ease with the singular-authorship model associated with Godard's cinema. Nevertheless, it is sometimes hard not to think of plunderphonics in the unclassifiable, inter-media multiplicity that is Godard's late cinema. From *Histoire(s)* onwards, images are regularly dissociated from their sounds, shots are played and replayed, looped at varying rhythms, sometimes intermittently or backwards; audiovisual segments of various lengths are often decontextualized and recontextualized *ad libitum*, accompanied by textual cut-ups and quotations, voice-overs or rogue fragments of soundtrack from other, invisible scenes. One scene's diegetic sounds may become another's nondiegetic interventions, ultimately rendering all sound metadiegetic, and narrative film-music concepts less and less relevant. Any attempt at causal and semantic listening soon becomes suspended, giving way to a free-flowing, decentralized interplay of associations between and across auditory and visual stimuli, 'an aural river one can enjoy as it comes' (Griffiths 2000).

'Oh Language!': Speech, Noise and Silencing

When I hear what we call music, it seems to me someone is talking, and talking about his feelings, or about his ideas of relationships. But, when I hear traffic, the sound of traffic here on 6th Avenue for instance, I don't have the feeling that anyone is talking. I have the feeling that sound is acting, and I love the activity of sound. (JOHN CAGE IN GRANGE AND SEBESTIK 1992)

The time of phrases is over. (*ÉLOGE DE L'AMOUR*, 2001)

In the opening titles of *Histoire(s)* 1A, Godard employs not only plunderphonic-style sampling, but also visual irony to assume, somewhat reluctantly, the role of a historiographer/narrator who stammers, who finds it hard to project one single line of enquiry, incessantly reviewing and reassessing his material. Sounds always precede images in creating this context; an industrial-type rhythm occupies the auditory foreground, punctuated by images of a film reel being fast-forwarded and slowed down. This counterpoint gradually refers us to an electronic typewriter at which Godard is apparently typing (quoted) segments as he reads/narrates them, pausing to repeat words to himself before moving on. In the background, a fade-in to the opening bars of the final movement of Arthur Honegger's Third Symphony (*Symphonie liturgique*, 1946) accompanies the visual cue of a boom microphone entering the frame rather intrusively as Godard is typing. The auditory middleground is diegetic, but entirely self-referential; it is occupied by the sound of the boom mike as it is being set up, and gradually, with increasing intensity, the heavily amplified micro-sounds of Godard's uncomfortable pauses as he stops between sentences, wets his lips, takes a drag of smoke from his cigar and starts again.

Godard's pausing to smoke his cigar right before the film's title shot would be a typical example of what Chion (2009 [2003], 73) identifies as 'verbocentric' cinema, a typical practice since the advent of the sound film. Attention is guided towards speech, but this is done imperceptibly, and naturalized via a number of tropes, including a visual focus on the mouth and mouth-related activity, typically including smoking or drinking, in between phrases. The consistency of this association can only be subverted deliberately, through the introduction of noise, perceptible as interference or a break in the flow of verbal language, enough to distract or redistribute attention.

Godard's cinema thrives on this destabilization of speech via noise. By foregrounding stammering voices, for instance, signification in voice-over and dialogue – traditionally cinema's privileged semantic media – is compromised, and speech is submitted to the abstract sound-object aesthetic that permeates his films. To begin with, although language itself is still privileged both as aural and as visual device, dialogue is not. "'Conversation'", observes Alan Williams (1982, 193), 'is only one possible type of language use in a Godard film. There are also, most notably, *reading aloud, composing aloud for transcription, interviewing, giving a prepared speech or lecture, free association,* and *translation*' (italics in original).

All of these uses are explored to their limits in Godard's later films, and, most notably, all are being subjected to noise that takes them quite beyond Chion's tripartite model of theatrical, textual or emanation speech (2009 [2003], 67–9). This is done primarily through interference (of simultaneous or intermittently inserted audiovisual events, including concurrent translations in different languages), distortion (in the speech itself, through self-reflective pauses, breaks or wordplays; or in the editing, by processing the audio track), or even muting (either literal or metaphorical, by changing the volume and shifting attention to an alternative, preferred channel of sound other than the main speech). Furthermore, these speech processes are often further complicated, rhythmically and/or texturally, with another layer of recordings that expose filming and recording apparatus in action (tape loops, film rolls, microphones, cameras and, in later films, portable cameras or mobile phones).

In typical verbocentric cinema, audio, visual or combined events of short duration between or within dialogue can act as punctuation, emphasizing what is being said. Chion labels this kind of audiovisual insertion technique a 'scansion between the said and the shown' (2009 [2003], 386). Godard, according to Chion, also works with this scansion, but often hyperpunctuates, thus exaggerating this effect to the point of destroying dialogue altogether (*ibid.*, 489). In conjunction with these punctuating devices, he makes ample use of voice-off, off-screen speech along the lines of Chion's *acousmêtre*, which essentially represents an absence, a disembodied voice that is somehow more powerful than an embodied, present one (Bonitzer 1975; Chion 1999). Discursive expectations are further broken by Godard's characteristic preference for silent textual insertions, appearing as intertitles or superimposed on the frame on various occasions. In his later films, these often give rise to highly elaborate deconstructive wordplay, reminiscent both of the alliterations and correspondences found in French Symbolism, and the deconstructive syllable games of Dadaist sound poetry. For Godard, however, these often entail a semantic charge, perhaps more resonant of the kind of deconstruction associated with post-structuralist philosophy (see, for example, Derrida 1997). HELLAS, in *Film socialisme*, for instance, is reiterated in various permutations as HELL / AS and HÉLAS. Aside from its sonic value, this is also an affective commentary on Greece's implication in the collapse of the European communitarian ideal (see Emmelhainz 2014). In typical intertextual fashion, the pun reappears after a very abrupt burst of noise, during a reference to banks in *Adieu au langage*.

True, for all his emphasis on cutting and fragmentation, Godard emphasizes the continuum of events, or soundflow, in his films. He admits to working 'not with an idea of vertical sound . . . but horizontally, where there are many, many sounds but it's still as though every sound is becoming one general speech, whether it's music, dialogue or natural sound' (Sterritt 1998, 171). Yet to consider noise and silence in Godard's speech cinema solely in the context of punctuating techniques that cut into an otherwise consistent logocentric flow of meaning is not necessarily the most insightful way to approach his sound aesthetics; neither can we hope to achieve fuller understanding of his work by identifying – and taxonomically analysing – all of Godard's references. Cue-by-cue analyses or attempts to list, map out and explicate Godard's quotations, as, for example, the exhaustive 'skeleton key' to *Histoire(s)* by Céline Scemama (2006), have become increasingly rare for his later films, and even if they did happen, it is doubtful whether they would contribute to a richer audiovisual experience.

One of the main reasons for these aporias is Godard's consistent emphasis on relational ontologies – on meanings derived by dynamically experiencing, processing and renegotiating relations rather than describing fixed, self-contained formal entities. 'We are not looking for new forms, we are looking for new relationships' (1991 [1985], 83), he had exclaimed as a founding member of the Dziga Vertov group (1968–72), a radical film co-operative named after the pioneering Soviet director of the 1920s and '30s. Vertov's own early experiments with sound film had included a so-called symphony of noises (*Enthusiasm: Symphony of the Donbass*, 1930), and foreran both *musique concrète* and sound art by several years in making full compositional use of urban and industrial sounds (Smirnov 2013). In that sense, and given also his fascination with the act of listening, Vertov might be considered the only filmic predecessor to Godard's noise aesthetic.

Noise, then, is more than a punctuating device that helps delineate a particular form in Godard. It is a remedy against logocentricism, a medium of immersion into a kind of 'inter-consciousness' (Nechvatal 2011, 222), where relations are fostered and explored:

> Noise ... expresses the nature of the relation [between system and expression] and deconstructs the binary oppositions that generally channel our attention towards a discrete and isolated aspect of expression: form or content, for instance, or medium or message ... [T]here can be no absolute separation between content and form in a relational ontology, and it is precisely the deconstruction of such binaries to which noise points.
>
> (Hainge 2013, 17)

A significant realization that has emerged via the recent surge in theorizations of noise as an artistic medium and as a social and political practice is that noise is not entirely reducible to the extraneous event, the hiss or glitch that 'distorts' or 'breaks up' a sensory continuity. Rather, these are only moments when noise becomes apparent. In fact, at a time where all ontology is mediated, noise is an integral part of the media (Hainge 2013; Niebisch 2012). It also functions as an innuendo (Evens 2005), an indication to what is implicit, silenced or not yet envoiced:

> I am very interested in noise ... Even when a small blade of grass is growing,
> there is a noise between the grass and the earth ... A *souffle* [breath] ... a low-
> volume noise ... talk about, shall we say, a cup of coffee ... A signal between the
> transmitter and the receiver goes through a channel and noise is added ...
> A matter of signals. Conversation between intimates: a leakage between
> channels.
> (Godard in Sterritt 1998, 73)

Nowhere is this idea of noise as 'intimate leakage' or 'innuendo' more prevalent than in *Film socialisme* and *Adieu au langage*. However, although the two films share a visceral, confrontational approach to sound design that pushes cinematic sound to its boundaries, their creative exploration of noise begins from different entry points. In the former, the idea of noise as an inbuilt feature of the digital medium is explored to maximal effect, both through the use of handheld DV (digital video) cameras to shoot large portions of the film, and in the extremely distorted, peaked signal, low-end field recordings, dominated by wind sounds in the first chapter. From the very onset, the depiction of an idyllic cruise in the Mediterranean is thus turned into a long-drawn sonic and visual assault, an exercise in saturation, distortion, decay and disintegration, effected through the inbuilt limita-tions of a constantly failing technology.

In *Adieu au langage*, noise is further underlined through constant interruptions to the soundflow, and almost censorial mutings of signifying sounds, followed by loud, dislocated bursts. Perhaps in line with the film's emphasis on metaphor, a recurring chapter title along with the usual deconstructive wordplays (ADIEU – AH DIEUX – AU LANGAGE – AH LANGAGE, etc.), noise in *Adieu* also entails a more overt transposi-tion of ambient sound contexts across spaces and semantic categories. Domestic interiors are loud, full of high-attack, aggressively amplified sounding objects. Exteriors are less resonant, more lo-fi and constantly mediated, subjected to extradiegetic 'cut-ups', musical or not. Entire audi-tory environments seem to escape their diegetic associations and the temporal flow they would be expected to serve, and are 'dislocated' or interchanged between interior and exterior locations, Europe and Africa, past and present, men and women, animal and human agency, relativizing binaries and forging mischievous 'links between things that have never been linked before and do not seem disposed to be so' (*Histoire(s)* 4B, 1998).

Epilogue: 'I Did Not Say "Look"; I Said "Listen"'

'Allow yourself a margin of indefiniteness', Godard is heard saying, see-mingly to himself, in the first few moments of *Histoire(s)* 1A. The lines

inevitably bring to mind Cage's notion of indeterminacy, and of experimentation as 'an act the outcome of which is unknown' (1961, 13). This
experimental side to Godard's otherwise highly controlled, concentrated
practice leads him to turn a blind eye towards fundamental formal rules
and conventions and 'consider what "good craftsmanship" traditionally
excludes' (Bordwell 2014). In his late cinema he keeps in line with both the
experimental and the improvisatory aspect of early *concrète* aesthetics by
essentially playing with sound, much more than composing it, or composing with it. Consequently, although some authors (Sterritt 1999, 110;
A. Williams 1982) have attempted to compare Godard's use of sound
with serial composition, the analogy is significantly misplaced. It may
apply to a general 'feel' of serialism (pointillistic, with an emphasis on
isolated, disjunct utterances across many different timbres and registers
and separated by long silences), but certainly not to the technical and
aesthetic implications of setting up a system for the strict manipulation of
note rows, or with the political repercussions of meticulously serializing all
given parameters of a soundwork.

A more flexible analogy could be drawn with Robert Wilson's notion of
theatrical sounds as a kind of 'weather' (Sterritt 1999, 238), where the focus
is on nuance and flow between sonic events, rather than on self-contained
meaning in each sound *per se*. In that respect, Tim Ingold's plea for
a vocabulary that will rely on meteorology for the description of auditory
space is perhaps a more useful framework for exploring Godard's sound
aesthetics:

> We do not touch the wind, but touch in it; we do not hear rain, but hear in it.
> Thus wind, sunshine and rain, experienced as feeling, light and sound,
> underwrite our capacities, respectively, to touch, to see and to hear. In order to
> understand the phenomenon of sound (as indeed those of light and feeling), we
> should therefore turn our attention skywards, to the realm of the birds, rather
> than towards the solid earth beneath our feet.   (Ingold 2007, 12)

For Godard, the very role of cinema since its earliest days has been 'to
rescue all these voices from their silent obscurity and to project them on
the white sky of the only museum where the real and the imaginary meet at
last' (Narboni and Milne 1972, 236). With his implicit reference to
Malraux's notion of an imaginary museum, the director clearly presup-
poses a cinematic experience that is immersive and dynamic, but also
bordering on the metaphysical. Godard's cinema may be employing all
the raw, playful techniques associated with amateur consumer electronics,
but at heart remains a single-authored project, with one man assuming
total control over as many parameters of the final outcome as possible; in
so doing, his practice exposes the uneasy aspect of auteurism inherent even

in historical *concrète* practices. This is perhaps where Godard has failed to keep up with the times. Besides, 'there are now so many cameras in the world that if the notion of the Director is to retain any artistic merit, it requires going beyond retaining control over what is filmed' (Gittins 2012).

Cinema is for Godard the last representative of high art (J. S. Williams 2000, 113); its status is akin to the sublime. In short, it can therefore never be entirely comprehended in an intelligible manner, but only experienced partially and fleetingly through the senses, with fragments of meaning only glimpsed at or, more aptly, overheard. And yet we cannot stop trying to make sense; not even at a time when all language has become so deeply industrialized and so widely consumed that it has been rendered 'provisional'; when 'the coming together ... of words and thoughts' has become 'a transient coupling, waiting to be undone' (Goldsmith 2011, 220). 'I don't know what precisely Godard is saying with "Goodbye to Language"', writes a recent critic, 'but I'm eager to continue listening' (Fragoso 2015). Perhaps, for all of the limitations in Godard's approach, this is ultimately one of his greatest cumulative achievements: encouraging an audience to bypass a century of image-dominated, logocentric cinema in order to listen, and keep listening – even if 'maybe nothing has been said' (*Éloge de l'amour* 2001).

19 Hans Werner Henze and *The Lost Honour of Katharina Blum*

ANNETTE DAVISON

After the Second World War, a number of European filmmakers looked to modernism as a means of asserting their difference from mainstream filmmaking. Some, such as Jean-Luc Godard, took a modernist approach to the organization of a film's component elements, including sonic and musical material. Others, for example Godard's compatriot, Alain Resnais, strove to use modernist musical materials by European art-music composers – including Hans Werner Henze – to enable them to create soundtracks that might retain a degree of independence from the other components of the film (see R. S. Brown 1994, 186). This chapter offers an exploration of these issues through the case-study of a score by Henze for a film of the New German Cinema: Volker Schlöndorff's and Margarethe von Trotta's *The Lost Honour of Katharina Blum* (*Die verlorene Ehre der Katharina Blum*; 1975), an adaptation of Heinrich Böll's novel *The Lost Honour of Katharina Blum, or: How Violence Develops and Where It Can Lead* (1975 [1974]).

Modernist Films – Modernist Scores

Modernism is, of course, notoriously difficult to define, though there have been attempts to identify the aesthetic core of an 'ideal' example of a modernist art work, given the canonization of particular works as archetypally modernist. For Andreas Huyssen, the following are prominent within this core: intense experimentalism, an 'adversarial' stance towards mass culture and a 'rejection of all classical systems of representation' (1986, 197). As a key form of mass communication, cinema is dependent upon industrial production practices and modern developments in technology. Thus, although in general terms it is a clear exemplar of social modernity, examples of modernist cinema are more narrowly defined: usually in terms of the negation or disruption of 'classical' cinema and its association with notions of stability or continuity. As a result, the various cinemas which are believed to offer an alternative to the classical, such as postwar European art cinema, have often been categorized as modernist. Such generalizations are not always

[308]

helpful, however: on the one hand, the notion of the 'classical' is itself open to a range of interpretations; on the other, only a fraction of European cinema is modernist in this manner.

Geoffrey Nowell-Smith offers a useful distinction between the various European cinema movements: where 'national cinemas' in postwar Europe worked to assert themselves in relation to competition from elsewhere (in many cases, American cinema), 'new cinema' movements, such as the French New Wave and New German Cinema, 'attempted to assert their place in relation to the national mainstream' (1998, 7). After the war, mainstream filmmaking in France and Germany tended to focus on high production-value literary adaptations and escapist fantasies respectively, and in general avoided confrontational considerations arising from the conflict. Younger filmmakers were thus drawn together through a shared rebellion against an older generation who, in the main, refused to deal with the war in their films.

By the beginning of the 1960s in West Germany, a new generation had begun to search for fresh images and sounds. A number of these directors, such as Jean-Marie Straub and Danièle Huillet (both born in France but deeply influenced by German thinking), took a radically modernist approach to filmmaking (Turim 1984, 335–58; Roud 1971; Walsh 1974). In their films, convention is undermined through direct confrontation and by encouraging active audience engagement by making intellectually demanding works, such as *History Lessons* (1972). Such films were highly influential in terms of interest from younger filmmakers but they failed to gain a large audience in Germany. Other filmmakers of this generation, including Schlöndorff, were more interested in re-establishing trust between the German public and the image, which they felt had been betrayed by Nazi propaganda films. They hoped to coax this audience back into cinemas to see films made in Germany, about Germany. In focusing on accessibility and reopening a dialogue with the public, this group of filmmakers were less concerned with producing films with a radically modernist aesthetic, particularly in terms of the narrative or visuals, though a number of these filmmakers sought scores and sound-tracks that might engage in criticism of, rather than conform to, classical conventions.

In *Composing for the Films* (2007 [1947]), Theodor Adorno and Hanns Eisler explored the possibility of creating modernist film music in theoretical terms. The first part of their book offers a critique of classical Hollywood cinema and its scoring practice, in order to challenge the passive and uncritical engagement between the viewer and the film text they believed it encouraged, through what Adorno and Eisler saw as the debasement of music's potential. This is followed by prescriptions for film scoring which are concerned with the placement of music within the film, the aim of pulling the viewer out of an easy engagement with the film, and the replacement of the outmoded language of diatonic harmony used frequently in film music of the period. Through the use of the new musical materials developed from the dissolution of tonality, a more 'dynamic' and less conventional sound would be possible: 'new musical resources', which do not require harmonic resolution nor organization into symmetrical phrases, since such resources do not require the same kinds of extension as tonal music and are also capable of more concentrated forms of expression (Adorno and Eisler 2007 [1947], 3–4, 21–9).

Adorno and Eisler asked that music and picture 'correspond', 'however indirectly or even antithetically', but also required that music should not confirm or duplicate the screen action in any way, thus avoiding redundancy (*ibid.*, 47). Montage was considered to offer potential, as Sergei Eisenstein had also suggested a few years earlier, since it would allow the various media to maintain independence from one another, yet also be taken in combination as a whole which would add up to more than the sum of its parts (Eisenstein 1942 and 1949; Eisenstein *et al.* 1928). For Adorno and Eisler, the relationship between music and image must demonstrate the divergence of the filmic media in material form, and should therefore be organized according to models of 'question and answer, affirmation and negation, appearance and essence' rather than parallelism or similarity (2007 [1947], 47). Music should avoid 'sneaking in' under dialogue and sound effects; instead it should suddenly appear, disappear and/or be used to 'outshout' the image. In this way the heterogeneity of music and image would be highlighted, and the apparent unity of the sound and image components in mainstream films would be exposed as constructed and, thus, artificial.

Some commentators have noted that Adorno's and Eisler's prescriptions for the exposure of the 'divergence of the media' in cinema are 'eerily prophetic' of the formal organization found in the films and soundtracks of Godard, for example (Gorbman 1991, 281; R. S. Brown 1994, 175–234; Davison 2004, 75–116). Broadly speaking, however, relatively few films organize musical and sonic materials in such a modernist manner. By contrast, dissonant or atonal musical material is a common feature of scores composed (or compiled) for certain film genres (such as film noir, horror, science fiction), as well as films that explore 'madness', paranoia or mental illness. Tonal music is commonly also a feature of such scores, providing contrast or relief; for example, to indicate moments of safety in dangerous situations, or sanity in the context of madness. This is not the case in *Katharina Blum*. Although Henze's atonal orchestral underscore is supplemented by popular music, the latter primarily forms part of the background against which the action takes place, though certainly its apparent joviality begins to take on sinister overtones as the film develops. Rather, it is a contrast within Henze's atonal score that presents the aim of Böll's novel directly and makes explicit the reason for Katharina's violent act. As the following analysis demonstrates, however, the character of the score and its organization are more complex than what might otherwise have been a rather familiar binary coding.

Protest, Terrorism and West Germany in the 1970s

Böll's novel is rooted firmly in the political unrest of the Federal Republic of Germany (FRG) in the early 1970s. Following student uprisings and demonstrations against the Vietnam War in the late 1960s, the FRG authorities became increasingly worried by a rise in anti-authoritarian behaviour among young people, students and, in particular, terrorists, notably the Baader–Meinhof group (as it was labelled by the press), later to become the Rote Armee Fraktion (RAF). In the FRG, Vietnam was not the only issue they protested, as Sarah Colvin explains: 'Their parents' generation had failed to demonstrate the political conscience necessary to nip Nazi empire-building in the bud, and the new generation was driven by a powerful need to act, and be seen to act, differently' (2009, 9). When a student protester was shot and killed by a policeman during a demonstration against the Shah of Iran during his visit to Berlin in 1967, and a student leader was shot by a right-wing activist the following year, some protesters began to question the effectiveness of nonviolent action. A discussion of violence as a legitimate response to state intervention began. In a collectively authored article, 'Gewalt', published in *Konkret*, violence was discussed as 'an instrument we shall neither categorically reject nor use arbitrarily, one whose effectiveness and revolutionary legitimacy we need to learn to understand in a process of theoretical reflection and practical use' (cited in *ibid.*, 37). Members of the Rote Armee Fraktion believed capitalism to be an inherently violent system, and that the establishment had to be provoked into revealing its true self. Counter-violence was seen as the only means to enable this provocation. A series of arson attacks targeted department stores and buildings belonging to the right-wing press, owned by Axel Springer, in response to sensationalist reporting about the threat of protests and demonstrations.

The state reacted harshly to the escalation. Böll, among others, criticized the response as heavy-handed, suggesting that democracy was being defended by anti-democratic practices (van der Will 1994, 223). In January 1972, he wrote an article for the liberal weekly *Der Spiegel* in which he attacked the Springer-owned newspaper *Bild-Zeitung* for its unbalanced and irresponsible reportage of the Baader–Meinhof terrorists, which he called 'naked fascism: incitement, lies, garbage' (Böll 1972; Harris 1994). There was no evidence to link the group to the crimes of which they were accused by the *Bild-Zeitung*. Böll urged a more responsible discussion of the problems terrorism caused and a means of ending the cycle of violence: he believed that opening lines of communication with the terrorists would help to avoid further intensi-fication of the crisis, and that they deserved a fair trial, which the Springer press was making impossible. Instead, the crackdown intensi-fied and terrorist activity increased. The state brought out a decree 'against extremists in civil and public services': 'Der Radikalernerlaß' ('Radicals Decree'; see van der Will 1994, 220). Intellectuals were accused of sympathizing with the left and harbouring terrorists. The universities, in particular, were seen as a threat to the status quo. Böll was persecuted by the media for his views, particularly by the *Bild-Zeitung*, which accused him of supporting terrorism. His telephone was tapped by the authorities and his son's flat searched (Harris 1994, 199). Böll stated that his novel was motivated by the case of Professor Peter Brückner and his alleged connection with Baader–Meinhof, rather than his own defamation by the Springer press: '[Brückner] gave them a place to stay, something entirely natural, and was destroyed psychologically because of it ... That is the starting point of the problem: not the [Baader–Meinhof] group itself, but people who are treated as lepers' (Böll cited in Conard 1992, 118). *The Lost Honour of Katharina Blum* was Böll's response: an exploration of what would happen if such irresponsible journalistic practices were inflicted upon an unknown innocent person.

Heinrich Böll's *The Lost Honour of Katharina Blum*

The novel begins with a clinical description of Katharina's murder of the tabloid journalist, Werner Tötges, the motivation for which is then revealed through evidence and documentation collected by the novel's narrator concerning the days prior to the shooting. Four days before, Katharina spent the night with a man she had met for the first time that evening: Ludwig Götten. He is described as an army deserter, a bank robber and a suspected terrorist. Although Götten is under round-the-clock surveillance, he escapes from Blum's apartment block. The police suspect Katharina of aiding his escape. Armed police search Katharina's apartment. She is taken to the police station for questioning. Tötges sensationalizes elements of Katharina's life in his report on the allegations, such as a neighbour's mention of a regular 'gentleman visitor'. It is later suggested that Tötges's immoral and insensitive actions led to the death of Katharina's mother, whom the journalist tricked his way into hospital to see, though she was critically ill and recuperating from a serious operation.

The novel begins with the following 'disclaimer':

> The characters and action in this story are purely fictitious. Should the description of certain journalistic practices result in a resemblance to the practices of the *Bild-Zeitung*, such resemblance is neither intentional nor fortuitous, but unavoidable.   (Böll 1994 [1975], preface; US edition)

The statement was not included in the first London publication of the novel's English-language translation due to fears of libel on the part of the British publisher (Harris 1994, 198). The book targets the excessive and destructive practices of licentious tabloid journalism. As indicated by the novel's subtitle – *How Violence Develops and Where It Can Lead* – Böll argues that forms of non-physical violence lead ultimately to physical retribution, in part the result of the media's 'corruption and co-optation of language' and its erosion of language as a means to express reality (Rectanus 1986; Zipes 1977, 78–9). After interrogation by the police, Katharina becomes the focus of a smear campaign by the *News* (the neutral translation for *Bild-Zeitung*), which results in abuse and obscene proposals from the public. With no means available to her to restore her honour, Katharina murders the *News* journalist.

By contrast to Tötges's 'fast and loose' relationship with the truth, the novel's narrator is obsessed with objectivity, presenting the 'brutal facts' without sensation. The narrator draws upon different types of documentation – formal reports of surveillance and interrogation, tabloid journalism, conversations – foregrounding a focus on language through the variety of modes of articulation presented. As Richard Kilborn points out, although precise information is given throughout with regard to sources, the narrator's relationship to his/her object of study is inconsistent, shifting from the view of the establishment to considering Katharina with sympathy and compassion (1984, 15). Böll thus encourages the reader to view the apparent objectivity of the narrator's approach with scepticism. Similarly, the narrator's 'objective' reporting incorporates a tangential exploration of aesthetics (for example, what the red blood of the victim looked like on his white carnival outfit). Kilborn suggests the narrator be understood not so much as a mouthpiece for the author, but rather as a representative of that society which is the subject of the author's probing and satirical attack.

The narrator's obsession with factual detail and almost idolatrous attitude to any form of official documentation implies a disturbing complicity with the system and ideology of a state about which Böll clearly has major reservations.

(Kilborn 1984, 17–18)

Katharina is depicted as hardworking and is well loved by those close to her. She is shown to be honest, and is obsessed with the accuracy of the transcription of her interrogation statement. By contrast, the head of the police investigation, Bezzmeine, and the journalist Tötges are depicted as straightforwardly 'bad', as are Lüding (owner of the *News*) and Sträubleder (the 'gentleman visitor'). As the novel develops, a network of collusion and influence between the police, the press and the law is revealed.

Katharina Blum and New German Cinema

As part of Schlöndorff's initiative to present his audiences with work that was more accessible than radical modernism would permit, the films he directed in the 1970s were about Germany, were set in Germany, used German actors and were often adaptations of German literary texts. What differentiated his work within New German Cinema was a willingness to use storytelling and techniques of filmmaking that were representative of the conventions of classical Hollywood or French commercial cinema, while others structured their filmmaking in a more complicated, even oppositional relation to these conventions.

Katharina Blum was the first film on which von Trotta received a directorial credit. Although she had worked ostensibly as an actress over the previous decade, she had also been developing a career as a screenwriter and film director alongside Schlöndorff, her then husband. The couple had already optioned Böll's previous novel, *Gruppenbild mit Dame* (*Group Portrait with Lady*, 1971), though the project did not come to fruition. When Böll began writing *Katharina Blum*, he told them he was writing something that he thought would be of interest given their political views, and that adapting it for the cinema would enable him to convey his ideas to a wider public (Schlöndorff in Habich 2008). Schlöndorff and von Trotta were sent galley proofs of *Katharina Blum* two months before it was published, and they co-wrote an initial screenplay that was then developed in collaboration with Böll. The novelist contributed additional dialogue (for example, to the scene where Katharina shoots the journalist), helped to devise new scenes that weren't in the book, and wrote the satirical epilogue heard at Tötges's burial. He also stipulated the age ranges of the characters for the screen: they had to be young enough to have avoided involvement with the Third Reich (Kilborn 1984, 10). Otherwise, the directors were left to 'get on with it' (Schlöndorff in Habich 2008).

While the form and style of Böll's novel are intricately interwoven with the political position it expresses, the film adaptation is less subtle: the complex chronology of the novel is presented in a more or less straightforward linear form, for example. Tension is intensified gradually and the film culminates with the murder of the journalist. *Katharina Blum* becomes a thriller. Although adapting a novel for the screen inevitably involves making explicit certain features of the story that may be impressionistic or indefinite in written form, Schlöndorff's approach to filmmaking also contributed to the film's directness (Elsaesser 1989, 123). The novel's narrator is consumed by the task of establishing the (apparently) objective facts, whereas the film depicts a series of clandestine procedures directly (such as the alleged tapping of phones) and makes explicit the illegal passing of information between press and police and vice versa. Although some critics complain that the novel's complexity is diminished in the film (see, for example, Zipes 1977, 80–4), others draw attention to the success of the film's medium-specific alternatives to the novel's literary style and organization. Hans-Bernhard Moeller and George Lellis suggest that the film's self-reflexivity enables the viewer to avoid simple identification with Katharina, or to become totally absorbed by thriller conventions, for example. This is achieved by emphasizing the power of the gaze (placing the spectator into a position of collusion with the wider public depicted in the film) and the 'disparity between the real Katharina Blum and mediated images of her' (Moeller and Lellis 2002, 139). Taken together, these strategies 'doubly [implicate] the voyeuristic spectator in the police-justice-press complex' (*ibid.*, 140).

The regular interjections of filmed surveillance, black-and-white photographs, close-ups of headlines and images from newspapers may be understood as equivalent to the narrator's intrusions detailing the different types of sources in the novel. Although historically black-and-white photography and filming have been understood to embody authenticity and truth as documentary evidence, here the distinction between 'truthful' and mediatized images is questioned. In the following analysis I turn from the film's visual strategy to its musical one and suggest that Henze's score is just as important to interpretations of the film.

Hans Werner Henze and *Katharina Blum*

A political composer with a socialist inclination, Henze was a logical choice to score *Katharina Blum*. He had composed several film scores since the mid-1960s, including two for films directed by Resnais and three directed by Schlöndorff, notably the latter's first solo feature, *Young Törless* (1966). Although Henze's music sounds modernist – particularly by comparison with much other film music – it is eclectic in style, leading analysts to describe his work as postmodern (for example, Whittall 1999, 314). Henze explored 12-note composition after attending the first of the Darmstadt Summer Schools, but rejected serialism and began to take a more pluralistic approach to musical materials. His works often combine reworkings of traditional formal frameworks, such as the sonata, with a flexible approach to harmony, drawing on both tonal and dodecaphonic musical worlds and also the lyricism of German lieder and Italian opera. (He moved to Italy in the 1950s.) Written just prior to his score for *Katharina Blum*, the song-cycle *Voices* (1973), in which he set texts by Ho Chi Minh, Hans Magnus Ensenzburger, Bertholt Brecht and others, presents the range of his eclecticism.

The filmmakers were keen to involve Henze early in the production process. Upon reading the script, the composer told Schlöndorff that the film was missing a scene: a second meeting between Katharina and Ludwig at the end. Henze's reasoning was driven by the notion of musical return and by his desire to 'compose an entire piece that can be considered a concert suite afterward', as with the score for *Young Törless* (Schlöndorff in Habich 2008). The scene was added. Schlöndorff indicated where music cues should be placed in the film but did not discuss the character and function of the music with the composer (Henze 2002). As is common, the score was composed at the end of the filmmaking process. It can be heard in approximately 25 of the film's 105 minutes (timings taken from StudioCanal Collection BluRay Disc LUK0909), and is scored for chamber orchestra with single brass and wind and an extensive percussion section: vibraphone, bongos, log drums, loo-jon, cymbals, tamtams, lotosflute, boo-bam, flexatone, Trinidad steel drum and watergong. A pianist doubles on celeste, and there is also a part for electric guitar. Henze later created a concert suite of seven movements – *Katharina Blum: Konzertsuite für kleines Orchester* (1975) – which contains the 'essence' of the film (Henze 1996, 254). Several cues from the film score appear more or less intact in the concert suite, including the first three movements: 'the poisoned river', 'the lovers' and 'lament'. The fourth and sixth movements – 'memories' and 'fear', respectively – are almost entirely comprised

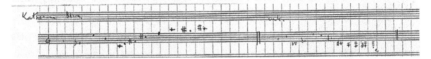

Figure 19.1 *The Lost Honour of Katharina Blum*: the original tone-row ('A') and its inversion, in Hans Werner Henze's manuscript sketch. Reprinted with the kind permission of Hans Werner Henze and the Paul Sacher Foundation.

of material from the film's cues (with the exception of the final 16-bar section of movement 4, and 8 bars in movement 6).

Sketch materials for the film score reveal the influence of 12-note compositional techniques: a note row is presented, along with its inversion in materials labelled 'Katharina Blum: Sketches and pages discarded from the original film score for Schlöndorff' (Igor Stravinsky Collection, Paul Sacher Foundation, Basel; see Figure 19.1). Eleven transpositions of the row and its inversion are also provided on a single sheet of a paper: each begins a semitone lower than the one above, and is related to the original row (or its inversion, respectively) by virtue of the following series of interval-classes: < 4 1 5 1 2 4 5 4 4 1 2 >. Thus, in the case of each of the 'transpositions', the second note is four semitones higher or lower than the first, followed by a semitone higher or lower than that one, and so on, culminating in the presentation of each of the twelve chromatic pitches once. Henze thus uses the notion of the row quite flexibly to generate musical materials: rather than strict transposition (or inversion), which would involve moving the entire ordered series up or down by a fixed interval, this more flexible form of transposition allows individual intervals to be inverted rather than transposed strictly, and the same is true of the row inversions.

Henze envisioned three primary musical themes in his score: the 'poisoned river', the Rhine, which Ludwig crosses at the start of the film; a lyrical theme for the lovers, Katharina and Ludwig; and a theme for the 'violence, the violence of the architecture, the tower block [Katharina] lives in, the violence of the press that attacks her, the violence of the police force who blow in her front door' (Schlöndorff in Habich 2008). The first of the cue categories forms the film's main-title music and references *Das Rheingold*. As Henze explained, 'At the beginning, when Götten crosses over the river, I see *The Rhinegold*, Wagner. I won't compose that, I'll let it be heard, because to me that's the poisoned river. This isn't the Nibelungs anymore. Instead it's the poisoned climate of our republic' (Schlöndorff paraphrasing Henze in Habich 2008).

The prelude to *Das Rheingold* takes the form of an extended elaboration of an E♭ major triad, driven upwards from the riverbed to the wave formations of sextuplet semiquavers at its surface. Henze's atonal cue also rises in pitch from a low-register opening, and also features interpolated bars of arpeggiated sextuplet semiquaver figures on an E♭ triad in wave formations, first on alto flute and bass clarinet, then flute and clarinet. After the second of these *Rheingold* references, the cue culminates in a chaotic and partially improvised sequence: wind, brass and string players select the duration of their specified pitches (within an overall time limit), and marbles are thrown onto the upper strings of the piano, which are then brushed (to produce glissandi) and plucked.

As the cue is heard, the title and credits are superimposed in striking red and blue type over filmed action on a ferry crossing the Rhine, during which Ludwig is introduced as the object of surveillance. A passenger appears to film the scenery with a domestic video camera, though interpolated shots of the footage in black and white reveal Ludwig to be the focus. These alternate with shots filmed in colour from a more omniscient point of view. Sound effects are also heard during the course of the sequence, from the lapping of the water against the boat, to the ferry's engine and the video camera's whirr; the latter emphasizes the theme of surveillance. The sequence ends with Ludwig's escape: an image from the surveillance footage frozen as he speeds off in the car he steals, his face caught in the cross-hairs of the camera's viewfinder. Themes of surveillance and the presentation of individuals through mediated images are thus foregrounded from the outset.

Note-row materials feature briefly in one part of the cue: the inversions of AT2 (oboe, horn) and AT9 (clarinet) are heard in full in retrograde, as well as a fragment of the inversion of AT4, also in retrograde (bassoon, flute). (The label 'AT2' describes Henze's (flexible) transposition of row A, which begins at a pitch class two semitones lower, four lower in the case of AT4, and so on.) The row-derived materials stand out as they form the only extended melodic figures in the cue, and are heard as Ludwig moves closer to the video camera, culminating in the first close-up of his face.

The musical material associated with violence – and thus with the police, the tabloid press and the effects of their actions – is often loud, brash and involves brass and auxiliary percussion. It is fragmented in melodic terms, features clipped articulation and is atonal and often microtonal. Several cues within this grouping involve the intensification of a sustained dissonant chord or cluster, sometimes comprising eleven or twelve pitch-classes. This group of cues does not reference the note-row materials, which are reserved for melodic figures in cues associated with Ludwig (as above) and Katharina's relationship with Ludwig, which for Henze embodies '[e]verything of musical tenderness in the score' (1996, 254).

It is presumably no coincidence that the score's most concentrated manifestation of note-row materials occurs as we watch 'the lovers' enter Katharina's apartment building to spend the night together. This, the score's second cue, comprises a complete presentation of AT5 on alto flute, a repetition of pitches 11, 12 and 1 of that row, followed by an almost exact repetition of the opening melody; then, on viola, Henze's inversions of rows AT10 and AT11 are heard in full, again with some pitches repeated, as well as extended fragments of the retrograde of AT10 in order (0:08:59–0:10:06). Presentations of the row material are characterized by relatively large leaps between pitches. A regular pulse is avoided by the recurrent alternation between 3/8 and 4/8 time signatures and note durations that extend across barlines. These ungainly qualities work to balance the quiet, lyrical, legato character of these row-derived materials, here marked *dolce*. The repetition of the rows (in part or whole), in combination with the repetition of specific pitches mid-row, often a semitone or tone apart, assists in generating a sense of familiarity in these materials. Indeed, the same rows (and Henze's inversions of them) – AT5, AT10 and AT11 – are the most frequently heard across the score as a whole.

The police then assemble in riot gear, search Katharina's apartment and take her to the police station for interrogation. Cues to accompany violence are heard here for the first time, and they become more prevalent through the film. From this point the presentation of the note-row materials in cues associated with Katharina and Ludwig becomes increasingly fragmented: the row broken up, performed only in part or with parts of it performed by different instruments. The original row (A) is heard just once, as Katharina eats breakfast alone, oblivious to the huge numbers of police amassing outside her apartment. The row is distributed between bassoon (pitches 1–4, 9–12, 1) and electric guitar (pitches 5–8) (0:11:42–0:11:53). As Katharina is told to dress (though effectively she is strip-searched), AT5 is heard, distributed between cor anglais, trumpet and horn, and followed by fragments of AT4 on viola (0:14:02–0:14:56).

When Katharina sits alone in a police cell, a fragmented form of AT3 is heard, distributed between bassoon and flute, at the discovery of confetti in a handkerchief, which triggers a flashback to meeting Ludwig at the party (0:23:27–0:25:23). A melancholic melody is heard on solo violin: most of row AT11, followed by Henze's inversion of it, though in a more disrupted form. (These cues also appear in the Concert Suite, as bars 1–11 then 11–25 of movement 3, 'lament'.) The same melody is heard in a later cue on viola where it accompanies a second flashback, this time triggered when Katharina catches sight of a flower she wore the night she met Ludwig. Here, though, the memory is tainted: the flower lies among items on a bathroom shelf covered with fingerprint powder. The violin melody is transposed, though not uniformly, resulting in a slightly off-kilter version of its lament.

The last complete presentation of a row occurs when Ludwig is seen alone at night in a hiding place to which Katharina gave him access. He tells her on the telephone that he likes her 'very very much', but the call reveals his whereabouts to the authorities. The inversion of row AT10 is heard distributed between cor anglais, flute and then trumpet, followed by extracts and repetitions of its retrograde on trumpet and alto flute, completed by a final presentation of Henze's inversion of AT11 which moves between violin, flute, then trumpet (1:12:57–1:13:26). (The cue is heard in the Concert Suite as bars 18–26 of movement 4, 'memories'.)

As the police interrogation continues, the press begin their onslaught, and Katharina is subjected to gradually more insults and obscene propositions from members of the public. Violence cues are heard more frequently. One brief cue, which begins with the semitonal clashing of a flutter-tongued trombone played *sfff*, with double-bass marked *sfff*, then *pp* to *fffff*, followed by a gong beaten quietly with knuckles once per second, is repeated four times over a twenty-minute period, sometimes in an extended form. At this point it becomes apparent to Katharina that the police, the press, the church and the business community are supporting one another in their assault upon her. In a cue presented later, as Katharina reads a headline proclaiming 'Götten Caught, Mother Dead', scalic semiquaver sextuplets on flute and then viola, cycling up and down from the pitch D repeatedly, reference the semiquaver sextuplets of *Rheingold* in the main-title sequence. Henze's allusion to the Rhine in Wagner's *Ring* cycle – home to the gold that will ultimately cause the downfall of the Gods – is subtle: it implies that the media and other establishment institutions in the Republic function as toxic pollutants.

Through their association with particular narrative elements – police/press versus Katharina/Ludwig – musical oppositions structure the film's score between percussive violence and intricate row manipulations. These categories become blurred, however, when Katharina's suffering begins to crystallize into a plan for violent retribution. Ironically, by this point the police are no longer interested in her possible involvement. As we see Katharina prepare for the meeting she has organized with Tötges, she becomes detached from the note-row materials, and is aligned instead with compound cues previously associated with the police and the tabloid press. These can be found among the 'discarded pages' of materials held by the Paul Sacher Foundation, Basel.

A cue from the previous scene, in which Katharina read the *News*' headline, is presented again (1:30:09–1:30:52; 1:31:43–1:32:19), followed by the first three bars of a cue Henze labelled 'die Gewalt'

('Force'), previously heard when the guards first surrounded Katharina's apartment (from 0:10:07; then 1:32:19–1:32:26). The next cue is new (1:32:27–1:32:39), and is presented as Katharina awaits Tötges's arrival. Henze labelled it 'XV Katharina auf dem stuhl' ('Katharina on the chair'). The cue generates stasis. It is organized around high string harmonics, sporadic flutters of pitches on keyboards and guitar, with a more regular rhythmic accompaniment on timpani. As Tötges arrives, the cue segues into its final component (1:32:39–1:32:53), labelled 'Tötges'. This is a variant of the cue that accompanies Katharina's being escorted from her apartment building by the police early in the film (0:16:44–0:16:54). Photographers are on hand to capture the scene as Katharina is manoeuvred awkwardly into a police car due to the presence of a large crowd: interpolated black-and-white images depict her as aggressive. The same cue is repeated as photographers shadow Katharina, Else Woltersheim and Karl Beiters when they return to the police station for questioning. A voice-over reports Katharina's movements (0:54:13–0:54:22). A twelve-note chord builds in amplitude as Tötges enters Katharina's apartment, stopping abruptly as he closes the door.

These last three cues of the cue-compound return to accompany Tötges's funeral, underlining that the film – and its score – place the blame for Katharina's violent act with Tötges and the tabloid press. The bloated funeral oration, written by Böll for the film, emphasizes this via satire:

> The shots that killed Werner Tötges didn't hit him alone. They were aimed at Freedom of the Press, one of the most precious values of our young Democracy. And these shots – for us who stand here in grief and horror – they strike us, just as they struck him.

The impact of this coda is further strengthened by an intertitle that paraphrases the (non)disclaimer from the beginning of the novel: 'Similarities with certain journalistic practices are neither intended nor accidental, but inevitable'. Although the police play a greater role in the film than in the novel, here Böll refocuses attention on the press.

Conclusion

As a result of its complexity, unfamiliarity and unpredictability, Henze's score retains a vestige of apparent objectivity – of a cold, detached filmic component, working in combination with the subdued earth tones of 1970s film stock. It both reflects and mediates the sense of alienation depicted in the film: in terms of the bureaucratic police procedures to which Katharina is subjected; collusion between the police, the press and the church; and the inability of the law to protect Katharina from smears by the tabloid press or from the newspaper readers who judge and condemn her. The gestural qualities of much of the film's music – aggressive, repetitive and obsessive – support this interpretation, though it contrasts with the lyrical approach to the presentation of the note-row music associated with Katharina and Ludwig. Yet these cues also create a sense of distance between the depiction of Katharina and the film's audience, somehow capturing Katharina's outwardly cool, rationalizing character. It prevents the audience from sympathizing with her in an unthinking way, just as the placement and integration of music with image and narrative avoids generating straightforward emotional climaxes; the armoured raid on Katharina's apartment and Katharina's murder of the journalist are left unscored, for example.

This is not to say that Henze's score does not also exhibit practices that might be classified as mainstream: the association of cues with particular narrative elements, and the use of music to assist continuity and develop unity, for example. But the absence of music at dramatic and emotional climaxes, the choice of musical language and compositional techniques used, and the relative obtrusiveness of Henze's score all work against this. Even the potentially sentimental solo violin cue that accompanies Katharina's flashback to the party while she is locked in a prison cell (0:25:00–0:25:23) is prevented from descending into schmaltz through the use of partially dodecaphonic material, for example.

Writing in 1971, Henze explained that he found himself caught in the bind of the politically progressive composer: he wanted to write approach-able music, but did not want it to be appropriated by commercial forces or to be diluted in its effect (1971, 180). In *Katharina Blum*, his aim was that the film's score should 'comment on the action rather than … merely accompany it' (1996, 254). Schlöndorff states that, some time after the film was released, Henze confessed that when he saw the rough cut he thought the film was not working, and that it would be a 'terrible failure'; the composer 'tried to pump up [the] film with the music' in response (Schlöndorff in Habich 2008). Schlöndorff believes this explains the violent use of music in the film, 'which sometimes goes so far that the music becomes independent'.

Certainly the score generates distance, although this is complicated by the gestural lyricism of the note-row material, which supports the film in offering a somewhat more emotional engagement with Katharina than is offered in the novel, and which also enables the change of cue alignment (from lyrical melody to aggressive violence) to be recognized. The use of a note row to generate these cues would almost certainly go unnoticed by the vast majority of viewers, the impact of the cues more likely being the result of narrative placement and other properties of the music, such as gestural qualities, tempi or instrumentation. The reception of the score is complicated further by Henze's inflection of the various properties of these cues with contradictory signals in terms of cultural coding, for example. Its meaning is neither immediately apparent nor straightforward. For Paul Coates, this is because the score 'places shifting sand under the film's seeming certainties', generating an 'aura of art' that diminishes the film's melodramatic power (1994, 73). In the final analysis, Richard Falcon's view of the film is also appropriate to an analysis of its score: 'the questions start once the film is over' (1997, 170).

20 Tōru Takemitsu's Collaborations with Masahiro Shinoda

The Music for *Pale Flower, Samurai Spy* and *Ballad of Orin*

TIMOTHY KOOZIN

Films provided an important cultural component in the reassertion of a Japanese past following the Second World War. Japanese New Wave (*nūberu bāgu*) filmmakers in the 1960s further explored issues of history and cultural identity while confronting the societal consequences of modernization and the Cold War, purposefully deconstructing and questioning the monumental style associated with epic narratives of Japanese feudal culture. The avant-garde filmmakers creating 'aesthetic-political' films in Japan included Masahiro Shinoda, Hiroshi Teshigahara, Shōhei Imamura and Nagisa Oshima, with Tōru Takemitsu often creating music for their films. (For more on avant-garde filmmakers in Japan in the 1960s and their organization through the Art Theatre Guild, see Everett 2010, 38. Eric Cazdyn (2002) places the Japanese New Wave filmmakers within a broader context of cultural history.) An amazingly prolific composer, Takemitsu composed music for more than a hundred films while also establishing his international reputation as a leading composer of modern concert music. (For a comprehensive list of Takemitsu's film scores, see Burt 2001, 277–80.)

Takemitsu once stated that 'Writing music for films is like getting a visa to freedom' (Richie 2002, 7–8). It provided him with opportunities to explore a broad array of musical styles, experiment with new techniques and engage with his own compositional past through borrowings and interrelationships that span his film and concert works. Takemitsu drew from his own concert music as well as non-Western, popular, film noir, jazz, pre-classical, romantic and modernist idioms in his collaborations with filmmakers. Takemitsu's approach to musical sound reflects a humanistic and inclusive aesthetic view that all human sounds and sounds in nature 'should be valued equally' and all musical traditions should be 'treated as cultural treasures for all mankind' (2004, 199–201). Soundtrack composition provided Takemitsu with a medium in which he could directly explore negotiations of difference involving sounds, silences and cultural traditions in the construction of meaning.

This essay focuses on three films Takemitsu created with Shinoda: *Pale Flower* (*Kawaita hana*; 1964), *Samurai Spy* (*Ibun Sarutobi Sasuke*; 1965) and *Ballad of Orin* (*Hanare goze Orin*; 1977). Takemitsu wrote music for sixteen of the thirty-five films Shinoda made. Theirs was a creative relationship that spanned almost all of Takemitsu's career and encompassed multiple film genres. The three films discussed represent genres central to Japanese film that would interest Takemitsu throughout his career: the film noir gangster film, the samurai film and the *jidai-geki* historical period film which places traditional Japanese musical and theatrical idioms in a filmic context. Working closely with the director throughout the filmmaking process and enjoying a level of creative control not often afforded to film composers, Takemitsu was able to shape artistically the entire soundscape in their collaborations.

In an interview with Audie Bock, Shinoda once said, 'If my films had to be perfect reconstructions of reality, I would not make them. I begin with reality and see what higher idea comes out of it' (Richie 2001, 204). Ideally complementing this approach, Takemitsu uses the soundtrack to question the authority of the real. Takemitsu creates an allegorical subtext to parallel the filmic narrative through use of musical topics that expressively explore boundaries of historical and musical temporality. Through electronic manipulation of source sounds, he transforms and elevates experientially 'real' sounds to form a modernist soundscape. As source sounds are defamiliarized to form a *musique concrète* aural canvas, the viewer is provoked to hear sounds of the real world in terms of their musical organization. This chapter explores how Takemitsu's creative shaping of the whole soundtrack serves expressive purposes that align with Shinoda's aesthetic-political aims, revealing inner psychological states, conveying ritualistic affinities to cultural traditions and projecting irony in order to provoke awareness of deeply ingrained aspects of human experience that might otherwise remain suppressed and unseen.

Pale Flower and the Liminality of Film Noir

Shinoda has acknowledged the dark symbolist poems of Baudelaire's *Les Fleurs du mal* (*The Flowers of Evil*, 1857) – decadent and erotic poetry with anti-heroes including gamblers, prostitutes and industrial workers, presenting a powerful critique of nineteenth-century French urban modernity – as a strong influence in his conception of the dystopian crime drama *Pale Flower* (Stephens 2011). Shinoda believed that the criminal culture of the Yakuza gangsters (organized crime groups that originated as early as the seventeenth century, whose modern members still identify with a strict samurai code of conduct) is one place in the contemporary world where a Japanese ceremonial structure is still sustained. The film is visually striking in its use of film noir elements to explore a hidden culture in which 'violence is choreographed in a traditional fashion' (Richie 2001, 205). Perversely, an act of violence, even a masochistic act of self-destruction, can then be understood as an aesthetic response to ceremony. Infused with symbolist sensibility and modernist angst, the film presents this dark and nihilistic hidden world as a reflection of a dominant industrialized culture that is dysfunctional and oppressive.

Shinoda called Takemitsu's soundtrack for *Pale Flower* the first avant-garde score for a Japanese film (Grilli 2011; according to the credits, Yuji Takahashi also composed some of the music). The director has explained how he was asked by Takemitsu to record for him all the sounds of the shooting. Takemitsu then assembled material for the soundtrack, using sounds that the director might have discarded. Table 20.1 shows the organization of sounds in the opening scenes. The protagonist, Muraki, is just out of prison after serving a three-year sentence for a gang-related killing. As he arrives in Tokyo on a train, we hear his dark inner thoughts. His observations on the bleak urban scene around him reveal his ironic predicament. The commuters at the train station have made personal sacrifices for the sake of industrial socialization that Muraki finds pointless, but he has made terrible sacrifices for the sake of hierarchic loyalty to his Yakuza clan, who have compromised him psychologically. As he observes those around him with detachment, Muraki thinks to himself, 'Nothing has changed.' He will repeat this statement several times, like a returning musical motive, in his conversations with others, underscoring his personal isolation and growing realization that his dutiful sacrifice was pointless. Ambient source sounds are alternately silenced, to underscore Muraki's social estrangement, or punctuated and altered electronically, so that the sounds of the 'real' world are made strange and remote. As indicated in Table 20.1, patterns of repetition in sound accompanying the credits delineate a ternary (ABA) musical form in the soundtrack. (Takemitsu also explores the boundaries between source sounds and electronic musical composition in his score for Masaki Kobayashi's film *Kwaidan* (*Kaidan*) from 1964, the same year as *Pale Flower*. See Burt 2001, 45–6.)

Muraki lives in detachment from any moral values or social structure that might enable him to re-enter society. Trapped within an intermediary passage between the everyday world and his dark inner world, he is a 'liminal' character, balanced at a threshold on the margins of society. *Pale Flower* resonates with liminal qualities also found in American film noir, in which, as R. Barton Palmer explains, characters typically 'find themselves straddling the border between competing forms of identity, as they often enter into perilous *rites de passage* through a nightmarish version of contemporary urban reality' (2007, 66). The restless anxiety of Muraki's liminal state is evident in his inability to emerge from a nightmarish

Table 20.1 *Sound organization in the opening sequence of* Pale Flower.

-----------	Out of prison
0:00:32	The train station: Whistle, rhythmic train sounds, voiceover of Muraki
0:00:45	Punctuating noise (turnstile gate?), busy streets. in a commuter train
0:01:40	Whisper: "Somebody died, but nothing has changed."
-----------	The gambling den
0:01:48	Dealer vocalization: "Place your bets."
0:02:34	Muraki to the younger gangster: "I see nothing has changed."
0:03:28	Muraki and Saeko gamble. Faster dealer vocalization
0:05:05	Dealer's ending punctuation: "We have a game."
-----------	Film credits (a)
0:05:06	Small drums, castanets, tap dancing (represents the gambling cards)
0:05:18	Long tones in high winds
0:05:27	Dealer vocalization: "Place your bets."
0:05:33	Dissonant blast with descending slide: brass and saxes
-----------	(b)
0:05:45	Pitch-bend sax chords: (moaning, taunting)
0:06:16	Brass in dissonant counterpoint
0:06:30	Abrupt silence
0:06:32	Very loud dissonant blast with descending slide: brass and saxes
-----------	(a)
0:06:39	Small drums, castanets, tap dancing
0:06:50	Long tones in high winds
0:07:05	Dealer ending punctuation
0:07:17	Tap dancing with clear metrical pattern
-----------	Scene change
0:07:25	A street at night: diegetic music from a bar off-screen

psychological inner world. In appropriating source sounds and transforming them musically, Takemitsu creates a modernist musical soundscape to depict a liminal world hovering between the real and the unreal.

The scene shifts from the external space of the Tokyo train station to the very private interior space of a gambling den, where Muraki will reconnect with his Yakuza associates. The starkly expressionist geometric confinement of the gambling room and the symmetry of seated gamblers parallel the rigid rules and decorum of the card game. The hard, domino-sized cards (*hanafuda*) rattle when shuffled. Takemitsu uses this sound as the basis for a highly abstract *musique concrète* passage, layering electronically altered sound patterns of the *hanafuda* together with percussion sounds. Takemitsu also uses the sounds of tap dancing, which he felt would complement and extend the sounds of the shuffling cards (Grilli 2011).

Example 20.1 Rhythmic patterns in the dealer's vocalization in *Pale Flower*.

Example 20.2 Wind dissonance from *Pale Flower*.

Another principal sound source in the opening is the dealer, who vocalizes a repetitive and musical chant in moderating the game, somewhat like the stylized and ritualistic chant of an auctioneer moderating bids. As shown in Example 20.1, distinct rhythmic patterns in the dealer's vocalization emerge and grow faster in tempo as the game unfolds. The gambling den is a liminal social space in which participants perform according to the rules of a ritualized game while suspending their real identities and masking their inner emotions. Visually acute in the patterned movements of the game and the concealment of cards under participants' clothing, the effect is not unlike the stylized movements and design elements in Kabuki theatre. This expresses the message that even the dark, secretive world of the gambling den has its stylized aesthetic tradition. Takemitsu's collage of source sounds, *musique concrète* and percussion forms an aural commentary on the aesthetic rituals that legitimize the cold and predatory reality of the winner-take-all game.

As the camera focuses on one of the gamblers – the female protagonist of the film, Saeko – the percussive music builds to an intense blast of brass and saxophones, as shown in Example 20.2. The music is coldly dissonant and extreme, with exaggerated pitch bends. Referencing both expressionistic and free jazz idioms, this chaotic music projects the psychological angst that is masked by the formality of the seated players. As the game ends, the dealer provides the punctuation that closes the scene. A clear metrical pattern emerges in the tap-dancing sounds, forming an aural transition to the street scene that follows.

There are scenes throughout the film, striking in their visual and sonic impact, that show Muraki and Saeko to be lost in an existential abyss where the only real pleasure is in the thrill attained through exposure to danger. When the leader of Muraki's Yakuza gang declares that a rival leader must be killed, Muraki volunteers to commit the murder. As a final fatalistic gesture, Muraki brings Saeko to watch the murder act. This is the culmination of their intense, mutually destructive relationship. The music heard as Muraki ascends a staircase to enter the public restaurant where he will kill the rival gang leader is 'Dido's Lament' from Henry Purcell's opera, *Dido and Aeneas* (c. 1684). The borrowing of this tragic music is ironic on multiple levels. Muraki is sacrificing himself by committing the murder in public before an audience. In Purcell's aria, Dido is a virtuous heroine consoling her loyal handmaiden as she prepares to die. There is none of Dido's selfless virtue in Muraki's gesture of violence, which is ritualized as a performed spectacle through the presence of the operatic music. Muraki is, in a sense, emasculated, as he is held in the gaze of others while we hear the soprano aria. The music enhances the aesthetic ritual and tragic tone of Muraki's violent act while, at the same time, it introduces an intrusive authority of Western high-art tradition. This simultaneously presents and critiques Muraki's action as a ceremonial sacrifice, ironically projecting the broader allegory of social dislocation and dysfunctionality at a time of growing industrialization and Western dominance in Japan during the Cold War era. The descending bass line of the lament provides a disorienting counterpoint as Muraki makes the liminal ascent on the stairway to commit the murder. Stabbing the rival boss to death, Muraki stands transfixed, as we hear Purcell's choral music that follows the aria. While Purcell's text entreats the angels to watch over Dido in death, we observe Muraki, aglow with backlighting, presented as a sacrificial martyr engaged in a gesture of annihilating grace. But it is an ironic and empty gesture, without heroic affirmation. The tragic outcome of his life serves no purpose. As he has recurringly stated himself, 'Nothing has changed.' The film as a whole depicts Muraki in a liminal state bounded by his release and subsequent return to prison. Allegorically, his predicament represents the malaise of Japan as a demoralized culture. The chaotic brass and saxophone music returns at the ending, as Muraki crosses the liminal boundary, returning to the dark living death of imprisonment.

Samurai Spy: Confronting the Absurdity of Political Violence through Parody

Shinoda and Takemitsu followed *Pale Flower* with two collaborations that critically engage with the samurai genre, *Assassination* (*Ansatsu*; 1964) and *Samurai Spy*. In contrast to *Assassination*, a serious drama of declining moral and political authority set at a time of civil unrest, *Samurai Spy* combines the spy and samurai genres to form a parodic and darkly comical view of the samurai during peacetime. The director explains, 'Actually, when making *Samurai Spy*, I wanted to show that the samurai swordplay genre was over. I felt that telling political stories was a lot better' (Shinoda 2005). Based on a legendary story of a heroic seventeenth-century warrior, Sasuke Sarutobi, the film comically interjects the present to provide a powerful analogy to the real-life instabilities and intrigues of the Cold War. Shinoda reimagines Sasuke as a deeply conflicted protagonist, a samurai with no appetite for war. Sasuke sends information he gathers on the movements of rival clans to his master, but he doesn't know the purpose in doing so, since there has been no war for fourteen years. To his friend, Mitsuaki, a double agent, Sasuke says, 'You see things in terms of war. Or money . . . Why do you divide men into enemy and friend? That is an idea caused by war. I don't like it. Even if it is an unstable peace, I have lived in peace.'

After the story is set up in the opening minutes of the film, music enters with the on-screen credits in a way that completely disrupts any trace of historical realism. In a clear reference to 1960s-style spy-film music, a bossa-nova bass pattern begins, accompanied with smooth sounding strings (see Example 20.3). Shinoda (2005) stated that Takemitsu's music 'sounded positively Cuban', explaining that the classically trained performers had some difficulty with the Cuban jazz idiom at first. The smooth, dark character of the music and the jazzy bass riff provide the underpinnings for a jazz flute solo, played by Sadao Watanabe, a Japanese saxophonist and flautist known internationally for jazz bossa-nova recordings. The topical markers of Cold War spy-film music used in *Samurai Spy* also resonate with music elements in television shows of the era.

Example 20.3 Bossa-nova cue from *Samurai Spy*.

For example, the upbeat bass riff with smooth strings is reminiscent of the music for the British spy series *The Avengers* (ITV, 1961–69), and the use of low sustained flute to signify mystery and intrigue is foregrounded in music for the original *Mission Impossible* series (CBS, 1966–73). (Kihachi Okamoto's *Kill!* (*Kiru*; 1968) is another film from this period notable for its satirical treatment of the samurai genre, with a score by Masaru Satō that creatively integrates musical elements of the Italian spaghetti western.)

The change in the music from one topical field to another is essential in expressing comic irony that establishes how a historical genre of intrigue and violence is relevant to contemporary times. Low chromatic flute sounds are used as a topical filmic signifier to suggest mystery and clandestine violence, for example, near the beginning (at 0:03:21) when a captured spy's throat is cut. This scene closely parallels a scene near the end (at 1:38:00), a close-up on Sasuke being strangled by the arch-villain in the film. In an ironic reversal of the expected outcome, Sasuke is suddenly aided by an unlikely rescuer, a younger spy, Saizo. Shifting from the tragic to the comic in a sudden twist of fate, the jazzy flute music returns to close the film.

The flute is also used in ceremonial music situated diegetically within the film. Implications in the drama are communicated through musical topicality, associating pentatonic melody with indigenous ceremonial traditions, chromatic tonality with mystery and danger, and jazz modality with transgressive resistance. Takemitsu's beautifully subtle string writing also enhances the dramatic atmosphere. Low pizzicato strings combined with large drums provide rumblings of sound suggestive of a mysterious pre-modern world, while dissonant sustained strings infuse battle scenes with modern subjectivity.

As the hunt for a murderer intensifies, the action shifts to an outdoor ceremony with a procession of dancers and singers. Like a scene in a James Bond spy thriller, the carnival-like ceremonial music masks the actions of the spies, providing an ironic counterpoint to their clandestine operation. Wooden and metal percussion instruments heard previously in nondiegetic music have now entered into the filmic action. The implication is that covert political violence is now erupting into open warfare. Previously abstract sound objects are now grounded in observed reality, suggesting that mysteries in the plot may also soon be revealed.

The festival depicted in the film is based on an actual festival at Suwa Shrine, a major Shinto shrine in Nagasaki. The Nagasaki *kunchi* festival served the purpose of promoting indigenous religion while suppressing conversion to Christianity, which was outlawed by an edict in 1614, the year the Suwa Shrine was established. The persecution of Christian samurai is one of the themes woven into the complex plot of *Samurai Spy*. Situating the historically real festival within the dramatic action of the film, Shinoda prefigures techniques he would further explore three years later in

Double Suicide (*Shinjū Ten no Amijima*; 1969), his critically acclaimed film treatment of an eighteenth-century Bunraku puppet-theatre piece by Chikamatsu Monzaemon (1653–1725) with a score by Takemitsu. *Samurai Spy* has enigmatic masked figures dressed in black who move in and out of the action with unknown purpose and are visually similar to the *kuroko* puppeteers that Shinoda utilizes to explore liminal boundaries between the real and the non-real in *Double Suicide*. (For a study of Takemitsu's score for *Double Suicide*, see Everett 2010.) Shinoda returned to Chikamatsu in *Gonza the Spearman* (*Yari no gonza*; 1986), a version of a 1717 puppet play, also with music by Takemitsu.

When the battle moves out into the countryside in *Samurai Spy*, there is a climactic scene of combat viewed from a great distance. The shot is so widely panoramic that the battling warriors appear as mere specks moving in the landscape. In an example of Takemitsu's highly expressive use of silence, all sounds of combat are erased. (For a discussion of similar distancing effects that occur in other battle scenes, notably in Akira Kurosawa's *Ran* (1985) – also scored by Takemitsu – see Deguchi 2010, 60–3.) This distancing in visual and aural treatment creates a perceptual gap that undermines the viewer's involvement in any dramatic realism. The break in realistic artifice emphasizes detached spectatorship and provokes reflection, forming a commentary on the absurdity of senseless violence in warfare. When it seems that Sasuke will fail in his heroic effort to protect Omiyo, an orphan girl under his care he has now pledged to marry, the younger samurai, Saizo, appears, killing the villain and saving the day. Unexpectedly escaping death, the warrior hero also escapes the established confines of the genre. Sasuke survives his final battle to marry and achieve the peaceful life he has wished for, thereby evading his presumed fate as a samurai for life. The return of the opening music with bossa-nova bass line, jazz flute solo and smooth strings powerfully signals the sudden shift in the narrative trajectory of the film. Through Takemitsu's parodizing deployment of musical styles, *Samurai Spy* attains the narrative structure of a comic romance, in which an unlikely hero privileges higher truths of personal integrity and love, ultimately prevailing over the exposed absurdities of political authority. (Takemitsu similarly uses parody in his music for the 1993 murder mystery, *Rising Sun*, his only score for a Hollywood film; see Koozin 2010, 65–78.)

Ballad of Orin: Shinoda's 'Melody in Grey'

Also called *Banished Orin* and subtitled 'Melody in Grey', *Ballad of Orin* has the quality of a mythic ballad or legendary story. Donald Richie (2001,

206) has observed that Orin is like the long-suffering heroines found in earlier films by Kenji Mizoguchi, with distanced, aesthetically balanced scenes and camera movements that seem to lead the tragic heroine to her eventual destruction. A blind orphan girl who receives training as a singer and shamisen player, Orin lives by a tradition of rural song performance known as *goze*. (The *goze* were organized groups of blind itinerant female musicians that existed from medieval times into the twentieth century: see Knecht 1979, 139–42.) Orin's story personifies the theme of individual freedom and local cultural tradition under the threat of growing militarism in the modern age. Takemitsu's music for the film is crucial in projecting Orin's life as one of personal and artistic expression positioned in resistance to authority. In terms of narrative structure, it presents the transvaluation of the pastoral over the industrial.

The film explores ambiguities and tensions in engaging with tradition, authority and otherness, as Orin gains entry into contained places of power and affluence not as an equal, but in a socially ambiguous role as a performing artist, afforded some protection under the *goze* tradition, but still vulnerable as an unprotected itinerant female. Ironically, Orin presents a threat to society, as an independent woman possessing nurturing connections to place and tradition that others of higher authority lack. The audiences who provide her with food and shelter are often depicted as boorish and disengaged, reflecting a fractured society of impoverished nostalgia that is disconnected from any active engagement with cultural memory.

Scenes in which Orin performs for gatherings of military leaders underscore her repressive status as a *goze*. She sometimes performs songs that comment ironically on her own predicament. While men grope at her and ply her with alcohol in attempts to take advantage of her sexually, she sings sad songs of unfortunate girls who are forced into prostitution. Later, while with her companion, Tsurukawa, she sings, 'how cruel is the fate of the sister and brother', comparing the gossiping talk of others to 'the trills that the bird make'. This is a reference to Orin and Tsurukawa, who travel together platonically as 'sister and brother', since rules of *goze* social conduct forbid them from living as the lovers they would wish to be.

The film portrays a powerful rebuke of militarized industrial modernization by depicting the tragic oppression encountered by women at different stages of life in a dysfunctional society. As shown in Table 20.2, this is projected through recurring music that unifies spacio-temporal shifts in depicting Orin and other women she encounters in the life cycles of childhood, young adulthood, old age and death. This music projects a richly sonorous pastoralism that heightens the visually striking images of Orin's perilous journey through the ravishingly beautiful natural

Table 20.2 Ballad of Orin: *Orin in society and nature.*

Opening music

0:00:16   Sounds of the sea shore, waves, and wind
Voiceover of Orin telling the story of her youth.

0:02:17   Oboe melody (a-b), harp ostinato, strings, bird calls.
Orin, age 6, walking in the snow, led by Saito the druggist to the Goze house. Opening title and credits.a

0:03:22   Double reeds
Spatio-temporal shift to sunny landscape, waves of grasses moving in the wind.

0:03:29   High strings melody (a)
Nesting baby birds, fed by the parent bird. Arrival at the goze house.

0:03:41   Horns (b), strings, female choral voices
Mountain landscape, greenery in the mist.

0:03:51   Strings; music ends
A small hut. Orin, in the present time, 20 years later.

Cyclic recurrences of music

Oboe melody (a-b), harp ostinato, strings, bird calls:

0:02:17   Orin, age 6, walking in the snow, led by Saito the druggist to the Goze house. Opening title and credits.

0:30:15   Orin coming of age, menstrual blood seen in the snow as she walks.

1:10:07   Orin is raped in the woods.

1:29:29   Orin with another goze at a seaside cliff, lamenting the death of an elderly woman and her granddaughter.

1:56:30   Orin has died. Her broken shamisen, her bones, final images of sea and landscape. Ending credits.

Expressive oppositions in the music for *Ballad of Orin*

singing	travelling
voice and shamisen	flute and harp
diegetic, dramatic	non-diegetic, pastoral
localised	unbounded in time and space
performed by Orin and others	depicts Orin
prescribed social and physical space	open, natural space
varied music (stanzas)	recurring music (refrain)
containment	escape from containment

landscape. Caught in an ironic dilemma, Orin must charm the men around her to gain a hand-out as a performing artist while evading those who would compromise her sexually and even persecute her as a criminal. The cycles of social containment and escape in Orin's journey are powerfully represented in images and sound. As she flees the confining dangers of civilization, she retreats into a harsh and inhospitable landscape that is as dangerous as it is beautiful. As summarized in Table 20.2, the binary opposition of two musical types, that which Orin performs while visiting restrictive interior social spaces and that which depicts her as an inhabitant of boundless outdoor spaces, is essential in projecting her struggle. The timing of musical exchanges, between the diegetic music of the social world and nondiegetic music of the natural world, creates a musical discourse that spans the entire film. This can be interpreted as a kind of ballad form, with varied music of social spaces alternating with recurring refrain-like music heard as Orin travels in the wilderness.

There is an ironic musical dialectic between the stylized expression of Orin's performances as a *goze*, in which she creates a theatrical reality, effectively rendering her own personal feelings and hardships invisible, and the depictions of her struggle to survive and maintain her individual selfhood in natural and social environs fraught with danger. Ironically, the artistic profession that provides for her survival is both expressive and repressive. The breathtaking landscapes accompanied with Takemitsu's evocative music also show the dualism of a natural world that is beautiful and dangerous. Wide shots position Orin as small and vulnerable as she travels through the wilderness, not unlike a bird, connecting to the *musique concrète* layerings of bird sounds that add a spatial and animistic aesthetic dimension to the music of her itinerant travels.

The diegetic music of social spaces performed by Orin and by other practitioners of traditional arts interjects a transgressive and aesthetically distanced commentary in the film. When Orin and Tsurukawa visit villages seeking work, they encounter a carnivalesque outdoor world of tradesmen selling their wares, wandering performers and crowds of people from every social status, including soldiers and gangsters. As Orin is taken by the police for questioning about crimes allegedly committed by Tsurukawa (at 1:20:30), a pair of dancing street musicians chant in Brechtian commentary on Western industrialization, blindness and cycles of human suffering:

> Oh, it's confusing, it's confusing, this present world is confusing.
> They say Westernization is under way, but you can't judge only by what you see.
> Gas and electricity are amazing, steam engines are wonderful,
> But are they just flash and show, like gilding or puffed tempura?
> People keep complaining about the bad economy,
> Unaware of being caught in an endless cycle of cash shortages.
> Oh, it's confusing, it's confusing, love and duty are also confusing.
> Are people blinded by their selfish desires? Oh, all people are confusing.

Liberating moments of carnival provide aesthetic distancing as we view musical and theatrical performances within the filmic action that comment on a militarized industrial society corrupt and harmful to the indigenous social fabric of the community. This creates a social discourse in the film, as authoritarian exhibition of power is countered by transgressive enactment of locally grounded artistic expression.

Conclusion

Shinoda's characters embody a radical politics of subjectivity and selfhood that opposes constraints of social authority. The vivid portrayal of resistance across varying historical filmic genres provokes the viewer to reconsider the present in a new light. Recognizing the importance of his collaborative relationship with Takemitsu, the director once said, 'To have been able to get Takemitsu to create the music for my films, I think that's one of the luckiest things that happened to me. So after he passed away, I quickly lost my passion for making films' (Shinoda 2005). The artistic freedom Takemitsu had in crafting the whole soundtrack enabled him to explore musically the contested terrain of tradition and modern subjectivity, with musical references that cross cultural and temporal boundaries, and sonic experiments in *musique concrète* that transform and elevate the real into an artistic expression of the unreal and unseen. Takemitsu's mastery in creating a dialogic narrative through interactions of musical style paralleled Shinoda's commitment in exploring tradition and modernity through innovation in established filmic genres. In showing how expressions of cultural tradition and modernity are interrelated, even as they are fractured and contested across aural and visual domains, they created films that are artistic, vibrant and still relevant today.

21 Welcome to Kollywood
Tamil Film Music and Popular Culture in South India

MEKALA PADMANABHAN

The southern cities of Chennai, Hyderabad, Kochi and Bangalore – releasing movies in Tamil, Telugu, Malayalam and Kannada languages, respectively – contribute 55 per cent of India's copious film output, whereas the Mumbai-based Hindi film industry, globally known as Bollywood, contributes between 15 and 20 per cent of the annual total (www.filmfed.org/IFF2014 .html). Nonetheless, Bollywood's prominence in the international media has, to some extent, shaped the nature of Indian film-music scholarship since the 1980s. The prevalent tendency is to group India's commercial films under the umbrella of Bollywood, often neglecting the country's leading regional cinemas. Film songs from the south, which outpace Bollywood, have not merited much more than a passing acknowledgement in mainstream film-music surveys. However, there are encouraging signs of change, as evidenced in three recent publications which feature discussions of Tamil film music: Mark Slobin's *Global Soundtracks* (2008), Joseph Getter's essay on the subject in Gregory Booth's and Bradley Shope's *More than Bollywood* (2014) and Tina K. Ramnarine's forthcoming *Global Perspectives on the Orchestra: Essays in Collective Creativity and Social Agency*.

The spectacular song and dance sequences in Indian cinema contribute to its uniqueness in a competitive global market. As Farah Khan, Bollywood's leading choreographer, once observed: 'What is saving Indian Cinema from being engulfed by Hollywood is our song and dance routines because they just can't imitate that' (Kabir 2001, 15). The ability of music directors to assimilate innumerable types of musical traditions within and beyond India has given film songs the staying power to flourish as popular mass entertainment. It is also a primary reason that makes Indian film songs a fascinating subject for study.

It is widely acknowledged by scholars that one of the fundamental discernible features in Indian film music is the synthesis of 'native and foreign' stylistic traits (Arnold 1988, 177–8; Morcom 2001, 64; Getter and Balasubrahmaniyan 2008, 121–2). Contemporary Indian film soundscapes also draw upon the sonic resources of South African, Latin American, Arabic and Chinese cultures in addition to their own. Creative practices in Indian film music have always been a complex process of interaction, interpretation and adaptation of new musical cultures not demarcated by geographical borders (see Ramnarine 2011). Moreover, it is impossible to ignore the distinct characteristics each region contributes to the genre. For example, Tamil has a rich cultural, linguistic and literary heritage dating as far back as the fourth century BC. In terms of lyrics and music, there are idiomatic means of expression that are both traditional and culturally unique to the language and place.

The main objective of this chapter is to investigate this idea further. In the state of Tamil Nadu, as elsewhere in southern India, film music has become synonymous with regional popular culture. The present chapter first examines the relevant socio-cultural and historical factors that have played an important role in the emergence of film songs as an influential medium in Tamil Nadu's 'pop' culture. The second part of the chapter explores how the confluence of Indian music, Western art, jazz and popular genres has shaped music creation in Tamil film orchestras over the last half-century. Against this background, the final discussion addresses two questions: How does the intercultural style of the music fit into the on-screen narrative? And how do music directors navigate the complex issues of regional ethnicity and cultural identity in film songs?

Introducing Kollywood

The lively seaside metropolis of Chennai, formerly Madras (until 1996), has been the location for a thriving Tamil film industry for nearly a century. Today's Chennai bears little resemblance to the Madras presidency in colonial India c. 1900 but its association with the movie industry has remained unchanged. The moniker Kollywood is (like Bollywood) an obvious derivative of Hollywood, with the 'K' referring to a suburb in Chennai – 'Kodambakkam' – a neighbourhood where the largest percentage of people who worked in the film industry lived. Even today it remains a home to music directors, actors and technicians. Between 1940 and 1960, many of Chennai's finest film and recording studios were located here. Owing to urban development over the last thirty years, several studios have become defunct and current production units are spread across Chennai (Sreevatsan 2011).

Tamil Film Songs: A Historical Perspective

Film historians have established that the earliest talkies closely followed the dramatic conventions of the already existent theatrical tradition of stage dramas in India (Barnouw and Krishnaswamy 1980 [1963]; Chandravarkar

1987; Bhaskaran 1991, 1996). In Tamil Nadu, the 'company drama' that surfaced in the 1890s owed its development to Parsi theatrical troupes from North India that had regularly performed in the south from 1870 onwards (Hughes 2007, 6). By 1900, it had developed into a commercial mass-entertainment enterprise leading to the establishment of numerous professional and amateur drama companies in Chennai. Dramatic content of the plays was drawn from Hindu mythology and epics. There was a mixture of dialogue and song, accompanied by musicians on the harmonium and *tablā*, as well as other traditional instruments. With the plots covering familiar stories, the musical components provided fresh entertainments. As Bhaskaran relates, the 'emphasis was on singing, not on drama. When a character died on the stage after singing a song, he would get up without any hesitation to respond to cries of "once more" and start singing all over again' (1991, 755). The overwhelming demand for songs in these staged performances is evident in contemporaneous comments:

> It is not unusual for people in the gallery . . . to shout to the hero or heroine, asking them to sing some particular song, which would have no connection to the play . . . The request must be immediately complied with, failure to do which, would result in the pelting of stones which were kept for the purpose . . . which would make it impossible for the play to proceed.
>
> (Myleru 1934, 75; cited in Hughes 2007, 7)

The playwright (*vāttiyār*) was also the music composer and lyricist; and songs were modelled using the South Indian Carnatic vocal idiom (Bhaskaran 1991, 755). In the south, Carnatic music was a classical art that had been entirely transmitted orally for several centuries. As a result, extant performance-related documentary evidence is available only from the sixteenth century onwards. Fostered primarily through royal patronage and temple performances, it was a genre that came to the public concert stage only in the early twentieth century (Subramanian 2006). Therefore, the adaptation of Carnatic style in stage songs might have begun as an effort to appeal to connoisseurs of art while promoting the company drama as an 'elite' form of entertainment. After 1910, influenced by the North Indian stage music, the Tamil drama songs began integrating *rāgas* from the Hindustani tradition and the Maharashtrian *bhavgeet*, into their *natya sangeeth* (dance music). (See Hughes 2007, 7; Bhaskaran 1991, 755.) Other modes of musical expression from the indigenous Tamil folk theatre such as *Therukoothu* (street drama and dances) found their way into comical songs (Bhaskaran 1991, 755). In short, the song in Tamil company dramas had become a hybrid of both North and South Indian music.

The contemporaneous Tamil theatre thus provided the primary musical and dramatic model for the early Tamil talkies. Ardeshir Irani, the

Mumbai producer of the first Tamil talkie *Kalidas* (1931), once remarked that having 'no dialogue writer, no lyricist, no music director ... everything had to be planned and started from scratch' (Ramachandran *et al.* 1981, 16). Irani recalled that he had searched and selected the songs and tunes from the stage dramas, and recorded the music with a minimal orchestra comprising a harmonium, *tablā* and violin. While the stage tradition laid the foundation for talkies, the advent of gramophone contributed to the evolution of Tamil film songs as a new product for mass entertainment.

From Gramophone Recordings to the Twenty-First-Century 'Audio Launch'

At the turn of the century, gramophone businesses in colonial South India primarily catered to the tastes of European consumers. Between 1910 and 1920, companies like HMV began to explore the commercial possibilities of South Indian music, which resulted in what Hughes calls the 'music boom' during the 1920s (Hughes 2002, 2007; Bhaskaran 1991, 1996). To summarize Hughes: well-known songs and singers from the stage became a splendid asset for gramophone sales. Theatrical songs covered a wide spectrum of musical and poetic expression; they included songs based on seventh-century Tamil devotional poems like *Tēvāram*, Carnatic music both vocal and instrumental, secular vernacular folk songs and comedic recitations. In the decade preceding the talkies, the recording industry had developed a market for Tamil songs independent of the dramatic context. The gramophone trade also played a pivotal role in launching the musical careers of many famous stage personalities and enabling their transition into film acting. Prominent examples include K. B. Sundarambal and S. V. Subbiah Bhagavathar, who achieved, as Hughes labels it, 'gramophone fame' and great success in films.

From the mid-1930s, several renowned Carnatic singers and musicians, including M. S. Subbalakshmi, D. K. Pattamal, G. N. Balasubramaniam, V. V. Sadagopan, Papanasam Sivan and Musiri Subramania Iyer, triumphed as actors, singers, lyricists and music directors. Even today, well-known Carnatic artistes such as Nithyasree Mahadevan, Charulatha Mani and P. Unnikrishnan frequently perform in film songs that require a specific vocal timbre or convincing performances of *rāga*-based or *rāga*-like songs.

In addition to bringing fame and popularity to the artists, the gramophone recordings also changed song structure, performance practice and aesthetics. On a practical level, the 78 rpm gramophone records could accommodate only three- or four-minute songs. In Carnatic music, there are song-types called *kritis* that are in three parts. (For further on this, and on other matters discussed in this essay, see Padmanabhan, forthcoming.) The singer or instrumentalist begins with an introductory improvised melodic expansion using the *swaras* (solfeggio syllables) of the *rāga* called *alapana*. The sections within the song itself are called *pallavi* (to blossom), *anupallavi* (*anu*, meaning to follow) and *caranam* (feet) – the terms referring to both the text and musical structure. In the *pallavi* and *anupallavi*, the performer uses improvisatory techniques such as *sangati* (subtle melismatic variations) alongside exploration of the various vocal registers using the *rāga*. At the end of the *anupallavi* exposition the *pallavi* returns, before moving on to the *caranam*. The *caranam* is analogous to a verse – usually comprising four lines of text. A song can have one to three or more *caranams*, each exploring the *rāga* further. At the end of each *caranam* the *pallavi* recurs like a refrain.

When performed on stage, the drama songs in Carnatic style included the improvisatory *rāga* explorations of the *alapana* and *pallavi–anupallavi*, extending the duration of a song to as long as thirty minutes. Due to the brevity of the gramophone recordings these passages were shortened or omitted and the result was a condensed version of the stage song (Hughes 2007, 8–10). Despite the technological advances of the twenty-first century, Tamil film songs rarely exceed the five-minute mark. Similarly, in spite of cross-cultural influences the basic *pallavi–caranam* structure has remained intact, albeit with some modifications. In fact, one could even say that the introductory *rāga alapana* has over the years transformed into what is known among Tamil film musicians as 'humming' or 'intro humming'. The term refers to a short introductory *a capella* melodic vocal phrase (without words) that sometimes precedes songs. Since the mid-1990s, it is not unusual to incorporate 'digital samples not composed and recorded by the composer, often repeated at later points within the song' (personal interview with S. Divakar, Chennai, 29 November 2013). To the unfamiliar listener, today's Tamil film songs resemble a strophic setting of a verse–refrain format with orchestral interludes in between. A large number of songs loosely follow the structure outlined in Figure 21.1.

intro humming (optional) → 1st BGM → *pallavi* → 2nd BGM →

1st *caranam* → *pallavi* → 3rd BGM → 2nd *caranam* → *pallavi* →

4th BGM or end music → 3rd *caranam* (optional)

Figure 21.1 Typical structure of Tamil film songs.

In the Tamil film industry, the abbreviation BGM (for background music) is used to identify the instrumental passages within the song, whereas the term 're-recording' refers to background music that accompanies the dialogue portions in the cinema.

S. G. Kittappa's 1925 gramophone rendering of the song 'Enthan kāmi catyapāmā katavai tiṟava' ('My dearest Sathyabama please open the door') illustrates these aspects (see Table 21.1, no. 1 (at end of this chapter), for video link). The song text portrays Lord Krishna trying to mollify his third wife, Sathyabama, after a domestic spat. Although the vocal melody uses the Carnatic manner of singing, the *sangati* ornamentations are minimalized. The opening line of the *pallavi* is repeated several times with subtle melodic variations on the words 'katavai tiṟava' ('please open the door') to express the pleading quality implicit in the Tamil text. The skeletal instrumental accompaniment for the song is the harmonium and the South Indian drum (*mirutaṅkam*) used in Carnatic concerts. Incidentally, Kittappa's song was reorchestrated a half-century later in *Sri Krishna Leela* (*The Playfulness of Lord Krishna*, 1977) by the music director S. V. Venkaratarman.

While the earliest songs from the talkies (1931–5) are not preserved, examples like these provide a glimpse into the fledgling stages of the Tamil film song. Moreover, their relevance is also apparent for present-day period films. Gnana Rajasekaran's (2014 Tamil) biopic, *Ramanujan*, on the life of the renowned South Indian mathematician Srinivasa Ramanujan (1887–1920) is an example. The first part of the film chronicles Ramanujan's life in Kumbakonam and Madras in c. 1900, to which the music director Ramesh Vinayakam added an authentic ambience:

> The one thing we must thank the British for is the gramophone. Since Carnatic music is an oral tradition and not a notated one, and is taught by rote, we do not know how people sang or how it sounded around 1897. I used early gramophone recordings to get an idea about the type of orchestration and sounds to use for the songs in the film.
>
> (Personal interview with Ramesh Vinayakam, Chennai, 13 February 2015)

Gramophone artists like Kittappa were also significant in shaping the musical awareness of the general public while the technology facilitated accessibility to the music. In the words of the Tamil scholar Va.Ra. (1947): 'Prior to Kittappa, most music maestros (*vitvāṉkaḷ*) behaved as though [music] was not essential or intelligible to the uneducated masses (*pāmaramakkaḷ*). But, Kittappa proved that even they had the ability to appreciate music' (Vamanan 2004, 52).

The central aesthetic in Carnatic music is the concept of *bhakti*, the Hindu notion of devotion to God, and this underpins all song texts.

As a result, the style suited the religious stories and mythological plots of early Tamil cinema. Towards the end of the 1930s, secular solo, duet and choral songs became a part of films. Song texts addressed a wide range of secular topics such as love, philosophical musings on life experiences, as well as poetry espousing Gandhian ideals reawakening pride in indigenous Tamil heritage and increasing patriotic fervour. The secular nature of the lyrics and stories demanded a different means of musical expression, which, as we will see later, was achieved by absorbing musical elements from other cultures.

Just as the drama songs of the previous decade had become a marketable commodity, so did the film songs of the 1930s. Gramophone recordings created a life for film songs outside the confines of the movie theatre. This set the precedent for the subsequent 'cassette culture' (Manuel 1993) of the 1970s and 1980s and mass dissemination of the genre in the digital age. Collectively, these developments have shaped film-music marketing in Tamil Nadu. What is striking is that, in the twentieth century, Tamil cinema promoted the film song, but in the internet era, the song now promotes the cinema!

The present trend in Kollywood is to hold a public 'audio launch' in the weeks prior to the release of the film. The concept is similar to Hollywood's 'red carpet' movie previews with A-list celebrities, but the difference is the focus on the film's song. The music director and film director receive top billing in promotional banners, radio and TV advertisements. Audio launches are fundamentally variety shows with live performances of the film's songs with orchestra, alongside performances of the music director's previous hits. Interspersed between song performances are choreographed group dances, plus speeches by the film actors, music director and film director. The speeches are an opportunity to share interesting details about the music and filmmaking processes with the audience in order to pique their curiosity about the movie. In short, the events are a public relations and marketing strategy to promote both the CD and the movie. Audio launches of big-budget blockbusters are broadcast on local TV networks at weekends. Over the last few years, production companies with a stake in the CDs, like Sony India, have uploaded the mp3 recordings onto YouTube to increase visibility for the film.

In Tamil Nadu, the largest audio launches are held in Chennai. The size and length of the event are directly proportionate to the celebrity status of the music director, actors and film directors in Kollywood. Recent examples include Ilayaraja's audio launch of *Nee Thāne En Pon Vasantham* (*You Are My Golden Springtime*; 2012) and A. R. Rahman's music for the 'romantic-thriller' *I* (2014). Both were massive events open to the public and held at the Jawaharlal Nehru Indoor Stadium. The star attraction for Ilayaraja's event was the orchestra of freelance European musicians under the baton of Nick Newland, whose London-based company Anglo-Indian Music Productions had hired the musicians for the re-recording of the soundtracks in the United Kingdom. For Oscar winner Rahman's launch, the star attractions besides Rahman himself included Arnold Schwarzenegger and the Tamil Nadu's 'Super Star Rajnikanth', as well as other luminaries from the film industry.

The supremacy of film songs as the dominant popular culture in present-day Tamil Nadu has been aided by technological advancements. Music directors have at their disposal a plethora of digital and acoustic instruments as well as a wide spectrum of musical styles with which to conceptualize their film score. The seeds for creating a popular genre primarily based on the concept of fusion have grown by leaps and bounds in Tamil film music over the last century.

At its inception, Tamil film songs were already a hybrid mixture of Hindustani, Carnatic and Tamil folk styles. The lack of studio facilities in Madras (Chennai) resulted in the use of studios in Bombay (Mumbai) and Calcutta (Kolkata). This meant Tamil film productions sometimes used North Indian film directors such as Ardeshir Irani, Manik Lal Tandon or the Irish-American Ellis Dungan, and the habit of reusing hit melodies from Hindi films was a regular practice that developed as a result. However, the gradual assimilation of musical styles beyond India, particularly from Western art and popular music, can be partially attributed to the gramophone circulation in Madras. An Irish music scholar, Margaret E. Cousins, who lived in Madras between 1915 and 1935, wrote: 'The impact on the minds of musicians and of the public of gramophone records and broadcasting of the music of other systems both East and West must inevitably give a new ideal to the playing of Indian instruments, both singly and in combination' (1935, 70–1). In fact, it appears from her writing that Cousins foresaw the development of a unique Indian orchestral sound as a result of exposure to new kinds of music. She predicted:

> there will arise a need for forms of musical expression in which many people can join actively and yet with their own distinctive characteristics, and this will preclude the expansion of the Indian orchestra from its limited latency into powerful patency of emotional effects through that unity of the orchestra which includes diversity of types of sound, of rhythm, of pitch, and of melodic outline. I believe that Indian music will evolve the art of writing melodies … India has instruments of very beautiful and expressive tone. It is the genius for fusion that strikes one as lacking. (Cousins 1935, 71)

Although Cousins was speaking about the Carnatic tradition, the idea of 'fusion' found its application in Tamil film music. Today, the expansion of the orchestral palette to which Cousins alluded has also occurred in the genre. The ensuing discussion traces the development of Tamil film-music orchestral sounds over the last eighty years. To a considerable extent, the stylistic evolution and synthesis of intercultural influences has been made possible by the inclusion of keyboard instruments.

Keyboard Instruments in Tamil Film Orchestras

Since 1931, two instruments have maintained their hegemony in the Tamil film-music soundscape: keyboards and strings. From traditional harmoniums, acoustic pianos and organs to their subsequent electronic counterparts, keyboard instruments have remained integral to the creative process and music in Tamil films. Their inclusion in Tamil film music has diversified orchestral colour and timbre while simultaneously shaping approaches to composition and performance. Additionally, music technology and sound-recording advancements have played a role in these developments.

The establishment of the first recording studio in South India, Srinivasa Cinetone (1934) in Madras, quickly led to the rise of at least nine recording studios in the city by 1937 (Bhaskaran 1991, 756). Incidentally, the first instance of playback singing occurred in the 1938 movie *Nandakumar* (Guy 2007). For music directors, this improvement in sound recording gave them freedom to use any instrument irrespective of size and also the facility to have a larger orchestra. As a result, we find the earliest audible exemplars of the acoustic piano in Tamil songs of the late 1940s.

Immediately following India's independence (1947), when the Governor's Music Band and military bands were discontinued, several Goan and Anglo-Indian pianists and musicians who played Western instruments were unemployed. In Madras, many of them found jobs as entertainers at the city's cosmopolitan Gymkhana Club. Frank Dubier, a contemporaneous jazz musician on the Madras scene, notes: 'most western musicians held two jobs – serenading foodies by night and working for films during the day' (Frederick 2010). V. S. Narasimhan, a well-known violinist and composer who has worked in the Tamil film music industry for over forty years, shared his studio experiences in the late 1950s (personal interview, Chennai, 26 February 2013). He recalled that the music directors would instruct pianists to play 'some chords' to round out the orchestral sound and provide harmonic support for the song melody. In accordance with the instructions, they would improvise and play basic diatonic progressions or arpeggios in the instrumental interludes within songs, never venturing into chromatic harmony or modulations. Such improvised approaches to film-song composition and orchestration were quite common in studio recordings for several years. Conversely, R. Chandrasekhar, a veteran guitarist, electronic keyboardist and sound engineer, remembers music directors – for instance, T. G. Lingappa in the 1950s and 1960s – providing written-out scores to film musicians in both Western and Carnatic notations and the studio recording being a 'very disciplined process' (personal interview, 11 February 2015).

Gemini Studios's 1949 box-office hit *Apoorva Sagotharargal (Amazing Brothers)*, an adaptation of Alexandre Dumas's *The Corsican Brothers*, is perhaps one of the earliest films to feature the acoustic grand piano on and off screen (Guy 2008). The song 'Māṇum mayilum āṭum cōlai' ('The groves where the deer and peacocks dance') begins with an ascending and descending scalic flourish between the lower and higher registers on the piano and continues as though spontaneously trying to improvise a tune in the first thirty-five seconds of the song. In the following orchestral passage, the entry of the *tablā* sets the rhythm while the piano introduces the melody of the *pallavi*. An interesting feature of this introduction is the way S. Rajeswara Rao uses the piano. Musically, the brief improvisation in the beginning bears a striking similarity to the harmonium idiom one would encounter in early company-drama songs. On screen is a romantic scene with the hero and heroine at the piano playing these melodies (Table 21.1, no. 2). Film historian Randor Guy notes:

> A duet meant for the Hindi version was composed on the piano by Rajeswara Rao, and Vasan liked it so much he wanted it for the Tamil version too. This song was added after the shoot was over! Acharya invested the song sequence with fine creative touches - Radha's hand covering Bhanumathi's and both their hands gliding across the ivory keys of the piano! (Guy 2008)

Songs like these set the trend for the acoustic piano to be seen on screen and heard in Tamil movies. Furthermore, it appears that the concept of using the piano keyboard like a harmonium caught on, particularly in films of the early 1950s. T. R. Papa's song 'Eṇṇa eṇṇa iṇpamē' ('What joy!') from *Anbu* (*Love*; 1953) also employs the harmonium technique in the prelude (first BGM). Visually, the playful interaction between lovers resembles the narrative of the preceding example (Table 21.1, no. 3). In the second BGM, the function of the piano is not melodic or harmonic, but rhythmic. This passage employs idiomatic Western pianistic technique, evident in the swiftly repeated chords, followed by two repetitions of a virtuosic motif in the treble and a glissando punctuating the beginning of the *caranam*. Even such innocuous uses of the piano, other foreign instruments and musical mannerisms stirred up a colossal controversy in Indian broadcasting history.

In the first decade of independent India, when nationalistic fervour was at its highest, Dr B. V. Keskar, the Minister of Information and Broadcasting, a staunch admirer of Indian classical music, was openly critical of the mixture of 'Western and Eastern music in film song' (*The Hindu*, 29 September 1953; Punathambekar 2010, 190). Keskar's stance gained support from a number of ardent devotees of the classical-music traditions. The argument had several facets but began with the use of Western instruments in film music and educational institutions. Calling for the immediate ban of all Western instruments, R. Ranjan, a prominent actor, dancer and musician from Madras, noted: 'with the adoption of the tempered scale of the west, our musicians become oblivious to the delicacies and subtleties of the 22-*sruti* scale ... ' (Barnouw and Krishnaswamy 1980 [1963], 207–10). Such opinions brought radical changes in All-India-Radio amounting to a ban of film-music programmes between 1952 and 1957, by which time the Indian government realized they were losing audiences and advertising revenue to the neighbouring Radio Ceylon (Sri Lanka) and film-music programmes were once again reinstated (Lelyfeld 1994, 117–21; Punathambekar 2010, 191; Weidman 2012, 259).

Western concepts of harmony, melody and homophonic texture begin to emerge in Tamil film songs in the late 1950s. A good example is G. Ramanathan's 'Ciṉṉa peṇāṉā pōtilē' ('When I was a little girl') from *Aravalli* (1957) – the Tamil version of the popular Jay Livingston and Ray Evans 1956 hit 'Que Sera Sera'. The Tamil song begins with soft xylophone tremolos and the strings before settling into the same waltz rhythm and melody as the English original (Table 21.1, no. 4). In addition to the re-orchestration, even the lyricist P. Kalyanasundaram takes his lead from the original text:

Tamil text transliteration	Translation
ciṉṉa peṇ āṉa pōtilē,	When I was a little girl,
aṉṉai iṭam nāṉ uravāṭiṉēṉ,	I asked my mother,
eṉ eṉṉaṅkaḷ yāvum iṭērumō?	Will all that my heart desires come true?
am'mā ni col eṉṟēṉ.	Mother, you tell me I said.

The use of homophonic texture, simple piano accompaniment and the concept of functional harmony becomes more pronounced in the 1960s. Master Venu's music for the song 'Ēṉ inta iravu, ēṉ inta kaṉavu' ('Why this night? Why this dream?') from *Puthiya Pathai* (*New Path*; 1960) displays the assimilation of the prevalent composition techniques in Western popular songs of the time (Table 21.1, no. 5). The first BGM begins with a soft melody in the violin accompanied by gentle arpeggios in the piano. After a brief silence, two bars of waltz rhythms in the guitar and piano lead to the first vocal phrase. It is one of the few Tamil songs that maintains the homophonic texture from beginning to end.

By the mid-1960s, the acoustic piano had acquired a prominent role both visually and musically – a trend that continues to the present day. The powerhouse duo primarily responsible for showcasing the piano in Tamil film music was the Viswanathan-Ramamurthy partnership, famously dubbed as Mellisai Mannargal (Kings of Light Music). In keeping with their title, their songs incorporated jazz idioms, such as syncopation, jazz-style piano breaks, flashy glissandos and toe-tapping rhythms suited for singing and dancing. For example, the song 'Uṉṉai oṉṟu kēṭpēṉ' ('I will ask you one thing') in the film *Puthiya Paravai* (*New Bird*; 1964) begins with a ragtime piano introduction (Table 21.1, no. 6). The syncopated piano octaves recede into the background when the voice enters but resurface prominently in the second BGM. Incorporation of jazz traits expanded the orchestral complement to include brass, double-bass and percussion sections. Other music directors such as Veda and V. Kumar also worked similar ideas into their film songs in the late 1960s and early 1970s.

The use of functional harmony and the beginnings of a Western symphonic approach to orchestration in Tamil film music manifest clearly for the first time in Ilayaraja's music of the late 1970s and early 1980s. The solo piano introduction to his 1980 song 'Eṉ vāṉilē orē veṇṇilā' ('In my sky there is but one moon') in *Johnny* begins with continuous triplet arpeggiation of the tonic triad in the bass supporting the tentative variants of the song melody in the upper registers (Table 21.1, no. 7). The second BGM that begins at 50″ and ends at 1′31″ initially starts as a repeated two-note semitone motif in the piano. The flute reinterprets the semitone idea as a trill an octave lower leading to the violin entry. The solo violin uses the trill as a starting point to embark freely on a new melodic idea with the harmonic support of the full string section (1′07″ to 1′20″). There is an ascending scale figure in the strings just before the piano entry at 1′20″. A short melodic motif is tossed back and forth like a dialogue between the piano and strings and the BGM ends with the return of the triadic arpeggio in the piano (1′31″). Overall, the passage just described draws on the conventions of Western classical symphonic and solo concerto idioms.

According to Ilayaraja, 'Lack of harmony and counterpoint in Indian music is an aspect pointed out by foreigners. However, that is wrong. To illustrate that I have used strong harmonic backgrounds and western techniques in songs' (1984, 74–6). Ilayaraja's 'western' style fuses compositional techniques of Western art music with the melodic and the orchestral inspiration he drew from the French easy-listening composer Paul Mauriat (*ibid.*, 13). This mode of orchestration is variously juxtaposed with instrumentation of the disco-pop era alongside moments from vernacular South Indian folk or Carnatic idiom (Table 21.1, nos. 8 and 9). In short, Ilayaraja's BGMs in the 1980s were a veritable medley of many musical styles in equal measure and were seminal in revitalizing the southern film-music industry. In recent years, there has been a perceptible change in his orchestration. For instance, in *Megha* (*Clouds*; 2014) the songs display a focused uniformity in texture, style, dynamics and subtle integration of new melodic ideas throughout. This is a contrast to earlier works when the orchestra was in the foreground only in the BGM sections.

The arrival of electronic keyboards in the late 1970s revolutionized the sound world of Tamil films in much the same manner that jazz elements had in the previous decade. Tamil films in the early 1980s weaved disco club scenes, pop or rock concerts and film-music recording studios into the narrative, providing music directors ample room in which to explore the sound world of Western pop idioms. However, Ilayaraja also found the means to incorporate the new sound in Tamil songs set in rural dramatic contexts. An illustration is the first thirty seconds of the first BGM of 'Potti vacca mallikai moṭṭu' ('The hidden jasmine flower') in the 1983 film *Man Vasanai* (*Scent of the Land*; see Subramaniam 2014). This passage begins with an electronic drone over which the synthesized melody emerges and subsequently mingles with flute (Table 21.1, no. 10). Perhaps because of pastoral references in Indian mythology, rural scenes in Tamil films often feature flute melodies.

Over the last two decades, the advent of MIDI technology, digital sampling and various music-composing software packages has had a significant impact on the Tamil film orchestra. An added dimension to the orchestral sound is the concept of 'texturing' or 'layering'. According to A. R. Rahman, a film song based on 'pure melody does not work for music tastes today' (Kabir 2011, 82). He explains:

> there's also a way of creating a palette of sounds without compromising on the core melody. You want people to relate to melody and when you have a great melody and sweeping harmony, you can help to hold attention by adding a driving rhythm. The rhythm is there for listeners who get restless and don't necessarily enjoy pure melody . . . When you layer a song, you can fully occupy the listener's mind. (Kabir 2011, 82)

The orchestration for the song 'Muṉpē vā eṉ aṉpē vā' ('Come to me, my love') from *Sillunu Oru Kaadhal* (*Love like a cool breeze*; 2006) is a good illustration of how layering works in practice (Table 21.1, no. 11).

Although the inclusion of Western instruments and styles might have begun as a novelty, over time they played a decisive role in changing compositional aesthetics in Tamil film music and songs.

Similarly, music technology has also transformed creative practices and music making significantly. Notwithstanding all these creative changes, Tamil film songs, for the most part, have continued to retain their cultural identity. The concluding discussion investigates how elements of regional culture have become integral to the nature of Tamil film music.

Conclusion: Creativity and Cultural Identity in Tamil Film Music

In the digital age, Tamil film music has become a profitable commodity not only in the regional and national market, but also globally among Tamil diaspora communities and even mainstream Hollywood. There appears to be an increasing awareness of the importance of conveying the nuances of the Tamil cultural milieu despite the intercultural nature of its compositions. Vinayakam's film score and songs for the 2014 biopic *Ramanujan*, mentioned earlier, serve as an excellent model for discussion.

In accordance with the events of Ramanujan's life, the movie was filmed in India and at Cambridge University. Therefore, the film director Rajasekaran wanted a mix of 'Western and Indian music for the score' (personal interview with Vinayakam, Chennai, 13 February 2014). As Vinayakam wanted to capture a European sound for the narrative in Cambridge, the recording for the UK scenes was done with session musicians of the German Pops Orchestra, at Bauer Studios, Ludwigsburg: see Figure 21.2. Consequently, the film score for the Cambridge scenes utilized not only Western art-music elements but also included a range of musical expression drawn from the South Indian cultural context. Additionally, to preserve the historical accuracy of the soundscape, instrumentation was limited to acoustic instruments available in the early twentieth century. Vinayakam's score showcases different facets of regional identity in the portrayal of Ramanujan's character and the cinematic landscape. Ramanujan first appears on the screen as a precocious child from a devout Hindu Brahmin family during the devotional *bhajan*-style opening number 'Narayana', set in a South Indian temple. Here again the traditional Indian instruments and semi-classical vocal style converge to convey the audible impression of the 'Hindu-Brahmin' cultural norms.

Regardless of his mathematical genius, Ramanujan remained deeply religious, adhering to the norms of Hindu Vaishnavaite traditions even during his Cambridge days. Vinayakam wanted to emphasize this trait in the song 'Viṅkaṭanta jōtiyāy' ('Thou art a luminous light

Example 21.1 Ramesh Vinayakam, 'Viṇkaṭanta jōtiyāy', bars 20-7. © 2014 by Ramesh Vinayakam. Used by permission.

Piano and strings

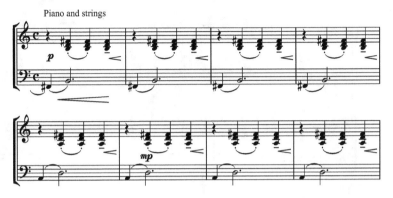

Figure 21.2 Ramesh Vinayakam's recording session for *Ramanujan* (2014) at Bauer Studios, Germany.

beyond galaxies'; personal interview, 13 February 2014). He achieves this by juxtaposing a soaring Carnatic-style vocal melody in the *pallavi* passage, expertly rendered by the Carnatic exponent P. Unnikrishnan, over the subdued rhythmic pulse of the strings and piano starting on the off-beat. Furthermore, the pronounced rhythmic disjunction between voice and orchestra within the cinematic structure mirrors the cultural polarities between the East and West (see Example 21.1 and 26″ to 1′20″ in Table 21.1, no. 12). Dramatically, the rhythmic independence of the vocal

Example 21.2 Ramesh Vinayakam, 'Viṇkaṭanta jōtiyāy', bars 44-51. © 2014 by Ramesh Vinayakam. Used by permission.

line serves to highlight Ramanujan's autodidactic genius that defied all logic. In the second BGM, the orchestral writing becomes animated due to the sharing of syncopated melodies between the woodwinds, piano and strings. Moreover the syncopations resolve rhythmic tension between the voice and accompaniment for the rest of the song (see Example 21.2;

Table 21.1, no. 12). In the finished soundtrack, one hears the almost imperceptible chimes of the triangle punctuating the end of vocal phrases. From the Tamilian cultural perspective, its inclusion can be interpreted as a nuanced reference to the small handheld cymbals (*jalra*) used for rhythmic support in *bhajans*.

Vinayakam's song text used three verses from the soulful devotional Tamil poetry of the seventh or eighth century AD to enhance the sonic references further. The poem *Tiruccantaviruttam* by Vaishanvite Saint Thirumazhisai Azhwar praises the incomparable virtues of the Hindu god Lord Vishnu in 120 verses. Vinayakam stated that he chose the excerpts for the *caranam* because the poetic alliteration sounded like number recitations that fitted the cinematic context, given Ramanujan's fascination with mathematics (personal interview, Chennai, 13 February 2014). Within the literary context, the alliteration, in fact, alludes to hidden theological and philosophical references to other Hindu Vedic texts. Even if contemporary Tamil movie audiences are unaware of such literary nuances, most will recognize the song as a prayer to Lord Vishnu, which is evident in the *pallavi* text:

Tamil Transliteration	English Translation
viṉkaṭantajōtiyāy viḷaṅkuñāṉamūrttiyāy	(Thou art) the radiant form beyond the cosmos, who possesses all knowledge of the universe,
paṅkaṭantatēcamēvu pāvaṉacanātanē	(Thou art) beyond all characteristic sounds of Vedas and destroyer of all flaws,
eṉkaṭantayōkiṉōṭu īrāṉtucenṟumāṉiyāy	(Thou) who despite Thy glorious attributes went begging for alms, assuming the form of a dwarf, ['dwarf' refers to Lord Vishnu's *Vāmana* incarnation]
maṉkaṭantavaṉṉaṉīṉ naiyārmatikavallarē	And then proceeded to measure the earth, Who can comprehend Thy mysterious ways?

Within the boundaries of the storyline, the functional role of the song, as Vinayakam pointed out, was to illuminate Ramanujan's unchanged character and beliefs. Outside the cinematic structure, the song assumes a different role independent of the narrative – a prayer. One of the most attractive aspects of the *Ramanujan* score is the balance it achieves between the foreign and native elements while retaining its cultural associations. The instrumental tracks on the audio CD reveal Vinayakam's attention to details that might not be overtly expressed in the narrative. An illustration is 'One to Zero', in duple time, that begins with a mathematical pattern shared between the lower and upper strings. One note in the violins is answered by two notes in the lower

Example 21.3 Ramesh Vinayakam, 'One to Zero', bars 1–8. © 2014 by Ramesh Vinayakam. Used by permission.

strings, which are answered by three notes in the upper strings and so forth (see Example 21.3).

Over the last century, musical creativity in Tamil films has undergone a metamorphosis from both artistic and practical perspectives. Nonetheless, the most successful music directors have always been able to find creative ways to retain the regional flavour even while adapting musical influences from other cultures. In recent years, this aspect has worked to their advantage in terms of CD sales, box-office receipts and even the ability to reach global audiences irrespective of nationality. As a result, Tamil film songs are now finding their way into mainstream Hollywood productions such as *The Accidental Husband* (2008) and more recently Walt Disney's *Million Dollar Arm* (2014). Speaking about the importance of maintaining cultural identity in his music, Ilayaraja once remarked: 'We compose in accordance with our culture, people, society, and place; and when we do so it could reach global audiences. However, there cannot be a common type of music for everybody. Creativity is a universal instinct, but creations are innumerable' (Prem-Ramesh 1998, 81). The 'innumerable' film songs have continued to thrive because the feelings that they evoke resonate in some way with the life experiences of Tamil people. It is this aesthetic that has enabled Tamil film music to emerge as a dominant force in mass popular culture in South India.

Table 21.1 *Sources for Tamil film songs.*

No.	Song Title	Literal Translation	Video URL
1	'Enthan kāmi catyapāmā katavai tiṟava'	'My dearest Sathyabama please open the door'	http://www.youtube.com/watch?v=meTvDhvt2V4
2	'Māṉum mayilum āṭum cōlai'	'The grove where the deer and peacocks dance'	www.youtube.com/watch?v=p5jC-zUnUE
3	'Eṉṉa eṉṉa iṉpamē'	'What joy!'	www.youtube.com/watch?v=qH6dfw4rgrc
4	'Ciṉṉa peṇāṉā pōtilē'	'When I was a little girl'	http://www.youtube.com/watch?v=yNKqxRfrXh0
5	'Ēṉ inta iravu, ēṉ inta kaṉavu'	'Why this night? Why this dream?'	www.youtube.com/watch?v=hkrzWeGagvE
6	'Uṉṉai oṉṟu kēṭpēṉ'	'I'll ask you one thing'	www.youtube.com/watch?v=WxD3YWmTJFE
7	'Eṉ vāṉilē orē veṇṇilā'	'In my sky, there is but one moon'	http://www.youtube.com/watch?v=72IlNd1fDOk
8	'Maṭai tiṟantu tāvum nati alai nāṉ'	'I am like a river flowing after the floodgates open'	www.youtube.com/watch?v=adef3uDP7bw
9	'Itu oru poṉ mālai poḻutu'	'This is a golden twilight time'	www.youtube.com/watch?v=UmfXm2T8OQs
10	'Potti vacca mallikai moṭṭu'	'The hidden jasmine flower'	www.youtube.com/watch?v=o4Os96UGTwc
11	'Muṉpē vā eṉ aṉpē vā'	'Come to me my love'	www.youtube.com/watch?v=-Z-Wq6xX_Ew
12	'Viṅkaṭanta jōtiyāy'	'Thou art a luminous light beyond galaxies'	www.youtube.com/watch?v=T8AB5dcEtAs

Works Cited

Academy of Motion Picture Arts and Sciences Research Council, 1938. *Motion Picture Sound Engineering*, New York: D. Van Nostrand Company, Inc.

Adams, John, 2009. CD liner notes to *Adams: City Noir*, Deutsche Grammophon 0289 479 0632 2 DDD GHD (2010), performed by the Los Angeles Philharmonic, conducted by Gustavo Dudamel

Adorno, Theodor and Hanns Eisler, 2007 [1947]. *Composing for the Films, with a new introduction by Graham McCann*, London: Athlone Press

Adorno, Theodor and Max Horkheimer, 2002 [1947]. *Dialectic of Enlightenment*, trans. E. Jephcott, Stanford: Stanford University Press

Allison, Tanine, 2015. 'Blackface, *Happy Feet*: The Politics of Race in Motion Capture and Animation', in North *et al.* 2015, 114–26

Alter, Nora M., 2012. 'Composing in Fragments: Music in the Essay Films of Resnais and Godard', *SubStance* 41/2 (Issue 128), 24–39

Altman, Rick, 1980. ed. 'Special Issue: Cinema/Sound', *Yale French Studies* 60
   1987. *The American Film Musical*, Bloomington and Indianapolis: Indiana University Press
   2004. *Silent Film Sound*, New York: Columbia University Press
   2013. 'The Musical as International Genre: Reading Notes', in Creekmur and Mokdad 2013, 257–64

Anderson, Tim, 1997. 'Reforming "Jackass" Music': The Problematic Aesthetics of Early American Film Music Accompaniment', *Cinema Journal* 37/1, 3–22

Arijon, Daniel, 1976. *Grammar of the Film Language*, London: Focal Press

Armour, Nicole, 2001. 'Back in the Moulin Rouge: Everything Old Is New Again', *Cinema Scope* 7 (Spring), 8–11

Arnheim, Rudolph, 1933 [1932]. *Film*, trans. L. M. Sieveking and Ian F. D. Morrow, London: Faber and Faber
   1957. *Film as Art*, Berkeley: University of California Press
   2002 [1932]. *Film als Kunst*, Frankfurt: Suhrkamp

Arnold, Alison, 1988. 'Popular film song in India: A case of Mass Market Music Eccleticism', *Popular Music* 7/2, 177–88

Arvey, Verna, 1937. 'Composing for the Pictures by the Noted Austrian Master Erich Korngold. An Interview', *Etude* 55/1 (January), 15–16, http://thompsonian.info/korngold-etude-Jan-1937.html (13 August 2015)

Attali, Jacques, 1985. *Noise: The Political Economy of Music*, Manchester: Manchester University Press

Attinello, Paul, Janet K. Halfyard and Vanessa Knights, 2010. eds. *Music, Sound and Silence in* Buffy the Vampire Slayer, Farnham: Ashgate

Aucoin, Don, 2006. 'The Pornification of America', *Boston Globe*, 24 January, www.boston.com/yourlife/articles/2006/01/24/the_pornification_of_america/?page=full (28 May 2015)

Babb, Paul and Gay Owen, 1988. *Bonzo: The Life and Work of George Studdy*, Shepton Beauchamp, Somerset: Richard Dennis

Baker, Michael Brendan, 2011. 'Rockumentary: Style, Performance, and Sound in a Documentary Genre', PhD diss., Montreal: McGill University

Bal, Mieke, 2009. *Narratology: Introduction to the Theory of Narrative*, 3rd edn, Toronto: University of Toronto Press

Balázs, Béla, 1970 [1952]. *Theory of the Film: Character and Growth of a New Art*, trans. Edith Bone, New York: Dover

Baraka, Amiri [LeRoi Jones], 1963. *Blues People*, New York: William Morrow

Barker, Jennifer M., 2009. *The Tactile Eye: Touch and the Cinematic Experience*, Berkeley: University of California Press

Barnouw, Erik and Subrahmanyam Krishnaswamy, 1980 [1963]. *Indian Film*, 2nd edn, New York: Oxford University Press

Barrios, Richard, 1995. *A Song in the Dark: The Birth of the Musical Film*, New York: Oxford University Press

Barthes, Roland, 1977. *Image-Music-Text*, essays selected and trans. by Stephen Heath, London: Fontana Press

Bartkowiak, Mathew J., 2010. ed. *Sounds of the Future: Essays on Music in Science Fiction Film*, Jefferson, NC: McFarland

Bartoli, Claire, 1997. 'Interior View', trans. John M. King. CD liner notes to *Jean-Luc Godard: Nouvelle Vague* (ECM 1600/01), 68–94

Baudry, Jean-Louis, 1976. 'The Apparatus', *Camera Obscura* 1/1, 104–26

Bazin, André, 1985. 'On the politique des auteurs', *Cahiers du cinéma* 70 (April 1957), reproduced in Hillier 1985, 248–59

2005 [1967]. *What Is Cinema?*, vol. 1, trans. Hugh Gray, Berkeley: University of California Press

Beckman, Karen, 2014. ed. *Animating Film Theory*, Durham and London: Duke University Press

Behlmer, Rudy, 1986. *Inside Warner Bros. (1935–51)*, London: Weidenfeld and Nicolson

Bellman, Jonathan, 1998. ed. *The Exotic in Western Music*, Boston: Northeastern University Press

Belton, John, 1999. 'Awkward Transitions: Hitchcock's *Blackmail* and the Dynamics of Early Film Sound', *Musical Quarterly* 83/2, 227–46

Bergstrom, Janet, 2005. 'Murnau, Movietone, and Mussolini', *Film History* 17/2, 187–204

Beynon, George W., 1921. *Musical Presentation of Motion Pictures*, New York: Schirmer

Bhaskaran, Theodore S., 1991. 'Music for the Masses: Film Songs of Tamil Nadu', *Economic and Political Weekly* 26/11–12, 755–58

1996. *The Eye of the Serpent: An Introduction to Tamil Cinema*, Madras: East West Books

Biancorosso, Giorgio, 2001. 'Beginning Credits and Beyond: Music and the Cinematic Imagination', *ECHO: A Music-Centered Journal* 3/1, www.echo.ucla.edu/Volume3-Issue1/biancorosso/index.html (29 May 2015)

2002. 'Where Does the Music Come From? Studies in the Aesthetics of Film Music', PhD diss., Princeton: Princeton University

2009. 'The Harpist in the Closet: Film Music as Epistemological Joke', *Music and the Moving Image* 2/3, 11–33

Biesen, Sheri Chinen, 2014. *Music in the Shadows: Noir Musical Films*, Baltimore, MD: Johns Hopkins University Press

Blake, Larry, 1984a. 'Mixing Dolby Stereo Film Sound', in Lambert 1984, 1–10
    1984b. 'Re-Recording and Post Production for Disney's Fantasia', in Lambert 1984, 19–24

Boehlert, Eric, 2006. 'Conservatives Attack Animated Penguin Movie as Global-Warming Propaganda', *Media Matters for America*, 30 November, http://media matters.org/research/2006/11/30/conservatives-attack-animated-penguin-movie-as/137421 (28 May 2015)

Böll, Heinrich, 1972. 'Will Ulrike Meinhof Gnade oder freies Geleit?' ('Does Ulrike Meinhof Want Mercy or Safe Conduct?'), *Der Spiegel*, 10 January
    1974. *Die verlorene Ehre der Katharina Blum, oder: Wie Gewalt entstehen und wohin sie führen kann*, Köln: Kiepenheuer & Witsch
    1975. *The Lost Honour of Katharina Blum, or: How Violence Develops and Where It Can Lead*, trans. Leila Vennewitz, London: Secker and Warburg
    1994 [1975]. *The Lost Honor of Katharina Blum, or: How Violence Develops and Where It Can Lead*, trans. Leila Vennewitz, New York: Penguin Books

Bologna, Corrado, 1992. *Flatus vocis. Metafisica e antropologia della voce*, Bologna: Il Mulino

Bonitzer, Pascal, 1975. 'The Silences of the Voice', reprinted in Rosen 1986, 319–34

Booth, Gregory D. and Bradley Shope, 2014. eds. *More than Bollywood: Studies in Indian Popular Music*, New York: Oxford University Press

Borde, Raymond and Etienne Chaumeton, 1955. *Panorama du Film Noir Américain*, Paris: Les Éditions de Minuit
    1996 [1955]. 'Towards a Definition of Film Noir', trans. Alain Silver, in Silver and Ursini 1996, 17–25
    2002 [1955]. *A Panorama of American Film Noir 1941–1953*, trans.
    Paul Hammond, San Francisco: City Lights Books

Bordwell, David, 1980. 'The Music Analogy', *Yale French Studies* 60 (special issue Cinema/Sound), 141–56
    1985. *Narration in the Fiction Film*, Madison: University of Wisconsin Press
    1996. 'Contemporary Film Theory and the Vicissitudes of Grand Theory', in Bordwell and Carroll 1996, 3–36
    2014. 'Say hello to GOODBYE TO LANGUAGE', blog post, www.davidbordwell .net/blog/2014/11/02/say-hello-to-goodby-to-language/ (1 May 2015)

Bordwell, David and Noël Carroll, 1996. eds. *Post-Theory: Reconstructing Film Studies*, Madison: University of Wisconsin Press

Bordwell, David and Kristin Thompson, 2010. *Film Art: An Introduction*, 9th edn, New York: McGraw-Hill

Bordwell, David, Janet Staiger and Kristin Thompson, 1985. *The Classical Hollywood Cinema: Film Style and Mode of Production to 1960*, New York: Columbia University Press

Born, Georgina and David Hesmondhalgh, 2000. eds. *Western Music and Its Others: Difference, Representation, and Appropriation in Music*, Berkeley: University of California Press

Bould, Mark, 2013. 'Genre, Hybridity, Heterogeneity: or, the Noir-SF-Vampire-Zombie-Splatter-Romance-Comedy-Action-Thriller Problem', in Spicer and Hanson 2013, 33–49

Bould, Mark, Kathrina Glitre and Greg Tuck, 2009. eds. *Neo-Noir*, London: Wallflower Press

Box Office Mojo, 2015. www.boxofficemojo.com (28 May 2015)

Branigan, Edward, 1992. *Narrative Comprehension and Film*, London and New York: Routledge

Braudy, Leo and Marshall Cohen, 2009. eds. *Film Theory and Criticism: Introductory Readings*, 7th edn, New York and Oxford: Oxford University Press

Brody, Richard, 2014. 'Getting Jazz Right in the Movies', *New Yorker Online*, www.newyorker.com/culture/richard-brody/whiplash-getting-jazz-right-movies (13 October 2014)

Brophy, Philip, 2001. ed. *Cinesonic: Experiencing the Soundtrack*, Moore Park, NSW: Australian Film Television and Radio School

Brown, Julie, 2010. 'Carnival of Souls and the Organs of Horror', in Lerner 2010, 1–20

Brown, Noel, 2012. *The Hollywood Family Film: A History, from Shirley Temple to Harry Potter*, e-book, London: I. B. Tauris

Brown, Royal S., 1980. 'Music and *Vivre sa vie*', *Quarterly Review of Film Studies* 5/3 (Summer 1980), 319–33; reprinted in R. S. Brown 1994, 188–99

   1994. *Overtones and Undertones: Reading Film Music*, Berkeley and Los Angeles: University of California Press

Brownrigg, Mark, 2003. 'Film Music and Film Genre', PhD diss., Stirling: Stirling University

Buchan, Suzanne, 2013. *Pervasive Animation*, London and New York: Routledge

Buhler, James, 2001. 'Analytical and Interpretive Approaches to Film Music (II): Analysing Interactions of Music and Film', in Donnelly 2001, 39–61

   2010. 'Wagnerian Motives: Narrative Integration and the Development of Silent Film Accompaniment, 1908–1913', in Gilman and Joe 2010, 27–45

   2014a. 'Ontological, Formal, and Critical Theories of Film Music and Sound', in Neumeyer 2014, 188–225

   2014b. 'Psychoanalysis, Apparatus Theory, and Subjectivity', in Neumeyer 2014, 383–417

Buhler, James and David Neumeyer, 2014. 'Music and the Ontology of the Sound Film: The Classical Hollywood System', in Neumeyer 2014, 17–43

Buhler, James, David Neumeyer and Rob Deemer, 2010. *Hearing the Movies: Music and Sound in Film History*, New York: Oxford University Press

Buhler, James, David Neumeyer and Caryl Flinn, 2000. eds. *Music and Cinema*, Hanover: University Press of New England/Wesleyan University Press

Bull, Michael and Les Back, 2003. eds. *The Auditory Culture Reader*, Oxford: Berg

Bullerjahn, Claudia, 2008. 'Gender-Konstruktion durch Filmmusik. Eine analytische Betrachtung am Beispiel der Vertonung von Frauenfiguren in Filmen von Alfred

Hitchcock und im neueren Frauenfilm', *Kieler Beiträge zur Filmmusikforschung* 2, 7–26, www.filmmusik.uni-kiel.de/artikel/KB2-Bullerjahnarc.pdf (29 May 2015)

2014. *Grundlagen der Wirkung von Filmmusik*, 2. unveränderte Auflage, Augsburg: Wißner-Verlag

Burt, Peter, 2001. *The Music of Tōru Takemitsu*, Cambridge: Cambridge University Press

Burton-Page, Piers, 1994. *Philharmonic Concerto: The Life and Music of Sir Malcolm Arnold*, London: Methuen

Buskin, Richard, 1994. *Beatle Crazy! Memories and Memorabilia*, London: Salamander

Butler, David, 2002. *Jazz Noir: Listening to Music from* Phantom Lady *to* The Last Seduction, Westport, CT: Praeger Press

Butler, Michael, 1994. ed. *The Narrative Fiction of Heinrich Böll*, Cambridge: Cambridge University Press

Byrnes, Paul, 2015. '*Happy Feet*: Curator's notes', *Australian Screen*, http://aso.gov .au/titles/features/happy-feet/notes/ (28 May 2015)

Cage, John, 1961. *Silence: Lectures and Writings*, London: Marion Boyars

Campbell, Edward, 2013. *Music After Deleuze*, London: Bloomsbury

Carlyle, Angus, 2007. ed. *Autumn Leaves: Sound and the Environment in Artistic Practice*, Paris: Double Entendre

Carpitella, Diego, 1985. 'Il mito del primitivo nella musica moderna', in *Studi Musicali* 14/1, reprinted with variations in Nuova Consonanza, ed., *Il mito del primitivo nella musica moderna (Parte I), XXVI Festival*, Rome: Semar, 1989, 13–27

Carr, Roy, 1996. *Beatles at the Movies: Scenes from a Career*, London: UFO Music Ltd.

Carroll, Brendan, 1997. *The Last Prodigy: A Biography of Erich Wolfgang Korngold*, Portland, OR: Amadeus Press

Carroll, Noël, 1996. *Theorizing the Moving Image*, Cambridge: Cambridge University Press

Cazdyn, Eric, 2002. *The Flash of Capital: Film and Geopolitics in Japan*, Durham, NC: Duke University Press

Cecchi, Alessandro, 2010. 'Diegetic versus Nondiegetic: a Reconsideration of the Conceptual Opposition as a Contribution to the Theory of Audiovision', *Worlds of AudioVision*, www-5.unipv.it/wav/index.php?option=com_content&view=ar ticle&id=71&lang=en (17 July 2015)

Cenciarelli, Carlo, 2012. 'Dr Lecter's Taste for "Goldberg", or: The Horror of Bach in the Hannibal Franchise', *Journal of the Royal Musical Association* 137/1, 107–34

Chandravarkar, Bhaskar 1987. 'The Tradition of Music in Indian Cinema: Birth of the Film Song', *Cinema in India* 1/2, 7–11

Chatman, Seymour, 1978. *Story and Discourse: Narrative Structure in Fiction and Film*, Ithaca and London: Cornell University Press

Chattah, Juan, 2006. 'Semiotics, Pragmatics and Metaphor in Film Music Analysis', DPhil diss., Florida State University

Chion, Michel, 1994. *AudioVision: Sound on Screen*, trans. Claudia Gorbman, New York: Columbia University Press

1995a. *La musique au cinéma*, Paris: Fayard

1995b. *David Lynch*, trans. Robert Julian, London: British Film Institute

1999. *The Voice in Cinema*, trans. Claudia Gorbman, New York: Columbia University Press

2009 [2003]. *Film: A Sound Art*, trans. Claudia Gorbman, New York: Columbia University Press

Cholodenko, Alan, 1991. *The Illusion of Life: Essays on Animation*, Sydney: Power Publications

2007. *The Illusion of Life II: More Essays on Animation*, Sydney: Power Publications

Clair, René, 1953. *Reflections on the Cinema*, trans. Vera Traill, London: William Kimber

Clark, L. E. and John K. Hilliard, 1938. 'Types of Film Recording', in Academy of Motion Picture Arts and Sciences Research Council 1938, 23–43

Coates, Paul, 1994. *Film at the Intersection of High and Mass Culture*, Cambridge: Cambridge University Press

Cohan, Steven, 1997. *Masked Men: Masculinity and the Movies in the Fifties*, Bloomington and Indianapolis: Indiana University Press

Cohen, Annabel, J., 2010. 'Music as a Source of Emotion in Film', in Juslin and Sloboda 2010, 879–908

2014. 'Film Music from the Perspective of Cognitive Science', in Neumeyer 2014, 96–130

Cohen, Danny, 2011. 'Is the Background Music Too Loud?', www.bbc.co.uk/blogs/legacy/tv/2011/03/is-the-background-music-too-loud.shtml (15 June 2015)

Cohen, Karl F., 1997. *Forbidden Animation: Censored Cartoons and Blacklisted Animators in America*, Jefferson, NC: McFarland

Cohen, Thomas F., 2009. *Playing to the Camera: Musicians and Musical Performance in Documentary Cinema*, London and New York: Wallflower

Colpi, Henri, 1963. *Défense et illustration de la musique dans le film*, Lyon: SERDOC

Colvin, Sarah, 2009. *Ulrike Meinhof and West German Terrorism: Language, Violence, and Identity*, Rochester: Camden House

Comisso, Irene, 2012. 'Theory and Practice in Erdmann/Becce/Brav's *Allgemeines Handbuch der Film-Musik* (1927)', *Journal of Film Music* 5/1–2, 93–100

Conard, Robert C., 1992. *Understanding Heinrich Böll*, Columbia, SC: University of South Carolina

Conley, Tom and T. Jefferson Kline, 2014. eds. *A Companion to Jean-Luc Godard*, West Sussex: Wiley-Blackwell

Connor, Steven, 2013. 'Sounding Out Film', in Richardson *et al.* 2013, 107–20

Conrich, Ian and Estella Tincknell, 2006. eds. *Film's Musical Moments*, Edinburgh: Edinburgh University Press

Cook, Nicholas, 1998. *Analysing Musical Multimedia*, Oxford: Clarendon Press

Cooke, Mervyn, 2008. *A History of Film Music*, Cambridge: Cambridge University Press

2010. ed. *The Hollywood Film Music Reader*, New York: Oxford University Press

2015. 'Water Music: Scoring the Silent World', in Rogers 2015, 104–22

Cooper, David, 2001. *Bernard Herrmann's* Vertigo: *A Film Score Guide*, Westport, CT, and London: Greenwood Press

   2005. *Bernard Herrmann's* The Ghost and Mrs. Muir: *A Film Score Guide*, Lanham, MD: Scarecrow Press

Copeland, Peter, 1991. *Sound Recordings*, London: The British Library

Copjec, Joan, 1993. ed. *Shades of Noir*, London: Verso

Copland, Aaron, 1949. 'Tip to Moviegoers: Take off Those Ear-Muffs', *New York Times*, 6 November, section 6, 28–32; reprinted in Cooke 2010, 320–26

Coryton, Demitri and Joseph Murrells, 1990. *Hits of the 60s: The Million Sellers*, London: B. T. Batsford

Coulthard, Lisa, 2013. 'Dirty Sound: Haptic Noise in New Extremism', in Vernallis *et al.* 2013, 115–26

Cousins, Margaret E. 1935. *The Music of the Orient and Occident: Essays Towards Mutual Understanding*, Madras: B. G. Paul

Coyle, Rebecca, 2009a. 'Special Issue: Thwack! Hearing the motion in animation (editorial)', *Animation Journal* 17, 3–6

   2009b. 'Spooked by Sound: The Blair Witch Project', in Philip Hayward 2009, 213–28

   2010. ed. *Drawn to Sound: Animation Film Music and Sonicity*, London and Oakville: Equinox

Crafton, Donald, 1996. '*The Jazz Singer*'s Reception in the Media and at the Box Office', in Bordwell and Carroll 1996, 460–81

   1997. *The Talkies: American Cinema's Transition to Sound, 1926–1931*, New York: Simon & Schuster

Crawford, Merritt, 1931. 'Pioneer Experiments of Eugene Lauste in Recording Sound', *Journal of the Society of Motion Picture Engineers* 17/4, 632–44

Creed, Barbara, 1986. 'Horror and the Monstrous-Feminine: An Imaginary Abjection', *Screen* 27/1 (January–February), 44–71

Creekmur, Corey K. and Linda Y. Mokdad, 2013. eds. *The International Film Musical*, Edinburgh: Edinburgh University Press

Dalmia, Vasudha and Rashmi Sadhana, 2012. eds. *The Cambridge Companion to Modern Indian Culture*, Cambridge: Cambridge University Press

Daniel, Estelle, 2000. *The Art of Gormenghast: The Making of a Television Fantasy*, London: Harper Collins

Danly, Linda, 1999. ed. *Hugo Friedhofer: The Best Years of His Life: A Hollywood Master of Music for the Movies*, Lanham, MD: Scarecrow Press

Daubney, Kate, 2000. *Max Steiner's* Now, Voyager: *A Film Score Guide*, Westport, CT, and London: Greenwood Press

Davis, Miles, 1988. *Ascenseur pour l'échafaud: Complete Recordings* (Fontana CD 840 813-2)

Davis, Nick, 2012. 'Inside/Outside the Klein Bottle: Music in Narrative Film, Intrusive and Integral', *Music, Sound, and the Moving Image* 6/1, 9–19

Davison, Annette, 2004. *Hollywood Theory, Non-Hollywood Practice: Cinema Soundtracks in the 1980s and 1990s*, Aldershot: Ashgate

   2007. 'Copyright and Scholars' Rights', *Music, Sound, and the Moving Image* 1/1, 9–13

De Fornari, Oreste, 1984. *Tutti i film di Sergio Leone*, Milano: Ubulibri

De la Motte-Haber, Helga and Hans Emons, 1980. *Filmmusik. Eine systematische Beschreibung*, Munich and Vienna: Carl Hanser Verlag

De Melis, Francesco, 1989. 'Leone e Morricone. Silenzio di suoni', *Dolce vita* 3/22–3, 12–14

Deaville, James, 2010. 'The Beauty of Horror: Kilar, Coppola, and Dracula', in Lerner 2010, 187–205

Deguchi, Tomoko, 2010. 'Gaze from the Heavens, Ghost from the Past: Symbolic Meanings in Toru Takemitsu's Music for Akira Kurosawa's Film, *Ran* (1985)', *Journal of Film Music* 3/1, 51–64

Demers, Joanna, 2010. *Listening Through Noise: The Aesthetics of Experimental Electronic Music*, Oxford: Oxford University Press

Derrida, Jacques, 1997. *Of Grammatology*, corrected edition, trans. Gayatri Chakravorty Spivak, Baltimore, MD: Johns Hopkins University Press

Dietz, Rob, 2006. 'Beck Gives Thumbs Down to Penguin Movie *Happy Feet* – "an animated version of *An Inconvenient Truth*"', *Media Matters for America*, 21 November, http://mediamatters.org/research/2006/11/21/beck-gives-thumbs-down-to-penguin-movie-happy-f/137371 (28 May 2015)

Donnelly, Kevin, 2001. ed. *Film Music: Critical Approaches*, New York: Continuum
2005. *Music in Film and Television: The Spectre of Sound*, London: BFI
2010. 'Hearing Deep Seated Fears: John Carpenter's *The Fog* (1980)', in Lerner 2010, 152–67

Donnelly, Kevin J. and Philip Hayward, 2013. eds. *Music in Science Fiction Television: Tuned to the Future*, Routledge: New York

Drake, Philip, 2003. ' "Mortgaged to Music": New Retro Movies in 1990s Hollywood Cinema', in Grainge 2003, 183–201

Duchen, Jessica, 1996. *Erich Wolfgang Korngold*, London: Phaidon

Duncan, Dean, 2003. *Charms that Soothe: Classical Music and the Narrative Film*, New York: Fordham University Press

Dusapin, Pascal, 2006. 'Telling a tale of Faustus . . .'. Liner notes for DVD of *Faustus, The Last Night* (Naïve M0 782177), 15–19

Dyer, Richard, 1981. 'Sweet Charity', *The Movie: The Illustrated History of the Cinema*, Issue 75, London: Orbis Publishing, 1484–5
1985. 'Entertainment and Utopia', in Nichols 1985, 200–32
2001. *The Culture of Queers*, New York: Routledge
2011. *In the Space of a Song: The Uses of Song in Film*, New York: Routledge

Edison, Thomas A., 1888. Handwritten Patent Caveat 110, filed 17 October 1888, Thomas A. Edison Papers Digital Edition PT031AAA, http://edison.rutgers.edu (1 September 2016)

Eisenstein, Sergei M., 1942. *The Film Sense*, trans. Jay Leyda. San Diego, CA: Harcourt Brace & Company
1949. *Film Form: Essays in Film Theory*, trans. Jay Leyda. San Diego, CA: Harcourt Brace & Company

Eisenstein, Sergei M., Vsevolod I. Pudovkin and Grigori V. Alexandrov, 1928. 'A Statement [on Sound]', trans. Jay Leyda, in Weis and Belton 1985, 83–5

Elsaesser, Thomas, 1989. *New German Cinema: A History*, London: British Film Institute

Elsaesser, Thomas and Malte Hagener, 2010. *Film Theory: An Introduction through the Senses*, New York and London: Routledge

Emmelhainz, Irmgard, 2009. 'Before Our Eyes: Les Mots, Non Les Choses. Jean-Luc Godard's *Ici et Ailleurs* (1970–74) and *Notre Musique* (2004)', PhD diss., University of Toronto

⎯⎯ 2014. 'Jean-Luc Godard: To Liberate Things from the Name that We Have Imposed on Them (Film . . .) to Announce Dissonances Parting from a Note in Common (Socialisme)', in Conley and Kline 2014, 527–45

Engel, Lehman, 1975. *The American Musical Theater*, London: Macmillan

Erdmann, Hans, Giuseppe Becce and Ludwig Brav, 1927. *Allgemeines Handbuch der Film-Musik*, 2 vols, Berlin-Lichterfelde: Schlesinger'sche Buch

Erlmann, Veit, 2004. ed. *Hearing Cultures: Essays on Sound, Listening, and Modernity*, Oxford: Berg

Evens, Aden, 2005. *Sound Ideas: Music, Machines and Experience*, Minneapolis: University of Minnesota Press

Everett, Yayoi Uno, 2010. 'Infusing Modern Subjectivity into a Premodern Narrative Form: Masahiro Shinoda and Toru Takemitsu's Collaboration in *Double Suicide* (1968)', *Journal of Film Music* 3/1, 37–49

Everett, Yayoi Uno and Frederick Lau, 2004. eds. *Locating East Asia in Western Art Music*, Middletown, CT: Wesleyan University Press

Falcon, Richard, 1997. '"The Obscure Object of Redemption" in Two Adaptations of Heinrich Böll', in Huber and Conard 1997, 163–72

Farmer, Brett, 2000. *Spectacular Passions: Cinema, Fantasy, Gay Male Spectatorships*, Durham, NC: Duke University Press

Fenimore, Ross J., 2010. 'Voices That Lie Within: The Heard and Unheard in *Psycho*', in Lerner 2010, 80–97

Feuer, Jane, 1993 [1982]. *The Hollywood Musical*, 2nd edn, Bloomington: Indiana University Press

Fielding, Raymond, 1967. ed. *A Technological History of Motion Pictures and Television*, Berkeley: University of California Press

Fischer, Lucy, 1977. 'René Clair, *Le Million*, and the Coming of Sound', *Cinema Journal* 16/2, 34–50

Fleeger, Jennifer, 2009. 'Opera, Jazz, and Hollywood's Conversion to Sound', PhD diss., University of Iowa

⎯⎯ 2014a. *Sounding American: Hollywood, Opera, and Jazz*, New York: Oxford University Press

⎯⎯ 2014b, *Mismatched Women: The Siren's Song Through the Machine*, Oxford: Oxford University Press

Flinn, Caryl, 1992. *Strains of Utopia: Gender, Nostalgia, and Hollywood Film Music*, Princeton: Princeton University Press

⎯⎯ 2013. 'Musical Feeling: Pride and Shame', Keynote, Queer Sounds and Spaces symposium, University of Turku, Finland, October

Ford, Fiona, 2011. 'The Film Music of Edmund Meisel (1894–1930)', PhD diss.,
University of Nottingham, http://eprints.nottingham.ac.uk/12271/
(13 August 2015)

Forlenza, Jeff and Terri Stone, 1993. eds. *Sound For Picture*, California: Hal Leonard

Fragoso, Sam, 2015. 'Dispatch from Ebertfest: Goodbye to Understanding with Jean-
Luc Godard', www.rogerebert.com/festivals-and-awards/ebertfest-goodbye-to-
understanding-with-jean-luc-godard (17 April 2015)

Franklin, Peter, 2011. *Seeing Through Music. Gender and Modernism in Classic
Hollywood Film Scores*, New York: Oxford University Press

   2014. *Reclaiming Late-Romantic Music. Singing Devils and Distant Sounds*,
Berkeley, Los Angeles and London: University of California Press

Frayling, Chistopher, 2000. *Sergio Leone. Something to Do with Death*, London:
Faber and Faber

   2008 [2005], *Sergio Leone. Once Upon a Time in Italy*, London: Thames & Hudson

Frayne, John G., 1976. 'Motion Picture Sound Recording: A Capsule History',
Journal of the Audio Engineering Society 24/6, 512–16

Frederick, Halsey A., 1928. 'Recent Advances in Wax Recording', *Transactions of the
Society of Motion Picture Engineers* 12/35, 709–29

Frederick, Prince, 2010. 'Memories of Madras-Bands, Banquet and Bach',
The Hindu, 6 April, www.thehindu.com/features/metroplus/memories-of-
madras-bands-banquet-and-bach/article389583.ece (3 March 2015)

Fuchs, Maria, 2014. '"The Hermeneutic Framing of Film Music Practice":
The *Allgemeines Handbuch der Film-Musik* in the Context of Historico-
musicological Traditions', in Tieber and Windisch 2014, 156–71

Furniss, Maureen, 1998. *Art in Motion: Animation Aesthetics*, London and Sydney:
John Libbey

   2008. *The Animation Bible*, London: Laurence King

Gabbard, Krin, 1996. *Jammin' at the Margins: Jazz and the American Cinema*,
Chicago: University of Chicago Press

   2004. *Black Magic: White Hollywood and African American Culture*, New
Brunswick, NJ: Rutgers University Press

Gallez, Douglas W., 1970. 'Theories of Film Music', *Cinema Journal* 9/2, 40–7

Garcia, Desirée J., 2014. *The Migration of Musical Film: From Ethnic Margins to
American Mainstream*, New Brunswick, NJ: Rutgers University Press

Garity, William E. and J. N. A. Hawkins, 1941. 'Fantasound', *Journal of the Society of
Motion Picture Engineers* 37/8 (August), 127–46

Garofalo, Marcello, 1999. *Tutto il cinema di Sergio Leone*, Milano: Baldini & Castoldi

Gaudreault, André, 2009 [1988]. *From Plato to Lumière: Narration and Monstration in
Literature and Cinema*, trans. T. Barnard, Toronto: University of Toronto Press

Gaumont, Leon, 1959. 'Gaumont Chronochrome Process Described by the
Inventor', reprinted in Fielding 1967, 65–7

Gelmis, Joseph, 1971. *The Film Director as Superstar*, London: Secker and Warburg

Genette, Gérard, 1980 [1972]. *Narrative Discourse*, trans. J. E. Lewin, Cambridge:
Cambridge University Press

Gengaro, Christine Lee, 2012. *Listening to Stanley Kubrick: The Music in His Films*,
Plymouth: Scarecrow

Gerstner, David A. and Janet Staiger, 2003. eds. *Authorship and Film*, New York: Routledge

Getter, Joseph, 2014. 'Kollywood Goes Global: New Sounds and Contexts for Tamil Film Music in the 21st Century', in Booth and Shope 2014, 60-74

Getter, Joseph and B. Balasubrahmaniyan, 2008. 'Tamil Film Music: Sound and Significance', in Slobin 2008, 114-51

Giddins, Gary, 2006. 'Miles Goes Modal', bonus feature on DVD of *Elevator to the Gallows* (dir. Louis Malle, 1958), Criterion Collection 335

Gilman, Sander L. and Jeongwon Joe, 2010. eds. *Wagner and Cinema*, Bloomington: Indiana University Press

Gittins, Sean, 2012. '*Film Socialisme*', *Philosophy Now* 89, https://philosophynow.org/issues/89/Film_Socialisme (1 May 2015)

Glynn, Stephen, 2013. *The British Pop Music Film: The Beatles and Beyond*, London: Palgrave Macmillan

Godard, Jean-Luc, 1968. 'Interview-montage with Abraham Segal', *Image et son* 215 (March)

 1991 [1985]. *Godard par Godard: Des années Mao aux années 80*, Paris: Flammarion

Godsall, Jonathan, 2013. 'Pre-existing Music in Fiction Sound Film', PhD diss., Bristol: University of Bristol

Goldmark, Daniel, 2001. 'Happy Harmonies: Music and the Animated Hollywood Cartoon', PhD diss., Los Angeles: University of California

 2005. *Tunes for 'Toons: Music and the Hollywood Cartoon*, Berkeley, Los Angeles and London: University of California Press

Goldmark, Daniel and Yuval Taylor, 2002. eds. *The Cartoon Music Book*, Chicago: A Cappella

Goldmark, Daniel, Lawrence Kramer and Richard Leppert, 2007. eds. *Beyond the Soundtrack: Representing Music in Cinema*, Berkeley and Los Angeles: University of California Press

Goldsmith, Kenneth, 2011. *Uncreative Writing: Managing Language in the Digital Age*, New York: Columbia University Press

Goldwasser, Dan, 2006. 'Toe Tappin' and Knee Slappin' with John Powell', *soundtrack.net* (November), www.soundtrack.net/content/article/?id=211 (28 May 2015)

Gomery, Douglas, 1976. 'Tri-Ergon, Tobis-Klangfilm, and the Coming of Sound', *Cinema Journal* 16/1, 51–61

 1980. 'Economic Struggle and Hollywood Imperialism: Europe Converts to Sound', *Yale French Studies* 60, 80–93

 1992. *Shared Pleasures: A History of Movie Presentation in the United States*, Madison: University of Wisconsin Press

 2005. *The Coming of Sound: A History*, New York: Routledge

Gorbman, Claudia, 1980. 'Narrative Film Music', *Yale French Studies* 60 (special issue Cinema/Sound), 183–203

 1987. *Unheard Melodies: Narrative Film Music*, Bloomington: Indiana University Press

 1991. 'Hanns Eisler in Hollywood', *Screen* 32/3, 272–85

 2000. 'Scoring the Indian: Music in the Liberal Western', in Born and Hesmondhalgh 2000, 234–53

2001. 'Drums along the LA River: Scoring the Indian', in Janet Walker 2001, 177–95

2007. 'Auteur Music', in Goldmark *et al.* 2007, 149–62

2015. 'The Master's Voice', *Film Quarterly* 68/2, 8–21

Grainge, Paul, 2003. ed. *Memory and Popular Film*, Manchester: Manchester University Press

Grange, Ann and Miroslav Sebestik, 1992. 'John Cage, Composer. NYC, 4 February 1991', in *Écoute*, http://vimeo.com/12597582 (28 October 2014)

Graser, Marc, 2014. 'Disney Brands Generate $40.9 Billion from Licensed Merchandise in 2013', *Variety*, 17 June, http://variety.com/2014/biz/news/dis ney-brands-generate-record-40-9-billion-from-licensed-merchandise-in-2013-1201221813/ (28 May 2015)

Greenwood, Jonny, 2005. *Popcorn Superhet Receiver*, for string orchestra, London: Faber Music

2011. *48 Responses to Polymorphia*, for string orchestra, London: Faber Music

Gregory, Richard L., 1987. ed. *The Oxford Companion to the Mind*, Oxford: Oxford University Press

Greydanus, Steven D., 2006. '*Happy Feet* (2006)', *Decent Films: SDG Reviews. Film appreciation and criticism informed by Christian faith*, http://decentfilms.com /reviews/happyfeet (28 May 2015)

Griffin, Sean, 2014. 'Don't Fence Me In: B Studio Musicals' Appeal to Marginalized Audiences', Society for Cinema and Media Studies Annual Conference, Chicago (20 March)

Griffiths, Paul, 2000. 'Godard's Mix of Movies and Music', *New York Times*, 2 July, http://www.nytimes.com/2000/07/02/movies/music-godard-s-mix-of-movies-and-music.html (2 January 2015)

Grilli, Peter, 2011. Commentary to DVD of *Pale Flower* (dir. Masahiro Shinoda, 1964), Criterion Collection 564

Gutiérrez, Laura G., 2010. *Performing Mexicanidad: Vendidas y Cabareteras on the Transnational Stage*, Austin: University of Texas Press

Guy, Randor, 2007. '*Nandakumar* (1938)', *The Hindu*, 12 October, www.thehindu .com/todays-paper/tp-features/tp-cinemaplus/nandakumar-1938/arti cle3023893.ece (3 March 2015)

2008. '*Apoorva Sagotharargal* (1949)', *The Hindu*, 27 June, www.thehindu.com /todays-paper/tp-features/tp-cinemaplus/apoorva-sahodarargal-1949/arti cle3023062.ece (3 March 2015)

Haas, Michael, 2014. *Forbidden Music: The Jewish Composers Banned by the Nazis*, New Haven, CT: Yale University Press

Habich, Christiane, 2008. *Erinnerungen an* Die verlorene Ehre der Katharina Blum (*Memories of* The Lost Honour of Katharina Blum), documentary film. Bonus feature on 2009 Blu-Ray disc *The Lost Honour of Katharina Blum* (StudioCanal Collection LUK0909)

Hacquard, Georges, 1959. *La musique et le cinema*, Paris: Presses universitaires de France

Hainge, Greg, 2013. *Noise Matters: Towards an Ontology of Noise*, New York: Bloomsbury

Halas, John and Joy Batchelor, 1954. 'Producing "Animal Farm"', *British Kinematography* 24/4 (April), 105–10

Halas, John and Roger Manvell, 1958. *The Technique of Film Animation*, London: Focal Press

Halas, Vivien and Paul Wells, 2006. *Halas and Batchelor Cartoons: An Animated History*, London: Southbank Publishing

Halfyard, Janet K., 2004. *Danny Elfman's* Batman: *A Film Score Guide*, Lanham, MD: Scarecrow Press

    2009. 'Music of the Night: Scoring the Vampire in Contemporary Film', in P. Hayward 2009, 171–85

    2012. ed. *The Music of Fantasy Cinema*, London: Equinox

Hall, Mordaunt, 1926a. 'Amazing Invention Coupling Sound with Screen Images Stirs Audiences', *New York Times*, 15 August, X2

    1926b. 'The Vitaphone and "The Better 'Ole"', *New York Times*, 8 October, 23

    1928. 'The Reaction of the Public to Motion Pictures with Sound', *Transactions of the Society of Motion Picture Engineers* 12/35, 603–13

Hamilton, Andy, 2007. 'Music and the Aural Arts', *British Journal of Aesthetics* 47/1, 46–63

Hanson, Helen, 2009. 'Paranoia and Nostalgia: Sonic Motifs and Songs in Neo-Noir', in Bould *et al.* 2009, 44–60

Harmetz, Aljean, 2002 [1992]. *The Making of* Casablanca. *Bogart, Bergman and World War II* [originally published as *Round up the Usual Suspects*], New York: Hyperion

Harris, Nigel, 1994. '*Die verlorene Ehre der Katharina Blum*: The Problem of Violence', in M. Butler 1994, 198–218

Hartmann, Britta, 2007. 'Diegetisieren, Diegese, Diskursuniversum', *montage/av* 16/2 (special issue Diegese), 53–69

Haworth, Catherine, 2012. 'Introduction: Gender, Sexuality, and the Soundtrack', *Music, Sound, and the Moving Image* 6/2, 113–35

Hayward, Philip, 2004. ed. *Off the Planet: Music, Sound and Science Fiction Cinema*, Eastleigh: John Libbey

    2009. ed. *Terror Tracks: Music, Sound and Horror Cinema*, Equinox: London

    2010. 'Polar Grooves: Dance, Music and Musicality in *Happy Feet*', in Coyle 2010, 90–103

    2013. 'Whimsical Complexity: Music and Sound Design in "The Clangers"', in Donnelly and P. Hayward 2013, 36–51

Hayward, Susan, 1996. *Key Concepts in Cinema Studies*, London: Routledge

Hegarty, Paul, 2007. *Noise/Music: A History*, London: Bloomsbury Continuum

Heldt, Guido, 2013. *Music and Levels of Narration in Film: Steps across the Border*, Bristol and Chicago: Intellect

Heldt, Guido, Tarek Krohn, Peter Moormann and Willem Strank, 2015. eds. *Martin Scorsese. Die Musikalität der Bilder*, Munich: edition text + kritik

Henriques, Julian F., 2003. 'Sonic Dominance and the Reggae Sound System Session', in Bull and Back 2003, 451–80

Henze, Hans Werner, 1971. 'Art and Revolution', reprinted in Henze 1982, 178–83

    1982. *Music and Politics: Collected Writings 1953–1981*, trans. P. Labanyi, London: Faber and Faber

1996. *Hans Werner Henze: Ein Werkverzeichnis, 1946–1996 [Hans Werner Henze: A Catalogue of Works, 1946–1996]*, Mainz and London: Schott

2002. Personal communication with Annette Davison by email via Christa Pfeffer, 19 June

Hickman, Roger, 2009. 'Wavering Sonorities and the Nascent Film Noir Musical Style', *Journal of Film Music* 2/2–4 (Winter), 165–74

Hillier, Jim, 1985. ed. *Cahiers du Cinéma. The 1950s: Neo-Realism, Hollywood, New Wave*, Cambridge, MA: Harvard University Press

Hochberg, Julian, 1987. 'Perception of Motion Pictures', in Gregory 1987, 604–8

Hogan, Mike, 2012. 'Paul Thomas Anderson, "The Master" Director, On Joaquin Phoenix, Dianetics and His "Natural Attraction" for Redheads', www.huffingtonpost .com/2012/09/11/paul-thomas-anderson-the-master_n_1874053.html (31 October 2014)

Holbrook, Morris B., 2011. *Music, Movies, Meanings, and Markets: Cinemajazzmatazz*, New York and London: Routledge

Horton, Robert, 1995. 'Music Man', *Film Comment* 31/6, 2–4

Hubai, Gergely, 2012. *Torn Music: Rejected Film Scores, a Selected History*, Los Angeles: Silman-James Press

Hubbert, Julie, 2011. ed. *Celluloid Symphonies: Texts and Contexts in Film Music History*, Berkeley: University of California Press

Huber, Lothar and Robert C. Conard, 1997. eds. *Heinrich Böll on Page and Screen: The London Symposium*, London: Institute of Germanic Studies, University of London, and University of Dayton Review 24/3

Hughes, Stephen P. 2002. 'The "Music Boom" in Tamil South India: Gramophone, Radio and the Making of Mass Culture', *Historical Journal of Film, Radio and Television* 22/4, 445–73

2007. 'Music in the Age of Mechanical Reproduction: Drama, Gramophone and the Beginnings of Tamil Cinema, *Journal of South Asian Studies* 66/1, 3–34

Hupfeld, Herman, n.d. [c. 1942]. 'As Time Goes By', words and music, London and Sydney: Chappell & Co. Ltd.; New York: Harms Inc.

Huron, David, 2002. 'Listening Styles and Listening Strategies'. Paper presented at the Society of Music Theory 2002 Conference, www.musiccog.ohio-state.edu /Huron/Talks/SMT.2002/handout.html (30 April 2015)

Hutchings, Peter, 2004. *The Horror Film*, Harlow: Pearson

Huyssen, Andreas, 1986. *After the Great Divide: Modernism, Mass Culture, Postmodernism*, Bloomington: Indiana University Press

Igma, Norman, 1988. 'Plunderphonics: an Interview with Transproducer John Oswald', www.plunderphonics.com/xhtml/xinterviews.html (30 April 2015)

Ihde, Don, 2007. *Listening and Voice: Phenomenologies of Sound*, New York: State University of New York

Ingold, Tim, 2007. 'Against Soundscape', in Carlyle 2007, 10–13

Ilayaraja, 1984. *Caṅkīta Kaṇavukaḷ*, Madras: Kalaignan Pathipagam

Jacobs, Lea, 2012. 'The Innovation of Re-Recording in the Hollywood Studios', *Film History* 24/1, 5–34

James, Alan, 1998. '*Godzilla*: A Monster Mix', *Audio Media* 91 (June), 84–6

Jameson, Fredric, 1991. *Postmodernism, or, the Cultural Logic of Late Capitalism*, London and New York: Verso

Jaszoltowski, Saskia, 2013. *Animierte Musik – Beseelte Zeichen. Tonspuren anthropomorpher Tiere in Animated Cartoons*, Stuttgart: Franz Steiner Verlag

Jewell, Richard B., 1995 [1984]. 'How Howard Hawks Brought Baby Up: An Apologia for the Studio System', in Staiger 1995, 39–49

Johnston, William A., 1928. 'The Public and Sound Pictures', *Transactions of the Society of Motion Picture Engineers* 12/35, 614–19

Jousse, Thierry, 1990. 'Godard à l'oreille', *Cahiers du cinéma* (special out-of-series issue: Spécial Godard: 30 ans depuis), supplement to *Cahiers du cinéma* 437 (November 1990), 40–3

    2000. CD liner notes to *Les Écrans Sonores De Jean-Luc Godard* (Signature CD SIG 11002)

Jullier, Laurent, 2004. 'JLG/ECM', in Temple *et al.* 2004, 272–87

Juslin, Patrik and John Sloboda, 2010. eds. *The Oxford Handbook of Music and Emotion: Theory, Research, Applications*, Oxford: Oxford University Press

Kabir, Nasreen Muni, 2001. *Bollywood: The Indian Cinema Story*, Basingstoke and Oxford: Pan Macmillan

    2011. *A. R. Rahman: The Spirit of Music*, Noida: Om Books International

Kael, Pauline, 1994. *For Keeps: 30 years at the Movies*, New York: E. P. Dutton

Kahn, Douglas, 1999. *Noise, Water, Meat: A History of Sound in the Arts*, Massachusetts: MIT Press

Kalinak, Kathryn, 1992. *Settling the Score: Music and the Classical Hollywood Film*, Madison: University of Wisconsin Press

    2007. *How the West was Sung: Music in the Westerns of John Ford*, Berkeley: University of California Press

    2012. ed. *Music in the Western: Notes from the Frontier*, New York and London: Routledge

Karlin, Fred and Rayburn Wright, 1990. *On The Track: A Guide to Contemporary Film Scoring*, New York: Schirmer Books

Kassabian, Anahid, 2001. *Hearing Film: Tracking Identifications in Contemporary Hollywood Film Music*, New York and London: Routledge

    2013. 'The End of the Diegesis as Know It?', in Richardson *et al.* 2013, 89–106

Keating, AnaLouise, 1998. '(De)Centering the Margins?: Identity Politics and Tactical (Re)naming', in Stanley 1998, 23–43

Kennedy, Joseph P., 1927. ed. *The Story of the Films: As Told by Leaders of the Industry to the Students of the Graduate School of Business Administration, George F. Baker Foundation, Harvard University*, Chicago and London: A. W. Shaw

Kenny, Tom, 1993. 'The Doors', in Forlenza and Stone 1993, 66–71

Kessler, Kelly, 2010. *Destabilizing the Hollywood Musical: Music, Masculinity and Mayhem*, Basingstoke, UK: Palgrave Macmillan

Keuchel, Susanne, 2000. *Das Auge hört mit . . . Rezeptionsforschung zur klassischen Musik im Spielfilm*, Bonn: ARCult-Media

Kilborn, Richard, 1984. *Whose Lost Honour? A Study of the Film Adaptation of Böll's 'The Lost Honour of Katharina Blum'*, Glasgow: Scottish Papers in Germanic Studies, vol. 4

King, Claire Sisco, 2010. 'Ramblin' Men and Piano Men: Crises of Music and Masculinity in The Exorcist', in Lerner 2010, 114–32

Kinnard, Roy, 1995. *Horror in Silent Films: A Filmography, 1896–1929*, Jefferson, NC: McFarland Classics

Kirby, Alan, 2009. *Digimodernism: How New Technologies Dismantle the Postmodern and Reconfigure Our Culture*, New York and London: Continuum

Klapholz, Jesse, 1991. '*Fantasia*: Innovations in Sound', *Journal of The Audio Engineering Society* 39/1–2, 66–70

Klein, Bethany, 2010. *As Heard on TV: Popular Music in Advertising*, 2nd edn, Farnham: Ashgate

Klein, Norman, 1993. *Seven Minutes; The Life and Death of the American Animated Cartoon*, London: Verso

Kloppenburg, Josef, 2000. ed. *Musik multimedial: Filmmusik, Videoclip, Fernsehen*, Laaber: Laaber-Verlag

Knapp, Raymond and Mitchell Morris, 2011. 'Tin Pan Alley Songs on Stage and Screen Before World War II', in Knapp *et al.* 2011, 81–96

Knapp, Raymond, Mitchell Morris and Stacy Wolf, 2011. eds. *The Oxford Handbook of the American Musical*, Oxford: Oxford University Press

Knecht, Peter, 1979. Review of *Watashi wa goze. Sugimoto Kikue kôden* (*I Am a Goze. The Story of Sugimoto Kikue*) by Ôyama Mahito and *Goze: Mômoku no tabi geinin* (*Goze: Blind Itinerant Entertainers*) by Saito Shinichi, *Asian Folklore Studies* 38/1, 139–42

Knight, Arthur, 2002. *Disintegrating the Musical: Black Performance and American Musical Film*, Durham, NC: Duke University Press

Knights, Vanessa, 2010. '"Bay City Rollers. Now That's Music": Music as Cultural Code in *Buffy the Vampire Slayer*', in Attinello *et al.* 2010, 1–14

Koozin, Timothy, 2010. 'Parody and Ironic Juxtaposition in Toru Takemitsu's Music for the Film *Rising Sun*', *Journal of Film Music* 3/1, 65–78

Korngold, Luzi, 1967. *Erich Wolfgang Korngold: Ein Lebensbild*, Vienna: Verlag Elisabeth Lafite

Kracauer, Siegfried, 1961. *Nature of Film: The Redemption of Physical Reality*, London: Dennis Dobson

Kreimeier, Klaus, 1996. *The UFA Story: A History of Germany's Greatest Film Company 1918–1945*, trans. Robert Kimber and Rita Kimber, New York: Hill and Wang

Kraft, James P., 1996. *Stage to Studio: Musicians and the Sound Revolution, 1890–1950*, Baltimore, MD: The Johns Hopkins University Press

Krutnik, Frank, 1991. *In a Lonely Street: Film Noir, Genre, Masculinity*, London: Routledge

Kulezic-Wilson, Daniela, 2011. 'Soundscapes of Trauma and the Silence of Revenge in Peter Strickland's *Katalin Varga*', *New Soundtrack* 1, 57–71

Lack, Russell, 1997. *Twenty Four Frames Under*, London: Quartet Books

Laing, Heather, 2004. *Gabriel Yared's* The English Patient: *A Film Score Guide*, Lanham, MD: Scarecrow Press

2007. *The Gendered Score: Music in 1940s Melodrama and the Woman's Film*, Aldershot and Burlington, VA: Ashgate

Laird, Paul, 2011. 'Musical Styles and Song Conventions', in Knapp *et al.* 2011, 33–44

Lambert, Kenneth, 1938. 'Re-recording and Preparation for Release', in Academy of Motion Picture Arts and Sciences Research Council 1938, 67–78

Lambert, Mel, 1984. ed. *Film Sound Today: An Anthology of Articles from Recording Engineer/Producer*, Hollywood: Reveille Press

Larkin, Mark, 1929. 'The Truth About Voice Doubling', *Photoplay Magazine* (July), 32–33, 108–10

Larsen, Peter, 2005. *Film Music*, London: Reaktion

Larson, Randall D., 1985. *Musique Fantastique: A Survey of Film Music in the Fantastic Cinema*, Metchuen, NJ: Scarecrow Press

Leadley, Simon, 2006. 'Happy Feet', *Audio Technology* 52, 52–8, www.audiotechnology .com.au/PDF/FEATURES/AT52_Sound_for_Happy_feet.pdf (28 May 2015)

Lees, Gene, 1975. 'Adventures of a Black Composer in Hollywood', *New York Times*, 16 March, Section 2, 21

　　2011 [1967]. 'The New Sound on the Soundtracks', in Hubbert 2011, 323–9

Lehman, Frank Martin, 2012. 'Reading Tonality through Film: Transformational Hermeneutics and the Music of Hollywood', PhD diss., Cambridge, MA: Harvard University

　　2013a. 'Transformational Analysis and the Representation of Genius in Film Music', *Music Theory Spectrum* 35/1, 1–22

　　2013b. 'Hollywood Cadences: Music and the Structure of Cinematic Expectation', *Music Theory Online* 19/4, www.mtosmt.org/issues/mto.13.19.4/mto.13.19.4.leh man.html (29 May 2015)

Leinberger, Charles, 2004. *Ennio Morricone's* The Good, the Bad and the Ugly: *A Film Score Guide*, Lanham, MD: Scarecrow Press

Lelyfeld, David, 1994. 'Upon the Subdominant: Administering Music on All-India-Radio', *Social Text* 39, 111–27

Leone, Sergio *et al.*, n.d. *C'era una volta Sergio Leone* (DVD set), DSC125492, n.pl.: CVC

Lerner, Neil, 2001. 'Copland's Music of Wide Open Spaces: Surveying the Pastoral Trope in Hollywood', *Musical Quarterly* 85/3, 477–515

　　2005. '"Look at that big hand move along": Clocks, Containment, and Music in *High Noon*', *South Atlantic Quarterly* 104/1, 151–73

　　2010. ed. *Music in the Horror Film: Listening to Fear*, New York: Routledge

　　2013. 'Hearing the Boldly Goings: Tracking the Title Themes of the *Star Trek* Television Franchise, 1966–2005', in Donnelly and P. Hayward 2013, 52–71

Lescarboura, Austin C., 1921. *Behind the Motion-Picture Screen*, 2nd edn, New York: Scientific American Publishing Company

Leslie, Esther, 2002. *Hollywood Flatlands: Animation, Critical Theory and the Avant-Garde*, London and New York: Verso

Levinson, Jerrold, 1996. 'Film Music and Narrative Agency', in Bordwell and Carroll 1996, 248–82

Lewis, Hannah, 2014. '"The Realm of Serious Art": Henry Hadley's Involvement in Early Sound Film', *Journal of the Society for American Music* 8/3, 285–310

Lexmann, Juraj, 2006. *Theory of Film Music*, Frankfurt: Peter Lang

Leydon, Rebecca, 2004. 'Forbidden Planet: Effects and Affects in the Electro Avant Garde', in P. Hayward 2004, 61–76

Licht, Alan, 2007. *Sound Art: Between Music, Between Categories*, New York: Rizzoli

Lindsay, Vachel, 1916. *The Art of the Moving Picture*, New York: MacMillan

Link, Stan, 2004. 'Sympathy with the Devil? Music of the Psycho Post-*Psycho*', *Screen* 45/1 (Spring), 1–20

    2010. 'The Monster and the Music Box: Children and the Soundtrack of Horror', in Lerner 2010, 38–54

Lissa, Zofia, 1965 [1964]. *Ästhetik der Filmmusik*, German trans., Berlin [DDR]: Henschelverlag

Locke, Ralph P., 2009. *Musical Exoticism: Images and Reflections*, Cambridge: Cambridge University Press

London, Kurt, 1936. *Film Music: A Summary of the Characteristic Features of Its History, Aesthetics, Technique and Possible Developments*, London: Faber and Faber

Long, Michael, 2008. *Beautiful Monsters: Imagining the Classic in Musical Media*, Berkeley: University of California Press

MacCabe, Colin, Mick Eaton and Laura Mulvey, 1980. *Godard: Images, Sounds, Politics*, London: Macmillan

MacDonald, Ian, 1994. *Revolution in the Head: The Beatles' Records and the Sixties*, London: Fourth Estate

Macey, David, 2001. *Dictionary of Critical Theory*, London: Penguin

MacNab, Geoffrey, 2015. '*March of the Penguins* Director to Close Cannes with Climate Change Film *Ice and the Sky*', *Independent* (London), 17 May, www .independent.co.uk/arts-entertainment/films/news/march-of-the-penguins-director-to-close-cannes-with-climate-change-film-ice-in-the-sky-10256805 .html# (28 May 2015)

Maddox, Garry, 2006. 'The Penguin Suite', *Sydney Morning Herald*, 2 December, www.smh.com.au/news/film/the-penguin-suite/2006/11/30/1164777710443 .html (28 May 2015)

Manuel, Peter 1993. *Cassette Culture: Popular Music and Technology in North India*, Chicago: Chicago University Press

Manvell, Roger and John Huntley, 1957. *The Technique of Film Music*, London: Focal Press; revised and enlarged edition, New York: Communication Arts Books/Hastings House

Marks, Laura, U., 2000. *The Skin of the Film: Intercultural Cinema, Embodiment, and the Senses*, Durham, NC: Duke University Press

    2002. *Touch: Sensuous Theory and Multisensory Media*, Minneapolis: University of Minnesota Press

Marks, Martin Miller, 1997. *Music and the Silent Film: Contexts and Case Studies, 1895–1924*, New York: Oxford University Press

    2000. 'Music, Drama, Warner Brothers: The Cases of *Casablanca* and *The Maltese Falcon*', in Buhler *et al.* 2000, 161–86

Marshall, Bill and Robynn Stilwell, 2000. *Musicals: Hollywood and Beyond*, Exeter: Intellect Books

Martin, Adrian, 2001. 'Musical Mutations: Before, Beyond and Against Hollywood', in Brophy 2001, 67–104

Martin, Jean, 2015. 'Peter Strickland's Film Soundtracks. A World of Dreams, Nostalgia and Fear', *Glissando* 26 (Soundscape), 160–7

Marvin, H. B., 1928. 'A System of Motion Pictures with Sound', *Transactions of the Society of Motion Picture Engineers* 33, 86–102

Marwick, Arthur, 1998. *The Sixties: Social and Cultural Transformation in Britain, France, Italy and the United States, 1958–74*, Oxford: Oxford University Press

Massawyrm, 2006. 'Massawyrm Cuts Off George Miller's HAPPY FEET And Tries To Feed Them To Him!!', *Ain't It Cool News*, 14 November, www.aintitcool.com /node/30704 (28 May 2015)

McCarty, Clifford, 1989. ed. *Film Music I*, New York and London: Garland

McDonald, Matthew, 2012. 'Mountains, Music, and Murder: Scoring the American West in *There Will Be Blood* and *No Country for Old Men*', in Kalinak 2012, 214–27

McQuiston, Kate, 2013. *We'll Meet Again: Musical Design in the Films of Stanley Kubrick*, New York: Oxford University Press

Medhurst, Andy, 1995. 'It Sort of Happened Here: the Strange, Brief Life of the British Pop Film', in Romney and Wootton 1995, 60–71

Melly, George, 1972. *Revolt Into Style: The Pop Arts in Britain*, Harmondsworth: Penguin

Melnick, Ross, 2012. *American Showman: Samuel 'Roxy' Rothafel and the Birth of the Entertainment Industry*, New York: Columbia University Press

Mera, Miguel, 2007. *Mychael Danna's* The Ice Storm: *A Film Score Guide*, Lanham, MD: Scarecrow Press

Mera, Miguel and Ben Winters, 2009. 'Film and Television Music Sources in the UK and Ireland', *Brio* 46/2, 37–65

Merlin, Didi, 2010. 'Diegetic Sound. Zur Konstitution figureninterner- und externer Realitäten im Spielfilm', *Kieler Beiträge zur Filmmusikforschung* 6, 66–100, www .filmmusik.uni-kiel.de/KB6/KB6-Merlinarc.pdf (29 May 2015)

Metz, Christian, 1971. *Langage et cinéma*, Paris: Librairie Larousse
    1974 [1968]. *Film Language: A Semiotics of the Cinema*, trans. M. Taylor, New York: Oxford University Press

Miceli, Sergio, 1988. 'I suoni di Giano. Sul comporre di Ennio Morricone'; in *Trento Cinema. Incontri internazionali con la musica per il cinema*, Catalogo, Trento: n.p., 70–81

Miceli, Sergio, 1994. *Morricone, la musica, il cinema*, Milano/Modena: Ricordi/ Mucchi
    2010. *Musica e cinema nella cultura del Novecento*, third expanded edn., Roma: Bulzoni
    2011. 'Miceli's Method of Internal, External, and Mediated Levels: Elements for the Definition of a Film-Musical Dramaturgy', ed. and trans. by Gillian B. Anderson with the assistance of Lidia Bagnoli, *Music and the Moving Image* 4/2, 1–29
    2013. *Film Music. History, Aesthethic-Analysis, Typologies*, ed. and trans. Marco Alunno and Braunwin Sheldrick. Milan and Lucca: Hal Leonard MGB/ LIM Editrice

Miklitsch, Robert, 2009. 'Audio noir: Audiovisuality in Neo-Modernist Noir', in Bould *et al.* 2009, 28–43

Miller, Cynthia J., 2010. 'Seeing Beyond His Own Time: The Sounds of Jerry Goldsmith', in Bartkowiak 2010, 210–22

Miller, Cynthia J. and A. Bowdoin Van Riper, 2010. '"It's Hip to Be Square": Rock and Roll and the Future', in Bartkowiak 2010, 118–33

Mirka, Danuta, 1997. 'The Sonoristic Structuralism of Krzysztof Penderecki', PhD diss., Katowice: Akademia Muzyczna; http://eprints.soton.ac.uk/71829 (12 August 2015)

    2000. 'Texture in Penderecki's Sonoristic Style' *Music Theory Online* 6/1, www .mtosmt.org/issues/mto.00.6.1/mto.00.6.1.mirka_frames.html (31 October 2014)

Moeller, Hans-Bernhard and George Lellis, 2002. *Volker Schlöndorff's Cinema*. Carbondale: Southern Illinois University Press

Monaco, James, 1981. *How to Read a Film*, New York and Oxford: Oxford University Press

Moore-Gilbert, Bart and John Seed, 1992. eds. *Cultural Revolution? The Challenge of the Arts in the 1960s*, London: Routledge

Morcom, Anna 2001. 'An Understanding between Bollywood and Hollywood? The Meaning of Hollywood-style in Hindi Films', *British Journal of Ethnomusicology* 10/1, 63–84

Morgan, Daniel, 2012. *Late Godard and the Possibilities of Cinema*, Berkeley: University of California Press

Morgan, K. F., 1929. 'Scoring, Synchronizing, and Re-Recording Sound Pictures', *Transactions of the Society of Motion Picture Engineers* 13/38, 268–85

Moritz, William, 2004. *Optical Poetry: The Life and Work of Oskar Fischinger*, Bloomington: Indiana University Press

Morricone, Ennio and Sergio Miceli, 2013 [2001]. *Composing for the Cinema: The Theory and Praxis of Music in Film*, lessons transcribed by Rita Pagani and ed. by Laura Gallenga; ed. and trans. by Gillian B. Anderson. Lanham, MD: Scarecrow Press

Morton, Lawrence, 1951. 'Film Music: Art or Industry?', *Film Music Notes* 11/1 (September–October), 4–6

Mukamel, Roy, Arne D. Ekstrom, Jonas Kaplan, Marco Iacoboni and Itzhal Fried, 2010. 'Single-Neuron Responses in Humans during Execution and Observation of Actions', *Current Biology* 20, 750–6

Murphy, Scott, 2006. 'The Major Tritone Progression in Recent Hollywood Science Fiction Films', *Music Theory Online* 12/2, www.mtosmt.org/issues/mto.06.12.2/ mto.06.12.2.murphy_frames.html (29 May 2015)

    2012. 'The Tritone Within: Interpreting Harmony in Elliot Goldenthal's Score for *Final Fantasy: The Spirits Within*', in Halfyard 2012, 148–74

    2014a. 'Transformational Theory and Film Music', in Neumeyer 2014, 471–99

    2014b. 'A Pop Music Progression in Recent Popular Movies and Movie Trailers', *Music, Sound, and the Moving Image* 8/2, 141–62

Murray, Robin L. and Joseph K. Heumann, 2011. *That's All Folks? Ecocritical Readings of American Animated Features*, Lincoln: University of Nebraska Press, ProQuest ebrary (28 May 2015)

Myleru, C. R., 1934. 'The Tamil Drama (Part 2)', *Journal of Annamalai University* 3/ 1, 71–8

Narath, Albert, 1960. 'Oskar Messter and His Work', reprinted in Fielding 1967, 109–17

Narboni, Jean and Tom Milne, 1972. eds. *Godard on Godard*, New York: Da Capo Press

Naremore, James, 2008. *More Than Night: Film Noir in its Contexts*, updated and expanded edn, Berkeley: University of California Press

    2013. 'Foreword', in Spicer and Hanson 2013, xix–xx

Naumburg, Nancy, 1937. ed. *We Make the Movies*, New York: W. W. Norton

Neaverson, Bob, 1997. *The Beatles Movies*, London: Cassell

Nechvatal, Joseph, 2011. *Immersion Into Noise*, Ann Arbor: M Publishing/Open Humanities Press

Neer, Richard, 2007. 'Godard Counts', *Critical Inquiry* 34/1, 135–73

Ness, Richard R., 2008. 'A Lotta Night Music: The Sound of *Film Noir*', *Cinema Journal* 47/2, 52–73

Nettl, Bruno, 1989. 'Mozart and the Ethnomusicological Study of Western Culture (an Essay in Four Movements)', *Yearbook for Traditional Music* 21, 1–16

Neumeyer, David, 1997. 'Source Music, Background Music, Fantasy and Reality in Early Sound Film', *College Music Symposium* 37, 13–20

    2000. 'Performances in Early Hollywood Sound Film: Source Music, Background Music, and the Integrated Sound Track', *Contemporary Music Review* 19/1, 37–62

    2004. 'Merging Genres in the 1940s: The Musical and the Dramatic Feature Film', *American Music* 22/1, 122–32

    2009. 'Diegetic/Nondiegetic: A Theoretical Model', *Music and the Moving Image* 2/1, 26–39

    2014. ed. *The Oxford Handbook of Film Music Studies*, Oxford: Oxford University Press

    2015. *Meaning and Interpretation of Music in Cinema*, with contributions by James Buhler, Bloomington: Indiana University Press

Neumeyer, David and Nathan Platte, 2012. *Franz Waxman's* Rebecca: *A Film Score Guide*, Lanham, MD: Scarecrow Press

New Zealand Government, 2015. 'Film Case Study – *Happy Feet*', www.censor.org .nz/resources/case-studies/happy-feet.html (5 August 2015)

Nialler9, 2011. 'An Interview with Jonny Greenwood', http://nialler9.com/jonny-greenwood-interview (31 October 2014)

Nichols, Bill, 1985. ed. *Movies and Methods: Volume II*, Berkeley: University of California Press

Niebisch, Arndt, 2012. *Media Parasites in the Early Avant-Garde: On the Abuse of Technology and Communication*, New York: Palgrave Macmillan

Nonesuch Records, 2007. 'Nonesuch Journal Exclusive: An Interview with Jonny Greenwood', *Nonesuch Journal*, www.nonesuch.com/journal/nonesuch-journal-exclusive-an-interview-with-jonny-greenwood (31 October 2014)

Norden, Martin F., 2007. 'Diegetic Commentaries', *Offscreen* 11/8–9 (Forum 2: Discourses on Diegesis – On the Relevance of Terminology), www.offscreen.com /biblio/pages/essays/soundforum_2 (29 May 2015)

North, Daniel, Bob Rehak and Michael Duffy, 2015. eds. *Special Effects: New Histories, Theories, Contexts*, London: British Film Institute

Nowell-Smith, Geoffrey, 1998. 'Introduction', in Nowell-Smith and Ricci 1998, 1–16

Nowell-Smith, Geoffrey and Stephen Ricci, 1998. eds. *Hollywood and Europe: Economics, Culture, National Identity 1945–95*, London: British Film Institute

'Open Forum', 1928. *Transactions of the Society of Motion Picture Engineers* 12/36, 1128–41

Orr, John, 1993. *Cinema and Modernity*, Cambridge: Polity Press

Osmond, Andrew, 2007. 'Happy Feet', *Sight & Sound* 17/2, 56–7

Oswald, John, 1985. 'Plunderphonics, or Audio Piracy as a Compositional Prerogative'. Paper presented at the Wired Society Electro-Acoustic Conference, Toronto, www.plunderphonics.com/xhtml/xplunder.html (29 April 2015)

Padmanabhan, Mekala, forthcoming. 'Orchestra and Song: Musical Narratives in Tamil Films', in Ramnarine, forthcoming

Palmer, R. Barton, 2007. 'The Divided Self and the Dark City: Film Noir and Liminality', *symplokē* 15/1–2 (*Cinema without Borders*), 66–79

Pasquariello, Nicholas, 1993. '*Indiana Jones and the Last Crusade*', in Forlenza and Stone 1993, 57–61

Pauli, Hansjörg, 1976. 'Filmmusik: ein historisch-kritischer Abriß', in Schmidt 1976, 91–119

    1981. *Filmmusik: Stummfilm*, Stuttgart: Klett-Cotta

Peirse, Alison, 2013. *After* Dracula: *The 1930s Horror Film*, London: I. B. Tauris

Pfeil, Fred, 1993. 'Home Fires Burning: Family Noir in *Blue Velvet* and *Terminator 2*', in Copjec 1993, 227–59

Phillips, Klaus, 1984. ed. *New German Filmmakers: From Oberhausen through the 1970s*, New York: Ungar

Pike, Deidre M., 2012. *Enviro-Toons: Green Themes in Animated Cinema and Television*, e-book, Jefferson, NC: McFarland & Company, Inc.

Pisani, Michael V., 1998. '"I'm an Indian Too": Creating Native American Identities in Nineteenth- and Early Twentieth-Century Music', in Bellman 1998, 218–57

    2005. *Imagining Native America in Music*, New Haven, CT: Yale University Press

Place, Janey and Lowell Peterson, 1996 [1974]. 'Some Visual Motifs of *Film Noir*', in Silver and Ursini 1996, 64–75

Plantinga, Carl and Greg M. Smith, 1999. eds. *Passionate Views: Film, Cognition, and Emotion*, Baltimore, MD: Johns Hopkins University Press

Platte, Nathan, 2010. 'Musical Collaboration in the Films of David O. Selznick, 1932–1957', PhD diss., University of Michigan, http://deepblue.lib.umich.edu/handle/2027.42/75870 (17 July 2015), published by Proquest: UMI Dissertation Publishing, 2011

    2011. 'Dream Analysis: Korngold, Mendelssohn, and Musical Adaptations in Warner Bros.' *A Midsummer Night's Dream (1935)*', *19th-Century Music* 34, 211–36

    2012. 'Conducting the Composer: David O. Selznick and the Hollywood Film Score', in Wierzbicki 2012, 122–37

    2014. 'Before *Kong* Was King: Competing Methods in Hollywood Underscore', *Journal of the Society for American Music* 8/3, 311–37

Porcile, François, 1969. *Présence de la musique à l'écran*, Paris: Éditions du CERF

Porfirio, Robert, 1992. '*Stranger on the Third Floor*', in Silver and Ward 1992, 269

 2013. 'The Strange Case of Film Noir', in Spicer and Hanson 2013, 17–32

Powdermaker, Hortense, 1951. *Hollywood, the Dream Factory: An Anthropologist Looks at the Movie-Makers*, London: Secker & Warburg

Powrie, Phil and Guido Heldt, 2014. 'Introduction: Trailers, Titles, and End Credits', *Music, Sound, and the Moving Image* 8/2 (special issue *Trailers, Titles, and End Credits*, ed. Powrie and Heldt), 111–20

Prem-Ramesh, 1998. *Iḷaiyarājā, icaiyiṉ tattuvamum aḻakiyalum*, Chennai: Chembulam Publications

Prendergast, Roy M., 1992 [1977]. *Film Music: A Neglected Art*, 2nd edn, New York: W. W. Norton & Co.

Punathambekar, Aswin, 2010. 'Ameen Sayani and Radio Ceylon: Notes towards a History of Broadcasting and Bombay Cinema', *Bioscope: South Asian Screen Studies* 1/2, 189–97

Putterman, Barry, 1998. 'A Short Critical History of Warner Bros. Cartoons', in Sandler 1998, 29–37

Raksin, David, 1989. 'Holding a Nineteenth Century Pedal at Twentieth Century-Fox', in McCarty 1989, 167–81

Ramachandran, T. M., Rani Burra and Mangala Chandran, 1981. eds. *Fifty Years of Indian Talkies, 1931–1981: A Commemorative Volume*, Bombay: Indian Academy of Motion Picture Arts & Sciences

Ramnarine, Tina K., 2011. 'Music in Circulation between Diasporic Histories and Modern Media: Exploring Sonic Politics in Two Bollywood Films *Om Shanti Om* and *Dulha Mil Gaya*', *South Asian Diaspora* 3/2, 143–58

 forthcoming. ed. *Global Perspectives on Orchestras: Essays in Collective Creativity and Social Agency*, New York: Oxford University Press

Rapée, Ernö, 1924. *Motion Picture Moods for Pianists and Organists*, New York: G. Schirmer

 1925. *Encyclopaedia of Music for Pictures*, New York: Belwin

Rectanus, Mark, 1986. '*The Lost Honour of Katharina Blum*: The Reception of a German Best-Seller in the USA', *German Quarterly* 59/2, 252–69

Reid, Mark, 2000. *Casablanca*, York Film Notes, London: York Press

Rhymes, Edward, 2007. 'A "Ho" by Any Other Color: The History and Economics of Black Female Sexual Exploitation', Black Agenda Report, *Alternet* (18 May), www.alternet.org/story/52067/a_%27ho%27_by_any_other_color%3A_the_ his tory_and_economics_of_black_female_sexual_exploitation (28 May 2015)

Richards, Jeffrey, 1992. 'New Waves and Old Myths: British Cinema in the Sixties', in Moore-Gilbert and Seed 1992, 218–35

Richardson, John, Claudia Gorbman and Carol Vernallis, 2013. eds. *The Oxford Handbook of New Audiovisual Aesthetics*, New York: Oxford University Press

Richie, Donald, 2001. *A Hundred Years of Japanese Film*, Tokyo: Kodansha International

 2002. 'Notes on the Film Music of Tōru Takemitsu', *Contemporary Music Review* 21/4, 5–16

Robertson, Pamela [Pamela Robertson Wojcik], 1996. *Guilty Pleasures: Feminist Camp from Mae West to Madonna*, Durham, NC, and London: Duke University Press

Robison, Catherine A., n.d. 'Carry Me Back to the Lone Prairie', www.countrymusic treasures.com/storybehindthesong/carry-me-back-to-the-lone-prairie.html (24 September 2015)

Rodman, Ronald, 2010. *Tuning In: American Narrative Television Music*, New York: Oxford University Press

Rogers, Holly, 2015. ed. *Music and Sound in Documentary Film*, New York and Abingdon: Routledge

Rogin, Michael, 1992. 'Blackface, White Noise: The Jewish Jazz Singer Finds His Voice', *Critical Inquiry* 18/3, 417–53

Romney, Jonathan and Adrian Wootton, 1995. eds. *Celluloid Jukebox: Popular Music and the Movies Since the 50s*, London: British Film Institute

Rosar, William H., 1983. 'Music for the Monsters: Universal Pictures' Horror Film Scores of the Thirties', *Quarterly Journal of the Library of Congress* 40/4, 391–421

Rosen, Philip, 1986. ed. *Narrative, Apparatus, Ideology: A Film Theory Reader*, New York: Columbia University Press

Ross, Alex (2008) 'Welling Up', *New Yorker*, www.newyorker.com/magazine/2008/ 02/04/welling-up (31 October 2014)

Rosten, Leo C., 1941. *Hollywood: The Movie Colony, the Movie Makers*, New York: Harcourt

Roud, Richard, 1971. *Jean-Marie Straub*, London: Secker and Warburg/British Film Institute

Roustom, Kareem, 2014. 'Michel Legrand scores *Une Femme est Une Femme*', in Conley and Kline 2014, 71–89

Sabaneev, Leonid, 1935. *Music for the Film: A Handbook for Composers and Conductors*, trans. S. W. Pring, London: Pitman

Sandler, Kevin, 1998. ed. *Reading the Rabbit: Explorations in Warner Bros. Animation*, New Brunswick, NJ: Rutgers University Press

Sapiro, Ian, 2013. *Ilan Eshkeri's* Stardust: *A Film Score Guide*, Lanham, MD: Scarecrow Press

Saunders, Bret, 2005, 'Saxman's Role as Himself in "Terminal" Opened Doors', *Denver Post*, 16 January, www.bennygolson.com/articles/IBBOB%20DENVER% 20POST%20%20ARTICLE%201-16-04%20.htm (3 March 2015)

Scemama, Céline, 2006. *Histoire(s) du cinéma de Jean-Luc Godard: La force faible d'un art*, Paris: L'Harmattan, http://cri-image.univ-paris1.fr/celine/celine.html (30 April 2015)

Schaeffer, Pierre, 1946. 'L'élément non visuel au cinéma', *Revue du cinéma* 1, 45–8; 2, 62–5; 3, 51–2

Schatz, Thomas, 1989. *The Genius of the System: Hollywood Filmmaking in the Studio Era*, New York: Henry Holt and Company

Schelle, Michael, 1999. *The Score: Interviews with Film Composers*, Beverly Hills: Silman-James Press

Scheurer, Timothy E., 2008. *Music and Mythmaking in Film: Genre and the Role of the Composer*, Jefferson, NC: McFarland

Schmidt, Hans-Christian, 1976. ed. *Musik in den Massenmedien Rundfunk und Fernsehen*, Mainz: Schott

Schmidt, Lisa M., 2010. 'A Popular Avant-Garde: The Paradoxical Tradition of Electronic and Atonal Sounds in Sci-Fi Music Scoring', in Bartkowiak 2010, 22–43

Schneider, Enjott, 1986. *Handbuch Filmmusik. Musikdramaturgie im Neuen Deutschen Film*, Munich: Ölschläger

Schuller, Gunther, 1989. *The Swing Era*, New York: Oxford University Press

Scott, Derek B., 2001. *The Singing Bourgeois: Songs of the Victorian Drawing Room and Parlor*, 2nd edn, Aldershot, UK: Ashgate

Selby, Andrew, 2009. *Animation in Process*, London: Laurence King
    2010. *Animation Portfolio*, London: Laurence King

Sheer, Miriam, 2001. 'The Godard/Beethoven Connection: On the Use of Beethoven's Quartets in Godard's Films', *Journal of Musicology* 18/1, 170–88

Shinoda, Masahiro, 2005. 'Video Interview', DVD of *Samurai Spy* (dir. Masahiro Shinoda, 1965), Criterion Collection 312

Silver, Alain, 1996. 'Introduction', in Silver and Ursini 1996, 2–15

Silver, Alain and James Ursini, 1996. eds. *Film Noir Reader*, New York: Limelight Editions

Silver, Alain and Elizabeth Ward, 1992. eds. *Film Noir: An Encyclopedic Reference to The American Style*, revised edn, Woodstock: Overlook Press

Simpson, Philip, Andrew Utterson and K. J. Sheperdson, 2004. eds. *Film Theory: Critical Concepts in Media and Cultural Studies*, 4 vols, London and New York: Routledge

Sinclair, Craig, 2003. 'Audition: Making Sense of/in the Cinema', *Velvet Light Trap* 51 (Spring 2003), 17–28

Skinner, Frank, 1950. *Underscore*, New York: Criterion Music Corp.

Slobin, Mark, 2008. ed. *Global Soundtracks: Worlds of Film Music*, Middletown, Connecticut: Wesleyan University Press

Slowik, Michael, 2014. *After the Silents: Hollywood Film Music in the Early Sound Era, 1926–1934*, New York: Columbia University Press

Smirnov, Andrey, 2013. *Sound in Z: Experiments in Sound and Electronic Music in Early 20th-century Russia*, London: Koenig Books & Sound and Music

Smith, Jeff, 1996. 'Unheard Melodies? A Critique of Psychoanalytic Theories of Film Music', in Bordwell and Carroll 1996, 230–7
    1999. 'Movie Music as Moving Music: Emotion, Cognition, and the Film Score', in Plantinga and Smith 1999, 146–67
    2009. 'Bridging the Gap: Reconsidering the Border between Diegetic and Nondiegetic Music', *Music and the Moving Image* 2/1, 1–25

Smith, Steven C., 1991. *A Heart at Fire's Center: The Life and Music of Bernard Herrmann*, Berkeley: University of California Press

Sobchack, Vivian, 1992. *The Address of the Eye: A Phenomenology of Film Experience*, Oxford: Princeton University Press
    2001. *Screening Space: The American Science Fiction Film*, 2nd, enlarged edn, New Brunswick: Rutgers University Press
    2004. *Carnal Thoughts: Embodiment and Moving Image Culture*, Berkeley: University of California Press

2005. 'When the Ear Dreams: Dolby Digital and the Imagination of Sound', *Film Quarterly* 58/4, 2–15

Spicer, Andrew and Helen Hanson, 2013. eds. *A Companion to Film Noir*, Chichester: Blackwell Publishing Ltd.

Spottiswoode, Raymond, 1935. *A Grammar of Film: An Analysis of Film Technique*, London: Faber and Faber

Spring, Katherine, 2013. *Saying it With Songs: Popular Music and the Coming of Sound to Hollywood Cinema*, New York: Oxford University Press

Sreevatsan, Ajai 2011. 'Heritage walk around old studios', *The Hindu*, 22 August, www.thehindu.com/news/cities/chennai/heritage-walk-around-old-studios/arti cle2381749.exe (3 March 2015)

Staiger, Janet, 1995. ed. *The Studio System*, Rutgers Depth of Field Series, New Brunswick: Rutgers University Press
2003. 'Authorship Approaches', in Gerstner and Staiger 2003, 27–57

Stam, Robert and Toby Miller, 2000. *Film and Theory: An Anthology*, Malden, MA, and Oxford: Blackwell

Stanley, Sandra Kumamoto, 1998. ed. *Other Sisterhoods: Literary Theory and U.S. Women of Color*, Bloomington and Indianapolis: Indiana University Press

Steiner, Max, 1937. 'Scoring the Film', in Naumburg 1937, 216–38
1939a. *The Oklahoma Kid*. Manuscript pencil draft, MSS 1547, The Max Steiner Collection, Film Music Archives, L. Tom Perry Special Collections [LTPSC], Harold B. Lee Library, Brigham Young University
1939b. *Dodge City*. Manuscript pencil draft, MSS 1547, LTPSC
1941. *The Bride Came C.O.D.* Manuscript pencil draft, MSS 1547, LTPSC
1942. *The Gay Sisters*. Manuscript pencil draft, MSS 1547, LTPSC
1963-4. 'Notes To You. An Unpublished Autobiography', MSS 1547, LTPSC

Stenzl, Jürg, 2010. *Jean-Luc Godard – musicien. Die Musik in den Filmen von Jean-Luc Godard*, Munich: edition text + kritik

Stephens, Chuck, 2011. 'Loser Take All', liner notes to DVD of *Pale Flower* (dir. Masahiro Shinoda, 1964), Criterion Collection 564

Sterritt, David, 1998. ed. *Jean-Luc Godard: Interviews*, Jackson: University Press of Mississippi
1999. *The Films of Jean-Luc Godard: Seeing the Invisible*, Cambridge: Cambridge University Press

Sterritt, David and Jürg Stenzl, 2010. *Jean-Luc Godard – musicien: Die Musik in den Filmen von Jean-Luc Godard*, Munich: edition text + kritik

Stilwell, Robynn J., 2007. 'The Fantastical Gap between Diegetic and Nondiegetic', in Goldmark *et al.* 2007, 184–202
2011. 'The Television Musical', in Knapp *et al.* 2011, 152–66

Stine, Whitney, 1974. *Mother Goddam: The Story of the Career of Bette Davis*, with a running commentary by Bette Davis, New York: Hawthorn Books

Stokes, Jordan Carmalt, 2013. 'Music and Genre in Film: Aesthetics and Ideology', PhD diss., New York: City University of New York

Studwell, William E., 1994. *The Popular Song Reader: A Sampler of Well-Known Twentieth-Century Songs*, Binghamton, NY: Haworth Press

Subramaniam, Divakar, 2014. 'Tirai icaiyai puraṭṭi pōṭṭa elakṭrōṇik kī pōrṭu', *Dinamalar*, 23 December, www.dinamalar.com/news_detail.asp?id=1145011 (3 March 2015)

Subramanian, Lakshmi, 2006. 'Court to Academy: Karnatic Music', *India International Centre Quarterly* 33/2, 125–38

Sutcliffe, Tom, 2000. *Watching*, London: Faber and Faber

Szwed, John, 2002. *So What: The Life of Miles Davis*, New York: Simon & Schuster

Tagg, Philip, 1990. '*The Virginian*, Horse Music and the Love of the West', part of a project financed by The Humanities Research Council of Sweden, Göteborg: private publication, 6–23

2000. *Kojak: 50 Seconds of Television Music. Towards the Analysis of Affect in Popular Music*, 2nd edn, New York: Mass Media Scholars' Press

Tagg, Philip and Bob Clarida, 2003. *Ten Little Tunes: Towards a Musicology of the Mass Media*, New York and Montreal: Mass Media Scholars' Press

Takemitsu, Toru, 1995. *Confronting Silence: Selected Writings*, Berkeley, CA: Fallen Leaf

2004. 'On Swari', trans. and annotated by Hugh De Ferranti and Yayoi Uno Everett, in Everett and Lau 2004, 199–207

Temple, Michael and James Williams, 2000. eds. *The Cinema Alone: Essays on the Work of Jean-Luc Godard, 1985–2000*, Amsterdam: Amsterdam University Press

Temple, Michael, James Williams and Michael Witt, 2004. eds. *For Ever Godard: The Work of Jean-Luc Godard, 1950 to the Present*, London: Black Dog Publishing

Tieber, Claus and Anna K. Windisch, 2014. eds. *The Sounds of Silent Films: New Perspectives on History, Theory, and Practice*, Basingstoke, UK: Palgrave Macmillan

Thomas, Frank, and Ollie Johnston, 1981. *Disney Animation: The Illusion of Life*, New York: Abbeville Press

Thomas, Tony, 1973. *Music for the Movies*, South Brunswick and New York: A.S. Barnes and Company, London: Tantivy Press

1997. *Music for the Movies*, 2nd edn, Los Angeles: Silman-James Press

Thompson, Emily, 2004. 'Wiring the World: Acoustical Engineers and the Empire of Sound in the Motion Picture Industry, 1927–1930', in Erlmann 2004, 191–209

Thompson, Kristin, 1980. 'Early Sound Counterpoint', *Yale French Studies* 60, 115–40

1988. *Breaking the Glass Armor: Neoformalist Film Analysis*, Princeton, NJ: Princeton University Press

Tieber, Claus and Anna K. Windisch, 2014. eds. *The Sounds of Silent Films: New Perspectives on History, Theory and Practice*, Basingstoke and New York: Palgrave Macmillan

Tilton, Roger, 1956. 'Jazz Dance', *Film Music* 15/4, 19

Tinkcom, Matthew, 1996. 'Working Like a Homosexual: Camp Visual Codes and the Labor of Gay Subjects in the MGM Freed Unit', *Cinema Journal* 35/2 (Winter), 24–42

Travis, Peter, 2008. '*There Will Be Blood*', *Rolling Stone*, www.rollingstone.com/movies/reviews/there-will-be-blood-20080118 (31 October 2014)

Tredell, Nicolas, 2002. ed. *Cinemas of the Mind: A Critical History of Film Theory*, Cambridge: Icon

Truax, Barry, 2001. *Acoustic Communication*, Westport: Greenwood Publishing

True, Lyle C., 1914. *How and What to Play for Moving Pictures: A Manual and Guide for Pianists*, San Francisco: Music Supply

Turim, Maureen, 1984. 'Jean-Marie Straub and Danièle Huillet: Oblique Angles on Film as Ideological Intervention', in Phillips 1984, 335–8

Tuska, Jon, 1984. *Dark Cinema: American Film Noir in Cultural Perspective*, Westport, CT: Greenwood Press

Ursini, James, 1996. 'Angst at Sixty Fields Per Second', in Silver and Ursini 1996, 274–87

Vamanan, 2004. *Tirai icai alaikal*, vol. 1, Chennai: Manickavasagar Pathipagam

van der Will, Wilfried, 1994. 'Fürsorgliche Belagerung: the Citizen and the Surveillance State', in Butler 1994, 219–38

Van Vechten, Carl, 2012 [1916]. 'Music for the Movies', reprinted in Wierzbicki *et al.* 2012, 18–22

Vernallis, Carol, Amy Herzog and John Richardson, 2013. eds. *The Oxford Handbook of Sound and Image in Digital Media*, New York: Oxford University Press

Walker, Janet, 2001. ed. *Westerns: Films Through History*, New York and London: Routledge

Walker, John, 1985. *The Once & Future Film: British Cinema in the Seventies and Eighties*, London: Methuen

Walsh, Martin, 1974. 'Political Formations in the Cinema of Jean-Marie Straub', *Jump Cut* 4, 12–18

Warner, Harry M., 1927. 'Future Developments', in Kennedy 1927, 319–35

Weaver, John Michael, 1993. 'Post-Production Pioneer James G. Stewart', in Forlenza and Stone 1993, 12–17

Weidman, Amanda, 2012. 'Musical Genres and National Identity', in Dalmia and Sadhana 2012, 247-63

Weis, Elisabeth and John Belton, 1985. eds. *Film Sound: Theory and Practice*, New York: Columbia University Press

Wells, Paul, 1998. *Understanding Animation*, London and New York: Routledge
2002. *Animation and America*, Edinburgh: Edinburgh University Press
2009. *The Animated Bestiary: Animals, Cartoons, Culture*, New Brunswick, New Jersey and London: Rutgers University Press
2014. '"I Can't Abide Cartoons!": Animation, Gravity and the Five Degree Space', *Animation Process, Practice & Production* 3/1 and 2, 3–15

Wells, Paul and J. Hardstaff, 2008. *Re-Imagining Animation*, Lausanne: AVA Academia

Whitmer, Mariana, 2012. *Jerome Moross's* The Big Country: *A Film Score Guide*, Lanham, MD: Scarecrow Press

Whittall, Arnold, 1999. *Musical Composition in the Twentieth Century*, New York: Oxford University Press

Wierzbicki, James, 2010. 'Lost in Translation? Ghost Music in Recent Japanese Kaidan Films and Their Hollywood Remakes', *Horror Studies* 1/2, 193–205

2012. ed. *Music, Sound and Filmmakers: Sonic Style in Cinema*, New York: Routledge

Wierzbicki, James, Nathan Platte and Colin Roust, 2012. eds. *The Routledge Film Music Sourcebook*, New York and London: Routledge

Williams, Alan, 1982. 'Godard's Use of Sound', *Camera Obscura* 3–4 (2–3–1 8–9–10), 192–209

Williams, James, 2000. 'European Culture and Artistic Resistance in *Histoire*(s) *du cinéma* Chapter 3A, *La monnaie de l'absolu*', in Temple and J. S. Williams 2000, 113–40

Williams, Tony D., 1995. *The Penguins: Spheniscidae*, Oxford and New York: Oxford University Press

Willman, Chris, 1997. 'He Shoots, He Scores: Making the "Jerry Maguire" Soundtrack', *Entertainment Weekly*, 17 January, 25

Wily, Roland John, 1985. *Tchaikovsky's Ballets:* Swan Lake, Sleeping Beauty, Nutcracker, Oxford: Clarendon Press

Winters, Ben, 2007. *Erich Wolfgang Korngold's* The Adventures of Robin Hood*: A Film Score Guide*, Lanham, MD: Scarecrow Press

2008. 'Corporeality, Musical Heartbeats, and Cinematic Emotion', *Music, Sound, and the Moving Image* 2/1, 3–25

2010. 'The Non-Diegetic Fallacy: Film, Music, and Narrative Space', *Music & Letters* 91/2, 224–44

2012. 'Musical Wallpaper? Towards an Appreciation of Non-narrating Music in Film', *Music, Sound, and the Moving Image* 6/1, 39–54

Witt, Michael, 2013. *Jean-Luc Godard, Cinema Historian*, Bloomington: Indiana University Press

Wolf, Stacy, 2015. 'Backstage Divas: The Passionate Attachments of After-School Musical Theatre Teachers'. Paper presented at the Association for Theatre in Higher Education 2015 Conference, Montreal

Wolfe, Charles, 1990. 'Vitaphone Shorts and *The Jazz Singer*', *Wide Angle* 12/3, 58–78

Wulff, Hans Jürgen, 2007. 'Schichtenbau und Prozesshaftigkeit des Diegetischen: Zwei Anmerkungen', *montage/av* 16/2 (special issue Diegese), 39–51

Wulff, Hans Jürgen, Susan Levermann, Patrick Niemeier and Willem Strank, 2010–11. eds. *Kieler Beiträge zur Filmmusikforschung* 5/1–4 (four special issues on the rockumentary), www.filmmusik.uni-kiel.de/beitraege.php (29 May 2015)

Yacavone, Dan, 2012. 'Spaces, Gaps, and Levels: From the Diegetic to the Aesthetic in Film Theory', *Music, Sound, and the Moving Image* 6/1, 21–37

Zipes, Jack, 1977. 'The Political Dimensions of *The Lost Honor of Katharina Blum*', *New German Critique* 12 (Autumn), 75–84

Reference Index of Films and Television Programmes

All films and television programmes mentioned in this volume are listed here, together with some pertinent additional information. For films this consists of any relevant translations of titles or foreign release titles, the year of first public screening (which may be earlier than that of general release), the name of the director and the country of origin. Similarly, entries for television programmes indicate the year of first broadcast, the original broadcast channel and the country of origin. In all cases, the country names have been abbreviated to the internationally recognized two-letter codes from ISO 3166.

General Index

Cambridge Companions to Music

Topics

The Cambridge Companion to Ballet
Edited by Marion Kant

The Cambridge Companion to Blues and Gospel Music
Edited by Allan Moore

The Cambridge Companion to Choral Music
Edited by André de Quadros

The Cambridge Companion to the Concerto
Edited by Simon P. Keefe

The Cambridge Companion to Conducting
Edited by José Antonio Bowen

The Cambridge Companion to Eighteenth-Century Music
Edited by Anthony R. DelDonna and Pierpaolo Polzonetti

The Cambridge Companion to Electronic Music
Edited by Nick Collins and Julio D'Escriván

The Cambridge Companion to Film Music
Edited by Mervyn Cooke and Fiona Ford

The Cambridge Companion to French Music
Edited by Simon Trezise

The Cambridge Companion to Grand Opera
Edited by David Charlton

The Cambridge Companion to Hip-Hop
Edited by Justin A. Williams

The Cambridge Companion to Jazz
Edited by Mervyn Cooke and David Horn

The Cambridge Companion to Jewish Music
Edited by Joshua S. Walden

The Cambridge Companion to the Lied
Edited by James Parsons

The Cambridge Companion to Medieval Music
Edited by Mark Everist

The Cambridge Companion to the Musical, second edition
Edited by William Everett and Paul Laird

The Cambridge Companion to Opera Studies
Edited by Nicholas Till

The Cambridge Companion to the Orchestra
Edited by Colin Lawson

The Cambridge Companion to Percussion
Edited by Russell Hartenberger

The Cambridge Companion to Pop and Rock
Edited by Simon Frith, Will Straw and John Street

CPSIA information can be obtained
at www.ICGtesting.com
Printed in the USA
LVHW010424040121
675641LV00017B/463

9 781107 476493